TEACHING ESL COMPOSITION

PURPOSE, PROCESS, AND PRACTICE

Second Edition

Dana R. Ferris
California State University, Sacramento

John S. Hedgcock
Monterey Institute of International Studies

LEA

LAWRENCE ERLBAUM ASSOCIATES, PUBLISHERS
2005   Mahwah, New Jersey   London

This book was typeset in 10/12 pt. Palatino Bold, Italic
The heads were typeset in Twentieth Century.

Copyright © 2005 by Lawrence Erlbaum Associates, Inc.
All rights reserved. No part of this book may be reproduced in
any form, by photostat, microform, retrieval system, or any
other means, without prior written permission of the publisher.

Lawrence Erlbaum Associates, Inc., Publishers
10 Industrial Avenue
Mahwah, New Jersey 07430
www.erlbaum.com

Cover design by Kathryn Houghtaling Lacey

Library of Congress Cataloging-in-Publication Data

Ferris, Dana.
    Teaching ESL composition : purpose, process, and practice /
Dana Ferris, John S. Hedgcock.—2nd ed.
        p.   cm.
    Includes bibliographical references (p.   ) and index.
    ISBN 0-8058-4467-8 (pbk. : alk. paper)
    1. English language—Study and teaching—Foreign speakers.
    2. English language—Composition and exercises—Study and teaching.
    I. Hedgcock, John.   II. Title.

PE1128.A2F47   2004
808'.0428—dc22   2004041156

Books published by Lawrence Erlbaum Associates are printed on
acid-free paper, and their bindings are chosen for strength and durability.

Printed in the United States of America
10 9 8 7 6 5 4 3 2 1

TEACHING ESL COMPOSITION

PURPOSE, PROCESS, AND PRACTICE

Contents

v

Preface

In keeping with the spirit of the first edition, this second edition of *Teaching ESL Composition: Purpose, Process, and Practice* aims to present pedagogical approaches to the teaching of ESL composition in the framework of current theoretical perspectives on second language (L2) writing processes, practices, and writers. It should therefore appeal to at least four different audiences:

1. Teacher–educators and graduate students in TESOL preparation programs
2. In-service ESL and EFL instructors currently engaged in teaching writing and related literacy skills
3. Mainstream composition teachers who wish to learn more about meeting the diverse needs of ESL writers
4. Researchers involved in describing L2 writing and investigating ESL composition pedagogy.

The text addresses the needs of the first three groups by providing overviews of research related to ESL writing, as well as numerous opportunities to reflect on, develop, and practice the teaching skills needed for effective ESL composition instruction. We hope that researchers in the field will also appreciate the current syntheses and analyses of the literature on various topics in ESL literacy and composition. Preview and postreading review questions in each chapter are intended to stimulate readers' thinking about the material presented. Application Activities at the end of each chapter are designed to serve as "hands-on" practice for pre- and in-service teachers and as resources for teacher educators. The Application Activities also provide a range of ideas for evaluating primary research on key issues raised in the chapters. Because of the book's dual emphasis on theory and practice in ESL composition, it is appropriate as a primary or supplementary text for courses focusing on L2 writing theory as well as practicum courses that emphasize or include literacy instruction.

As a discipline, L2 writing still is viewed by some as an emergent field. Consequently, few resources have been produced to help pre- and in-service teachers become experts in a discipline that is becoming recognized as a profession in its own right. Therefore, one of our primary goals is to furnish readers with a synthesis of theory and practice in a rapidly evolving community of scholars and professionals. We have consistently and intentionally focused on providing apprentice teachers with practice activities that can be used to develop the complex skills entailed in teaching L2 writing. Although all the topics discussed are firmly grounded in reviews of relevant research, a feature that we feel distinguishes this book from others is its array of hands-on, practical examples, materials, and tasks. By synthesizing theory and research in a way that preservice teachers can understand, we have endeavored to craft chapter content and exercises in a way that enables readers to see the relevance of the field's knowledge base to their own current or future classroom settings and student writers.

The book as a whole moves from general themes to specific pedagogical concerns. Chapter 1 begins with an argument for the importance of theory as it shapes pedagogical practice. After a historical overview of L1 and L2 composition theory, the discussion focuses on influential orientations in writing pedagogy and literacy instruction. The chapter highlights the precepts of process-oriented pedagogies and the implications of postprocess models, culminating in an in-depth discussion of the issues and variables unique to L2 writers and ESL composition instruction. Chapter 2 aims to present a perspective on L2 composition instruction firmly grounded in the precept that literacies are socially constructed. We propose that educators should view the teaching of writing as inherently connected to (and dependent on) the cultivation of reading and other literacy skills.

On the basis of the socioliterate premises outlined in chapters 1 and 2, chapters 3 and 4 address fundamental concerns related to approaching any ESL literacy course that prominently features writing: needs assessment, syllabus design, textbook and materials selection, lesson planning, and task construction. The remaining chapters then focus on specific topics of persistent interest to L2 composition instruction: teacher response to student writing (chapter 5), peer response (chapter 6), development of grammar and editing skills for writing (chapter 7), models of writing assessment (chapter 8), and the role of technology in L2 writing instruction (chapter 9).

Although the organization of individual chapters varies somewhat according to topic, all contain the following components:

- **Questions for Reflection.** These prereading questions invite readers to consider their own prior experiences as students and writers and to anticipate how these insights might inform their own teaching practices;
- **Reflection and Review.** These follow-up questions ask readers to examine and evaluate the theoretical information and practical suggestions provided in the main discussion;
- **Figures and Appendices.** These textual illustrations provide sample authentic activities, lesson plans, ESL student writing, and so on, which teachers can use and adapt in their own classrooms;
- **Application Activities.** Application Activities follow each "Reflection and Review" section, presenting a range of hands-on practice exercises. Tasks include evaluating and synthesizing published research, writing commentary on sample student papers, developing lesson plans, redesigning classroom activities, and executing classroom tasks.

NOTES ON THE SECOND EDITION

Readers familiar with the first edition of this book will no doubt observe that the second edition appears to follow the blueprint of the original. Indeed, a comparison of the Tables of Contents would suggest very few differences. However, such a superficial comparison would fail to reveal both the advances our discipline has made in the past seven years and the evolution of our own thinking as writing instructors and teacher educators.

We are gratified by the positive response this book has received from teacher educators and their students. We are especially appreciative of the thoughtful reviews commissioned by Lawrence Erlbaum Associates from at least eight different teacher educators who used the book in their courses. Together with our own experiences using the text in our courses over the years, we have been privileged to make a fair assessment of what worked well in the first edition and what could benefit from some rethinking.

The strong consensus was that our theory-to-practice approach to the text matched the needs of its target audience, and that the blend of research reviews and practical suggestions for teaching struck an appropriate balance. The distribution of topics and themes across the nine chapters has not changed radically from that of the first edition, largely because we—and users of the book who offered such constructive feedback—found that the organization worked successfully in our courses. Reviewers spoke appreciatively of the Questions for Reflection at the beginning of each chapter and the Reflection and Review Questions at the end of each chapter. Evaluators also praised the sample materials provided in the figures and appendices. In the second edition, therefore, we have attempted to maintain our emphasis on the interdependent relationship between theory and instructional practice. Of course, we have updated all the research summaries to consider the new work that has appeared since the first edition was completed in 1997. We also have included reflection questions again, with some minor changes and additions.

Reviewers graciously offered suggestions for improvement that we attempted to address in our revisions. First, chapter 9 (Technology in the writing class) desperately needed updating. Readers accurately noted that the chapter was out of date even before it was published. Although research and practice related to the use of computers in the L2 writing courses continue to change rapidly, we have at least made a good faith effort to bring this discussion into the 21st century!

Some reviewers felt overwhelmed by the number and variety of Application Activities at the end of each chapter. In particular, they felt that the activities calling for data collection were too ambitious and unlikely to be used by most readers. We have therefore streamlined the number and type of Application Activities, keeping those that appeared to be most helpful, namely, hands-on practice exercises and critical analyses of primary research.

Finally, considering reviewers' comments as well as our own experiences with the text, we have substantially revised chapters 2, 5, and 7, and have reorganized the topics in chapters 3 and 4. We hope that the finished product will both please the users of the first edition and win the text some new friends.

As writers, researchers, teachers, and teacher-educators, we find that the field of L2 composition offers both challenges and rewards. We hope this book not only will provide its readers with accurate information, meaningful insights, and practical ideas, but also will convey our enthusiasm for this rapidly evolving, engaging field of intellectual inquiry and professional practice.

DANA'S ACKNOWLEDGMENTS

I am grateful to my graduate students and colleagues at California State University, Sacramento, who have helped me to conduct the primary research reflected in this book and in my other writings and to pilot classroom materials found in this second edition. In particular, I thank the three graduate students who allowed me to use their work in chapter 6 (Appendix 6A): Suzie Dollesin, Patricia Doris, and Sarah Oettle. I learn new things from my students—both ESL writers and future writing teachers— every day, and I am so thankful for the opportunity to have my thinking and practice informed and challenged by them.

On a personal level, I thank my advisor and mentor, Professor Robert Kaplan, for all of his encouragement over the years. Furthermore, I dedicate my efforts in this second edition to the memory of Professor David Eskey of the University of Southern California, who also had a profound influence on my academic career. Finally, I extend my love and gratitude to my husband, Randy Ferris, and my daughters, Laura and Melissa Ferris.

JOHN'S ACKNOWLEDGMENTS

Special thanks are due Joe and Shiela Mark for their support of this project through a Faculty Development Award I was honored to receive for a much needed course release during the Spring 2002 semester. The grant enabled me to lay crucial groundwork for this revision and affirmed their confidence in the worthiness of the project. Like Dana, I am also indebted to the students in my teacher education courses at the Monterey Institute of International Studies who worked with the first edition and offered constructive feedback on our draft material. Finally, I extend my sincerest thanks to Simon Hsu, whose optimism and perpetual moral support calmed my nerves and cheered me up.

JOINT ACKNOWLEDGMENTS

We owe much to the unfailing reassurance, patience, and grace of our editor, Naomi Silverman, whose steady guidance made the development of this edition rewarding and enjoyable. We

appreciate and admire Naomi not only for her professional ex-
pertise, but also for the profound respect that she demonstrates
for the authors with whom she works. We acknowledge the
assistance of Lori Hawver, Erica Kica, and Sarah Wahlert of
LEA; Jessica Williams, University of Illinois at Chicago; Nancy
Hayward, Indiana University of Pennsylvania; May Shih, San
Francisco State University; N. Ann Chenoweth, Carnegie Mellon
University; Teresa Pica, University of Pennsylvania; and Andrea
G. Osburne, Central Connecticut State University.

Dana Ferris
John Hedgcock

Chapter 1

Theoretical and Practical Issues in ESL Writing

Questions for Reflection

- *What do you remember about the primary language writing instruction you received during your primary, secondary, college, or even graduate education? What were the principal features of the method or methods used by your instructors?*
- *What aspects of that writing instruction contributed most (or least) to your expertise as a writer in your primary language? Why?*
- *In your experience as a writer, have you become aware of any explicit or implicit theories of writing that might have motivated the instruction you received? Were there any instances in your formal education in which writing teachers exposed their philosophy concerning the teaching of writing? If so, what were the stated principles and how did they influence your learning?*
- *If you have received formal instruction in a foreign or second language, were you provided training as a writer of that language? If so, compare that experience to your experience as an apprentice writer in your primary language. Describe specific similarities and differences.*

THE VALUE OF THEORETICAL KNOWLEDGE

Teacher preparation manuals conventionally begin with a theoretical background that explains and justifies the premises of the instructional approaches to be presented. This practice sometimes frustrates pre- and in-service teachers who may wish to forgo a careful study of abstract theories in favor of acquiring practical strategies for effective classroom teaching. This book aims to provide its readers with a principled set of instructional tools for teaching writing to secondary and postsecondary learners of English as a Second Language (ESL) and English as a Foreign Language (EFL).[1] To achieve this goal, we first lay a foundation of theoretical principles and historical precedents so that readers can make informed decisions about the pedagogical processes and procedures presented throughout the chapters of this book. By acquainting themselves with the historical and philosophical origins of the discipline of second language (L2) writing, readers can approach current instructional paradigms from a well-grounded, critical standpoint (Matsuda, 2003b; Polio, 2003).

We believe that the development of effective instructional skills for the L2 composition classroom relies partly on an explicit awareness of the fundamental precepts that guide prevailing beliefs and practices in the field (Hedgcock, 2002; Kroll, 2003b). Our current understanding of composing processes and methods for teaching them is evolving and disparate. Consequently, teachers must "consider a variety of approaches, their underlying assumptions, and the practices that each philosophy generates" (Raimes, 1991, p. 412). A knowledge of formally articulated paradigms, theories, models, and precepts enables teachers to discover and build on their own theories (Grabe & Kaplan, 1997; Johnson, 1996; Tsui, 1996; Yates & Muchisky, 2003). This knowledge also enables teachers to appreciate the strengths and weaknesses of their own teaching, a dimension of teacher education that encourages teachers "to become critical and reflective practitioners, researchers of their own professional life, and agents of change" (van Lier, 1994, p. 7).

Formal theories, in tandem with the insights of empirical research, can and should play a vital role in our thinking about instructional planning, practice, and assessment (Sasaki, 2000). In a persuasive argument for the utility of theory in composition teaching, Zebroski (1986) characterized the ways in which theory served his day-to-day teaching:

> Theory has helped me to excavate and to uncover my own assumptions about writing. It has aided me in crafting a more coherent and unified course structure. It has encouraged me to try out some new methods of teaching writing. It has helped me to relinquish control and to emphasize classroom community. (p. 58)

Instead of viewing theory as abstract and distant from the challenges we face as novice and expert teachers, we should recognize its enormous practical utility: Without the knowledge provided by theoretical principles, we lose sight of a crucial tool for responsible instructional planning and classroom decision making. As Lewin (1951), a pioneer in social psychology, wrote, "There is nothing so practical as good theory" (p. 7).

THEORY AND RESEARCH IN ESL COMPOSITION INSTRUCTION

Despite its brief history as a discipline, L2 writing lacks a tidy corpus of conclusive theory and research on which to base a straightforward introduction to processes of learning and teaching. The field can boast an impressive body of research, yet a single, comprehensive theory of L2 writing is perhaps a long way off—if, in fact, a singular theory is even a suitable aim. Indeed, Cumming and Riazi (2000) cautiously observed that the field currently lacks a coherent understanding of "how people actually learn to write in a second language" and of how teaching contributes to this learning (p. 57).

Nonetheless, L2 writing instruction as a discipline is far from atheoretical. Substantive L2 composition research did not appear until the 1980s, but its current theoretical frameworks can be traced to advances in first language (L1) rhetoric and composition research, applied linguistics, and TESOL (Grabe & Kaplan, 1996, 1997; Hedgcock, in press; Leki, 2000; Matsuda, 1998, 1999, 2003a, 2003b; Raimes, 1991, 1998). The following sections examine major approaches to L1 rhetoric and composition, focusing on those paradigms and approaches that have played influential roles in shaping theory development and praxis in L2 writing. Throughout this survey, it should be remembered that no singular theory or paradigm is necessarily autonomous or self-contained. In fact, we should expect to find a number of common features and overlapping points of view, even among so-called "competing theories" (Knoblauch & Brannon, 1984).

Product-Oriented Instructional Traditions in L1 Rhetoric and Composition

From the early 20th century into the 1960s, the principles governing composition instruction in U.S. schools, colleges, and universities were rooted largely in an educational philosophy that featured the reading and analysis of literature. In this tradition, native speakers (NSs) of English were required to read novels, short stories, plays, essays, and poetry. They then analyzed these works in written compositions or "themes." Pedagogical practice emphasized the understanding and interpretation of canonical literary texts. Consequently, little, if any, instructional time was devoted to planning, drafting, sharing, or revising written products (Babin & Harrison, 1999; Berlin, 1984, 1987; Grabe & Kaplan, 1996; Graves, 1999; Kroll, 2001; Matsuda, 2003b). Paradoxically, however, students were expected to master a range of school-based written genres (e.g., narration, exposition, argumentation) that embedded functions such as description, illustration, process analysis, and comparison and contrast.

To enable students to achieve this mastery, many 20th century textbooks followed what was then a conventional model of instruction. Initially, the teacher introduced and defined a rhetorical form, pattern, or "mode" (e.g., comparison) in terms of rigidly established rules or formulas. Students then read a work of literature, which they discussed and analyzed in class. Next, the teacher assigned a composing task based on the literary text, referring back to the rhetorical description introduced earlier. This sequence often was accompanied by a linear outline or template for students to follow in constructing their essays or themes. In the final phase of the instructional sequence, the teacher evaluated the students' assignments before initiating a similar cycle based on a new literary text.

This model of composition instruction, known by some as the "traditional paradigm" in U.S. English language education (Berlin, 1987; Bloom, Daiker, & White, 1997; Clark, 2003b, 2003c, 2003d) and by others as the "product approach" (Kroll, 2001), was not grounded in a fully articulated theory of education or cognitive development. Indeed, the traditional paradigm reflected a perspective in which school-based essays and themes were viewed as static representations of students' learning and content knowledge. Therefore, in product-oriented writing classrooms, little if any effort was dedicated to the strategies and other cognitive operations involved in putting pen to paper (or fingers to the keyboard) and drafting a coherent, meaningful piece of connected discourse.

The Process Movement and Allied Pedagogies in L1 and L2 Composition

The 1960s, 1970s, and 1980s witnessed a highly influential trend in L1 composition pedagogy and research. "Process approaches," as they now are broadly labeled, emphasized the individual writer as a creator of original ideas. It was believed that written discourse encoded these ideas, serving as a vehicle for exploring oneself, conveying one's thoughts, and claiming one's individual voice, or authorial persona, as a writer. Process-oriented writing pedagogies focused particular attention on procedures for solving problems, discovering ideas, expressing them in writing, and revising emergent texts—typically, in isolation from any cultural, educational, or sociopolitical contexts in which writing might take place (Canagarajah, 2002; Casanave, 2003; Hyland, 2003).

Faigley (1986) divided process writing proponents into two distinct categories: expressivists and cognitivists. Expressivists (Elbow, 1973, 1981a, 1981b; Macrorie, 1984; Murray, 1985; Zamel, 1982, 1983) viewed composing as "a creative act in which the process—the discovery of the true self—is as important as the product" (Berlin, 1988, p. 484). Based on the belief that writing instruction should be nondirective and personalized, expressionism writing instruction involved tasks designed to promote self-discovery, the emergence of personal voice, and empowerment of the individual's inner writer. Elbow (1981b), for example, enthusiastically advocated journal writing and personal essays as tasks in which students could "write freely and uncritically" to "get down as many words as possible" (p. 7). Expressivism therefore explicitly valued fluency and voice (Elbow, 1981b, 1999) as the chief tools for achieving writing proficiency (Hillocks, 1995; Hirvela & Belcher, 2001; Ivanic, 1998; Sharples, 1999; Soven, 1999; Zamel, 1976, 1982, 1983).

Cognitivism, sometimes described as a "writing as problem solving" approach, has affected theory construction in L2 writing pedagogy in even more marked ways. At the same time, some cognitivist approaches share with expressivism an explicit appreciation of novice writers' composing processes as recursive, personal, and "inner directed" (Bizzell, 1992). Cognitivists placed considerably greater value than did expressivists on high-order thinking and problem-solving operations. These operations included planning, defining rhetorical problems, positioning problems in a larger context, elaborating definitions, proposing solutions, and generating grounded conclusions (Emig, 1983; Flower, 1985, 1989; Hayes & Flower, 1983).

Hallmarks of cognitivist approaches to teaching L1 and L2 writing as a process include invention and prewriting tasks, drafting of multiple versions of writing assignments, abundant text-level revision, collaborative writing, feedback sessions, and the postponement of editing until the final stages of the composing cycle (Atkinson, 2003b; Clark, 2003b; Murray, 1992; see chapters 3, 4, and 5). Cognitivist rhetoricians and L2 writing practitioners thus focused principally on developing writers' intramental processes, particularly cognitive and metacognitive strategies for creating, revising, and correcting their texts independently (Bereiter & Scardamalia, 1987; Berlin, 1988; de Larios, Murphy, & Marín, 2002; Flower, 1989; Ransdell & Barbier, 2002a, 2002b). From a cognitivist, process-based perspective, writing is "essentially learnt, not taught, and the teacher's role is to be nondirective and facilitating, assisting writers to express their own meanings through an encouraging and cooperative environment with minimal interference" (Hyland, 2003, p. 18).

L1 and L2 Writing in the Post-Process Era

Although the literature of the past several decades strongly implies that the process movement entails a singular, homogeneous method of instruction, it is no exaggeration to suggest that the number of "process approaches" might equal the number of classroom writing teachers. That is, practitioners interpret and adapt aspects of process models, hybridizing principles and practices in ways that suit their beliefs, teaching styles, classroom contexts, and students (Blanton, Kroll, Cumming, & Erickson, 2002). Nonetheless, most implementations of process-based pedagogies share a number of fundamental, recursive practices such as prewriting, peer and teacher feedback, and revision (Cumming, 2003). As teaching practice and beliefs about process have evolved away from the process movement's expressivist and cognitivist core, L1 rhetoricians (Clark, 2003b; Glenn, Goldthwaite,

& Connors, 2003; Gottschalk & Hjortshoj, 2004; Kent, 1999; Tobin, 1994; Trimbur, 1994) and L2 writing specialists (Atkinson, 2003a, 2003b) have tried to characterize what they term the "post-process" era. Post-process scholarship aims, among other things, to expose the shortcomings of current process-oriented conceptualizations, "highlight the rich-multifocal nature of the field," and "go beyond now-traditional views of L2 writing research and teaching" (Atkinson, 2003b, p. 12).

Like many popular and influential educational trends, process-oriented approaches (expressivist and cognitivist alike) have been challenged on ideological, social, cultural, ethical, theoretical, empirical, and pedagogical grounds. Atkinson (2003b), for example, observed that process paradigms represent text construction as a solitary, asocial, and decontextualized activity. Because process models assume that written production emanates from within the individual, they tend to "disempower teachers and cast them in the role of well-meaning bystanders" (Hyland, 2003, p. 19). In addition to minimizing teacher authority in composition instruction (Bizzell, 1992; Cope & Kalantzis, 1993), the inductive, discovery-based nature of process-oriented practice typically avoids prerevealing learning aims (Feez, 2002; Hasan, 1996).

With their strong emphasis on idea generation, self-discovery, and problem solving, process pedagogies also tend to imply that "'product' is not important" (Delpit, 1988, p. 287). Conveying such a message can be particularly damaging to minority and non–native-speaker (NNS) writers who have not been socialized into adopting, let alone embracing, the nondirective, discovery-based precepts and practices of process writing. In fact, many process approaches "draw heavily on inaccessible cultural knowledge" (Hyland, 2003, p. 21), which well-intentioned teachers may falsely assume all students have available to them. Indeed, prototypical components of process-based instruction (e.g., personal writing, multiple drafting, extensive revision, minimal form-focused feedback) can be mystifying to NNS writers, particularly those in EFL and multilingual contexts in which prevailing educational traditions do not support such practices (Holliday, 1994).

Along similar lines, just as the promotion of voice in L1 composition pedagogy has come into question (Bowden, 1999, 2003), L2 experts have challenged the appropriateness of this abstract metaphor in ESL and EFL writing instruction (Atkinson, 2000; Belcher & Hirvela, 2001b; Ramanathan & Atkinson, 1999b;

Ramanathan & Kaplan, 1996a). Development of one's voice is undeniably a vital component of writing proficiency. Stapleton (2003), for example, acknowledged that voice "should be brought into the mainstream of L2 writing pedagogy either via consciousness raising or through the specific teaching of certain features" (p. 187). However, he offered a strong caution regarding voicist pedagogies, warning that overplaying the voice metaphor "sends the message to teachers that voice is critically important, and this message, if passed down to students, may result in learners who are more concerned with identity than ideas" (p. 187).

Some of the groundwork for constructing a post-process framework was laid by cognitivists who recognized that writing, as a form of literacy, is an inherently social, transactional process that involves mediation between the writer and his or her audience (Bazerman, 1988; Bereiter & Scardamalia, 1987; Cope & Kalantzis, 1993; Flower, 1994; Gee, 1996, 1998). As a transactional activity, writing represents a process that must be undertaken with the reader's background knowledge, needs, interests, and ideologies in mind. By understanding their readers and by anticipating reader expectations, writers shape their texts so that they meet these expectations effectively (Hinds, 1987; K. Hyland, 2000, 2003; Johns, 1997, 2003). According to this social constructionist view, the audience or target discourse community largely determines knowledge, language, and the nature of both spoken and written discourse (Bruffee, 1986; Coe, 1987; Cope & Kalantzis, 2000; Prior, 2001).

A discourse community comprises a minimum number of expert members and frequently a larger number of apprentice members who operate on the basis of implicit and explicit public goals (Swales, 1990, 1998). It is informative to examine discourse communities because their members develop and use speech and writing systems that often are specific to a particular community's needs, goals, and ideologies (Gee, 1999). Within these systems, we often find participatory mechanisms used by community members to transmit information and feedback (e.g., meetings, print publications, and electronic messages) as well as text types and genres that promote collective goals (e.g., letters, newspapers, books, and journal articles) with particular formal (rhetorical, grammatical, lexical) features (Freedman & Medway, 1994a, 1994c; Johns, 1995a, 2002b, 2003).

The access of novice writers to academic discourse communities depends fundamentally on the mastery of certain communication skills. These skills might include the writing of expository or persuasive essays for college composition courses (Bizzell, 1992), the preparation of empirical research reports for the physical sciences (Bazerman, 1985, 1988, 1998; Myers, 1990), or the composition of documents in the workplace (Bhatia, 1993, 1999). Given these institutional, educational, and social demands, composition instruction must provide novice writers with opportunities for practicing and appropriating the content knowledge, language, and rhetorical expertise represented in the academy and in the specific disciplines that students wish to join (Berkenkotter & Huckin, 1995; K. Hyland, 2000; Johns, 1997; Reid, 1989; Spack, 1988). These multiple communicative functions and transactions coincide with a broad conceptualization of contemporary rhetoric, that Williams (1996) defined as "the conscious control of language to bring about an intended effect in an audience" (p. 27).

Pedagogical models have been proposed to assist writers in gaining control over language and written genres, and in becoming apprenticed to the discourse communities associated with these genres (Bishop & Ostrom, 1997; Briggs & Bauman, 1992). Because L2 writing pedagogy has in many respects paralleled L1 composition in terms of theory and practice (Leki, 1991b, 1992; Matsuda, 1999, 2003b; Raimes, 1998), the next section explores ideological, theoretical, and methodological developments as they pertain specifically to the teaching of composition in ESL and EFL classrooms.

The Emergence of a Discipline: Issues and Methods in L2 Writing

Based on presumed and observed similarities between L1 and L2 composing processes, ESL writing instruction in the early 1980s largely replicated L1 classroom practice (Leki, 1992; Matsuda, 2003b). Not only did research in L1 composition and rhetoric provide sound theoretical underpinnings for L2 composing pedagogy, emergent L2 writing research also began to show that ESL writers already proficient in writing in their primary languages tended to display strategies and skills parallel to those displayed by native English-speaking writers. For instance, Cumming (1989) and Zamel (1976, 1982, 1983) demonstrated that ESL writers with well-developed L1 writing abilities tended to transfer L1 skills and strategies to their L2 composing processes. The ESL students in these investigations displayed skills that included planning, grappling successfully with specific writing tasks, organizing their ideas, and revising their texts to reflect their intentions as writers. Cumming (1989) also reported that the ability of his intermediate- and advanced-level writers to practice these strategies as they composed in English was an independent function of their measured ESL proficiency. This study and others like it led some L2 writing researchers and practitioners to conclude that ESL students' needs are essentially comparable with those of basic L1 writers in terms of composing processes and their instructional needs.

Nonnative linguistic proficiency does not seem to prevent ESL writers from becoming effective writers of English, yet many such learners require assistance in developing written fluency and practice with a range of composing strategies and written genres. Some experts (Jones & Tetroe, 1987; Zamel, 1983) have argued that the primary needs of ESL writers consist of extensive and directed practice with global writing functions, as opposed to more extensive language instruction. Research involving ESL writers who are inexperienced writers in their L1s tends to suggest that, like their NS peers, NNSs may lack a sense of direction as they undertake composing tasks, may experience difficulty categorizing and sequencing information according to reader expectations, and may often get stalled at intermediate steps in their composing and revision processes (Bereiter & Scardamalia, 1987; Bosher, 1998; Cumming, 1989; Raimes, 1985). Consequently, less experienced L1 and L2 writers may focus prematurely—and with less than satisfactory results—on microlevel features such as grammatical, lexical, and mechanical accuracy, as opposed to discourse-level concerns such as audience, purpose, rhetorical structure, coherence, cohesion, and clarity (Cumming, 1989; Jones, 1985; New, 1999). Given that novice L1 and L2 writers appear to share such characteristics, many models of L2 composing pedagogy, particularly, those that emphasize process writing and multidrafting, assume that L2 writers benefit from the same instructional techniques as those used in L1 composition settings (Krapels, 1990; Leki, 1991b, 1992). Several recent studies (Lally, 2000a, 2000b; Ma & Wen, 1999; Olsen, 1999; Thorson, 2000) have nonetheless suggested that L2 writers may require targeted instruction aimed at the development of specific linguistic skills, rhetorical expertise, and composing strategies.

Shifts in Pedagogical Focus

Approaches to L2 composition reflect parallel (although by no means simultaneous) developments in L1 composition and rhetoric. Historical accounts of ESL writing theory and practice (Cumming, 2001; Hedgcock, in press; Leki, 2000; Matsuda, 2003a, 2003b; Raimes, 1998) provide meaningful insights into how ESL writing theory and practice have evolved and how the field has achieved status as a discipline in its own right. For the sake of expediency, we summarize major trends in ESL writing according to the following foci, which we link to relevant approaches, schools of thought, and ideologies.

Focus on Discursive Form, Traditional Form, and "Current–Traditional Rhetoric," 1966–.

Raimes (1991) and Matsuda (2003b) traced formally oriented L2 writing approaches to the audiolingual tradition in second language teaching (Fries, 1945), in which writing served essentially to reinforce oral patterns of the language being learned and to test learners' accurate application of grammatical rules (Rivers, 1968).

Early L2 composition pedagogy emphasized the production of well-formed sentences. A writing task that typifies this paradigm is the controlled composition, a narrowly focused paragraph- or essay-length assignment designed principally to give students practice with specific syntactic patterns (e.g., the past simple and past progressive in narration) as well as lexical forms (Kroll, 2001; Matsuda, 1999; Silva, 1990).

In an extension of this model, known as "current–traditional rhetoric" (Berlin & Inkster, 1980; Grabe & Kaplan, 1996; Silva, 1990), students also were instructed to generate connected discourse by combining and arranging sentences into paragraphs based on prescribed formulas. Representative composing tasks involved the imitation of specific rhetorical patterns (e.g., exposition, exemplification, comparison, classification, argumentation, and so forth) based on authentic samples and sometimes student-generated models (Barnett, 2002).

Focus on the Writer: Expressionism and Cognitivism, 1976–.

Congruent with process approaches to L1 composition (described earlier), a focus on the writer in L2 composition has drawn researchers' and teachers' attention to what writers "actually do as they write" (Raimes, 1991, p. 409). Researchers in this paradigm therefore attempted to characterize the heuristics, cognitive strategies, and metacognitive processes used by writers as they plan, draft, read, revise, and edit their texts (Cumming, 2001; Manchón, 2001; Ransdell & Barbier, 2002b). Classroom procedures associated with this writer-based orientation include practice with invention strategies (see chapter 4), creation and sharing of multiple drafts, peer collaboration, abundant revision, and implementation of editing strategies. Syllabi reflecting this approach may likewise allow writers to select their own topics and take more time to complete writing tasks than would be possible with a formally oriented approach.

Focus on Disciplinary Content and Discursive Practices, 1986–. Reservations concerning writer-centered instructional designs have been expressed by researchers and practitioners who argue that the "almost total obsession" (Horowitz, 1986c, p. 788) with how writers construct personal meaning overlooks the need of many NS and NNS writers to compose texts for academic or professional readers with particular expertise (Coe, 1987; Horowitz, 1986a; Hyland, 2000, 2003; Johns, 1997, 2003). In response to this perceived need, experts have proposed shifting the methodological emphasis in the direction of the knowledge and written genres characteristic of ESL students' specific areas of study and academic disciplines.

Instead of replacing writing processes with the pedagogical material characteristic of traditional English courses (i.e., language, literature, and culture), proponents of content- and genre-based instruction assert that ESL writing courses should feature the specific subject matter that ESL students must master in their major and required courses (Crandall & Kaufman, 2001; Dudley-Evans & St. John, 1998; Flowerdew, 2002; Johns & Price-Machado, 2001; Jordan, 1997; Kasper, 2000; Pally, 2000; Paltridge, 2002; Reppen, 1994/1995; Snow, 2001; Snow & Brinton, 1988, 1997). In this model, students in adjunct, multiskill, English for Academic Purposes (EAP), and English for Specific Purposes (ESP) courses are given assistance with "the language of the thinking processes and the structure or shape of content" (Mohan, 1986, p. 18). This focus on content does not preclude the use of writer-driven, process-oriented principles and procedures such as prewriting, revision, collaboration, and peer review (Guleff, 2002; Horowitz, 1986b; Johns, 2003). The fundamental emphasis "is on the instructor's determination of what academic content is most appropriate to build whole courses or modules of reading and writing tasks around that content" (Raimes, 1991, p. 411).

Focus on Readers and Discursive Communities: Social Constructionism, 1986–. Overlapping considerably with content-based models, reader- and discourse-based frameworks for ESL writing instruction have emerged partly in opposition to the prescriptions of writer-centered approaches, described by Horowitz (1986a) as a form of "humanistic therapy" (p. 789). Reader- and discourse-oriented composition pedagogy is founded instead on the social constructionist premise that NS and NNS writers need to be apprenticed into one or more academic discourse communities, and that writing instruction consequently should prepare students to anticipate, satisfy, and even challenge the demands of academic readers (i.e., their instructors and other authorities) as they generate their written products (Flower, 1979; Flower, Long, & Higgins, 2000; Hinds, 1987; Hyland, 2002; Johns, 1990; Pennycook, 2001).

Clearly, socioliterate approaches (Johns, 1997) are highly compatible with content-based approaches, ideologically and methodologically. Interestingly, some have interpreted the implementation of socioliterate pedagogies as entailing a return to a directive, prescriptive stance with respect to materials selection and classroom pedagogy (Benesch, 2001; Freedman & Medway, 1994b). To operationalize a reader-centered pedagogy emphasizing discipline-specific rhetorical forms, teachers need to collect texts and assignments from the relevant disciplines, analyze their purposes, assess audience expectations, and acquaint learners with their findings. According to this view, writing instruction most appropriately centers on identifying, practicing, and reproducing the implicit and explicit features of written texts aimed at particular audiences.

Focus on Sociopolitical Issues and Critical Pedagogy, 1990–.

With a number of scholars appealing to "Freirean notions of liberatory literacy practices" (Grabe & Kaplan, 1996, p. 32), the educational, ethical, and political dimensions of L2 writing instruction, including genre-oriented and socioliterate models, have come under careful scrutiny in recent years (Freire, 1970, 1985, 1994; Freire & Macedo, 1987). Zamel (1993), for instance, argued that academic literacy instruction should enable writers to comprehend, analyze, and negotiate the demands of academic disciplines.

Belcher and Braine (1995) pointed out that the teaching of academic literacy should no longer be understood as "neutral, value-free, and nonexclusionary" (p. xiii). Consequently, ESL/EFL writing specialists have begun to address issues of critical pedagogy, including critical needs analysis (Benesch, 1996), critical discourse analysis (Fairclough, 1995), critical writing about academic genres (Benesch, 2001; Hyland, 2002), the complexity of text appropriation and plagiarism (Bloch, 2001; Hyland, 2000; Pecorari, 2001; Pennycook, 1996), race and class issues (Canagarajah, 2002; Vandrick, 1995), gender equality and inequality (Belcher, 1997; Kirsch & Ritchie, 1995; Vandrick, 1994), and identity (Ivanic, 1998; Norton, 1997).

A major thread in applications of critical pedagogy to literacy instruction stems from the charge that social constructionist approaches have tended to overlook "sociopolitical issues affecting life in and outside of academic settings" (Benesch, 2001, p. xv). Whereas EAP and socioliterate approaches embrace the precept that writing and the teaching of writing always have social purposes, critical pedagogy challenges assumptions that those purposes are necessarily value free or beneficial to novice writers.

These ideological, theoretical, and methodological orientations do not reflect discrete historical periods, epistemological models, or ideological orientations. In other words, whereas each focus represents a distinct instructional purpose and area of core interest, we can see considerable chronological, conceptual, and practical overlap among them. The conflicts and compatibilities that exist among these orientations can certainly cause confusion among ESL writing teachers in search of answers to pedagogical questions.

Nonetheless, with the maturation of L2 writing as a discipline and profession, progress has been made, and it is increasingly possible to navigate a sometimes bewildering landscape of theories and practices (Kroll, 2003b). To make sense of a challenging and perplexing situation, Silva (1990) first proposed that L2 writing be approached systematically as "purposeful and contextualized communicative interaction, which involves both the construction and transmission of knowledge" (p. 18). Working within this framework, we then can consider the following components of composing processes as we assess research and theory, and in doing so, make sound decisions about our own teaching practices:

- *The ESL writer.*   The writer as a person (i.e., his or her personal knowledge, attitudes, learning styles, cultural orientation, orientations, evolving identity, language proficiency, and motivational profile, in addition to his or her composing strategies) (see chapter 3).
- *The NS reader as the ESL writer's primary audience.* The L1 reader's needs and expectations as a respondent

and as a potential evaluator of the ESL student's written products (see chapters 5, 6, and 7).

- *The writer's texts.* The writer's products as represented by their purposes, formal characteristics, and signifying constituent elements: genre, rhetorical form, discursive mode, coherence, cohesion, syntactic properties, lexical patterns, mechanical features, print-code properties, and so on (see chapters 2 through 7).
- *The contexts for writing.* Cultural, political, social, economic, situational, and physical dimensions of the writer's texts (see this chapter and chapter 6).
- *The interaction of all these components in authentic educational and disciplinary settings.*

Sources: Polio, 2003; Raimes, 1991; Silva, 1990.

We can begin to formulate our own operational theories of how ESL writers learn to write, and how we can shape our instruction to meet their needs effectively, by adopting a critical view of L2 composing theory and research. In addition, it is important for us to appreciate how this work has been informed by developments in L1 composition, rhetoric, and their allied fields. An operational understanding of theoretical and pedagogical paradigms can sensitize us to our students' strengths and weaknesses. It also can equip us to implement a balanced, informed, and effective pedagogy that takes into account the multiple dimensions of L2 writers' developing skills in composing.

Prior Knowledge and Its Implications for the Teaching of L2 Writing

A primary feature distinguishing NNS from NS writers lies in the prior experience they bring to the composition classroom. Differences in background knowledge and strategic proficiency manifest themselves in a variety of ways: in NNS students' responses to texts and topics, in their reactions to the activities of ESL writing classrooms, and in their familiarity with the rhetorical patterns of academic and professional discourse communities (Fig. 1.1).

This prior knowledge about texts, their purposes, their genre categories, and their formal properties are part of a learner's schema. A schema refers to an "organized chunk of knowledge or experience, often accompanied by feelings" (Weaver, 1994, p. 18). In psycholinguistic and cognitive approaches to L1 and L2

```
Knowledge brought to the writing class
    about reading and writing topics
    about written texts
    about rhetorical patterns of academic writing in English
    about the expectations of English-speaking academic readers
Reactions to the writing class
    about the role of personal expression in English writing
    about writing from sources and using the work of others
    about peer response and teacher-student conferences
    about teachers' response techniques
    about revision procedures
```

FIG. 1.1. Cultural and rhetorical differences between L1 and L2 writers.

reading, schema has been discussed in terms of both content and formal knowledge about texts (Aebersold & Field, 1997; Carrell, 1983a, 1983b; Carrell & Eisterhold, 1983; Chen & Graves, 1995; Grabe & Stoller, 2002b), particularly the facilitative effects of adequate schemata—and, conversely, the debilitating impact of the absence of sufficient schematic knowledge—among L2 readers and writers.

The notion of schema as it relates to formal instruction rests on several precepts: that literacy events involve an interaction between readers and texts (Rumelhart & McClelland, 1982), that readers' responses to and comprehension of a text vary according to individuals' schemata and other circumstances at the time of the interaction (Weaver, 1994), and that schemata include not only the content of a text, but also its organization (Carrell, 1987). For example, imagine that you are reading a recipe in a magazine, newspaper, or web page. What would you expect the content and the organization of that text to comprise? You probably would anticipate finding a list of necessary ingredients and then a sequential list of steps to follow in order to prepare the dish. A recipe that deviates from this expected structure might frustrate or confuse you. These expectations constitute your formal and content schemata. Of course, if you have never cooked a meal or baked a cake, your schemata related to recipes will be quite different from those of a skilled cook. Moreover, your experience with reading that text will vary depending on the circumstances: Are you merely glancing at the recipe to consider it for a future meal? Are you in the kitchen at this moment preparing dinner? The specific situation naturally will affect the level of concentration and attention to detail that you bring to the reading task.

The findings of L1 and L2 literacy research have generally demonstrated that "when content and form are familiar, reading and writing are relatively easy. But when one or the other (or both) are unfamiliar, efficiency, effectiveness, and success are problematic" (Reid, 1993a, p. 63). A major implication of schema theory is that teachers should take systematic steps to ensure that students find the texts and topics of a course accessible—cognitively, culturally, and educationally (Ediger, 2001; Moran, 2001). These goals can be achieved by selecting reading materials and writing tasks that allow learners to capitalize on their prior experience. Teachers can likewise devise in-class activities that develop and expand students' schemata. Specific suggestions for schema activation and development are presented in chapters 2, 3, and 4.

Contrastive Rhetoric and Its Implications for Teaching ESL Writing

As we have suggested, an important way that the schemata of L2 students differ from those of L1 writers involves their expectations about the structural properties and rhetorical functions of texts. The study of contrastive rhetoric (CR) aims to characterize these divergent expectations and their effects on L2 literacy development, including L2 writing skills. Connor (1996) wrote that "contrastive rhetoric maintains that language and writing are cultural phenomena. As a result, each language has rhetorical conventions unique to it. Furthermore, the linguistic and rhetorical conventions of the first language interfere with writing in the second language" (p. 5).

The Genesis of Contrastive Rhetoric. Kaplan's (1966) pioneering article is frequently considered to be a landmark work in the study of CR. At the time that Kaplan's article appeared, contrastive analysis (CA) and its application to foreign- and second-language instruction were very much in vogue. With the CA approach, linguists and materials developers compared the grammatical structures and phonological features of learners' L1s with those of the L2 they were trying to acquire. It was believed that CA could identify specific areas of difficulty (e.g., in syntax and speech production), and that direct instruction focusing on major contrastive features could facilitate and accelerate the language learning process (Gass & Selinker, 2001; Mitchell & Myles, 1998).

Against the backdrop of CA, Kaplan (1966) suggested that L2 students' L1s also exhibited contrasting rhetorical and logical patterns. His study featured a formal analysis of more than 600 texts written by NNS writers representing a range of primary languages. On the basis of his rhetorical analysis, Kaplan proposed the following generalizations: Arabic-speaking writers make extensive use of coordination (considered excessive by English-speaking readers), speakers of "Oriental" languages tend to circle around a topic instead of approaching it head-on, and speakers of French and Spanish tend to digress and introduce extraneous material more than NNS writers of English do.

The Impact of CR in ESL Writing Instruction. Kaplan's ground-breaking article ignited considerable interest in CR, which has since generated an impressive body of empirical research. In characterizing the impact of Kaplan's work, Hinkel (2002) noted that CR research

> pursues the goal of descriptive accuracy that originates in pedagogical necessity. He specified that L2 students enrolled in U.S. colleges and universities are expected to produce academic texts that are congruent with Anglo-American rhetorical paradigms. However, these students bring to the larger academic arena the fundamental discourse paradigms that reflect their L1 conventions of writing, and need to be taught the textual constructs accepted in writing in English. (p. 6)

With its focus on the written products of expert and novice writers (as compared with the writers themselves), CR has led to spirited discussions concerning the possible influences of L2 writers' primary languages, their knowledge of L1-specific rhetorical patterns, and their educational experiences on the construction of their written products. Although hardly uncontroversial, CR has contributed much to our understanding of rhetorical patterns in written text across a range of genres by accounting for the frequency of selected rhetorical features in written discourse, the conventions associated with particular written genres, and the patterns of text construction across numerous languages (Bräuer, 2000; Connor, 2003).

In the years after the publication of Kaplan's (1966) research, ESL and composition professionals interpreted his findings as suggesting a number of instructional implications. For instance, many teachers felt that the CR hypothesis pointed to the need among L2 writers for explicit instruction and modeling in the rhetorical patterns of English (Angelova & Riazantseva, 1999; Kirkpatrick, 1997). Not unexpectedly, this view dovetailed nicely with current–traditional approaches to writing instruction that prevailed in the 1960s and 1970s, and into the 1980s.

Nonetheless, as the CR hypothesis underwent increasing scrutiny, a number of reservations surfaced concerning its validity and empirical premises (Panetta, 2001). Kaplan's (1966) early work was criticized for the alleged imprecision of his analytic categories (e.g., his classification of all Asian writers in his sample under the broad category, of "Oriental") (Zhang, 1997). Critics have likewise asserted that Kaplan's early framework was overly simple, given his attempt to reconstruct L1 rhetorical patterns from compositions written in students' L2s (Holyoak & Piper, 1997). In addition, detractors have argued that CR models were deterministic, leading to rigid, ethnocentric views of English rhetorical patterns and potentially damaging stereotypes of ESL writers (Kachru, 1995; Kubota, 1997, 1999; Leki, 1997; Scollon, 1997; Wu & Rubin, 2000; Zamel, 1997).

Nevertheless, CR-based studies have produced useful evidence of differing rhetorical patterns across diverse languages, indicating measurable effects of L1-specific discursive and sentence-level patterns on the texts of ESL writers (Connor 1996, 2003; Connor & Kaplan, 1987; Kaplan, 1987, 1988; Leki, 1991b, 1992; Purves, 1988; Reid, 1993a). Hinds' (1983a, 1983b, 1987) investigations of Japanese and English argumentation styles provide a clear and persuasive example. In his studies, Hinds discovered that English-speaking readers expected writers to make clear, unambiguous statements of their points of view, usually near the beginning of a persuasive text. In contrast, he reported that Japanese-speaking writers elected to obscure their own opinions in their presentation of the various sides of an issue, taking a position only at the end of the text, if at all. Having probed his writers' and readers' perceptions of persuasive writing, he discovered that Japanese readers found the linear, deductive argumentation style associated with English-language texts to be dull, pointless, and self-involved. At the same time, English-speaking readers perceived Japanese argumentative patterns to be circuitous, abstract, and occasionally evasive.

The strong predictive claims made by early CR researchers no longer characterize this important line of empirical study in L2 writing (Connor, 2003; Hinkel, 2002; Kaplan, 2001), yet even the most conservative scholars acknowledge the descriptive value of careful CR research. According to state-of-the-art CR research, we cannot assume that all writers from a given linguistic or cultural background will experience the same difficulties in a given L2.

However, the knowledge that logical patterns of organization in written language differ cross-culturally and cross-linguistically can help both teachers and students understand issues and challenges involved in composing in an L2 (Angelova & Riazantseva, 1999; Kirkpatrick, 1997). Leki (1991a) and Reid (1993a) suggested several ways in which an understanding of CR findings can inform L2 writing instruction. These suggestions are summarized in Fig. 1.2.

We believe that L2 writing teachers must be aware of the rhetorical knowledge that their novice writers bring to the composition course. This rhetorical knowledge may include formal and content schemata as well as implicit and explicit knowledge about text structure, genres, and their purposes. It is essential to recognize, however, that L2 writers' L1s, cultures, and prior educational experience do not predetermine their difficulties or abilities in mastering the genres and text structures that typify English-language writing (Atkinson, 1999). The backgrounds and knowledge bases of L2 writers' differ not only from those of NS writers of English, but also from those of other L2 writers. In other words, each L2 writer should be viewed in individual terms, not as a prototype representing a set of collective norms or stereotypes (Scollon, 1997). Individual differences across novice

---

Implications

1. Familiarity with CR findings can assist teachers in understanding some of the culturally and educationally based influences on rhetorical patterns in L2 students' written production.
2. An understanding of CR research can help teachers avoid stereotypes, leading them to view L2 writers as individuals who may or may not incorporate L1-based rhetorical patterns into their L2 writing.
3. Insights from CR may help L2 writers appreciate and understand L1-based cultural and educational factors that underlie their L2 written production.
4. CR findings can show students that their L2 writing development may be affected by cultural patterns and rhetorical practices rather than individual inadequacies (adapted from Leki, 1991b).

Applications

1. Teachers can collect literacy assignments across the curriculum to "become more informed about appropriate . . . academic discourse patterns" in the L2.
2. Teachers can analyze diverse assignments "to inform their . . . writing students about discourse differences and audience expectations."
3. Teachers then can plan activities and lessons around this information "to provide practice with the imposition of appropriate patterns upon experience and to offer opportunities for practice and experience with the new schema" (adapted from Reid, 1993b, p. 63; cf. Kirkpatrick, 1997).

FIG. 1.2.   Implications and applications of contrastive rhetoric.

L2 writers affect their abilities to comprehend, analyze, and respond to the texts they read, to function effectively in the L2 literacy classroom, and to construct original texts that fulfill the expectations of target language readers. Consequently, ESL writing teachers must consider the implications of schematic and rhetorical differences in the readings they select, the tasks they assign, the modes of instruction they deploy, the assessment instruments they use, and the feedback they offer their student writers.

THE UNIQUENESS OF ESL WRITERS: CLASSROOM IMPLICATIONS

The preceding discussion addressed aspects of L2 composing theory, research, and pedagogy that drew on parallels with L1 composition and rhetoric. It also dealt with ideological assumptions, empirical discoveries, and instructional approaches that make implicit and explicit distinctions between L1 and L2 composing processes and strategies, particularly with respect to CR research. Silva (1993) observed that "L2 writing is strategically, rhetorically, and linguistically different in important ways from L1 writing" (p. 696). It is, therefore, crucial for L2 writing teachers—as well as L1 composition instructors whose mainstream classes include L2 writers—to understand fundamental characteristics that distinguish L2 writers, and to appreciate the diversity of learners whom they may encounter in their composition courses. This variety of backgrounds, goals, and expectations on the part of novice ESL writers accentuates the complexity of an already challenging educational endeavor.

We embrace the precept that "there is no such thing as a generalized ESL student" (Raimes, 1991, p. 420). If ESL writers (or any other type of writer, for that matter) constituted a homogeneous group, our task as composition professionals might simply entail making decisions about the optimal instructional approach or approaches to adopt, on the basis of current expert knowledge (Kumaravadivelu, 2003). In fact, however, ESL instructors in many educational settings are keenly aware of the challenges posed by student populations that are heterogeneous in terms of linguistic, ethnic, and cultural background, not to mention language proficiency, literacy, educational attainment, and cognitive development (Cumming, 2001; Leki, 2000; Raimes, 1998; Spack, 1997b). Also of concern to classroom teachers are learners' attitudes toward learning, formal instruction, and the target subject matter, as well as students' motivation to acquire linguistic, cognitive, and academic skills. Other factors known to influence learning include age, academic goals, aptitude, anxiety, cognitive strategy use, language awareness, and social distance.

We mention these variables here to acknowledge the enormously complex challenges facing classroom teachers of ESL writers. At the same time, we suggest general directions for identifying, categorizing, and working with these multiple variables in planning and delivering instruction. The individual differences (ID) research in second language acquisition has shed considerable light on the multiple learner-specific, linguistic, and environmental factors bearing on L2 learners' success, or failure, in their efforts to acquire L2 knowledge and skills. In general, ID research has focused on how ID variables influence learner development, proficiency, and achievement, as measured in quantifiable performances (Ellis, 1994; Gass & Selinker, 2001; Lightbown & Spada, 1999; Mitchell & Myles, 1998; Skehan, 1989, 1991, 1998; Williams & Burden, 1997).

Notwithstanding a few notable exceptions (Lally, 2000b; Reid, 1995b), the L2 composition literature seldom draws upon this research, yet it is worthy of our attention because it offers a systematic framework for identifying roughly hewn, but easily identifiable, ID factors known to influence language proficiency, academic performance, and student predispositions toward writing processes and tasks. Of particular relevance to ESL composition are dimensions of learners' knowledge and prior training that have shaped their current linguistic capabilities, L1 and L2 literacy skills, metacognitive strategy repertoires, and language awareness. Figure 1.3 summarizes a few of the major features that may set ESL writers apart from NS writers.

As the previous sections on schema theory and CR observed in some detail, a chief characteristic distinguishing ESL writers from their NS peers is that ESL students come to the classroom with the ability to speak, and often write, one or more languages other than English. This multilingual, multicultural, and, in many cases, multiliterate, knowledge gives ESL students a unique status as learners that entails a set of linguistic, metalinguistic, cognitive, and metacognitive skills. This skill set may be very different from the skill sets of monolingual, NSs of English (Brisk & Harrington, 2000; Carrell & Monroe, 1995; Harklau, Losey, & Siegel, 1999). Based on the findings of CR research and genre analysis, we have suggested that this rich knowledge can both facilitate and impede progress in the development of L2 writing proficiency.

	NS Writers . . .	ESL Writers . . .
Knowledge of language and writing systems	• begin with "intact" knowledge of spoken and written English • are principally acquiring English composing skills • are familiar with the Roman alphabet and English orthographic conventions • produce sentence-level errors that are not influenced by knowledge of another language • are not influenced by rhetorical knowledge emanating from another language, writing system, or rhetorical tradition, although they may be unfamiliar with formal rhetorical conventions (i.e., organizational sequences, coherence and cohesion markers, and so forth).	• begin with an intact L1 and a developing knowledge of spoken and written English as a second language • are simultaneously acquiring language and composing skills • may or may not be familiar with the Roman alphabet and thus still may be acquiring English graphemic and orthographic conventions • may produce sentence-level errors influenced by their primary language(s) • may have L1-related rhetorical knowledge (i.e., organizational sequences, coherence and cohesion markers, and so forth) that could facilitate or possibly inhibit the learning of English rhetorical conventions.
Schematic and rhetorical knowledge	• have topical and schematic knowledge specific to English-speaking discourse communities, cultures, and educational systems • have access to (and perhaps some knowledge of) English-speaking readers' expectations • by virtue of educational experience in an English-speaking discourse community, have exposure to (and experience with) rhetorical conventions of school-based writing in English.	• may not have the same topical or schematic knowledge as NS writers because of educational experience (e.g., in an L1 discourse community) • may be unfamiliar with the expectations of English-speaking readers • may have little or no experience with rhetorical conventions of writing in English-speaking discourse communities; may have been trained in rhetorical conventions of a L1 educational tradition, which may contrast with those observed in English-speaking discourse communities.
Responses to composition instruction	• may have experience with personal writing and the development of individual voice • may have experience with peer response (and may expect it) • may have experience using published sources, paraphrasing, quoting, and so on • may have received instruction in how to avoid plagiarism • may have extensive experience with teachers' response and feedback styles (e.g., marginal notes, questioning, indirectness, and so forth) • may expect to revise assignments significantly.	• may have some experience with personal writing and expressing voice, or none at all (especially in school contexts) • may have little or no experience with peer response • may have little or no experience using published sources, paraphrasing, or quoting • may have undergone little or no instruction in how to avoid plagiarism • may have little or no experience with teachers' interactive response and feedback styles (e.g., marginal notes, questioning, indirectness, and so forth); may expect little or no feedback for revision • may not expect to revise assignments significantly (if at all).

FIG. 1.3. Overview of differences between novice NS and ESL writers.

SUMMARY

The individual cognitive, linguistic, ethnic, and socioeconomic background factors highlighted in the previous section (by no means an exhaustive survey) underscore the priority of taking into account students' unique personal and educational profiles, as well as the characteristics of particular educational institutions. Clearly, individual differences and institutional factors can have direct and rather specific implications for classroom practice in ESL and EFL environments. Despite the apparent parallels between the composing processes of L1 and L2 writers highlighted in the first part of this chapter, ESL writers represent a unique learner population (Silva, 1993, 1997). Therefore, the development of a sound approach to the teaching of ESL composition necessitates an appreciation of these unique features, as well as strategies for accommodating them. To synthesize this chapter's chief content, we present the following summary statements as a foundation for considering the topic-specific material outlined in the succeeding chapters:

- By virtue of their emergent L2 proficiency and literacy skills, ESL writers should not be expected to perform like their NS peers on writing tasks and tests designed for NS writers. We reject a deficit view of L2 writers, yet composition instructors should understand why ESL writers' texts can vary, qualitatively and quantitatively, from comparable NS writers' texts in terms of linguistic form, rhetorical structure, and even content.
- In their development of L2 literacy skills, ESL writers have needs specific to their status as NNS students. That is, in light of their implicit and explicit linguistic knowledge, prior educational experience, L1 and L2 literacy skills, cognitive development, and metacognitive skill and strategy use, ESL writers have unique instructional needs that may not be fully or effectively addressed in NS-oriented or mainstream composition courses.
- These particular needs can be accurately identified and appropriately accommodated by composition teachers equipped with theoretical and practical knowledge of L2 writing processes, as well as an awareness of the unique linguistic and cultural expertise of L2 writers.
- Apprentice ESL writers may require "more of everything" in terms of reading skill development, idea

generation techniques, planning heuristics, drafting practice, and feedback incorporation than their NS counterparts (Raimes, 1985, p. 250). Teachers of L2 composition may offer their students the greatest benefit by devoting "more time and attention across the board to strategic, rhetorical, and linguistic concerns" (Silva, 1993, p. 670).

- Instruction in L2 composition may be maximally effective when it intentionally directs writers' attention toward macro- and micro-level textual concerns, including audience expectations, rhetorical forms, lexicogrammatical variety, and formal accuracy.

REFLECTION AND REVIEW

1. Compare the following theoretical orientations toward L1 and L2 composition and rhetoric: traditional paradigms, current–traditional models, process approaches (expressivist and cognitivist perspectives), and post-process approaches (including social constructionist views). What theoretical, ideological, and practical characteristics do these models have in common?

2. To what extent do you feel that the following emphases in L2 writing instruction are complementary: focus on formal features of text, focus on the writer, focus on content, focus on readers and discursive communities, and, focus on sociopolitical issues and critical pedagogy? Explain your point of view by referring to your own experience as a student or teacher of writing.

3. Summarize and evaluate the cognitive, perceptual, communicative, and creative consequences and advantages of being bilingual or biliterate in monolingual and multilingual discourse communities. In what ways can bilingual and biliterate knowledge promote various types of learning, particularly learning to write?

Application Activity 1.1: Guided Retrospection

Directions: Reflect again on your experience as a writing student in an L1 or L2 setting, either in written form or in an informal discussion with a group of classmates. Explain how you would characterize the instructional approach or approaches used in these courses in terms of one or more of the major theoretical orientations presented in this chapter (i.e., traditional and current-traditional paradigms, process approaches [expressivist and cognitivist], and post-process models [including social constructionist approaches], and so on).

Application Activity 1.2: Classroom Observation Task

Directions: Individually or with a classmate arrange to visit at least one NS and one ESL composition class. Before going into the field to conduct your observations, select or develop a set of focused, easy-to-use classroom observation tools for capturing classroom behaviors and processes of specific interest to you (see, for example, Allwright & Bailey, 1991; Borich, 1999; or Wajnryb, 1992). Use these tools to focus your attention as you take field notes. After your observation, prepare a written observation report in which you describe and make inferences about the following:

1. Information concerning course level, the literacy curriculum, assignment types in progress, institution type, student demographics (ESL proficiency, gender ratio, L1 backgrounds), and so on
2. The contents, sequence, procedures, and tasks you observed during the lesson
3. The instructor's explicit and implicit objectives for the lesson and its component parts (i.e., tasks, activities, assignments)
4. The extent to which the instructor's objectives were met
5. The instructor's and the institution's dominating theoretical–ideological orientation toward literacy, writing in particular
6. Evidence of the students' learning as observed in their behaviors and written products. Use the preceding steps as basic guidelines for reporting and reflecting on your classroom observations. You also may wish to consider the following additional options for maximizing your observational experience:
   a. In one or more observations, focus on a single writer and his or her behaviors throughout the lesson. Interview the student before and after the lesson to capture his

or her impressions of the composition class, composing processes, and so forth.
b. Meet with the instructor before and after your observation to learn about his or her explicit expectations for, and perceptions of, the lesson that you examined. Compare the instructor's impressions with your own.
c. Compare a NS composition class to an ESL composition class in terms of long-term goals, lesson objectives, procedures, tasks, and student behaviors. Discuss the similarities and differences between the theoretical-ideological orientations of the classes.

Include an appendix with your field notes and any other materials related to the course (e.g., the syllabus, assignment sheets, and so forth) as part of your complete observation report.

Application Activity 1.3: Introspective Process Analysis

Directions

1. Select a substantial academic writing task that you have been assigned in one of your regular courses (e.g., a bibliographic essay, a term project, a position paper). Select an assignment that requires extended prose and involves revision (i.e., not a 24-hour take-home examination or a short homework assignment).
2. Maintain a chronological log in which you record notes on your processes, procedures, and decision making throughout the development of this assignment. At the beginning of this process, you may take notes on the task or assignment sheet itself. Date your log entries so that you can use them to compose a retrospective meta-analysis of your writing and revision processes. You should include this log as an appendix to your completed analysis.
3. Refer to the following questions and prompts repeatedly and systematically throughout the process of completing the writing assignment and your analysis of its evolution:

   a. What is your assigned topic and what are your purposes for writing?
   b. Whom do you envision as your audience? Explain.

c. How did you get started? Describe specific procedures.

d. Characterize the processes involved in producing a preliminary draft. Note the time, place, and length of time required to generate a draft. Describe brainstorming, planning, reading, and other processes involved. Record instances in which you made progress, took backward steps, abandoned your original plans, and so on. Always consider why you made these decisions.

e. Describe what you were pleased and displeased with upon completion of your preliminary draft.

f. Note your thoughts about your audience as you completed your preliminary draft and began revising it. Did your perceptions of the audience change? Why?

g. Characterize the process entailed in composing your second version. To what extent did it resemble the first draft? What changes did you make? Why?

h. If you received oral or written feedback from another reader (a friend, a classmate, your instructor), discuss how that feedback influenced your revision process.

i. If you went through more than one revision process, return to items d–h and record your impressions.

j. Perform a candid assessment of your effectiveness in addressing the assignment itself. To what extent did you accomplish the instructor's stated goals? How might you have altered your process? Describe your satisfaction with the final product.

k. Summarize the principal features of your composing process in completing this assignment, noting what you feel are its strengths and weaknesses.

l. How do your current impressions of your composing processes agree with your original beliefs about these processes? What have you learned from analyzing your process?

m. Characterize the foci of your writing processes. At what points are your writing processes predominantly form-directed, writer-based, content-focused, and reader-based?

4. On the basis of your journal reflections and findings, compose a first-person analytic commentary on your own writing and revision processes, synthesizing the central features listed in item 3.

NOTES

[1] It is difficult to arrive at an unproblematic yet accurate means of referring to the socioeducational status of English (Leki, 2001). Throughout this book, the acronym ESL refers inclusively to settings in which English is taught as a second language (i.e., in environments in which English is a dominant language), as an additional language (i.e., in plurilingual contexts such as India, Hong Kong, and Singapore), and as a foreign language (i.e., in nonanglophone environments where English is not a language of public life and in which access to English outside the classroom is limited). Although not optimal, the ESL label to a large extent describes the status of English in a broad range of situations, enabling us to avoid awkward typographic conventions such as "ESL/EFL," and so on.

Chapter 2

ESL Writing and L2 Literacy Development

Questions for Reflection

- *In what ways has your academic and other reading influenced your L1 and L2 writing proficiency?*
- *To what extent do your writing skills and styles match the kinds of reading you have done for academic and recreational purposes?*
- *Why might reading skill be an especially important factor in how ESL students become proficient writers of English?*

PERSPECTIVES ON L2 LITERACY DEVELOPMENT AND THE SOURCES OF LITERATE KNOWLEDGE

Readers eager to develop skills for teaching ESL composition might wonder why we dedicate an entire chapter to literacy and reading development in a book on L2 writing instruction. Our experience as academic writers and teachers of writing confirms our belief that meaningful writing instruction *is* literacy instruction and that one cannot successfully teach writing without also simultaneously teaching reading (Kroll, 1993). In other words, writing cannot and should not be isolated as a cognitive or academic activity because it fundamentally depends on writers' purposeful interactions with print, with fellow readers and writers, and with literate communities of practice (Carrell, Devine, & Eskey, 1988; Johns, 1997, 2003). Research and practical experience have demonstrated overwhelmingly that one cannot become a proficient writer in any language without also developing an array of literacy skills, including the ability to comprehend written text efficiently—fluently and accurately.

As a function of general language proficiency and cognitive development, reading has received considerable attention among researchers and teachers over the past several decades. Reading in any language was once portrayed as an individualized mental activity involving the decoding of print. Bernhardt (1991), for example, observed that the act of reading could be characterized as "an intrapersonal problem-solving task that takes place within the brain's knowledge structures" (p. 6). Indeed, the act of reading involves a transformation of the reader's state of knowledge. To understand this transformation, Just and Carpenter (1987) maintained that we must take into account the following components of the text processing operation:

- what information in the text starts the process
- how long the process takes
- what information was used during the process
- the likely sources of mistakes
- what the reader has learned when the process is finished. (p. 4)

This final component, "what the reader has learned when the process is finished," is widely believed to be the basis of how readers become *writers* because this acquired information contains print-encoded messages as well as clues about how the message's grammatical, lexical, semantic, pragmatic, and rhetorical constituents combine to make the message meaningful. Teachers interested in the learning and teaching of L2 composing skills should therefore understand reading–writing relationships, their socioeducational dimensions, and their implications for classroom instruction. Moreover, the acquisition of proficient literacy skills requires learners to recognize interconnections among the components and processes of literate activity. As Celce-Murcia and Olshtain (2000) pointed out,

> in the process of trying to understand a written text the reader has to perform a number of simultaneous tasks: *decode* the message by recognizing the written signs, *interpret* the message by assigning meaning to the string of words, and finally, *understand* what the author's intention was. In this process there are at least three participants: *the writer, the text,* and *the reader.* (p. 119)

This chapter examines themes in literacy research, summarizing selected empirical studies whose findings suggest directions for maximizing the dynamic interplay between reading and writing in the composition classroom.[1]

MODELS OF LITERACY AND THE TEACHING OF ESL WRITING

This section encapsulates generalizations that can be drawn from recent findings in literacy studies. The primary aim of our summary is to sketch a framework that will assist teachers in assessing literacy research, as well as methods and practices prescribed for ESL composition instruction. Empirical findings pointing to connections between reading skills and writing performance have led researchers to infer that efficient reading skills lay a foundation for the growth of both L1 and in L2 writing proficiency. This input-based view, sometimes described as the directional hypothesis (Eisterhold, 1990; Grabe, 2001a, 2003), presupposes that the emergence of composing skills must necessarily be preceded by the establishment of sound reading skills. The cultivation of this skills base presumably occurs through practice and abundant contact with print. Whereas this model has its strong advocates, research in L1 and L2 composition offers at least two alternative means of describing how reading and writing may be related: the nondirectional hypothesis and the bidirectional hypothesis.

The nondirectional model assumes a set of "common underlying processes" that underlie both reading and writing (Eisterhold, 1990, p. 93). Its chief pedagogical implication is that instruction should focus on constructing meaning in both reading and writing tasks. In the bidirectional view (as in the nondirectional model), practice in writing promotes the development of reading skills, just as improved reading proficiency can enhance writing skills (Zamel, 1992). The bidirectional model, however, holds that the reading–writing connection undergoes qualitative change as learners strengthen and diversify their literacy skills (Grabe & Stoller, 2002b; Heller, 1999; Peregoy & Boyle, 1997).

In alignment with the bidirectional hypothesis, the perspective taken in this chapter (indeed, throughout this book) is that teachers should not view ESL writing instruction merely as a linear process leading to the mastery of narrow forms of text production. Rather, professionals should approach the teaching of composition as an opportunity to build their students' academic, vocational, professional, social, and cultural *literacies*, which clearly are multiple and informed by numerous types of expertise. We thus embrace the premise that ESL writing instruction should support a diversity of literacy skills and practices. Such literacy practices often entail operations that are inherently much more complex than the mechanical reproduction of school-based genres.

Congruent with these broad, socially oriented conceptualizations of literacy, we encourage teachers to develop a diversified, flexible set of pedagogical principles (Hyland, 2002). Brown (2001, p. 40) recommended "an enlightened, eclectic approach" to L2 instruction. Similarly, we suggest that composition instructors nurture varied principles and strategies for teaching ESL writing to address divergent learner needs (Kumaravadivelu, 2003). An eclectic approach by no means implies randomness or a lack of theoretical drive. To the contrary, reasoned eclecticism requires principled decision making concerning the differential priorities that writing teachers assign to reading tasks and related literacy-oriented activities (Soven, 1999). The three reading–writing models outlined earlier can serve as guidelines for striking an appropriate pedagogical balance in designing syllabi, lessons, and tasks (see chapters 3 and 4). That is, we must provide meaningful input (in support of the directional hypothesis), promote the construction of meaning (in support of the nondirectional hypothesis), and maximize learners' evolving and interdependent reading and writing proficiencies (in support of the bidirectional hypothesis).

Equipped with the understanding that reading–writing relationships are multidimensional and may change as learners progress, teachers can adjust the weight given to reading tasks and writing practice according to the needs and expectations of their learners (Benesch, 1996; Pressley, 1998; Rodby, 1992). In a sense, every class of students represents a unique population with particular characteristics, such as age, general L2 proficiency, L1 literacy, L2 literacy, academic and professional objectives, and so forth (Corson, 2001; Harklau, Losey, & Siegel, 1999; Schleppegrell & Colombi, 2002). For example, low-proficiency secondary or precollege learners with limited ESL academic literacy skills may benefit from extensive and intensive reading coupled with abundant practice in writing for fluency. Advanced-level university students, on the other hand, may gain more substantially from intensive, discipline-specific reading, guided practice in reproducing key genres, and accuracy-oriented instruction. Such learners may profit from explicit grammar instruction and focused metalinguistic awareness raising (see chapter 7). Composition teachers should therefore make decisions about materials, classroom activities, and assignments based on these needs. Such decisions should also be informed by the multiple instructional options suggested by the directional, nondirectional, and bidirectional reading–writing models.

Although these models may differ in orientation, they are complementary and share an important fundamental principle: Writing skills cannot emerge by dint of practice alone. In other words, underlying each of these hypotheses is the premise that the ability to compose in any language cannot develop without knowledge of the forms, patterns, and purposes of written language. The principle that real learning depends on the provision of abundant, meaningful input is virtually axiomatic in the field of language education. Nevertheless, instructional practices in L1 and L2 composition have not always followed this principle. An attitude that persists in some institutions and among some educators is that one must learn to write before one can write. In this view, the most logical and practical way to turn nonwriters into writers is to teach them to write. Such an attitude is problematic and misguided because certain aspects of composing may not be "teachable" at all. Some researchers (Krashen, 1984; Smith, 1988, 1994) have even taken the controversial position that writing is essentially an acquired, "unteachable" set of skills that develops naturally as a result of extensive interaction with print and participation in authentic literacy events such as reading for information and further learning.

In keeping with both the nondirectional and bidirectional models, Zamel (1992) described tools for maximizing the transactional, mutually supportive relationship between reading and writing in the composition classroom. Just as reading is constructive and recursive, writing about texts enables us to reexamine them and allows us to confront uncertainties. As we engage purposefully with texts, we "reflect on the complexities, deal with the puzzlements, and offer approximative readings. By providing us a means for working out a reading, writing allows insights that may have been inaccessible or inchoate at the time the text was read" (p. 472).

According to this perspective, apprentice ESL writers benefit from engaging in reading-based writing tasks that encourage them to read like writers (Johns, 1997; Smith, 1984) and to write like readers (Bereiter & Scardamalia, 1984; Heller, 1999; Newell, Garriga, & Peterson, 2001). Beach and Liebman-Kleine (1986) claimed that the most effective writers learn "to imagine reader attributes and to use those attributes to assess their [own] writing" (p. 65). Such tasks may include reading for meaning, reading for details, inferencing, predicting, skimming, scanning, critical reasoning, journaling, and so forth. The Application Activities at the end of this chapter contain sample tasks and procedures that exemplify a number of these task types.

TRACING L1 AND L2 LITERACY CONNECTIONS: READING SKILLS AND WRITING PROFICIENCY

Carson and Leki (1993) observed that the profession of teaching English as a second language (TESL) or as a foreign language (TEFL) was "on the brink of an important new understanding of the connections between reading and writing" (p. 1). A decade later, Grabe (2003) assessed empirical insights into these connections, noting that "cumulative insights from this body of research have contributed to helping teachers find a variety of ways to exploit reading and writing connections" (p. 242). Because of the sheer quantity of research on L1 and L2 literacy, a comprehensive survey of this work is not possible in this discussion.[2] Nevertheless, we summarize some of the principal questions, hypotheses, and findings that bear on the teaching of ESL writing as a literate practice. Despite evidence supporting positive influences of reading on language and literacy development, we still lack a comprehensive understanding of exactly how the act of reading shapes literacy skills, particularly writing proficiency (Grabe, 2001a; Hayes, 1996). Consequently, many researchers have attempted to account for how writing proficiency develops as a result of readers' interactions with print.

The reciprocal relationships between reading and composing processes have, in fact, become a focal point of L1 and L2 literacy research. An influential trend in literacy research involves the scrutiny of quantitative and qualitative relationships between measures of reading ability or achievement and writing performance. In their synthesis of L1 reading–writing research, Shanahan and Tierney (1990) reported that measured reading and writing abilities achieve correlations scores between 0.50 and 0.70 (or approximately 25% to 50% shared variance). These and other empirical findings suggest that reading and composing both involve the construction of meaning, the development of complex cognitive and linguistic skills, the activation of existing knowledge and past experience, and the ability to solve problems to control thinking (Birch, 2002; Carson, 2001; Devine, 1993; Flower et al., 1990; Tickoo, 1995).

This rich body of literate knowledge and experience forms structures (schemata) that behave as open databases (Carrell, 1983a, 1983b; Carrell & Eisterhold, 1983; see chapter 1 for a discussion of schema theory). As readers read, they enter ideas in the form of words and sentence strings into these databases, which they subsequently search and modify as they encounter new textual information (Amsel & Byrnes, 2002; Mannes & St. George, 1996; Reid, 1993a). In activating, reworking, and building schemata, L1 and L2 readers engage in a dynamic, interactive process whereby they formulate meaning for a given passage or text. They construct meaning by storing new knowledge, sorting through banked knowledge, attending to textual clues about the writer's intended meaning or meanings, and assembling these data into coherent knowledge structures. If successful, this process leads to the transformation of existing knowledge into new understandings and ideas. Schema theory highlights important links between reading and writing by identifying the processes readers use to discover ideas and points of view that become available as subject matter for their writing. As readers consciously and unconsciously build more numerous and complex schemata, they develop a tacit (and sometimes explicit) awareness of written genres and the expectations of their readers (Chen & Graves, 1995; Dobson & Feak, 2001; Freedman, 1993; Goldman, 1997; Hyon, 2002; Johns, 1997; Newell, Garriga, & Peterson, 2001; Pang, 2002; Reid, 1993a).

Studies of L1 literacy development have largely borne out the productive interplay between reading and composing processes (Heller, 1999; Irwin & Doyle, 1992; Krashen, 1993; Nelson & Calfee, 1998; Perfetti, Rouet, & Britt, 1999; Pressley, 1998; Shanahan, 1984; 1990; Stotsky, 1983). This empirical research shows that L1 readers "develop a complex integration of information that can be learned, depending on the types of texts used and the types of tasks performed" (Grabe, 2001a, p. 19). However, ESL literacy acquisition involves an even more complex interaction of skills and knowledge than does L1 literacy acquisition, because literate L2 students may already have well-developed L1 literacy skills (and often literacy skills in other languages as well). At the same time, because ESL writers may have underdeveloped linguistic, rhetorical, academic, and strategic knowledge in English, we cannot assume reading–writing relationships to be as clear-cut for them as they might be for their NS counterparts. Cummins (1981, 1984) nonetheless presented a convincing case for the transfer of literacy skills from L1 to L2, maintaining that speakers of all languages share a common cognitive–academic language proficiency (CALP). The CALP model allows for the interlingual transfer of specific literacy skills and strategies, a process facilitated when the learner's linguistic and metalinguistic awareness is enhanced (Bernhardt & Kamil, 1995; Johns, 1995b; Parry, 1996). If such an interdependence model holds true, then L2 literacy development is likely to be influenced by literate knowledge and processes available in the L1.

The transfer of L1 literacy skills to the developing L2, however, is by no means automatic (Bell, 1995; Dong, 1998; Grabe & Stoller, 2002; Hulstijn, 1991; McLaughlin, 1987; Schunk, 2000). Cummins (1981) argued that learners must first attain a threshold level of L2 proficiency before they can efficiently transfer L1 literacy expertise into their emerging L2 skill repertoire (Alderson, 1984; Bossers, 1991; Carrell, 1991; Raimes, 1987). According to Cummins (1981), the cognitively demanding language processing involved in L2 reading and composing necessitates a functional level of linguistic control, text processing capability, fluency, and speed (Cziko, 1978; Fakhri, 1994; Mustafa, 1995).

Such a claim presents significant implications for ESL writing instruction. The threshold hypothesis challenges assumptions about the ease with which literacy skills can be transferred from a learner's primary language to the L2 knowledge base. Moreover, it highlights the complex nature of the knowledge systems that L2 students must manage as they read L2 materials and attempt to produce their own texts. Results reported by Carson, Carrell, Silberstein, Kroll, and Kuehn (1990), for example, have revealed multiple literacy components that may underlie the development of L2 composing skills. Deploying a sophisticated research design, Carson et al. (1990) collected L1 and L2 reading and writing performance data from 105 Chinese- and Japanese-speaking ESL students enrolled in U.S. universities. They examined relationships between L1 and L2 reading abilities, L1 and L2 writing abilities, L1 reading and writing abilities, L2 reading and writing abilities, and L2 proficiency, interlingual transfer, and intralingual transfer.

Confirming that interlingual transfer can occur, these researchers nonetheless noted that the patterns and strength of interlingual transfer were related to L1 background and prior educational experience, that is, the students' existing literacy repertoires. Whereas L1 reading skills appeared to transfer to L2 for both groups of students, only the Japanese students appeared to transfer L1 writing skills into English. For both Japanese and Chinese students, L1 reading and writing abilities were at least weakly related, as were L2 reading and writing abilities. The authors also claimed stronger relationships between interlingual reading abilities than between interlingual writing abilities. For the Chinese students, the relationship between L1 and L2 writing abilities was not significant.

Carson et al. (1990) described their investigation as exploratory, yet their results highlighted the complex interaction among factors underlying linguistic proficiency and literacy skills, including both reading and writing. As for the pedagogical implications of this study and others like it, some researchers (Bell, 1995; Dong, 1998; Parry, 1996) have suggested that L2 reading instruction should draw upon L1 reading skills, but that teachers should not expect all such skills to apply readily to L2 literacy tasks. Some L1 abilities and strategies (e.g., decoding, inferencing, syntactic parsing, semantic mapping) certainly may transfer to emergent L2 literacy (Edelsky, 1982; Johns, 1988). However, explicit instruction may be required to facilitate positive interlingual transfer (Alderson, 1984; Eisterhold, 1990; Grabe, 2001a; Grabe & Stoller, 2001; McLaughlin, 1987).

The potential for writing instruction to exploit learners' L1 literacy skills may be confined to certain L1 groups and possibly to novice-level learners. In contrast to the claims of Alderson (1984), Cummins (1981) and Cziko (1978) argued for a threshold level of L2 competence. In contrast Carson et al. (1990) maintained that, "whereas teachers may be able to exploit L1 literacy relationships in the transfer of L2 literacy practices at lower proficiency levels, they cannot do so reliably at more advanced L2 levels" (p. 261). With more linguistically sophisticated learners, teachers may need to rely more heavily on students' emergent

L2 literacy, as well as their linguistic and metalinguistic aware-ness. At lower proficiency levels, interlingual transfer may be more marked, whereas at more advanced levels, intralingual in-put may be more influential for the development of L2 literacy.

Regardless of our position with respect to the threshold of L2 proficiency, we will be better equipped to provide effective instruction when we understand that our learners require spe-cial support in developing literacy-related skills (Aebersold & Field, 1997; Birch, 2002; Grabe & Stoller, 2001, 2002b; Hyon, 2002; Pang, 2002; Urquhart & Weir, 1998). Earlier L1-based formula-tions of reading–writing relationships should be recognized and appreciated for alerting researchers and teachers to the neces-sity of promoting good reading habits and efficient reading skills among their students. For example, Stotsky's (1983) survey of L1 studies investigating reading–writing relationships suggested that good writers tend to be good readers, skilled writers read frequently and extensively, and effective readers tend to produce more sophisticated texts than do weaker readers. However, re-cent research in L2 literacy has highlighted the need to avoid oversimplifying the complex connections that hold among the multiple factors that make up L2 academic literacy (Belcher & Hirvela, 2001a; Goldman & Trueba, 1987; Grabe, 2001a).

ROLES FOR EXTENSIVE AND VOLUNTARY READING IN ESL COMPOSITION

A fundamental principle of L2 education is that students ac-quire more knowledge and learn more efficiently when abundant and meaningful input is available (Brown, 2001; Byram, 1997; Krashen, 1985a, 1985b; Lee & VanPatten, 2003; Savignon, 1997, 2001). The common wisdom of communicative language instruc-tion extends to the ESL composition setting, in which many teach-ers operate on the presupposition that nearly any type of reading is beneficial to apprentice writers. Numerous studies, for exam-ple, have indicated that extensive reading correlates highly with improved writing performance in L1 (Belanger, 1987; Stotsky, 1983) and in L2 (Krashen, 1984, 1993). Consequently, ESL writ-ing courses are sometimes founded on the premise that "writing competence results somehow from exposure to reading, and that good readers make good writers" (Carson, 1993, p. 85). Enthusi-astic reading proponents have further argued for the primacy of reading over explicit writing and grammar instruction in L2 class-rooms (Day & Bamford, 1998; Krashen, 1984, 1985b, 1993, 1994; McQuillan, 1994). Although the research literature offers some support for the view that reading is the single greatest factor in promoting compositional skills, this view merits cautious evaluation and interpretation. Teachers of ESL composition can benefit from understanding the advantages and limitations of empirical studies investigating reading–writing relationships, particularly as they pertain to the teaching of academic literacy. In the following discussion, we examine a sampling of these studies and their implications.

Not surprisingly, empirical studies frequently show that reading for academic, professional, and recreational purposes positively influences L1 and L2 development among children, adolescents, and adults, including those with only rudimentary literacy skills (Elley, 1991; Krashen, 1993; Nelson & Calfee, 1998). Partly on the basis of findings from this line of inquiry, Reid (1993a) claimed that "good writers are often good readers" (p. 43). If acquiring effective writing skills necessitates acquiring a high level of reading proficiency, then how do learners become good readers? According to Grabe and Stoller (2001), "one does not become a good reader unless one reads a lot" (p. 198). With these premises in mind, we can reasonably postulate a serial relationship in which extensive reading practice develops effective reading skills and effective reading skills eventually lead to the growth of proficient writing skills (assuming, of course, that this position in no way undermines the bidirectional hypothesis discussed earlier).

In an effort to explore this commonsense connection empirically, L1 and L2 literacy experts have undertaken experimental, quasi-experimental, and descriptive research designed to identify reading habits and behaviors leading to measurable gains in writing ability (Day & Bamford, 1998). Details of these important studies are unfortunately beyond the scope of this chapter. Nonetheless, their primary findings and implications strongly suggest that the ESL composition curriculum should systematically integrate reading activities that engage learners in purposeful interaction with authentic texts (see chapters 3 and 4).

For instance, L1 studies exploring the impact of voluntary and pleasure reading on writing performance, have regularly suggested that individuals who report reading extensively for school and for pleasure tend to perform better on reading and writing tasks than students who seldom or never read (Applebee, 1978; Birnbaum, 1982; Krashen, 1993; Stotsky, 1983). Rouet,

Favart, Britt, and Perfetti (1997) recently reported, for example, that efficient readers familiar with specific content areas use multiple texts and integrate knowledge more effectively into writing arguments than do novice readers.

A number of L2 studies following similar methods and aimed at learners of various ages have produced largely parallel results (Elley & Mangubhai, 1983; Flahive & Bailey, 1993; Hafiz & Tudor, 1989; Hedgcock & Atkinson, 1993; Krashen, 1988, 1993). Inquiry along these lines has lent considerable validity to the proposition that composing ability emanates partly, if not largely, from frequent, self-initiated reading, preferably over sustained periods. In an analysis of the reading habits and L2 writing performance of graduate ESL students, for example, Janopoulos (1986) reported statistically significant relationships between students' self-initiated reading patterns and standard composition scores. He concluded that "the amount of pleasure reading a . . . student does in English may be used as a reliable predictor of his/her English writing proficiency" (p. 767). Elley's (1991) synthesis of nine "book flood" studies conducted around the world similarly confirmed the "spread of effect from reading competence to other language skills—writing, speaking, and control over syntax" (p. 404).

Following a similar line of inquiry, Tsang (1996) compared three groups of secondary-level, Cantonese-speaking EFL learners, each of whom underwent distinct types of EFL literacy regimens. Unlike the groups that received regular instruction plus mathematics enhancement or regular instruction plus frequent writing practice, the group that underwent regular instruction plus extensive reading showed improvement in EFL writing performance. In line with claims that reading contributes more significantly to composing proficiency than even intensive writing practice, Tsang (1996) concluded that extensive reading exposed learners to an "appropriate model of the target language at an appropriate level . . . , improved general knowledge and thus helped develop content in writing . . . [and] exposed students to appropriate models of construction, agreement, tense, number, and word order/function" (p. 228).

Krashen (1984, 1989, 1993, 1994) summarized similar L1 and L2 investigations focused on reading–writing relationships, unequivocally arguing that "reading exposure is the primary means of developing language skills," including grammatical knowledge, vocabulary, and writing proficiency (Krashen, 1985b, p. 109). Controversial and subject to frequent criticism, Krashen's more extreme hypotheses are nonetheless important for ESL literacy teachers because they bring to light a fundamental premise: Composing skills must, to some extent, depend on learners' exposure to—and meaningful interaction with—print matter. Some have even argued that reading may actually make a more significant contribution to writing proficiency than the practice of writing, particularly when reading is self-initiated or self-selected (McQuillan, 1994; Smith, 1984). Underscoring the primacy of reading over writing practice, Smith (1988) even asserted that "no one writes enough to learn more than a small fraction of what writers need to know" (p. 19). Such claims should be viewed with caution, of course, especially when they pertain to L2 writers: There is no reason to assume that extensive reading of any sort automatically leads to competent reading or composing skills (Shanahan, 1984). In direct contradiction to Reid (1993a), Hughey, Wormuth, Hartfiel, and Jacobs (1983) argued, for example, that "being a good reader does not make one a good writer. Reading serves to give the writer ideas, data, model sentence patterns, and structures, but a student will be able to become a good writer only by writing" (p. 49).

The L1 and L2 literacy research to date generally supports a balanced approach to composition pedagogy, in which explicit instruction is carefully balanced with many types of literacy activities, notably reading (Grabe, 2003). Even at a young age, extensive, self-initiated exposure to print may thus heighten learners' awareness of the multiple functions of written language, the nature and purposes of relevant genres, and the linguistic features prevalent in particular text types. Research outcomes often reflect the principle that self-initiated reading is good and that more self-initiated reading is even better for the development of language and literacy skills (Krashen, 1993, 1994). As Smith (1988) observed, knowledge about written language and its use "must be found in what other people have written, in existing texts.... We learn to write without suspecting that we are learning or what we learn. Everything points to the necessity of learning to write from what we read, as we read" (p. 20). Flower and Hayes (1980) similarly argued that good writers demonstrate significant amounts of tacit knowledge concerning conventional and formal features of written text thanks to the act of reading. Using this unconscious knowledge "may be one way in which extensive reading affects a person's ability to write: A well-read person simply has a much larger and richer set of images of what a text can look like" (p. 28).

Because of ESL writers' unique and complex learner profiles (see chapter 1), the positive effects of self-initiated and assigned reading on their English writing proficiency are more difficult to discern than they are for L1 writers (Grabe, 2001a). The task of literate ESL writers involves challenges that L1 writers never confront (Grabe & Stoller, 2001). For example, ESL students often have well-developed L1 literacy skills (Bell, 1995; Carson et al., 1990). Nonetheless, their English literacy skills may require support "from a language system which, in the early stages at least, is insufficiently developed to allow those learners the full range of literacy practices to which they are accustomed" (Eisterhold, 1990, p. 94). Teachers of ESL composition must therefore take into account their students' not-yet-native-like knowledge of the structure and use of written English, in addition to the potential transfer or nontransfer of L1 literacy skills to L2 performance, as we discussed earlier.

Notwithstanding these potential instructional challenges, empirical findings still underscore the advantages enjoyed by ESL learners who read extensively in English over those learners who read little or not at all. Promoting literacy habits such as extensive reading is admittedly a serious challenge, particularly for practitioners with limited or no access to the material resources necessary for instituting a comprehensive and effective literacy enhancement program. Furthermore, large-scale and long-term voluntary reading programs sponsored by schools and local libraries are typically geared toward primary and secondary students (Day & Bamford, 1998; Krashen, 1993, 1994). Teachers of ESL writing in secondary and higher education may find it impractical to initiate or participate in such programs, largely because of preestablished curricular objectives or low student interest.

We further recognize that problems such as limited resources and access to English-language materials can be particularly acute in EFL settings. Small-scale efforts to encourage self-selected, extensive reading can nonetheless be practical in ESL programs in which teachers select their own instructional materials and participate in curricular decision making. It also is important to recognize the positive affective incentive associated with well-designed literacy enhancement programs. Numerous studies have indicated that L2 students find self-selected reading to be pleasurable and motivating. Such positive attitudes certainly are likely to facilitate ESL literacy acquisition to an even greater extent (Elley, 1991; Flahive & Bailey, 1993; Hafiz & Tudor, 1989; Lai, 1993; McQuillan, 1994; Verhoeven & Snow, 2001).

Grabe and Stoller (2001) presented the following list of "ideal conditions for extensive reading," acknowledging that individual instructors "can pursue only a subset of them":

1. Provide time for extended silent reading in every class session, even if it only involves reading from the textbook.
2. Create opportunities for all types of reading.
3. Find out what students like to read and why.
4. Make interesting, attractive, and level-appropriate reading materials available.
5. Build a well-stocked, diverse class library with clear indications of topic and level of difficulty for each text.
6. Allow students to take books and magazines home to read, and hold students accountable for at-home reading in some simple way.
7. Create incentives for students to read at home.
8. Have students share and recommend reading materials to classmates.
9. Keep records of the amounts of extensive reading completed by students.
10. Seek out class sets of texts (or at least group sets) that everyone can read and discuss.
11. Make use of graded readers, provided that they interest students, are attractive, create sufficient challenge, and offer a good amount of extensive reading practice.
12. Read interesting materials aloud to students on a consistent basis.
13. Visit the school library regularly and set aside time for browsing and reading.
14. Create a reading lab and designate time for lab activities.

(Grabe & Stoller, 2001, pp. 198–199)

We further suggest that an effective means of encouraging ESL learners to read English texts on their own is to dramatize the value of voluntary reading by describing, discussing, and modeling reading for personal enjoyment and enrichment (Dupuy, Tse, & Cook, 1996). For example, teachers can devote class time to exposing the short- and long-term benefits of reading for writing and learning. Teachers can likewise help students discover resources where texts of personal interest may be located. For example, ESL students may not realize that their school library or a municipal library subscribes to daily newspapers and popular magazines and is a good place to keep abreast of current events. The teacher also may discuss strategies for dedicating time to pleasure reading and for fitting it into a busy academic schedule. By addressing these issues in the writing class, teachers can accentuate the value of reading for all sorts of enrichment. For courses in which reading is an integral component of the composition curriculum, teachers may offer their students a range of texts from which they can make individual selections rather than require a single textbook or set of readings. Such an approach can work effectively for content-based courses, in which students might be further encouraged to seek out their own reading materials on the basis of topics to be covered in the course (Brinton, Snow, & Wesche, 1989; Kasper, 2000; Snow, 1998, 2001). Even for courses in which teachers' hands are tied in terms of materials selection, formal writing assignments (e.g., summaries, book reviews, essays, research reports) can be designed to allow students to choose their own sources and write about them in ways that purposefully engage them in reading.

The ability to read and make sense of any discipline's expertise and content knowledge entails a large number of microskills that may not be apparent to those of us who take such skills for granted. Grabe (2001a) distilled key characteristics of proficient reading in the following summary:

> The ability to read for basic comprehension is the skill that underlies most other purposes for reading. Basic comprehension requires rapid and accurate word recognition; fluency in processing words, sentences, and discourse cues; a large recognition vocabulary; a reasonably strong grasp of the structure of the language; an ability to integrate meanings from the text; an ability to make necessary inferences and connections to background knowledge; an ability to vary processes and goals strategically; and an ability to monitor comprehension.... These abilities also represent the foundation for reading to learn, critical reading, and reading to synthesize information, and they cannot be bypassed. (p. 18)

We can more fully understand the true complexity of these linked reading processes and work toward strategies for teaching them by recognizing essential microskills, many of which can be translated into guided instructional tasks appropriate for the composition classroom. Gunderson (1991) presented the following list of microskills, which he suggested were necessary for L1 and L2 readers who must cope with the complexity of academic reading materials:

Content Reading Skills

- Recognize the significance of the content.
- Read and interpret graphs.
- Recognize important details.
- Read and interpret charts.
- Recognize unrelated details.
- Read and interpret maps.
- Find the main idea of a paragraph.
- Read and interpret cartoons.
- Find the main idea of large sections of discourse.
- Read and interpret diagrams.
- Differentiate fact and opinion.
- Read and interpret pictures.
- Locate topic sentences.
- Read and interpret formulae.
- Locate answers to specific questions.
- Read and understand written problems.
- Make inferences about content.
- Read and understand expository material.
- Critically evaluate content.
- Read and understand argument.
- Realize an author's purpose.
- Read and understand descriptive material.
- Determine the accuracy of information.
- Read and understand categories.
- Use a table of contents.
- Adjust reading rate relative to purpose of reading.
- Use an index.
- Adjust reading rate relative to difficulty of material.
- Use a library card catalogue [or its electronic equivalent].
- Scan for specific information.
- Use appendices.
- Skim for important ideas.
- Read and interpret tables.
- Learn new material from text.

(Gunderson, 1991, pp. 145–146)

We have suggested that ESL composition teachers should systematically endeavor to strengthen reading–writing interactions by promoting multiple literacy practices among their students. At the same time, we caution against inappropriately subordinating writing practice to reading. As Scarcella and Oxford (1992) noted, "the more experience students have writing about specific topics in particular genres and contexts, the more confidence they gain and the more fluent their writing becomes" (p. 122). Like Grabe (2001a), we believe that an effective approach to literacy instruction entails a careful balance between reading and composing activities:

> A strong theory of learning . . . will highlight the need for exposure to print through reading practice; the learning of a large vocabulary; fluency in reading; practice and assisted learning with more complex and difficult texts and tasks; practice in using strategies to understand the text, establish goals, and monitor comprehension processes; and supporting interaction and discussion around textual meaning. . . . Writing about what is to be read or has been read is also a very good way to develop advanced academic reading abilities. (p. 19)

READING AND WRITING IN SOCIOLITERATE COMMUNITIES: GENRE-ORIENTED APPROACHES TO LITERACY DEVELOPMENT

The reciprocal connections between reading and writing outlined in the previous sections have a socioeducational dimension that merits further exploration (Bishop & Ostrom, 1997; McKay, 1993; Sudol & Horning, 1999; Wells, 1999). We have attempted to present a view in which the ability to use and produce written texts from a range of genres constitutes a major component of the skill complex known as "literacy." We have further suggested that literacies are multiple, that they are always embedded in sociocultural contexts, and that they develop as the result of a dynamic interaction of verbal activities, including reading, writing, and speech (Cope & Kalantzis, 1993, 2000; Fairclough, 2000; Pérez, 1998; Zamel & Spack, 1998). Congruent with this socially grounded perspective on literacy, we encourage L2 composition professionals to adopt an approach to writing instruction that nurtures learners' participation in a rich diversity of academic and nonacademic literacies, in addition to their proficiency in producing appropriate genres.

The following discussion focuses on cultivating ESL learners' awareness of formal (i.e., rhetorical and linguistic) conventions of written genres to promote the comprehension, analysis, reproduction, and critique of texts associated with those genres. Early definitions of genre focused principally on categories of literary text and subsequently on the lexical, grammatical, rhetorical, and discursive features of texts (Halliday & Hasan, 1989; Hyland, 2002; Johns, 2003; Swales, 1990). Although these functions still represent important aspects of genre studies, genre is better understood in dynamic and socially complex terms. Martin's (2002) concise definition of genre nicely encapsulates the field's current understanding of the construct. For Martin, genre entails "configurations of meaning that are recurrently phased together to enact social practices" (p. 269). Furthermore, although "abstract and schematic," genre knowledge, is "systematic" and "conventional, in that form and style may be repeated" (Johns, 1997, pp. 21–22).

We thus examine means of integrating reading tasks and skills practice into the teaching of written genres in ESL composition instruction, emphasizing that the acquisition of genre awareness and the ability to produce and reproduce genres necessitates both mastery of forms and mechanical operations and, perhaps more importantly, an appreciation of the complex psychological, sociocultural, educational, political, and ideological contexts in which texts are produced, transacted, challenged, and reformed (Bhatia, 1993; Casanave, 2002; Christie & Martin, 1997; Dias, Freedman, Medway, & Paré, 1999; Dias & Paré, 2000; Freedman & Adam, 2000; Johns, 1997; Paltridge, 2001, 2002).

Most of the L1 and L2 reading–writing studies cited in this chapter hint strongly at learners' vital need to become familiar with multiple genres, subgenres, and text types as they learn to compose in their primary and secondary languages (Grabe, 2002; Martin, 2002). Because this book is directed principally at classroom teachers, and because so much literacy research addresses the teaching and learning of literacy practices in primary, secondary, and tertiary institutions, the following discussion concentrates largely on the reading and production of school-based, academic genres. However, many of the principles and practices we examine can be adapted suitably to the development of professional, vocational, and other literacies.

Academic Literacies and Genre Knowledge

We have endeavored to show that literacy acquisition never occurs in a vacuum, and the acquisition of academic literacy skills is no exception (Christie, 1993; Jones, Turner, & Street, 1999; Weese,

Fox, & Greene, 1999). In schools, colleges, and universities, ESL writers read and write for specific purposes, all of which involve attaining some combination of developmental, academic, and sometimes professional goals. Ultimately, literacy instruction should enable learners to acquire skills, to develop strategies, and to master the discourse patterns (including spoken and written conventions) of the academic community in general and of the individual disciplines they will pursue (Berkenkotter & Huckin, 1995; Currie, 1993; Geisler, 1994; Hyland, 2000; Johns, 1997; Lewis, 2001; Mavor & Trayner, 2001; Spack, 1997a).

It is necessary for L1 and L2 students alike to achieve disciplinary awareness, genre knowledge, text comprehension, and production skills. To meet these objectives, learners must first understand that their formal education will involve them in reading and writing for tangible purposes. These purposes often are grounded in established ways of being and thinking, many of which may be tacit:

> Since any particular discourse is composed of the work of the people who read and write its texts, it follows that discourse in general—and, by extension, literacy—has a *social* as well as a cognitive dimension, a dimension that plays a major role in shaping the literate behavior of readers and writers in any real-world context. (Eskey, 1993, p. 224).

Teachers of ESL play a crucial role in bringing their learners into such discourses, given their responsibility for preparing their students to meet the demands and challenges of academic institutions. Facilitating this socialization process assumes that reading, as one component of academic literacy, involves cultural and sociocognitive interactions among readers, writers, and texts.

Reciprocally, socialization into academic literacy also presupposes that writing is not only a communication "technology" (Grabe & Kaplan, 1996), but also a social practice (Bazerman, 1994; Freedman & Medway, 1994a, 1994b, 1994c; Gee, 1998; Geisler, 1994; Ivanic, 1998; Kress, 1993; Miller, 1994a, 1994b; Prior, 1998; Weese et al., 1999). These precepts coincide with what Johns (1997) called "socioliterate views," which maintain that "literacies are acquired principally through exposure to discourses from a variety of social contexts. Through this exposure, individuals gradually develop theories of genre" (p. 14). A socioliterate view suggests central implications for literacy instruction:

> In our classrooms and on our campuses, we should assist students to draw from their past strategies and experiences and to develop new approaches to texts and tasks. Our classrooms should

encourage student research into their own literacy and text histories, into current approaches to literate practices, and into strategies that work in a variety of contexts. We should encourage the investigation and critique of the literacy practices of others, particularly of more advanced students and faculty....

[In a socioliterate approach] literacy classes become laboratories for the study of texts, roles, and contexts, for research into evolving student literacies and developing awareness and critique of communities and their textual contracts. Our literacy classrooms can become places in which students are able to assess their current practices and understandings and develop strategies for future rhetorical situations. (Johns, 1997, p. 19)

An obvious means of socioliterate ESL instruction, of course, is to apprentice writers into a community or communities of fellow readers and writers. Smith (1988) labeled this type of community a "literacy club." Gee (1999) referred to broader sorts of collective entities as Discourses "with a capital 'D'" (p. 13) and to literate communities as "literacies" (Gee, 1992, 1996, 1998). A closely related term sometimes used by genre analysts and researchers working in socioliterate paradigms is "community of practice," defined by Lave and Wenger (1991) as "a set of relations among persons, activity, and world, over time and in relation with other tangential and overlapping communities of practice" (p. 98). Johns (1997) situated the Lave and Wenger model with respect to socioliterate approaches to literacy education, maintaining that "communities of practice are seen as complex collections of individuals who share genres, language, values, concepts, and 'ways of being' (Geertz, 1983), often distinct from those held by other communities" (p. 52).

A primary challenge for ESL literacy teachers, therefore, is to demonstrate that reading and writing competence are vital to achieving membership in an educational literacy club, Discourse, or community of practice (e.g., a school, a college, a university, a field of study, or a profession). Therefore, practitioners need to promote reading as a way into the disciplines and to demonstrate that becoming an expert member of a literacy club or community of practice depends on completing literacy-based tasks (Guleff, 2002). "Almost every writing assignment in the disciplines requires reading; many reading assignments and examinations require writing" (Johns, 1993, p. 274). Spack (1993) explained that ESL composition instructors have an essential responsibility to facilitate students' acquisition of general knowledge about the purposes served by writing in these domains (Horowitz, 1986a,

1986b). She further asserted that writing instruction must move ESL students "back and forth along the continuum to grow as writers as they build enough local knowledge to enable them to perform effectively" (p. 183). That is, students refine their writing abilities through their classroom experiences and through immersion in a discipline, field of study, or profession (Dias & Paré, 2000).

Teachers of ESL composition can play an important part in helping their students to become members of any number of institutional and discipline-specific literacy clubs, Discourses, and communities of practice by acquainting learners with the enterprises and literacy practices of people who are already part of these communities (Adam & Artemeva, 2002; Delpit, 1998; Geisler, 1994; Goldstein, 1993; Hedgcock, 2002; Prior, 1998). Expert members of these communities (e.g., professors, teaching assistants, advanced students) as well as novices (e.g., peers) can serve ESL students "as their unsuspecting surrogates in the trial and error of learning" (Smith, 1988, p. 22) via their written products. Literacy educators must expose their learners to the texts that real academic writers (i.e., faculty members, researchers, textbook writers, policy-makers) write for the academy and that real academic readers (i.e., researchers, teachers, students) read for the purposes of learning and acquiring expertise in a given field (Prior, 1998). In so doing, teachers can show their ESL learners that "text is in fact the link between reading and writing as the complementary halves of literacy. . . . Text is where reader and writer meet and interact" (Eskey, 1993, p. 223). As such, text constitutes a transactional medium through which a kind of social behavior takes place: A text allows its writer to communicate a message to its reader, provided the reader can understand the core principles of how meaning is constructed by members of the literate audience envisioned by the writer (Bakhtin, 1981; Hansen, 2000; Johns, 2002a, 2003). Mastering the interpretation of text (i.e., learning to read and make sense out of someone else's writing) is a significant step toward achieving membership in the community of readers and experts for whom that text is meaningful. Indeed, achieving such mastery may guarantee membership in some literacy clubs (Smith, 1988) or Discourses (Gee, 1996, 1999).

Mastering the construction of text—learning and observing the conventions of a particular genre or text type—may similarly grant apprentice writers admission to the community of writers associated with that discipline or field of knowledge. Eskey

(1993) identified the sociolinguistic and psycholinguistic aspects of the reading–writing connection in relation to literacy clubs (e.g., academic institutions) by describing two of the ESL writing teacher's principal "jobs."

The first of these jobs entails motivating learners to develop reading and composing skills that accord with the conventions of *our* literacy club and its related discourse communities (Verhoeven & Snow, 2001). This responsibility involves demonstrating literacy skills, acquainting learners with the universe of texts available in the L2, and identifying how and why certain texts are valued (Martin, 2002). The second "job" of the ESL instructor consists of facilitating learners' acquisition of comprehension, problem-solving, and production skills such as "word and phrase recognition, reading rate development, grammatical sentence writing, and organizing discourse in accordance with the established conventions of some particular genre" (Eskey, 1993, p. 231).

Genre studies and socioliterate research thus emphasize the pedagogical imperative to show language learners that reading and writing can help them to acquire and display knowledge, as well as to become participants in a literate community of students, teachers, and scholars. As more seasoned members of literacy clubs and academic communities of practice ("old timers," as Lave and Wenger [1991] called them), ESL teachers are perhaps the most accessible models of literate behavior, or "surrogates," that their students can expect (Smith, 1988). In this role of surrogate, or facilitator, ESL composition teachers can make their learners aware of the social, personal, and educational uses of written language, bringing them into the community of people (experts and novices) who know how to read and write (Benesch, 2001; Hammond & Macken-Horarik, 1999). Instructors can achieve this aim by incorporating into their syllabi materials that exemplify the kinds of texts used, valued, and created by academic readers and writers for the purposes of acquiring and creating new knowledge (see chapters 3 and 4). It is only by understanding and adopting the behaviors and values of academic and professional disciplines and communities of practice that ESL students can join the ranks of expert readers and writers (Dias & Paré, 2000).

Promoting Academic Literacy: Insights from EAP, ESP, and Genre Studies

A major practical issue in preparing academic ESL learners concerns how composition instruction can help students to become readers and writers of the genres and texts associated with particular literacy clubs, Discourses, and communities of practice. Academic communities of practice may include computer science, engineering, technology, physics, biology, medicine, business, law, sociology, political science, history, journalism, literary study, education, and so on. Smith (1988) argued that it is critical for teachers to provide their learners with materials "that are relevant to the kind of writer [students] are interested in becoming" (p. 26), noting that text comprehension and production are always connected to real purposes, real writers, and real audiences (Berkenkotter & Huckin, 1995; Johns, 1995b, 1995c, 1997, 2002a; Swales, 1990, 1998). The social dimensions of text comprehension and production are especially pertinent to the discipline of writing instruction because, "in the real world where readers and writers mingle, individual texts do not stand alone." Texts constitute "a *genre* or . . . the *discourse* of some particular group of readers and writers who read and write the same kinds of texts, that is, the discourse of everything from personal letters to linguistics or physics" (Eskey, 1993, p. 223).

To comprehend and produce texts from target genres, novice L1 and L2 writers clearly need to acquire a working knowledge of the following elements:

1. The nature and purposes of the discipline or community of practice
2. The "membership rules" and value system of the discipline (Gee, 1992, 1999)
3. The primary content and general boundaries of the discipline's core knowledge—what Geisler (1994) called "domain content"
4. The formal characteristics of the genres and text types valued by expert members of the discipline or community of practice (e.g., rhetorical structure, register, stylistic features, preferred syntactic patterns, lexical choice, layout, mechanical and typographic conventions)
5. Audience expectations pertaining to the content, structure, form, and effect of texts and genres transacted within the community of practice
6. The text production and decoding strategies used by expert members.

In the case of learners acquiring school-based literacies (academic literacies) the curricular imperative, of course, is to provide appropriate content, representative models, linguistic and metalinguistic awareness, reading and writing experience, and strategic training as means of apprenticing students into the practices of academe and its many disciplinary communities.

English for Academic Purposes (EAP) and English for Specific Purposes (ESP)—ESL pedagogies designed specifically to address very similar curricular goals—represent well-established, genre-oriented traditions for Teachers of English to Speakers of Other Languages (TESOL), and Teachers of English as a Foreign Language (TEFL). Specifically, EAP aims to characterize the genres, standards, practices, and values of academic disciplines and their participants. Broadly speaking, the term EAP can be "applied to any course, module, or workshop in which students are taught to deal with academically related language and subject matter" (Brown, 2001, p. 123). Meanwhile, ESP refers to "programs . . . specifically devoted to professional fields of study" such as English for Agriculture or Business Writing, and to "disciplines in which people can get university majors and degrees" (Brown, 2001, p. 123). Johns and Price-Machado (2001), categorizing EAP as a subcategory of ESP, presented the following "absolute" and "variable" characteristics of ESP:

1. Absolute characteristics: ESP consists of language teaching which is
   a. designed to meet the specified needs of the learner
   b. related to content (i.e., in its themes and topics) to particular disciplines, occupations, or activities
   c. centered on the language appropriate to these activities in syntax, lexis, discourse, semantics, and the analysis of this discourse
   d. in contrast to "general English."
2. Variable characteristics: ESP may be, but is not necessarily
   a. restricted to the language skills to be learned (e.g., reading only)
   b. not taught according to any preordained methodology. (pp. 44–45)

Although detailed coverage of EAP and ESP research and pedagogy is beyond the scope of this chapter, insights from these influential domains of ESL instruction can be extremely valuable for composition teachers who wish to equip their students with a fuller range of socioliterate skills.[3] Since the genesis of EAP and ESP in the 1960s and their evolution through the 1970s, EAP and ESP pedagogies have relied heavily on needs and task analyses for curriculum design (Benesch, 1996; Leki & Carson, 1994; cf. chapter 3). Research in EAP and ESP, which proliferated in the 1980s and 1990s, has, among other things, examined how non-ESL faculty rank the importance of linguistic and critical skills in their classrooms, the writing tasks required of students in particular majors and disciplines, and the genres and text types that prevail in those disciplines (e.g., summary, analysis, critique, editorial, classification, argument; see Application Activity 2.5, as well as Figs. 4.6, 4.11, and 4.12).

These findings have enabled both teachers and researchers to identify the knowledge bases, cognitive skills, processes, strategies, and forms of sociocultural awareness that comprise academic literacy. Specialists in EAP and ESP have likewise proposed frameworks and tools for helping students to achieve both broad and narrow objectives in courses designed to promote specialized literacies (Johns, 1990; Prior, 1995b). Some researchers and teachers reject the presupposition that ESL students should be "taught" academic literacy or be forced to become members of an academic community of practice. Bizzell (1987), for example, argued that academic institutions and discourse communities should themselves adapt to the diversity of cultures that ESL learners represent (Corson, 2001; Leki, 1995b; Silva, 1993).

Eskey (1993) claimed that the knowledge and skills required to comprehend and produce or reproduce particular genres and text types, as well as those required for teaching them, "are best acquired by taking part in real, socially grounded communicative events like reading or writing for some authentic purpose or writing in a real genre for a real audience" (p. 224). Evidence for strong or even weak links between what learners read and what they write have potentially far-reaching implications for literacy instruction, and most especially for genre-based approaches. Smith (1988) offered the following commonsense recommendations for enhancing writers' genre knowledge:

> To learn how to write for newspapers you must read newspapers; textbooks about newspapers will not suffice. For magazines, browse through magazines rather than through correspondence courses on magazine writing. To write poetry, read it. For the typical style of memoranda that circulate in your school, consult the school files. (p. 20)

Smith's no-nonsense directive clearly implies an interaction between genre-specific reading and writing, a theme that has only recently been explicitly addressed among literacy researchers. Specific questions have emerged concerning the observable links between what learners read and how they write. Taking a non–school-based genre as a test case, let us suppose, for instance, that a learner who is an avid science fiction reader frequents commercial and noncommercial science fiction Web sites to read reviews posted by fellow science fiction aficionados. Let us further assume that our learner is highly intrinsically motivated to gain information about the latest science fiction titles and thus exposes him- or herself to large quantities of these book reviews over a sustained period. Presumably, this learner will learn to read and comprehend texts in this genre category quite efficiently.

Let us even further assume that this avid science fiction fan is driven to compose and post reviews of his or her own on selected Web sites and listservs as he or she becomes proficient in the science fiction Discourse, its genres and subgenres, and its associated cyberliteracies. Will this learner have at his or her disposal latent knowledge regarding the underlying and surface features of the online book review genre (e.g., rhetorical stance, organizational patterns, register, grammatical conventions, lexical choice)? If the answer to this latter question is yes (as Smith likely would predict), then the learner's writing should somehow manifest evidence of that knowledge. In other words, our hypothetical science fiction fan should be more proficient in producing book review samples than peers who have not exposed themselves to substantial quantities of this text type or genre.

Producing empirical evidence to support strong links between genre-specific reading and genre-specific writing ability unfortunately poses serious challenges for researchers (Grabe, 1991, 2001a, 2003; Hudson, 1998). Consequently, the few studies that have explored these relationships (Carson et al., 1990; Elley & Mangubhai, 1983; Flahive & Bailey, 1993; Hedgcock & Atkinson, 1993; Janopoulos, 1986) have yielded generally inconclusive results. One reason for which these connections are so difficult to unravel is that building genre knowledge involves highly abstract processes that experienced reader–writers may be unable to perceive or discern on a conscious level. As Smith (1988) wrote,

> even arbitrary rules, descriptions, and definitions evade us when it comes to such subtle matters as *style*, the intricate *registers* that depend upon the topic of discussion and the audience addressed, and the *schemas* [sic] appropriate to the particular medium being employed. (p. 19)

Although controversial, Smith's views on literacy development and his pedagogical directives have led to welcome calls for authenticity in L1 and L2 literacy education—calls echoed by a number of researchers and materials writers (Brinton & Master, 1997; Hedgcock & Pucci, 1993; Kasper, 2000; Larimer & Schleicher, 1999; Schleppegrell & Colombi, 2002; Snow & Brinton, 1997; van Lier, 1996). Smith's proposals also underscored the need to view texts and text types as unique, formal representations of the genres and discourse communities in which they are most commonly transacted (Biber, 1988; Connor, 1996). An educational implication of such a socioliterate view is that teachers and students should come to recognize the widely varying levels of rhetorical and linguistic complexity reflected in texts. In addition, the construction and meaningful interpretation of most texts involves a dynamic interaction of features, rules, and layers of meaning encoded in texts themselves. Moreover, as we have previously noted, the reader and the writer play equally active roles in conveying information, shaping meaning, and enhancing literacy skills.

Both EAP and ESP as well as related socioliterate approaches to ESL writing instruction operate on the premise that important dimensions of genre and literacy practice can be explicitly described and taught. In terms of writing instruction, an EAP or ESP orientation in particular involves the production of texts that are acceptable to academic readers (chiefly faculty in the disciplines, but also students' NS and NNS peers) (Dudley-Evans & St. John, 1998; Flowerdew, 1993; Johns & Price-Machado, 2001; Jordan, 1997). Achieving academic literacy thus has a discernibly pragmatic dimension in that successful academic writers must be skilled at meeting the expectations of their readers and achieving the conventional standards upheld by a community of practice.

To generate acceptable texts, students must therefore master the mechanical aspects of composing sentences, paragraphs, and larger units of discourse that correspond to the dominant genres of the academy, a specific field, or both (Hinkel, 2002). At the same time, "learning to write is part of becoming socialized to the academic community—finding out what is expected and trying to approximate it" (Silva, 1990, p. 17). As we have argued, reading is an obvious and accessible means of effecting this socialization. It is by reading and understanding that apprentice writers become experienced members of their target disciplinary communities, developing discursive schemata and views of what constitutes appropriate writing. Therefore, EAP pedagogies emphasize not only generic forms and purposes, strategies, and standards (none of which are necessarily static or fixed), but also the sociocultural and institutional currents that shape options and conventions for writing in academic disciplines.

Whereas EAP and ESP research initially emphasized the products of academic writers, its chief focus has shifted to include the readers and writers of academic texts as well as how they comprehend and compose such texts (Leki, 2000). This transition parallels in many respects the development of process orientations in composition instruction, as outlined in chapter 1. Although some tension has arisen between proponents of science- and technology-based writing on the one hand and humanities-based writing on the other (Spack, 1988), EAP practitioners generally recognize the importance of situating texts, as well as reading and composing processes, in their socioeducational contexts (Benesch, 1995, 2001).

Recent studies clearly demonstrate that writing tasks in academic disciplines are "cued, produced, and evaluated through complex, largely tacit, social and intellectual processes" (Prior, 1995a, pp. 48–49). Because of this complexity, EAP and ESP pedagogies are no longer confined to taxonomic, rule-oriented descriptions of disciplinary genres, nor to the mere specification and presentation of "academic writing tasks." For example, EAP professionals are increasingly called on to avoid static conceptualizations of communicative competence that suggest well-structured knowledge representations and instead to develop the communicative flexibility that students need to participate in the dynamic interactions of authentic, disciplinary contexts (Jordan, 1997). Prior (1995) maintained that by examining academic writing tasks as "speech genres" emerging in real situations with real participants, we can help students "to encounter the dialogic forces shaping academic activity and discourse, to see the situated interpretive and interactional work that generates meanings and texts, and to sense how that work is socially mediated or socially impeded" (p. 77).

Guidelines for Socioliterate Classroom Practices

Instruction in ESL composition should systematically equip novice writers with autonomous composing skills. As a means of going beyond traditional, current–traditional, and process-based paradigms (see chapter 1), however, we encourage teachers to avail themselves of the theories, materials, and pedagogical tools developed by experts in the fields of literacy, EAP, ESP, and genre studies. Although the books and articles cited in this chapter are intended to provide readers with tangible resources for building their own socioliterate repertoires, we acknowledge the need to sketch out general steps to lead readers toward actualizing a socioliterate pedagogy. In her influential book, Johns (1997) recognized the practical challenges of embracing a socioliterate approach by posing this question on behalf of literacy teachers: "Given the short time I have to work with my students, how can I best prepare them for the varied and unpredictable literacy challenges that they will confront in their academic and professional lives?" (p. 114).

To address this well-founded concern, Johns (1997) set forth the following three guidelines or "tenets" that lay groundwork for curricular planning and that point toward genre-based instructional activities:

1. "Draw from all possible resources" (p. 115).
   Involve students in the investigation of literacy practices and genre production processes. Consult and interview experts (e.g., faculty and staff members on campus, professionals in the disciplines) and apprentices (e.g., advanced students) by interviewing them, conducting surveys, and collecting sample texts and artifacts. Compile, analyze, and deconstruct data samples.
2. "Select reading texts carefully" (p. 117).
   Choose texts for "authenticity and completeness." Samples should be "full and unabridged, preserved just as they have been written" (p. 118). Aim for "teachability and appropriateness" (p. 118) by drawing selections from the genre categories that most appropriately reflect the target community of practice and that most suitably match students' literacy and linguistic needs. Assess "specific text-external factors" such as audience and purpose (p. 119). Study text samples written for both general and specialist readers. Students unfamiliar with a discipline may need to learn about its domain content and value systems before exploring discursive conventions. "Community-specific academic texts" (p. 119), on the other hand, enable students to analyze and decode

specialized rhetorical, grammatical, and lexical features unique to the Discourse. Seek out text samples with "visuals and other text-internal features" (p. 120) such as pictures, graphs, formulas, charts, and unique formatting features. Provide guidance in exposing "language-related text-internal factors" that might "prereveal information about textual content, organization, and argumentation" (p. 120). Such factors and features might include topic sentences, thesis statements, conclusions, headings, bold-faced and italicized type, and so on.

3. "Design carefully crafted writing assignments" (p. 122). Avoid essayist bias by "requiring different genres, writer roles, audiences, and purposes" in the design of authentic, communicative literacy tasks that entail genuine, pragmatic purposes such as requesting, complaining, complimenting, arguing, and the like. Induce students to assume "different roles as readers and writers" (p. 122) and provide practice writing to a variety of audiences. Construct tasks requiring learners to write "in different contexts and under varying constraints," from multidrafting to writing "quickly, under pressure" (p. 123). Build into assignments "a variety of conventions and values" (p. 123) so that students "deal with content issues in a variety of ways within a variety of texts and contexts" (p. 124).

Johns' (1997) tenets of socioliterate instruction exemplify the socially embedded nature of text construction and the genre systems that enable teachers and learners to penetrate disciplines, literacies, communities of practice, and their ideologies. Moreover, these pedagogical principles suggest that responsible L2 composition instruction, as an established category of literacy education, need not rely solely or principally on traditional, academic genres such as textbooks and literature. The latter should, of course, still be considered fair game in a socioliterate approach, although teachers should perhaps view these genres in more complex, sociocultural terms.

Geisler (1994), for example, cautioned against allowing the textbook genre to serve as a global surrogate for all academic genres and subgenres: "Textbooks, still the mainstay of the curriculum, are interpreted as containing the domain content upon which students will be tested. Writing, on the rare occasions it is used, serves to duplicate the knowledge structure of those texts." (p. 87). At the same time, "textbooks are socially constructed . . . and . . . can be analyzed and used for the advancement of genre knowledge" (Johns, 1997, p. 125). Literature, also a prominent component of many composition curricula, can likewise be approached from an exploratory, socioliterate perspective, which differs in significant ways from its treatment in traditional, current–traditional, and process-based models (Carter & McRae, 1996; Hirvela, 2001; Kramsch, 1993; Lazar, 1993; McKay, 2001; Vandrick, 2003).

SUMMARY

This chapter describes aspects of L1- and L2-based research on interactions between reading habits and skills on the one hand and the development of writing proficiency on the other. The theoretical formulations that have emerged from empirical studies (i.e., the directional, nondirectional, and bidirectional hypotheses) represent somewhat divergent conceptualizations of literacy development, yet they all suggest that the source of composing skills essentially resides in print matter and the ways in which literate people use it. Studies of L1 and L2 literacy further indicate that skilled writers tend to demonstrate more efficient reading skills than weaker writers. Proficient L1 and L2 writers are also more likely to have read extensively for school and for pleasure than their less proficient counterparts. Research thus points toward a complex, interactional model of reading–writing connections: "Reading and writing are literacy skills, acquired gradually and based on the transfer of skills from one mode to another" (Jabbour, 2001, p. 293). Studies of L2 reading and writing patterns, however, have revealed that literacy does not automatically transfer from L1 to L2. Moreover, the development of L2 writing skills may depend on a constellation of interdependent factors such as language proficiency, L1 and L2 reading ability, L1 and L2 writing proficiency, and exposure to particular genres of writing.

Despite somewhat inconclusive findings, ESL writing instructors have much to draw from current literacy research, particularly from research that views reading and writing as socially constructed practices. The skills of comprehending, using, and creating text are ways of achieving membership in Discourses, literacies, and communities of practice, which comprise readers, writers, teachers, scholars, and so on. As such, the acquisition of literacy skills can and should be viewed as a process of apprenticeship to practices enabling people to read, construct, and share different kinds of texts for real purposes. Inferences drawn from literacy research thus suggest the following implications for the teaching of ESL writing as a literacy:

- Teachers of ESL, realizing that effective writing instruction crucially depends on measuring and nurturing students' reading skills, should adjust the relative weight given to reading and writing assignments on the basis of their students' L2 proficiency levels, needs, and expectations.
- Skills for L2 writing cannot be acquired successfully by practice alone. Some aspects of composing are difficult to teach and must be acquired through sustained exposure to multiple varieties of text.
- To become successful writers of English, ESL learners need instruction involving cyclical iterations of reading and writing. Neither extensive exposure to reading materials nor large quantities of writing practice alone is sufficient: Both are necessary.
- Just as reading facilitates the development of writing skills, so writing develops proficiency in reading. Teachers should therefore consider writing activities that help students to prepare for, respond to, comprehend, and critique reading selections effectively.
- Secondary and postsecondary academic ESL instruction should include reading and writing tasks designed to prepare learners for the demands of the academy, for their individual disciplines, and for vocations and professions.
- Teachers of ESL should strive for authenticity in selecting texts from a variety of genres and in developing composing tasks.
- Teachers of ESL should expose their students to their own processes and practices of engaging in academic literacy events.

REFLECTION AND REVIEW

1. Consider your history as a reader and writer in your L1. Which of the three hypotheses outlined by Eisterhold (1990) (the directional, nondirectional, and bidirectional models)

best account(s) for your development as a writer? What evidence best supports your claim?

2. If you have L2 literacy experience, would you say that your L2 writing skills can be explained by the same model that you cited to explain your L1 writing skills? Why or why not? If you do not have L2 literacy experience, ask a nonnative speaker (NNS) of English (a classmate or other ESL learner you know) to describe for you the major sources of knowledge that have contributed to his or her ability to compose in English. Which of Eisterhold's (1990) hypotheses would be most consistent with the views expressed by your NNS informant?

3. What text genres do you read for pleasure? For information? For your courses? In what ways do you think this reading has contributed to your ability to compose academic and other kinds of texts? If you do not consider yourself an extensive reader, what do you think prevents you from reading voluntarily for personal enrichment or for enjoyment?

4. Reflecting on your recent experiences as a learner and academic writer, describe the genres and text types you have most often produced for your courses (e.g., summaries, reports, reviews, essays, annotated bibliographies, research papers). Have you had explicit instruction in how to construct such texts? If not, how did you learn to compose them? If you were asked by a novice how to compose such texts, what instructions would you give?

5. Consider the collective metaphors and constructs introduced in this chapter:

   a. Discourse (Gee, 1992, 1999)
   b. community of practice (Lave & Wenger, 1991)
   c. literacy (Gee, 1996, 1998)
   d. literacy club (Smith, 1988).

   To what literacy clubs, Discourses, literacies, or communities of practice do you belong? For example, do you consider yourself to be a member of the TESL/TEFL literacy club in your department or of a broader TESL/TEFL community of practice? Are you a parent, a cook, a surfer, a bird watcher, or a community volunteer? Can you identify the practices, values, and literacy skills that you and other members of these Discourses demonstrate? From the perspective of an outsider, what practices, behaviors, and ideologies signify these entities? What skills must one acquire to be regarded as a full-fledged insider in these communities of practice?

6. In your opinion, why should the notion of genre be an especially important consideration for teachers of ESL writing? For example, what are some pedagogical advantages of addressing the genres and text types that students are expected to read and reproduce for their academic coursework? What are some potential benefits of raising students' awareness of nonacademic genres and text types with which students are already familiar?

Application Activity 2.1: Encouraging Extensive, Self-Initiated Reading

Directions: Imagine that you are teaching a secondary or college-level ESL or EFL literacy course at an institution in your community. Identify the educational, vocational, and professional needs of the students, as well as their level of L1 and L2 literacy. In a small group or in your journal, brainstorm ideas for

a. helping students to find sources of engaging English-language texts (e.g., the campus or public library, used book stores, book sales, book exchange clubs, online communities of readers)
b. motivating students to read for pleasure and personal enrichment in English (Day & Bamford, 1998; Grabe & Stoller, 2001, 2002b; Verhoeven & Snow, 2001; Weinstein, 2001).

Application Activity 2.2: Maximizing Reading–Writing Relationships—Writing From Texts Using Reading Journals

Journal writing has become an increasingly popular instructional tool in L1 and L2 literacy instruction (Johns, 1997; Olshtain, 2001; Peyton & Reed, 1990). Reading journals serve as vehicles for ESL writers to respond to assigned and self-selected readings. They can thus serve as a logical component of a voluntary or mandatory reading program in a writing course, although writers may not immediately appreciate the benefits (Holmes & Moulton, 1995). To promote students' written fluency, critical thinking skills, engagement with texts, and latent knowledge of how written language conveys meaning, Zamel (1992) presented a number of approaches to giving students "experiences with the dialogic and dynamic nature of reading" (p. 472). Several of these approaches are summarized in the following task.

Many teachers recommend against using reading journals as evaluative tools. Instead of assigning grades for reading journals, teachers may require students to compose a specified number of entries based on a choice of prompts. Students whose entries are complete receive a full mark. Teacher response to reading journals consists of oral, handwritten, or word-processed comments to selected student entries. Teacher comments may consist of affirmations, queries, and personal reactions.

Directions: Individually or with a classmate, examine the following classroom tasks, which were adapted from Zamel (1992). Consider how you might put one or more of these ideas into practice in a real or hypothetical ESL literacy course, then assess their potential effectiveness. Identify the instructional advantages as well as the practical challenges.

- Ask students to maintain reading journals or logs in which they record and elaborate on what they read for school or for pleasure (e.g., textbooks, literary texts, newspapers, newsmagazines, Web sites).
- Give students the opportunity to write about information they find interesting, significant, perplexing, moving, or otherwise striking to help them realize that "their written reflection makes . . . understanding possible" (p. 474).
- Ask students to keep double-entry or dialectal notebooks. Instruct them to divide the pages of their notebooks or word-processing files into two vertical columns. In the left-hand column, they will copy or summarize passages of interest to them. In the right-hand column, they will respond to these entries by posing questions, paraphrasing, commenting, and so on. Encourage students to respond in the form of images and metaphors.
- Ask students to write entries that they might normally include as cryptic marginal notations in the original text. According to Zamel (1992), "this form of response allows students to consider, weigh, and interpret their reading and gives rise to reactions that they may not have been aware of" (p. 477).
- To make students aware of their associations with texts before they read them, ask students to write journal entries about an experience featured in a text they are about to read. This procedure can help them to construct and anticipate connections that they would not otherwise identify.

- Similarly, ask students to consider and weigh their own ideas about an issue before they read a text. This simple form of schema-raising can enable students "to approach the reading from a position of authority" (p. 478).
- To show students that readers use prediction to construct meaning, ask them to write speculatively about what will happen in a text and to compare these predictions with those of their peers and with the original text. "Written predictions of this sort literally transform student writers into authors of the text" (p. 479).
- Sequence journal entries around readings so that students address texts from diverse perspectives. Encourage students not only to view texts but also to "re-view" them using their new knowledge.

Application Activity 2.3: Writing-to-Read Task Development

Directions: Imagine that you have selected a brief literary text for your intermediate-level literacy course (e.g., a short story such as Shirley Jackson's "The Lottery," a poem such as Robert Frost's "Stopping by Woods on a Snowy Evening," an essay such as M. Scott Peck's "Stages of Community Making," or a chapter or excerpt from a content textbook). Individually or with a partner, develop prompts, tasks, and instructions for one or more of the following:

1. Double-entry dialogue journal
   Construct guidelines for a quarter- or semester-length double-entry reading journal assignment (see Application Activity 2.2). In addition, draft several sample writing prompts.
2. Marginal annotation
   Marginal annotation may include writing brief comments, notations, or symbols in text margins as a means of anticipating content, paraphrasing, and highlighting key information for future retrieval.
3. Write-before-you-read assignments
   To facilitate comprehension, instruct students to write informal responses to open-ended preview questions related to the topics and themes introduced in an upcoming reading assignment.

4. Prediction activities
Develop schema-raising tasks to "activate prior know-ledge" (Anderson, 1999, p. 9), scaffold students' prediction of text structure and content, and develop their strategic reading skills. Such tasks may include scanning titles and headings, working with graphic organizers, searching for specific discursive features, generating probing questions about the text, and so on.
5. Viewing reading from different perspectives
Ask students to assume different reader roles (e.g., topical expert or specialist, total novice) before undertaking a read-ing task.

Application Activity 2.4: Writing From Texts—A Sample Assignment Sequence

Spack (1993) proposed that ESL composition instruction should enable students to "write from and about written texts and gath-ered data" (p. 187). The following assignment outline, adapted from Spack's article, could center on a reading selection re-quired in a literacy or content course. It is intended to serve as a guideline, not as a self-contained, prescriptive set of instruc-tions.

Directions: Individually or with a partner, select a sample text ap-propriate for use in a low, intermediate, or advanced ESL literacy course. Using the following sequence as a starting point, sketch a teaching plan that addresses the specific needs of the students you have in mind.

1. Design and assign a "write-before-you-read" activity (see Application Activity 2.3). Ask students to produce a free-write, journal entry, or sequence of journal entries about an issue, idea, or experience featured in the target reading selection or selections.
2. Assign the text or texts as homework, allowing class time for students to begin the reading in class. Before students begin, instruct them to annotate the text in whatever way they choose as a means of encouraging them to use previewing and prediction strategies. If students are unfamiliar with annotation processes, provide them with sample techniques and model them.

3. Ask students to compose reading journal entries using one or more of the procedures suggested by Zamel (1992) (see Application Activity 2.2). To further students' engagement with the text, encourage them to express agreement or disagreement with the contents of the reading selection.

4. To aid students in exploring their understanding of the text and its intended meaning or meanings, request that they compose a summary of the reading (see Appendix 4), which they will bring to class to share with small peer groups. Students also could post their summaries to an electronic bulletin board or conference for classmates to preview.

5. Plan and supervise peer group discussions of the summaries. This task will send students "back into the text" (Spack, 1993, p. 191), dramatizing that the exchange of ideas, reactions, criticisms, and opinions is an integral part of intellectual life and of academic discourse (Blanton, 1993; Johns, 1997). Students will see that texts are the currency of academic discussion and debate. Moreover, by reading their peers' summaries, they will look at the reading selection with a degree of distance that they had not previously experienced.

6. Introduce a formal composing assignment in writing and ask the students to analyze the directions individually or in small groups. With the students, explicitly identify the audience of the text. Discuss the strategies they will use to meet the expectations of the audience (e.g., rhetorical approach, register, tone, evidence, length, citation style, language choice, lexical range). The writing assignment should be designed so that it requires students to delve deeply into the text, to reflect on it critically, and to situate it with respect to a literacy or discipline.

7. Ask students to draft a version of the assignment to be presented to their peers (and possibly to you). If practical, set aside some class time for this procedure.

8. Plan and supervise peer review sessions or teacher conferences (see chapter 6 for specific recommendations concerning peer response). As a prelude to the session, ask students to review their annotated reading selections, as well as their pre- and while-reading journal entries. Peer or teacher response should focus on the extent to which the writer has fulfilled the assignment, made use of the reading selection, and constructed the essay to meet audience expectations. After the feedback session, the students should make sure

they understand the feedback so they can incorporate it into a subsequent draft of the assignment. The revision cycle then continues at the teacher's discretion (see chapters 3 and 4).

Application Activity 2.5: Text Analysis

In contrast to "writing-to-read" tasks and assignments, which feature student interaction with substantive and autonomous texts, text analysis activities frequently involve briefer texts and require learners to read intensively rather than extensively. The sample text analysis task in Fig. 2.1 asks students to examine the rhetorical structure of an excerpt from a university-level textbook. As part of a series of similar assignments involving multiple skills, a major purpose of this exercise is to sensitize students to paragraph structure and evidential support. This task precedes a writing assignment in which students will be asked to incorporate the forms and styles that they identify in the passage.

Step 1. Simulation and practice

Directions:
a. Assume the role of an ESL student; then complete the following sample reading task.
b. When finished, compare your responses to those of a classmate.
c. After you share your results, devise a follow-up activity that could lead to an authentic, genre-based writing assignment in an intermediate or advanced ESL writing course (e.g., a memo, a summary, a paraphrase, a library investigation, an editorial, an informative or persuasive commentary).

Step 2. Authentic task development

Directions: Select an authentic text or passage from an academic or literary source (not an ESL or composition textbook). Using the sample exercise in step 1 as a departure point, design your own exercise with a view toward (a) facilitating genre analysis, (b) guiding focused discussion about texts, roles, and contexts (Johns, 1997), and (c) reproducing a text associated with an appropriate genre. Authentic sources might include textbooks from any academic discipline, scholarly articles and papers, articles and opinion pieces from the campus newspaper, downloaded

Textbook Passage for Analysis:
Definition Structure

Directions to students: *The following passage is from a popular introductory linguistics textbook. Please read the questions at the bottom of the page, then read the passage carefully. As you read, keep the questions in mind, note the sequence of information, and make note of unfamiliar vocabulary.*

LINGUISTIC KNOWLEDGE AND PERFORMANCE

Speakers' linguistic knowledge permits them to form longer and longer sentences by joining sentences and paraphrases together or adding modifiers to a noun. Whether you stop at three, five, or eighteen adjectives, it is impossible to limit the number you could add if desired. Very long sentences are theoretically possible, but they are highly improbable. Evidently, there is a difference between having the knowledge necessary to produce sentences of a language and applying this knowledge. It is a difference between what you know, which is your **linguistic competence,** and how you use this knowledge in actual speech production and comprehension, which is your **linguistic performance.**

Speakers of all languages have the knowledge to understand or produce sentences of any length. When they attempt to use that knowledge, though — when they perform linguistically — there are physiological and psychological reasons that limit the number of adjectives, adverbs, clauses, and so on. They may run out of breath, their audience may leave, they may lose track of what they have said, and of course, no one lives forever.

When we speak, we usually wish to convey some message. At some stages in the act of producing speech, we must organize our thoughts into strings of words. Sometimes the message is garbled. We may stammer, or pause, or produce **slips of the tongue.** We may even sound like Tarzan . . . who illustrates the difference between linguistic knowledge and the way we use that knowledge in performance.

(Fromkin, Rodman, & Hyams, 2003, pp. 12–13)

Questions to consider

1. What are the primary purposes or functions of this passage? For example, do you think the author's main objectives are to inform, persuade, or defend a position? Why?
2. Can you locate the following elements in the passage? How do you know where to look for them? What functions do they serve?
   a. Topic sentences
   b. Transitional expressions
   c. Definitions, explanations, paraphrases, and exemplifications
   d. Concluding or summarizing statements
3. What kind of evidence do the authors use to develop and illustrate their main points?

FIG. 2.1.   Sample text analysis task.

pages from reliable scholarly Web sites, sample student writing, and so on.

Adaptations of this task could be applied to a range of genres and text types, including literary passages, research materials, student compositions, and so forth. Many genres and text types have not been mentioned specifically in this chapter because of space limitations. The alphabetical list in Fig. 2.2 suggests some accessible text sources.

Reading-based approaches, methods, and tasks appropriate for use in the ESL composition classroom can be found in

Partial List of Genres and Text Types		
❑ advice books	❑ graffiti	❑ personal letters
❑ almanacs	❑ invitations	❑ policy briefs
❑ applications	❑ job announcements	❑ product advertisements
❑ biographies	❑ jokes	❑ proverbs
❑ business letters	❑ legal briefs	❑ recipes
❑ business plans	❑ legal notices	❑ religious tracts
❑ classified ads	❑ legal summonses	❑ résumés
❑ college handbooks	❑ legends	❑ sermons and homilies
❑ conference handouts	❑ letters of reference	❑ schedules
❑ diary entries	❑ local news reports	❑ service manuals
❑ fables	❑ memos	❑ society columns
❑ fairy tales	❑ myths	❑ travel narratives
❑ festschrifts	❑ obituaries	❑ want ads
❑ film reviews	❑ op-ed columns	❑ Web pages
❑ financial reports	❑ personal ads	

FIG. 2.2.   Accessible text sources.

numerous publications related to L1 and L2 literacy instruction. Readers are encouraged to consult the following resources for teaching ESL literacy: Aebersold and Field (1997), Anderson (1999), Belcher and Hirvela (2001), Birch (2002), Day (1993), Day and Bamford (1998), Dubin, Eskey, and Grabe (1986), Johns (1997), Jordan (1997), Pally (2000), Peregoy and Boyle (1997), Rodby (1992), Silberstein (1994), Snow and Brinton (1997), Swaffar, Arens, and Byrnes (1991), Urquhart and Weir (1998), Zamel and Spack (2002). Recent ESL literacy textbooks also can provide models for creating reading-to-write and writing-to-read tasks and assignments.

NOTES

[1]Carson and Leki (1993) and Grabe and Stoller (2001, 2002a, 2002b) provide in-depth accounts of the role of reading in ESL composition.

[2]See Belcher and Hirvela (2001a); Carson and Leki (1993); Grabe (2001a, 2003); Heller (1999); Nelson and Calfee (1998); and Rodby (1992).

[3]For EAP materials and practices, see Jordan (1997) and the quarterly journal, *Journal of English for Academic Purposes*. For ESP resources, see Dudley-Evans and St. John (1998); Hutchinson and Waters (1987); Johns and Price-Machado (2001); Orr (2002); Robinson (1991); and the quarterly journal, *English for Specific Purposes*.

Chapter 3

Syllabus Design and Lesson Planning in ESL Composition Instruction

Questions for Reflection

- *Recalling your experiences as a student, think about syllabi presented in courses you have taken. What made the useful syllabi useful? What was missing from the weaker ones? What elements do you consider to be essential in a course syllabus? Why?*
- *In what ways should the design of a writing course accommodate students' sociocultural backgrounds and educational needs? The requirements and philosophy of the educational institution?*
- *What features do you think makes the planning for a writing course distinct from that for other types of courses? How are composition courses like or unlike other courses in terms of how they are structured?*
- *In your view, what are the essential components of a successful lesson in a composition course? What activities should form the basis of such a lesson? How should they be sequenced? What skills should be practiced, and why?*
- *On the basis of your experience as a student and as a teacher (if applicable), identify the hallmarks of effective classroom instruction and management.*

The ESL/EFL writing class is perhaps best seen as a workshop for students to learn to produce academic essays through mastering techniques for getting started and generating ideas . . . drafting papers which they will anticipate revising, and learning to utilize feedback provided by the teacher and other students in the class to improve the writing assignment at hand. The goal of every course should be individual student progress in writing proficiency, and the goal of the total curriculum should be that student writers learn to become informed and independent readers of their own texts with the ability to create, revise, and reshape papers to meet the needs of whatever writing tasks they are assigned. (Kroll, 2001, p. 223)

SYLLABUS DEVELOPMENT: PRINCIPLES AND PROCEDURES

In keeping with the principles so clearly outlined by Kroll (2001) in the preceding excerpt, this chapter outlines a concrete yet flexible approach to planning instruction in ESL composition courses and provides tools for developing effective lessons. Rather than address global principles concerning the design of entire curricula, we concentrate chiefly on the day-to-day planning tasks of writing teachers: constructing course syllabi, sequencing components of a writing cycle, and designing lessons.[1] In the first section, we address the needs assessment process in detail, because understanding the unique characteristics of ESL writers is essential to shaping effective L2 composition instruction.

NEEDS ASSESSMENT: A TOOL FOR SYLLABUS DESIGN

In broad terms, needs assessment consists of "procedures for identifying and validating needs, and establishing priorities among them" (Pratt, 1980, p. 79). Because of the particular expertise required to teach writing to non-native speakers (NNSs) of English, we need a systematic way of inquiring into the diverse background features, skills, schemata, and expectations of ESL writers so we can take this information into account when planning instruction (Benesch, 1996; Johns & Price-Machado, 2001; Spack, 1997b). Generally, some of this information (e.g., institution type, students' target disciplines, their immigration status) is obvious to teachers and requires no data collection.

Specific demographic and proficiency-related characteristics of the learner population, however, may be available only by eliciting specific information directly from the students themselves and perhaps from institutional authorities.

Although other effective needs analysis tools exist (Brown, 1995; Dudley-Evans & St. John, 1998; Graves, 2000; Reid, 1995a), we concentrate in this chapter on those that are easy to construct, practical to administer, and simple to analyze in the context of an individual program or course: written questionnaires, informal interviews, and ongoing observation. Instead of presenting a static "one-size-fits-all" survey or interview format, we offer the variables in Fig. 3.1 and the explanations that follow as elements to consider in constructing needs analysis instruments tailored to your learner population, institutional setting, and teaching style.

Understanding the Learner Population

Figure 3.1 provides a general starting point for identifying students' instructional requirements by requesting information about factors known to influence the effectiveness of L2 composition instruction. This information should ultimately be used to design course syllabi and classroom tasks.

Institution Type. For the same reasons that we should not make pedagogical decisions without considering the diversity of learners in our classrooms, we should be mindful of the types of students described in the research literature (Browning, 1996; Graves, 2000; Nieto, 2002; Silva, 1993). One of the most obvious characteristics to consider is the type of institution in which students receive their English-language instruction. We can generally assume, for example, that college- and university-level ESL writers have had more experience with English and have developed more extensive academic literacy skills than high school ESL writers, simply by virtue of the length of their exposure to the language through formal schooling. Likewise, postsecondary students, by virtue of having elected to continue their studies beyond compulsory secondary education, may have varied educational and career goals in mind.

Even within postsecondary institutions, we also find diverse types of students. Students at Japanese universities enrolled in EFL writing courses, for instance, may have received little or no preparation as writers of English, despite continuous

Institution Type		
❑	Secondary school	
❑	Community college	
❑	College- or university-based intensive ESL/EFL program	
❑	Four-year college	
	❑	Lower division (freshman/sophomore)
	❑	Upper division (junior/senior)
❑	Comprehensive research university	
	❑	Lower division (freshman/sophomore)
	❑	Upper division (junior/senior)
	❑	Graduate degree/diploma
	❑	Other
Prior L1-Medium Educational Experience		
❑	None	
❑	Primary/elementary school	
❑	Secondary/high school	
❑	Adult school	
❑	Vocational/technical/trade school	
❑	Community college degree/diploma	
❑	College/university degree/diploma	
❑	Graduate degree/diploma	
❑	Other (e.g., Nondegree):	
Prior English-Medium Educational Experience		
❑	None	
❑	Primary/elementary school	
❑	Secondary/high school	
❑	Adult school	
❑	Vocational/technical/trade school	
❑	Community college degree	
❑	College/university degree	
❑	Graduate degree/diploma	
❑	Other:	
L1 Literacy Skills*		
Reading proficiency: ❑ High ❑ Mid ❑ Low		
Writing proficiency: ❑ High ❑ Mid ❑ Low		
English Language Proficiency and Literacy*		
ESL/EFL proficiency: ❑ High ❑ Mid ❑ Low		
Reading proficiency: ❑ High ❑ Mid ❑ Low		
Writing proficiency: ❑ High ❑ Mid ❑ Low		
Immigration Status (For students in anglophone settings)		
❑	Immigrant/permanent resident	
❑	International (student visa holder)	
Traditional/Nontraditional Status (Check one, if applicable)		
❑	Traditional (no interruption in secondary or postsecondary education)	
❑	Nontraditional/returning (one or more interruptions in secondary or postsecondary education)	

* These crude proficiency ratings are presented only for illustrative purposes. As we suggested in chapter 2, responsible treatment of learners' literacy skills requires attention to a wide range of influential sociocognitive and educational variables.

FIG. 3.1.　Inventory of institutional and educational variables.

study of English throughout secondary school. Meanwhile, other Japanese students, particularly those who have studied in English-medium institutions at home or abroad, may enter university EFL writing courses with rather extensive experience as writers of English. In the North American context, high schools and community colleges often serve a high proportion of immigrant students, depending on geographic location. In contrast, four-year colleges and research universities may attract a high proportion of international students. Many North American four-year and research institutions maintain steady populations of both types of student, although it is common for institutions in some areas to be dominated by either immigrant or international students with nonpermanent resident status. Community colleges often serve higher numbers of immigrant students because these institutions offer low-cost education and opportunities for students to transfer to four-year colleges and research universities upon completion of basic education requirements (Ching, McKee, & Ford, 1996).

We make a distinction between immigrant and international students in this discussion because immigrant students (some of whom may be the children of immigrants or immigrants themselves) may have permanent resident status. Meanwhile, international students usually enter English-speaking countries on student visas, complete their college or university studies, and subsequently return to their home countries.

Further distinctions are to be made between students taking courses in intensive English programs (IEPs) and their counterparts in traditional degree programs. Frequently, IEPs in anglophone settings are housed on college and university campuses, but may not award students college or university course credit (with the occasional exception of certain advanced-level courses). Many IEPs offer both academic and nonacademic ESL courses for international students as well as immigrant learners. Academic-track IEP courses often are geared toward providing students with the linguistic and academic skills they need to matriculate as regular students and to enter traditional degree programs (Gaskill, 1996). Nonacademic courses, meanwhile, frequently serve international students who intend to spend a limited time in an English-speaking environment to improve their English proficiency and then to return to their home countries. Clearly, the teaching of ESL writing in IEP courses needs to be geared specifically toward students' educational, professional, and personal goals.

In many English-medium educational institutions, ESL students may be assessed and placed into pre-academic, basic, or "remedial" courses designed to bring their oral–aural and literacy skills to a level at which they can enroll in regular content courses with students who are native speakers (NS) of English (Braine, 1996; DeLuca, Fox, Johnson, & Kogen, 2001; Harklau, Losey, & Siegel, 1999; Silva, Leki, & Carson, 1997). Frequently, students assigned to these courses are identified as weak in specific skill areas and allowed to take courses that count toward a degree or certificate only after they successfully pass these courses, successfully pass an in-house language proficiency test, or achieve a specified score on the Test of English as a Foreign Language (TOEFL) or other criterion-referenced test.

The implications for the teaching of writing in these circumstances are clear. Instruction must furnish students with the skills required to perform in subsequent ESL, "mainstream" English, and content courses in the disciplines, and for better or worse, to succeed on tests. In a number of institutions, successful completion of these courses entitles students to make the transition from the ESL track to the regular or "native" track, where no distinction is made between NNS and NS students, and where classes are made up of both learner types.

Other institutions, meanwhile, may offer ESL- or NNS-stream writing courses that parallel NS courses in terms of curriculum and assessment criteria. In principle, such courses are designed specifically with NNS learners' needs in mind and, like their mainstream counterparts, enable students to earn credit toward a degree. Instructors with ESL training or experience working with NNS writers often (and preferably) teach courses designated for ESL students. In NNS-stream courses that parallel NS courses, instruction often is determined largely by the mainstream curriculum and guided by the principles and techniques featured in equivalent courses. In some such cases, conflicts may arise between philosophies and approaches to the literacy tasks and writing processes that students must practice and master (Atkinson & Ramanathan, 1995; Johns, 2003; Kroll, 2001; Silva et al., 1997).

Prior Educational Experience. In addition to the numerous factors influencing the extent and type of writing instruction offered and required by schools, colleges, and universities, ESL students' formal educational backgrounds also must be considered. The inventory of student variables shown in Fig. 3.1 includes two broad categories aimed at capturing this information: prior L1-medium educational experience and prior English-medium educational experience. For each of these categories, students' levels of education or years of formal schooling offer only a rough index of students' experience and expertise as classroom learners, note-takers, discussion participants, readers, writers, test-takers, and so forth. Teachers of ESL need to bear in mind, of course, that their students' prior educational experiences might vary considerably from those provided by the ESL or EFL setting in which they currently are receiving instruction. Immigrant and international students pursuing an education in an English-medium institution, for example, may find that their prior training contrasts considerably with the form of instruction embraced in the ESL and EFL courses they are offered. Educational systems around the world vary widely in terms of approach, philosophy, and cultural orientation (Feagles, 1997; Reagan, 1996). Anticipating and understanding learners' prior experiences can be tremendously valuable to writing teachers, because many ESL students come from educational traditions in which school-based texts exemplify rhetorical patterns that are fundamentally distinct from those valued in English-medium Discourses and communities of practice (see chapters 1 and 2).

Moreover, in some non-Western educational models, writing processes may not be explicitly taught if, in fact, writing is even featured in the curriculum. Students trained in those traditions may sometimes view composing as incidental to the mastery of discipline-specific subject matter or enhancement of language proficiency (Leki, 2003). Such students may thus be unfamiliar (and possibly uncomfortable) with the numerous ways in which texts and iterative composing processes are used and taught in English-medium academic settings (Corson, 2001; Duszak, 1997; Matsuda & Silva, 1999; Raimes, 1985, 1998; Scollon, 1997; Scollon & Scollon, 1981).

Knowing about students' English-medium educational experiences can be equally informative, as teachers may need to accommodate their learners' familiarity with composing skills and strategies to prepare them effectively for writing at a more advanced level. For the university freshman composition instructor, for example, it is important to understand the extent to which his or her ESL writers are prepared to undertake the formal, academic writing often required in freshman-level courses, including personal and academic essays, literary analysis, and the like (see chapters 1 and 2). Students with a U.S. high school or community college background may already be familiar with these

English-based genres, although their level of proficiency in producing them is bound to vary. Students with no English-medium educational experience, on the other hand, may come into the freshman writing course with little or no explicit awareness of these pervasive rhetorical forms or knowledge of how to reproduce them, thus presenting underequipped composition teachers with potentially daunting challenges.

Language Proficiency and Literacy. Along with information regarding the type and extent of students' formal schooling, indications of their general ESL proficiency as well as their L1 and L2 literacy skills can offer ESL writing teachers vital information about where composition instruction should begin and how it should proceed (Benesch, 1996; Johns, 1997, 2003). Adult ESL learners, regardless of their L1 literacy level, have at least two bases of knowledge from which to draw in building their L2 proficiency: L1 knowledge and emergent L2 knowledge. Moreover, many classroom ESL and EFL learners are, in fact, fully multilingual, able to function in several languages. If they have attained a threshold of L1 literacy, L2 learners also can "draw on their literacy skills and knowledge of literacy practices from their first language (*interlingual transfer*), and they can also use the input from literacy activities—reading and writing (*intralingual input*)—in their developing second language" (Carson, Carrell, Silberstein, Kroll, Kuehn, 1990, p. 246). As noted in chapter 2, some researchers have maintained that L2 learners use both of these knowledge bases as they develop L2 literacy skills. Others, meanwhile, have claimed that the transfer of literacy skills from the primary language to an L2 is not automatic and that the relationship between the two literacies is complex and in need of extensive research.

It is nonetheless intuitively appealing to assume that text-based input influences the development of both reading and writing proficiency in a given language. For developing L2 writers, of course, the situation involves multiple dimensions of knowledge and skills: "One must take into account not only the learner's L2 . . . proficiency, but also the possibility of interaction of first language literacy skills with second language input" (Carson et al., 1990, p. 248). Clearly, these interactions cannot possibly be captured with a crude instrument such as a questionnaire, although a rough measure of students' current L1 and L2 literacy skills can provide basic information about their literacy profiles, as can a characterization of students' learning styles and study habits (see chapter 2).

Immigration Status. An additional background factor that we have set apart as a distinct factor concerns students' immigration status. Although relevant only to international and immigrant English-language learners, this ostensibly trivial piece of demographic information can be a tremendously significant determinant of an individual student's educational pathway. A student's immigration status can consequently present important implications for ESL writing instruction. Immigrant students' linguistic and educational histories, instructional needs, and career plans may differ widely from those of international students, who, as we have already noted, generally intend to return to their home countries upon completion of their studies in North America, the United Kingdom, Australia, New Zealand, or any other English-medium environment (Brindley, 2000; DeLuca et al., 2001; Harklau et al., 1999; Murray, 1996; Schleppegrell & Colombi, 2002; Silva et al., 1997).

As a supplement to information about students' prior educational experience, language proficiency, and literacy skills, immigration status can tell teachers a great deal about their students' personal histories and socioeconomic backgrounds, as well as the educational and professional futures they may envision for themselves. As we indicated earlier, immigrant students have (or may be in the process of obtaining) permanent residency status in the host countries where they are studying. In some cases, these students have lived in an anglophone setting for extended periods, in contrast to their nonimmigrant counterparts, who generally enter the host country on temporary student visas and do not intend to make the host country their permanent home. Immigrant students also may have left their primary language environments as refugees or may be the children of refugee parents. Such students may consequently be members of sizable and well-established ethnic and linguistic minority communities.

In many ethnolinguistic minority communities, ESL students' primary language or languages also may predominate in the home and in community-based Discourses. These broader Discourses may include formal communities of practice (e.g., cultural organizations, social clubs, religious institutions, aid agencies) in addition to less formal—although equally influential—social aggregations, from circles of family and friends, to neighborhoods, to street gangs, and so forth (Rampton, 1995; Romaine, 1995). This multilingual, multi-discursive situation may promote the development of bilingual (or multilingual) proficiency and multiliteracies among some learners (Cope & Kalantzis, 2000;

Fairclough, 2000). For others, meanwhile, competition can arise between languages, literacies, and Discourses, posing challenges in the educational setting (Grosjean, 1982; Harklau et al., 1999; Skutnabb-Kangas & Cummins, 1988; Stewart, 1993).

To illustrate the potential range of such educational challenges, some immigrant students who have resided for many years and have attended school in an anglophone setting may achieve a highly functional level of linguistic proficiency and academic literacy in English, enabling them to advance through ESL courses quickly and transition to NS-track courses. These students may complete their postsecondary education while maintaining, and even strengthening, their bi- or multilingualism and cultural ties to their home communities (Hakuta & D'Andrea, 1992).

For many other immigrant students, however, achieving bilingualism and biliteracy can be considerably more difficult and frustrating. Those with strong ties to a cohesive ethnic and linguistic community in which English is seldom or never used may find that the school, college, or university campus may be the only place in their daily lives where English is the primary medium of communication (August & Hakuta, 1997; Rampton, 1995). Consequently, such immigrant learners may have limited opportunities to use English for purposes other than those directly related to formal education and may therefore require substantial instructional support to compensate for these limitations. International ESL students enrolled in colleges, universities, and IEPs frequently report an analogous sense of social and linguistic isolation from English-speaking students and the wider community, often because both international and immigrant students may tend to socialize and find solidarity with peers from the same linguistic and sociocultural background. A result of this tendency is that ESL students may use their primary languages in their social interactions nearly everywhere but the educational setting.

This dualistic situation can pose problems of a slightly different nature for immigrant students than for international students. Immigrant students are faced with having to use English not only to complete their formal studies, but also to seek and secure employment, and to pursue careers and livelihoods in an English-speaking workplace. Many immigrant students also perform the difficult role of interpreter and translator for parents and extended families with severely limited English language skills. Moreover, the majority of immigrant students enrolled in educational institutions often struggle with economic and social hardships that their international peers may never experience. Many international students, for example, come from developed nations and have the economic resources to cover the cost of their foreign study, thanks to government sponsorships, family resources, or both. Immigration laws in most host countries, in fact, require student visa holders to demonstrate proof that they possess these financial means and that full-time student status is maintained throughout their course of study.

The circumstances of many (perhaps even most) immigrant students contrast sharply with those of international students. Because of the need to contribute financially to their family incomes or to support families of their own, immigrant learners enrolled in ESL programs at all levels of education may hold part- or full-time jobs. These financial and family-related obligations may place heavy demands on ESL students, for whom educational achievement may also be a palpably strong social value in their home communities. Not only may resident students face ever-present financial and educational pressures and hardships; they may likewise confront problems associated with being members of ethnolinguistic minority communities that do not enjoy equal, let alone privileged, social status with respect to dominant (anglophone) cultures and Discourses.

These divergent experiences clearly set resident student populations apart from international student populations and suggest the need for ESL teachers to adjust pedagogical assumptions accordingly. The content and assignments in a writing course designed for international students may be largely inappropriate for immigrant students. Consider, for example, a syllabus in which North American culture and literature serve as core content, in conjunction with writing tasks that involve students in making comparisons between the cultural practices of the target culture and the home culture. Whereas such a curriculum would probably serve the needs of newcomers to an English-medium cultural and educational environment, it would be of marginal relevance to ESL students who have lived and studied in the United States for quite some time, and for whom the "home country" is a distant memory. Recognizing and understanding the current personal, social, and economic conditions of immigrant and international students can help ESL teachers develop a sensitivity to the constraints that their students must overcome in their efforts to improve their linguistic and academic skills, including their composing proficiency (Valdés, 1992, 2000).

Traditional and Nontraditional Students. An additional factor that frequently is overlooked but can influence the character of learning and teaching in a given ESL setting has to do with learners' status as so-called "traditional" or "nontraditional" students. Traditional students (both NS and NNS) are sometimes described as such if they have experienced few if any interruptions in their progress from secondary school to (and through) postsecondary education. That is, traditional students are those who upon completion of secondary school proceed directly to a community college, four-year college, or research university, and from there, perhaps to a graduate or professional program. Because of this rapid progress from a secondary to a postsecondary institution, traditional students usually are young adults in their late teens or early twenties when they begin their postsecondary education.

Nontraditional or "returning" students, on the other hand, may have experienced one or more interruptions along their educational pathways. These interruptions can include substantial periods of full-time employment (and sometimes the pursuit of a new career), as well as considerable time devoted to caring for children, elderly family members, or both. These students, whose numbers are increasing rapidly in many educational institutions, thus represent a variety of age groups (Peterson, 1995; Stewart, 1993). Moreover, many nontraditional students reinitiate their formal studies while working and may likewise have personal, financial, and family commitments to fulfill.

These circumstances can sometimes have a direct and obvious impact on students' participation, motivation, confidence level, and performance in a composition course. Consider, for example, a returning immigrant student who undertakes part-time coursework toward an undergraduate degree after having successfully completed her ESL composition requirements 10 years before. Such a student may have decided to return to college for compelling personal or economic reasons, such as no longer having young children to care for, coupled with a desire to pursue a career outside the home. A student in this situation might understandably need special assistance and guidance in readjusting to the academic environment. It may also take time for her to reactivate literacy skills that have not been practiced in a long time. With a sensitivity to such circumstances, teachers can anticipate the academic, linguistic, sociocultural, and psychological obstacles faced by their students and can appreciate the challenging experiences that might strongly influence their students' progress as writers.

Learner Preferences, Strategies, and Styles.   A final but crucial dimension of needs assessment involves accounting for learners' predispositions toward aspects of classroom instruction and independent learning. Whereas the information targeted in Fig. 3.1 is primarily demographic, the learner variables included in the writing styles questionnaire (Fig. 3.2) address aspects of learners' predispositions, preferences, strategies, and styles that are subject to considerable change over time and that may be most productively measured locally in the classroom context. Research on learner strategies and styles (which is, unfortunately, too extensive to consider in detail here) consistently shows how these highly personal and dynamic variables affect learning processes in the classroom and beyond (Cohen, 1998; Gass & Selinker, 2001; Graves, 2000; Reid, 1995b; Skehan, 1989, 1991, 1998). This work also now suggests ways in which teachers can diagnose their students' styles and preferences, raise awareness of maximally productive strategies, and facilitate the acquisition of new strategies.

The sample questionnaire in Fig. 3.2, inspired by several instruments presented in Reid (1995b), was developed by an instructor who administered it on the first day of an advanced university course in Writing English for Academic Purposes (EAP) offered to international students. The prompts are clearly geared toward nonimmigrant students with limited experience in English-medium classrooms. The questionnaire items are specifically aimed at inviting students to report their perceived expertise as readers and writers, in addition to their views regarding collaborative work, drafting procedures, feedback, and revision. The instructor was able to use his students' responses to address these issues explicitly in the course and to plan instruction to accommodate the reported needs and preferences of the class. In other words, the questionnaire results not only served to guide the instructor's instructional planning, but also provided data on which students could subsequently reflect as a measurement of their literacy development as the course progressed. During periodic writing conferences, the teacher informally interviewed students' about their level of satisfaction with the course. At the end of the course, the instructor devised a retrospective assignment in which students wrote a comparison of their initial perceptions and their cumulative achievements.

By regularly considering formally and informally gathered self-report data about their students' work patterns, study habits, drafting styles, task type preferences, and so forth, teachers can

WRITING STYLES QUESTIONNAIRE

A. Student background information

Name: _____

Native country: _____

Native language(s): _____

B. Classroom work styles

DIRECTIONS: _This portion of the survey will help your instructor understand the ways in which you prefer to complete class assignments. Think about your most recent experiences in college or university classes. For each statement below, place a check mark(✓) in the cell that best describes your habits and preferences. Please be honest! Candid responses will give your instructor valuable information._

1 = Strongly agree	3 = Somewhat agree
2 = Agree	4 = Somewhat disagree

	5 = Disagree
	6 = Strongly disagree

		1	2	3	4	5	6
1.	In my native country, I had many opportunities to work with fellow classmates on projects and assignments.						
2.	Outside my native country, I have had opportunities to work with fellow classmates on projects and assignments.						
3.	In general, I enjoy working with other students in planning and completing academic assignments.						
4.	When I work with a partner or a small group, I usually produce better work than I do when working alone.						
5.	When I work with a partner or a small group, I usually concentrate better and learn more.						
6.	I am comfortable working with partners who are also nonnative speakers of English.						
7.	I prefer working with a partner or with a group when the teacher assigns specific roles to group members.						
8.	I hope we will do a lot of pair and group work in this course.						

C. Strengths, styles, and preferences

DIRECTIONS: _This portion of the survey is designed to help you and your instructor understand the ways in which you prefer to plan and complete writing assignments in English. Think about your most recent experiences in classes where you wrote academic papers. For each statement below, place a check mark (✓) in the cell that best describes your habits and preferences. Again, be honest! Candid responses will give your instructor valuable insight._

1 = Strongly agree	3 = Somewhat agree
2 = Agree	4 = Somewhat disagree

	5 = Disagree
	6 = Strongly disagree

		1	2	3	4	5	6
1.	I think I am a good academic writer in my native language.						
2.	I think I am a good writer of academic English.						
3.	I know how to use source material (e.g., textbooks, scholarly books, journal articles, news accounts, Web-based resources) effectively in my writing assignments.						
4.	One of my major strengths as a writer of English is producing interesting ideas.						
5.	I am skilled at organizing my ideas and expressing them logically.						

FIG. 3.2. Writing styles questionnaire for classroom use (Continued).

85

	1	2	3	4	5	6
6. I have learned about academic writing mostly through reading.						
7. When I write academic assignments, I am a good typist and an efficient computer user.						
8. I rearrange my ideas a lot when I am planning a text.						
9. When I revise a paper or draft, I often make a lot of changes.						
10. As I revise a paper, I like to add new material.						
11. When I write and revise a paper, I think carefully about what my reader wants to know from me.						
12. Before I revise a paper, I ask a classmate or friend to give me comments on it.						
13. My papers usually state a purpose explicitly.						
14. I use clear and succinct transitions between paragraphs.						
15. The paragraphs of my papers usually contain plenty of examples, explanations, and other evidence.						
16. I try hard to connect each of my paragraphs to my main purposes for writing.						
17. My concluding statements synthesize my main points and the evidence I have presented in my text.						
18. When I turn in papers, they contain mostly minor grammatical errors.						
19. My papers show that I have a strong command of English vocabulary.						
20. When I turn in papers, they have few spelling and punctuation errors.						
21. When I write an academic paper, I know how to use references, quotations, footnotes, bibliographic sources, and so on effectively.						
22. Generally, I learn a lot from the comments I get back from my instructor.						
23. I enjoy sharing my writing with other students and learn from reading the writing of my classmates.						
24. After getting an assignment back from my instructor, I usually learn things that I can apply to future writing assignments.						

D. Self-assessment and goals

DIRECTIONS: *Please complete the statements below with at least three points. Be as specific as you can.*

1. My greatest strengths as a writer of English include ...
   a.
   b.
   c.

2. Aspects of my writing that I would like most to improve in this course include ...
   a.
   b.
   c.

FIG. 3.2.   Writing styles questionnaire for classroom use.

design syllabi, plan lessons, construct assignments, lead activities that capitalize on students' strengths and overcome their weaknesses, and avoid student resistance to dispreferred task types. Instruments used to collect this information are perhaps most suitably and productively developed by adapting and combining styles and strategies resources already available.[2]

SETTING AND MEETING GOALS
FOR LEARNING AND TEACHING

Having collected systematic profile data on his or her student cohort, the teacher is minimally equipped to identify, articulate, and negotiate the desired outcomes (global and specific) of a literacy course. Goals are frequently recognized as global targets around which instructional programs and syllabi are designed. Brown (1995) defined *goals* as "general statements concerning desirable and attainable program purposes and aims based on perceived language and situation needs" (p. 71). The goals for a particular program and its course sequence should address the observed needs of the student population and the requirements of the educational institution, as identified by regular, methodical needs analyses (Frodesen, 1995; Graves, 2000; Kumaravadivelu, 2003; Nunan, 2001; Walker, 2003).

A goal summary for a premainstream, advanced academic ESL literacy course series, for example, might read something like this: "Students will be able to identify implicit relationships in academic English between parts of a concept: in a flow chart, in a table, and in an outline, as well as in the prose describing a chart or table in an essay" (Brown, 1995, p. 77). Such goal statements ideally reflect cognitive, linguistic, academic, and analytic skills that can be described, practiced, and assessed in the context of an instructional program and the courses it comprises.[3]

In many ESL and EFL settings, instructional goals are preestablished by administrators and institutions. The role of individual teachers is to work toward and accomplish these goals in the planning and execution of the courses they teach. However, embracing this role should not imply that teachers cannot play a part in shaping institutional, program-level goals or in using these goals to their advantage in developing syllabi and lesson plans. As Graves (2000) pointed out, "clear goals help to make teaching purposeful because what you do in class is related to your overall purpose. Goals and objectives provide a basis for making choices about what to teach and how" (p. 79). Instead of confining teachers' decision making, therefore, well-articulated goals should be viewed as tools for facilitating literacy instruction in the following ways:

1. Formalized goals articulate the purposes of the course and educational program.
2. Goal statements focus on what the course or program intends to accomplish, indicating the specific skills that students will acquire or perfect upon completion of the course.
3. Goals allow for the formulation of more precise and achievable instructional objectives.
4. Goals are dynamic—they evolve as a function of the changing needs of the students as their skills develop (Brown, 1995; Graves, 2000).

In the sections that follow, we look at procedures for constructing course syllabi and designing lessons. By planning instruction to meet specific learning objectives formulated on the basis of a solid needs analysis, teachers can bring about the realization of broader programmatic goals.

FROM GOALS TO OBJECTIVES: THE SYLLABUS AS A FRAMEWORK FOR INSTRUCTION

Whereas goals typically constitute general statements of a curriculum's purpose, *objectives* articulate "the particular knowledge, behaviors, and/or skills that the learner will be expected to know or perform at the end of a course" (Brown, 1995, p. 73). We use the term "instructional objective" in this discussion to describe the purposes of a course as outlined in a syllabus as well as the tools for devising units and lessons.[4] Objectives are thus fairly precise. Instructional objectives specify the following essential characteristics: performance (what the learner will be able to do), conditions (procedural and sociocognitive, within which the performance is expected to occur), and criteria (the quality or level of performance that will be considered acceptable) (Mager,

1975). The following sample goal statements illustrate how these components can be spelled out succinctly in a curriculum plan or course description:

> - "By the end of the course, students will have become more aware of their writing in general and be able to identify the specific areas in which improvement is needed" (Graves, 2000, p. 80);
> - "By the end of the course, students will improve their writing to the next level of the ACTFL [American Council of Teachers of Foreign Languages] Proficiency Guidelines Writing scale" (Graves, 2000, p. 80);
> - "By the end of the course, the students will be able to write the full forms of selected abbreviations drawn from pages 6–8 of the course textbook with 80 percent accuracy" (Mager, 1975, p. 74).

We underscore the specific, explicit wording of these statements, which articulate observable (and, ideally, measurable) learner behaviors or performances. We maintain that this level of precision is not only indispensable for lesson planning and teacher self-evaluation, but also crucial for fair, meaningful assessment (see chapter 8). The instructional objectives outlined in Fig. 3.3 represent a small but somewhat more extensive sampling of the types of functions that ESL writing syllabi at various proficiency levels and in various institutions might include.

Not all curriculum design experts, language educators, or rhetoricians advocate setting a priori instructional objectives. A principal objection to explicit aims relates to their negative association with behavioral psychology and the charge that stating objectives somehow trivializes classroom teaching by forcing instructors to focus only on narrowly defined skills and written products (Gronland, 1985; Hillocks, 1995). A further complaint maintains that explicit objectives limit teachers' freedom, constrain their decision making, and perpetuate the status quo (Benesch, 1996; Joseph, Bravmann, Windschitl, Mikel, & Green, 2000). We do not find these objections to be particularly persuasive. We argue that teachers should view objectives not as rigid, prescriptive targets, but as flexible guidelines keyed to performative outcomes embedded in the curriculum. As Brown (1995) pointed out, "objectives are most effective when a variety of different types are used and when the level of specificity for different

Course Type & Level	Sample Objectives as Outlined in Course Syllabus
Grades 9–12 ESL or EFL: Intermediate/High to Advanced	• Identify and summarize in writing main ideas of paragraphs and larger units of written discourse, including textbooks and literary passages. • Compose paragraph-length prose responses to specific questions in connected prose form. • Compose original expository and narrative texts (up to 500 words in length) on personal topics, academic content, and current events.
Adult/Vocational ESL: Low to Low Intermediate	• Transcribe simple words in dictation. • Compose lists of words that relate to a theme, semantic category, or pragmatic function. • Complete simple forms and documents, including bank deposit and withdrawal slips, postal forms, and so on. • Use simple illustrations and diagrams to compose simple descriptive sentences.
Pre-Academic Intensive ESL or EFL: Low to Low Intermediate	• Take legible notes on familiar topics. • Respond in complete sentences to personal and academic questions. • Compose simple letters, paraphrases, and summaries of biographical data as well as work and school experiences. • Compose descriptive, narrative, and expository paragraphs of 100 words or more based on simple, authentic texts.
Community College/University ESL: Intermediate to Advanced	• Take detailed notes on familiar and unfamiliar topics. • Respond in connected written discourse to text-based questions. • Compose summaries of biographical data and work/school experiences. • Compose paraphrases and summaries of extended academic prose (texts of up to 10 pages in length). • Compose descriptive, narrative, and expository essay-length texts (up to 500 words in length).
College/University ESL: Advanced (NS-track equivalent)	• Take detailed notes on familiar and unfamiliar topics. • Respond in connected written prose to text-based content questions. • Compose summaries of statistical and graphic data. • Compose paraphrases and summaries of extended academic or technical discourse (texts of up to 20 pages in length). • Compose descriptive, expository, analytic, and argumentative texts of 1,500 words or more.

FIG. 3.3.   Sample course objectives: ESL writing skills.

objectives is allowed to diverge" (p. 95). The explicit presentation of instructional objectives in a course syllabus enables teachers to

1. transform student needs into teaching points that can be organized into a teaching sequence
2. identify for students target skills that underlie instructional points
3. decide on the level of specificity for the teaching activities in the syllabus

4. adopt or adapt teaching materials that appropriately accommodate student needs and expectations
5. map out a blueprint for assessing student performance and progress
6. evaluate their own teaching effectiveness (Frodesen, 1995; Graves, 2000; Richards & Lockhart, 1994).

SYLLABUS DEVELOPMENT: NUTS AND BOLTS

Conducting a needs assessment can be an informative and rewarding process leading to the development and establishment of clear, measurable, and achievable course objectives. These objectives and their operationalization, of course, need to be formalized in writing on the course syllabus.

It is useful to think of a course syllabus as a document comprising two main parts. First, it can serve as a contract between the instructor and the students, summarizing course objectives and how they will be met (Hafernik, Messerschmitt, & Vandrick, 2002; Kroll, 2001). Second, a syllabus serves as an operational framework and planning tool. It structures and sequences instructional aims, units, lessons, assignments, classroom procedures, and assessment procedures for both the instructor and the students (Graves, 2000; Nunan, 1991a, 2001). The checklist in Fig. 3.4, although not exhaustive, offers a framework for providing students with all the information they will need about course objectives and content, workload, participation requirements, policies, assignments, and performance expectations. Figure. 3.4 also serves as an advance organizer for the discussion in the sections that follow. A sample syllabus for a community college composition course appears in Appendix 3A to exemplify the principles and practices outlined in this chapter.

THE COURSE SCHEDULE: PRIORITIZING, SEQUENCING, AND PLANNING FOR WRITING

Laying out a sequence of reading materials, classroom activities, and assignments can be one of the most challenging tasks facing novice and even experienced classroom teachers. Before

1. Descriptive information

☐ Course name, number, meeting time, and location
☐ Prerequisites and other requirements
☐ Instructor's name and contact information (office location, consultation hours, campus telephone number, and e-mail address)

2. Course goals and primary content

☐ Program-level and course goals
☐ Specific course goals, as well as general and specific course objectives
☐ Core course content, as well as aspects of literacy and composing processes to be presented, practiced, and assessed
☐ Dimensions of English rhetoric, textual analysis, grammar, and so forth, that will be directly addressed
☐ Description of what constitutes progress toward the achievement of course aims (see item (7))
☐ Quantity and scope of reading material to be covered in class activities and writing assignments

3. Reading materials

☐ Bibliographic information for all required and optional text sources, as well as details about their availability
☐ List of reading assignments, their sequence, page ranges, and deadlines (if this information can be determined in advance)

4. Writing assignments

☐ Number and description of writing assignments, including information about genre, length, use of published sources, and so on
☐ Description of how many and which assignments will involve multidrafting, peer response, teacher feedback, and so forth
☐ Indication of how many and which assignments will involve timed (in-class) or online writing
☐ Policies governing late work, revised assignments, collaboration, plagiarism, and so on
☐ Presentation requirements, including preferred style sheet (e.g., MLA, APA, Chicago, CBE), length criteria, text formatting, word-processing conventions, electronic file formatting, and so forth

5. Instructional processes and procedures

☐ Description of how class time will be allocated (e.g., balance of workshop activities, drafting, peer review sessions, class discussions, lecture, in-class writing, quizzes)
☐ Expectations concerning student preparedness and participation in discussions, group tasks, peer review sessions, contributions to electronic bulletin boards, and so on

6. Course requirements

☐ Summary of compulsory assignments and their deadlines
☐ Description of assessment criteria, including how student work will be evaluated
☐ Explanation of policies concerning attendance, participation, missed assignments, and so on

7. Assessment and grading procedures

☐ Explicit description of assessment criteria and how they will be applied to assignments
☐ Account of how final course grades are weighted (if applicable) and calculated
☐ Justification of assessment and marking procedures

8. Course schedule or timetable

☐ If practicable and appropriate, a session-by-session or week-by-week calendar of dates, themes, events, reading assignments, and deadlines (considerable flexibility often is required with course timetables to accommodate inevitable changes, delays, and negotiated syllabi)

FIG. 3.4. Syllabus checklist.

describing specific techniques for meeting these challenges, we offer some guiding principles to assist in laying groundwork for writing a syllabus and course outline. Figure 3.5 presents an overarching schema and set of suggested procedures for incorporating overlapping phases of a hypothetical composing sequence into a course outline (see chapter 1). We point out that the stages leading from prewriting through publishing are not mechanical, autonomous steps, but potentially overlapping and recursive phases and subprocesses (Clark, 2003d). Hillocks (1995) persuasively argued that conventional approaches to implementing so-called "process" models of composition instruction should be viewed with extreme caution, as we suggested in our discussion of process and postprocess pedagogies in chapter 1. "While the general model of the composing process is useful," wrote Hillocks (1995), "it cannot begin to account for variations in process that appear to be dependent on a variety of factors" (p. xix). Therefore, we wish to avoid trivializing the complexity of individual writers' evolving composing processes. We thus present the model in Fig. 3.5 not as a linear, operational design, but as a general guideline for structuring and sequencing classroom tasks and multiple drafting to serve a broad range of instructional contexts and student writer populations.

To operationalize this iterative writing process schema, we must first and foremost establish student and program goals as our highest priority, organizing our material, instructional procedures, and tasks accordingly (Jensen, 2001; Lee & VanPatten, 2003; Omaggio Hadley, 2001). Second, it is crucial that we understand how our planning decisions (including materials selection, sequencing, balance of instructional activity types, assignment development, and so on) will help our students to meet course objectives (see chapter 4). If textbooks and assignments are prescribed by an academic department, program, institution, or educational agency, our syllabi still will not write themselves. Our teaching will be most effective when we can justify—to ourselves and to our students—our planning decisions with direct reference to course objectives (Cumming, 2003). Third, flexibility is essential: As Tarvers (1993) aptly emphasized, "a ruthless sense of realism must go into planning [a] course schedule" (p. 42), because no timeline can be etched in stone.

Whereas some teachers can efficiently follow and complete a detailed, preplanned course timetable, many find it difficult to adhere so closely to a course outline that lays out a day-by-day, 10- or 15-week plan. Under ideal conditions, teachers can work with students to negotiate a syllabus, involving learners in decision making about literacy development tasks, reading selections, the nature and number of assignments, multidrafting processes, revision requirements, assessment criteria, portfolio contents, and so forth (Bamberg, 2003; Glenn et al., 2003; Nunan, 1991b, 2001). Under such circumstances, a quarter- or semester-length timetable is perhaps unnecessary. On the other hand, successfully delivering a negotiated syllabus requires even more

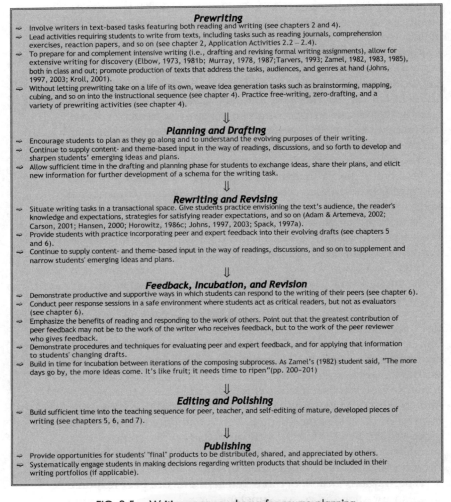

Prewriting

⇝ Involve writers in text-based tasks featuring both reading and writing (see chapters 2 and 4).
⇝ Lead activities requiring students to write from texts, including tasks such as reading journals, comprehension exercises, reaction papers, and so on (see chapter 2, Application Activities 2.2 – 2.4).
⇝ To prepare for and complement intensive writing (i.e., drafting and revising formal writing assignments), allow for extensive writing for discovery (Elbow, 1973, 1981b; Murray, 1978, 1987; Tarvers, 1993; Zamel, 1982, 1983, 1985), both in class and out; promote production of texts that address the tasks, audiences, and genres at hand (Johns, 1997, 2003; Kroll, 2001).
⇝ Without letting prewriting take on a life of its own, weave idea generation tasks such as brainstorming, mapping, cubing, and so on into the instructional sequence (see chapter 4). Practice free-writing, zero-drafting, and a variety of prewriting activities (see chapter 4).

⇓

Planning and Drafting

⇝ Encourage students to plan as they go along and to understand the evolving purposes of their writing.
⇝ Continue to supply content- and theme-based input in the way of readings, discussions, and so forth to develop and sharpen students' emerging ideas and plans.
⇝ Allow sufficient time in the drafting and planning phase for students to exchange ideas, share their plans, and elicit new information for further development of a schema for the writing task.

⇓

Rewriting and Revising

⇝ Situate writing tasks in a transactional space. Give students practice envisioning the text's audience, the reader's knowledge and expectations, strategies for satisfying reader expectations, and so on (Adam & Artemeva, 2002; Carson, 2001; Hansen, 2000; Horowitz, 1986c; Johns, 1997, 2003; Spack, 1997a).
⇝ Provide students with practice incorporating peer and expert feedback into their evolving drafts (see chapters 5 and 6).
⇝ Continue to supply content- and theme-based input in the way of readings, discussions, and so on to supplement and narrow students' emerging ideas and plans.

⇓

Feedback, Incubation, and Revision

⇝ Demonstrate productive and supportive ways in which students can respond to the writing of their peers (see chapter 6).
⇝ Conduct peer response sessions in a safe environment where students act as critical readers, but not as evaluators (see chapter 6).
⇝ Emphasize the benefits of reading and responding to the work of others. Point out that the greatest contribution of peer feedback may not be to the work of the writer who receives feedback, but to the work of the peer reviewer who gives feedback.
⇝ Demonstrate procedures and techniques for evaluating peer and expert feedback, and for applying that information to students' changing drafts.
⇝ Build in time for incubation between iterations of the composing subprocess. As Zamel's (1982) student said, "The more days go by, the more ideas come. It's like fruit; it needs time to ripen"(pp. 200–201)

⇓

Editing and Polishing

⇝ Build sufficient time into the teaching sequence for peer, teacher, and self-editing of mature, developed pieces of writing (see chapters 5, 6, and 7).

⇓

Publishing

⇝ Provide opportunities for students' "final" products to be distributed, shared, and appreciated by others.
⇝ Systematically engage students in making decisions regarding written products that should be included in their writing portfolios (if applicable).

FIG. 3.5.   Writing process schema for course planning.

scrupulous attention to curricular goals and course objectives because teachers must ensure that writers achieve the outcomes stated in the syllabus without the explicit structure of a detailed timetable (Jensen, 2001).

With these general planning precepts in mind, we can begin to lay out the work of a quarter or semester with the goals of our institutions and our students (as operationalized in our course objectives) as clear, measurable targets. It is useful to start the process with an academic calendar or planner showing the exact number of class meetings and holidays to be included in the timetable. Cancellations because of personal and professional commitments should then be noted, and any required make-up meetings should be built into the schedule. Class days also should be reserved for timed writings, midterms, examinations, and the like to give a clear picture of exactly how many meetings can be planned for teaching, workshops, feedback sessions, and so on.

We further suggest designating one or two sessions per term as "free" or "flex" (flexible) sessions if the academic calendar permits. Flex sessions can provide highly valuable padding that allows the teacher to carry over units, tasks, and assignments without having to rework the entire course timetable when a class falls behind schedule, as many inevitably do. If the course proceeds as planned, flex sessions can then be used for extra writing time, teacher–student conferences, portfolio preparation, and even working ahead.

Next, it is a good idea to schedule due dates for graded writing assignments, particularly if these deadlines are prescribed by the program, department, or institution. We recommend working backward from final submission deadlines to include intermediate deadlines for drafts, peer feedback sessions, editing workshops, student–teacher conferences, and so forth. The sample syllabus and course outline in Appendix 3A illustrates one way in which this "backtracking" planning method can be used. We recommend allocating adequate time for multidraft assignments and revised papers, particularly near the beginning of a term, when writing assignments tend to take longer to work through. Extra class periods may be necessary early on to discuss preliminary drafts, demonstrate and practice peer response techniques, and revise assignments in class or in the computer lab.

You will likewise find it valuable to build into the course timetable sufficient time for you and your students to read assigned texts, practice prewriting and drafting techniques, and work through peer response tasks. The timetable should also allow sufficient time for you to annotate and evaluate your students' work (see chapters 5, 6, 7, and 8). Allow as much time between sessions as practicable to make a multidraft approach worthwhile if multidrafting is a central feature of your course.

To maximize the multidrafting approach and provide sufficient incubation time between drafts, it can be useful to initiate a new writing assignment while the preceding one is still in progress. For example, it may be time efficient to collect a set of short papers for feedback or evaluation while students embark on an extended project or research assignment.

Once the core assignments are in place and the deadlines for preliminary work (readings, drafts, peer and teacher feedback, revision, and so on) are established, the course outline has at least a skeletal form that allows for the planning of discussions, lectures, student presentations, peer response workshops, online chats, quizzes, and other class activities. If reading figures prominently in the course objectives (as we strongly suggest it should), reading selections should be assigned with great care so that they correspond logically to the themes, genres, rhetorical patterns, and discursive forms to be featured in the syllabus, as well as the writing assignments and literacy tasks based on them (Johns, 1997; Kroll, 2001). Generally, reading selections in published anthologies and rhetorical readers (see chapter 4) are presented as units, linked topically, and connected to specific writing tasks (e.g., expository or argumentative essays).

Examples of themes included in recent ESL and NS composition textbooks include affirmative action, educational policy, environmental controversies, gender issues, globalization, human sexuality, immigration, language rights, multiculturalism, racism, and reproductive rights. Where such textbooks are not part of the curriculum, a thematic approach still may be used as the basis for syllabus design, with a thematic unit revolving around an identifiable topic or context (Snow, 1998, 2001; Snow & Brinton, 1997). As with writing assignments, reading assignments should be allotted generous time. Lengthy reading selections may need to be divided into smaller parts to enable students to complete them and to provide for effective treatment in class. Finally, lay your plan out so that you and the students can see the chronology of the entire term. Before finalizing the course schedule, check to see that adequate time has been allocated for especially labor-intensive literacy tasks such as extended reading selections, multi-draft writing assignments, and investigation projects. For multidraft assignments, track the sequence you have sketched out to ensure enough time for the necessary iterations of drafting, feedback, revision, and editing (Kroll, 2001).

LESSON PLANNING: PRACTICES AND PROCEDURES

Identifying Lesson Objectives

In the same way that the instructional objectives specified in a syllabus identify what knowledge and skills students will acquire by the end of a course, effective lesson objectives describe the observable behaviors that students will demonstrate at the end of a class period or unit (Brown, 2001; Jensen, 2001; Nunan, 2001; Raimes, 1983). If instructional objectives are clearly specified in the syllabus, identifying lesson objectives should be an easy task when it comes to planning individual class periods. Lesson objectives should emanate directly from instructional objectives and at least indirectly from program or course goals. Consider, for example, this instructional objective for a low to low-intermediate, pre-academic ESL writing course from Fig. 3.3: "Compose descriptive, narrative, and expository paragraphs." A corresponding performative objective for a lesson derived from this course aim might read "Compose a 200- to 250-word paragraph describing each writer's dormitory room, apartment, or house." The anticipated outcome is described in terms of an observable, measurable student performance as well as a written product with which students can work and that can ultimately be published, shared, and evaluated. The objective statement also should be worded with action verbs such as "compose" and "describe" (in contrast to verbs such as "learn" or "understand," which are difficult to observe and appraise).

Although many experienced and skilled teachers plan and execute productive lessons without writing out their objectives in detail, effective teachers do have a clear purpose in mind when they select and organize classroom tasks. As Purgason (1991) pointed out, "each activity needs to have a reason. A teacher must think through why that activity is important to the students and what they will be able to do when they finish it" (p. 423). Consequently, it is advisable for both novice and experienced teachers to articulate lesson objectives routinely in their planning (Brown, 2001; Cruickshank, Bainer, & Metcalf, 1999; Graves, 2000; Ur, 1996). Explicit, measurable objectives help teachers to unify the components of their lessons:

> In synthetic terms, lessons and units of work will consist, among other things, of sequences of tasks, and the coherence of such

lessons or units will depend on the extent to which the tasks have been integrated and sequenced in some principled way. (Nunan, 1989, p. 10)

Sequencing and Organizing a Lesson Plan

A lesson plan can take many forms, depending on the time constraints and personal style of the individual teacher. Regardless of how it appears, a lesson plan should provide the teacher with a "script" for presenting materials, interacting with students, and leading students through structured and unstructured activities. Much more than a mere step-by-step chronology of a classroom event, however, a lesson plan is a practical, tangible, and potentially dynamic tool for meeting student needs as operationalized in course objectives. It serves as a vital link between curricular goals and the learning we wish to bring about among our students. In this sense, the lesson is where the known (instructional objectives, texts, and so on) meets the unknown (the novice writers in our composition classes).

Hillocks (1995) noted that mapping out instruction is initially an exploratory endeavor: "At the beginning of a year or term, our students are likely to be new to us. We cannot begin planning, except with general outlines, until we know what students do as writers" (p. 132). Because we cannot possibly anticipate every aspect of what happens in our classrooms, we can think of lessons as opportunities for experimentation. Not all lessons or activities will succeed. We can be prepared for this outcome, however, by expecting the unexpected. We also can improve our teaching effectiveness by reflecting on what works well and what does not work so successfully with the students in our own classes (Bailey, Curtis, & Nunan, 2001; Bailey & Nunan, 1996; Richards & Lockhart, 1994).

Hillocks (1995) offered sound planning advice in noting that "the thoughtful teacher, in searching for ways to help students learn more effectively, will plan real trials (what researchers call quasi-experiments), determine what effect they have, even as the trial goes forward, and consider new options as a result" (p. 125). Most teachers, even those seasoned and self-assured enough to conduct entire lessons with no written notes, are aware of the benefits of advance planning, which can lead to a willingness to depart from their plans when necessary (Bailey, 1996). A written lesson plan, whether a general list of activities or a meticulously detailed sequence of procedures, facilitates processes such as postlesson evaluation, problem diagnosis, and skills enhancement.

The Mechanics of Lesson Planning

In purely mechanical terms, a lesson plan can be handwritten or word-processed on standard paper and formatted in any number of ways. Teachers working in highly "wired" environments can even prepare their class plans using interactive software such as Microsoft PowerPoint, enabling them to project outlines and materials onto a screen or an array of monitors. In contrast, a low-tech lesson plan can easily be printed out on notecards. In fact, for some teachers, it is enough to write out lesson notes before class as a way of putting the content and sequencing into their heads. In this way, they obviate the need for a written plan during the lesson.

Whatever form a lesson plan takes, it should be readable, convenient to refer to in class when needed, and usable as a future record of what took place. Instead of proposing a rigid or prescriptive model for planning ESL writing classes, we offer the following general outline and conceptual framework as options for individualizing daily lesson designs.[5] The outline in Fig. 3.6 includes practical and procedural aspects of the planning process that many teachers consider essential in constructing a lesson. Appendix 3B contains an example of an authentic lesson plan that reflects these principles, procedures, and formatting options. Figure 3.6 focuses principally on logistical elements, whereas Fig. 3.7 focuses on pedagogical moves and instructional procedures.

Although most of the items in Fig. 3.6 are self-explanatory, a few are worth elaboration. In addition to reviewing the lesson's objectives, making a note about the work that students did during the previous class and have done for homework can give us a realistic feeling for what kinds of reading, writing, discussion, and problem solving tasks students are ready for next. This review process is invaluable in managing time effectively. Preparing a list of equipment (e.g., overhead projector, transparencies, markers), materials, page numbers, and so on before class can avert the need to spend valuable class time getting organized. Having a prepared checklist of student work to return and collect can likewise save time, as can dispensing with announcements efficiently. Some teachers routinely write these on the board or an overhead transparency for students to read on their own. Others

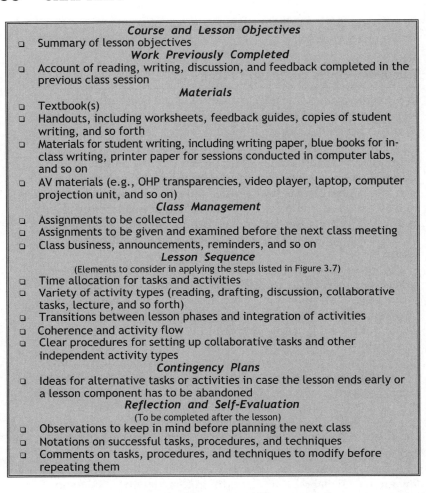

Course and Lesson Objectives
- Summary of lesson objectives

Work Previously Completed
- Account of reading, writing, discussion, and feedback completed in the previous class session

Materials
- Textbook(s)
- Handouts, including worksheets, feedback guides, copies of student writing, and so forth
- Materials for student writing, including writing paper, blue books for in-class writing, printer paper for sessions conducted in computer labs, and so on
- AV materials (e.g., OHP transparencies, video player, laptop, computer projection unit, and so on)

Class Management
- Assignments to be collected
- Assignments to be given and examined before the next class meeting
- Class business, announcements, reminders, and so on

Lesson Sequence
(Elements to consider in applying the steps listed in Figure 3.7)
- Time allocation for tasks and activities
- Variety of activity types (reading, drafting, discussion, collaborative tasks, lecture, and so forth)
- Transitions between lesson phases and integration of activities
- Coherence and activity flow
- Clear procedures for setting up collaborative tasks and other independent activity types

Contingency Plans
- Ideas for alternative tasks or activities in case the lesson ends early or a lesson component has to be abandoned

Reflection and Self-Evaluation
(To be completed after the lesson)
- Observations to keep in mind before planning the next class
- Notations on successful tasks, procedures, and techniques
- Comments on tasks, procedures, and techniques to modify before repeating them

FIG. 3.6. Lesson plan outline/checklist.

prefer to make announcements at the end of class, when they will not have to be repeated for latecomers. On an increasing number of campuses, instructors can also post informational messages on electronic bulletin boards or conferences dedicated to courses.

The core lesson elements in Fig. 3.6 refer to techniques for successfully executing the steps outlined in Fig. 3.7. The first of these core elements is time management, perhaps the single most pervasive challenge for teachers in carrying out their lesson plans. For this reason, a useful practice is to anticipate the time that each activity in a lesson will require, adding several additional

Lesson Phase	Teacher Actions	Student Actions
1. Activation of prior learning	• Helps students recall what they have learned or practiced in previous lesson(s) • Asks students to demonstrate new knowledge and skills	• Report on prior learning • Demonstrate new knowledge and skills through practice
2. Preview/warm-up	• Previews new lesson, connecting new material to material just reviewed or practiced • Checks students' understanding of material and concepts at hand • Guides students in anticipating lesson content by capturing their interest and stimulating thought about the topic and task	• Respond to preview • Respond to teacher's prompts
3. Lesson core: Instruction, procedures, participation	• Presents lecture, writing task, or activity • Communicates lesson objectives to students • Models task or activity, guiding students to engage with new concepts and practice relevant skills • Asks students to complete the task or activity individually or in groups • Provides opportunities for students to practice using new knowledge and skills independently • Encourages student involvement, participation, and interaction • Checks students' understanding of material and concepts at hand	• Respond to teacher's presentation (e.g., by taking notes, asking questions, and so on) • Observe modeling, ask questions • Undertake the task or activity individually or in groups • Complete the task or activity independently • Elicit teacher's assistance to complete the task, as needed
4. Closure	• Prompts students to reflect on what they have learned and practiced • Links new learning to prior learning	• Discuss or describe what they have learned or practiced • Discuss relationship of new learning to prior learning
5. Follow-up and preparation for next lesson	• Presents additional tasks or activities to practice same concepts • Introduces or lays groundwork for future tasks and learning objectives	• Complete additional tasks or activities • Take note to prepare for further learning

FIG. 3.7. Conceptual framework for lesson sequencing.

minutes to that total. This strategy gives teachers a way of estimating what can reasonably be accomplished in a single class period. A general rule to follow is that open-ended activities such as unstructured discussions of texts, group activities, peer response workshops, and student conferences frequently take much longer than teachers predict, partly because of the numerous unexpected questions that can emerge and partly because managing such activities requires added time. The same can often be said of untested classroom tasks (see chapter 4).

Related to the issue of time management is the principle that lessons should involve some degree of variety in terms of task type and interactional styles (Graves, 2000; Jensen, 2001).

In an ESL composition course, it is entirely appropriate that a significant amount of class time be dedicated to the practice of writing, to the discussion of writing processes, and to effective text construction strategies. At the same time, teachers should recognize that allocating large chunks of time to writing in class can result in unproductive use of instructional resources (e.g., teacher expertise, class discussion, peer interaction). The classroom should serve not only as a workshop environment, as Kroll (2001) maintained, but also as a setting for meaningful, socioliterate activity.

Similarly, because many composition courses are not only writing courses but also reading courses (see chapter 2), it is reasonable to dedicate a substantial portion of class time to responding to, analyzing, discussing, and writing about the required texts and genres featured in the syllabus (Feez, 1998; Glenn et al., 2004; Johns, 1997, 2003; Kroll, 2001; Williams, 1996). Class meetings should likewise reflect a careful balance between teacher talk and student talk, with group work, class discussion, and lecture appropriately balanced (Bamberg, 2003). Classroom activities also should be linked explicitly to one another and to the instructional objectives so that students can see that lessons are internally coherent and connected to both institutional goals and their own literacy goals (Benesch, 1996). Of course, implementing transitions to link lesson components and establish coherence requires skill on the part of the teacher, but transitions are a crucial part of the teaching process. Making explicit links is easier when classroom tasks have a discernible purpose and are introduced with transparent, easy-to-understand directions and procedures (see chapter 4).

Whenever practicable, lesson plans should involve careful, systematic thought about how classroom activities will be set in motion by the teacher and students. It also is sometimes necessary to have a contingency plan ready in the event that you have extra time or must abandon something you had planned because of some unexpected circumstance (Bailey, 1996; Ur, 1996). This alternate task or activity does not necessarily require elaborate advance preparation. Indeed, an alternate task could involve something as simple as asking students to compose a journal entry on the day's topic of discussion, free-write on an aspect of a recent reading assignment, or begin the next reading selection or homework exercise. The point here is that, although these are straightforward solutions to the problem of underplanning, they may not seem so straightforward when you reach the end of your lesson plan with 10 or 15 minutes to spare. When armed with a practical contingency plan, teachers can implement them rather seamlessly while engaging student writers in a valuable and productive literacy task that accomplishes much more than filling an unexpected time gap.

The postlesson reflection phase of instructional planning should not be seen as an addendum. On the contrary, we should view postinstructional evaluation as an integral part of meeting course objectives and of promoting our own professional development (Bailey et al., 2001). Teachers can take simple yet productive steps to evaluate a lesson plan at the end of a class session. For example, you can decide whether you would repeat the same procedures if you were to teach the lesson a second time or if you would make changes. "Ask yourself how well students responded to the activities you planned and try to diagnose the causes of problems you encountered" (Omaggio Hadley, 2001, p. 464). In addition to recording what worked and what did not work so well, you can note how long each activity took for future reference. Many teachers use their postlesson observations and assessments as starting points for planning the next class period. This cyclical practice provides the teacher and his or her students with a sense of continuity from one meeting to the next, facilitating the process of tracking progress through the syllabus.[6]

We now turn to the central pedagogical task of lesson planning: laying out the actual procedures involved in teaching a group of students in a meaningful literacy event such as writing and providing them with substantive writing practice in the course of a class period. The framework in Fig. 3.7 presents a general outline for a lesson sequence (i.e., that part of the class period focused not on logistics but on teaching, learning, interaction, and literate activity, including the production of written discourse).

After whatever preliminary business precedes the actual lesson (see Fig. 3.6 and the explanation that follows it), the sequence ideally begins with a procedure in which students are asked to recall what they have learned or practiced previously. This phase does not necessarily require an elaborate, comprehensive review. It may involve a 5-minute task in which students write a quick summary of the preceding day's discussion of a reading selection, compose a three-sentence reaction to the instructor's feedback on their last writing assignment, or complete a simple quiz on the text to be discussed in groups that day. These straightforward techniques can and should reactivate students' knowledge and awareness to facilitate the introduction of new knowledge and to promote the practice of new skills.

The preview phase is sometimes indistinguishable from the activation phase, although the preview phase tends to direct students' attention to what lies ahead. Activities that might logically follow the summary task described earlier could include a read-aloud of students' summaries in small groups or a brief discussion of the next writing assignment's literacy goals. A follow-up to students' three-sentence responses to comments on their essays may serve as an introduction to strategies for incorporating teacher feedback into a revised writing assignment. A review of reading quiz solutions would be a good way to use that exercise productively to initiate a more detailed analysis of the text or texts under study. Depending on students' understanding of the material at hand, this portion of the lesson could last from 5 to 15 minutes before giving way to the lesson core, in which new material is introduced and new skills are practiced.

At this point, the teacher might briefly expose his or her objectives to the students before getting into the heart of the lesson. In the case of the discussion of summaries and subsequent read-aloud activity, the teacher might initiate students into a writing assignment draft focused on the text that sparked the original discussion. One option would entail brainstorming writing topics, whereas another would involve instructing students to begin writing based on a choice of focused prompts. To use students' three-sentence reactions to essay feedback and his or her subsequent introduction to incorporation strategies, the teacher might instruct the class to begin working on revised drafts. Meanwhile, the teacher could discuss revision plans with students in mini-conferences. After correction of the reading quiz and a discussion of the solutions, the teacher might scaffold a class or group activity in which students perform a detailed analysis of the text. In all of these hypothetical situations, students become actively involved in tasks that require them not only to recycle familiar knowledge, but also to practice new skills and acquire new knowledge.

Like the activation and preview segments, the closure phase may require very little time. Closure is nonetheless an important process leading naturally and logically to the follow-up. In each case, closure may involve prompting students to identify what they have practiced and why, and clarifying for them the purposes that their work will serve. For the students who began composing initial assignment drafts in class, a natural extension of this task would involve completing the drafts and eliciting peer responses to them at the next class meeting. Students who were given instruction on incorporating feedback and who conferenced with the instructor may be asked to complete their revisions and reflect on the value of the feedback process. In the case of the students who practiced with text analysis, the teacher may assign a brief, structured written analysis for the next class (see Application Activity 2.5). Alternatively, the teacher might ask writers to apply the same analytic techniques to a different but related text in preparation for a class discussion. In all of these scenarios, the conclusion of each lesson requires the application of previously introduced skills and knowledge, and the laying of groundwork for future learning.

At this juncture, it is worth reiterating several related points made earlier in this chapter. The first is that, as with designing course syllabi, constructing lesson plans and putting them into action requires flexibility if the teacher is to achieve instructional aims, satisfy student needs, and avoid persistent frustration. The second point concerns the planning framework described in the preceding section and schematized in Figs. 3.6 and 3.7: The lesson design scheme we have sketched is intended to provide a general heuristic for developing lessons and making them successful. It should not be applied zealously or rigidly. Whereas we do hold that structure is necessary in planning and teaching writing courses, that structure should be adjusted to accommodate the wide-ranging needs of students and the unexpected events that are inevitable in any classroom. To paraphrase Hillocks' (1995) notion of lesson planning, the most effective teacher of writing is the one who designs lessons as "trials," expects lessons to produce unanticipated results, and applies those results in subsequent teaching. It is through this process that we discover "new options" (p. 125).

SUMMARY

Syllabus design and implementation constitute complex tasks for many composition teachers. To make these tasks more manageable, this chapter explores principles and procedures for constructing syllabi, course outlines, and lesson plans as a direct function of identifiable student and institutional needs. We present the following summary statements as a synthesis of the principles we have covered:

> • A clear understanding of learners' backgrounds, needs, expectations, styles, and strategies, as well as institutional requirements (as identified in systematic and ongoing needs analysis) is crucial to the formulation of achievable course goals and instructional objectives.
> • The most effective syllabi, course outlines, and lesson plans are those that accommodate multiple, recursive writing processes by allowing adequate time for reading and exploring genres, composing and revising drafts, giving and using feedback, and exploring new content.
> • Maintaining a clear sense of instructional objectives in constructing daily lesson plans enables the teacher to effect coherent instruction by connecting tasks within lessons and by linking each lesson to past and future lessons.
> • Flexibility is essential in all aspects of instructional planning.

REFLECTION AND REVIEW

1. In what ways can student background variables (e.g., primary language or languages, nature and length of prior education, educational and career goals, immigration status, motivational profile) affect students' potential performance in ESL and non-ESL literacy courses? How can a systematic characterization of students' backgrounds inform writing instruction?
2. Describe the roles played by goals and objectives in the planning of syllabi, course outlines, and lesson plans. Identify the advantages of linking goals and objectives to course content and classroom tasks.
3. In what ways can a syllabus and course outline assist the teacher in planning literacy instruction and writing practice? How can these tools assist students in their literacy skill development?
4. What are the principal components of a writing lesson?

5. Explain specific methods for operationalizing prewriting, composing, feedback, and revision tasks into a syllabus or lesson plan.
6. What are the short- and long-term benefits of constructing literacy lesson plans and reflecting on their effectiveness in a systematic manner?

Application Activity 3.1: ESL Writer Profile

Directions

1. Using the background and situational variables in Fig. 3.1 and the learning style and strategy variables in Fig. 3.2 as starting points, devise a questionnaire that you could administer to a prospective group of student writers at an institution with which you are familiar. Add specific items that pertain to the population and institution you have in mind. Your purpose in this task is to develop an instrument or prototype to use and adapt in your own classroom teaching and action research. Solicit feedback on your survey from your instructor, colleagues, classmates, and administrators. After your revisions, administer the questionnaire to one or more classes of ESL writers, tally the frequency data, and compose a demographic profile of the sample. In your report, suggest an instructional approach that you believe would be appropriate and effective for that group of writers.
2. As in the preceding task, use the background and style variables outlined in Figs. 3.1 and 3.2 as frameworks for developing a survey or interview protocol that you will use to conduct a case study of an ESL writer. Secure permission from your student to audiotape or videotape one or more interviews that focus on his or her background as a language learner and writer. In your analysis of the data, discuss how your student's primary language knowledge, sociocultural background, educational experiences, immigration status, motivational predispositions, and so forth have influenced his or her progress as an ESL writer. Capture his or her perceptions of the usefulness of the literacy instruction she or he has received. Suggest instructional implications based on the student's views of the effectiveness of his or her prior education.

Application Activity 3.2: Syllabus Assessment

Directions: Using the syllabus development tools and checklists in Figs. 3.3 and 3.4, compare the sample syllabus in Appendix 3A with a syllabus and course outline for a writing course at a local school or college. On the basis of the criteria outlined in this chapter and in Figs. 3.4 and 3.5, prepare a written or oral assessment of the strengths and weaknesses of the sample syllabi in light of what you know about the institution, the curriculum, and the learner population. In addition to the checklists, the following questions may help to scaffold your comparative analysis:

- What are the stated course goals and instructional objectives?
- To what extent do course content and organization coincide with goals and objectives?
- If you were to teach one of the courses, what changes would you make to the syllabus and why?

Application Activity 3.3: Assessing Lesson Plans

Directions: Compare the lesson plan formats suggested in Figs. 3.6 and 3.7 with the sample lesson plan in Appendix 3B. Alternatively, compare these with one of your own lesson plans, or with a lesson outline prepared by a colleague for an actual literacy course. On the basis of the criteria presented in this chapter, assess the strengths and weaknesses of the lesson plan in light of what you know about the course and the students. To what extent does the lesson plan address instructional objectives? What changes would you make to the lesson plan, and why?

Application Activity 3.4: Working With Lesson Plans

Directions

1. Using the lesson plan formats suggested in Figs. 3.5 and 3.7, outline a simple lesson for a literacy course in which you have conducted observations or worked as a practice

teacher or tutor. Alternatively, prepare a lesson outline for one of the following situations:

a. An introductory session on writing paragraph-length comparisons for a novice-level high school ESL or EFL literacy course
b. An advanced-level university IEP course on summarizing and paraphrasing sources (e.g., textbook chapters, scholarly articles and essays, Web pages) in short research papers (see Appendix 4)
c. A premainstream community college literacy course requiring students to paraphrase and quote from academic sources (see Appendix 4)
d. A mainstream university composition course made up of both NS and ESL writers who need help supporting assertions and arguments with persuasive evidence.

2. After writing (and, if possible, teaching) a lesson or unit using the suggested format, explain the revisions you would make to the format. Should any sections be added or omitted? What changes in the format would make the plan easier to use?

NOTES

[1] Additional sources on curriculum design include Brown (1995); Dubin and Olshtain (1986); Graves (1996, 2000); Markee (1997); Richards and Rodgers (1987); and Walker (2003).

[2] Reid (1995b) provided a wealth of similar instruments designed for classroom use, some of which specifically target the teaching of composition (e.g., Carrell & Monroe, 1995; Reid, 1995a). Other useful sources include Brown (1995); Dudley-Evans and St. John (1998); Graves (2000); Jordan (1997); Oxford (1990); and Oxford and Ehrman (1993).

[3] We avoid the term, "critical" here, not because we believe that "critical" skills have no place in the academic literacy curriculum, but because the term itself is notoriously ill-defined (Atkinson, 1997; Ramanathan & Kaplan, 1996b).

[4] For in-depth discussions of instructional objectives and their implementation, see Dubin and Olshtain (1986); Findlay and Nathan (1980); Finocchiaro and Brumfit (1983); Feez (1998); Graves (2000); Gronland (1985); Joseph et al. (2000); Nunan (1991c); Richards and Lockhart (1994); and Walker (2003).

[5] Guidelines for constructing classroom lesson plans can be found in Brown (2001); Cruickshank et al. (1999); Dubin and Olshtain (1986); Jensen (2001); Lee and VanPatten (2003); Nunan (1991a); and Purgason (1991).

[6] Systematic self-assessment tools can be found in Bailey et al. (2001); Gebhard and Oprandy (1999); and Richards and Lockhart (1994).

APPENDIX 3A: SAMPLE SYLLABUS AND COURSE OUTLINE

SYLLABUS AND COURSE OUTLINE
ENGLISH 110A—Composition I
Fall Semester 2004 Baxter Community College

English 110A, Section F — 4 semester units	Lydia Chang, Instructor
Class Meetings: MWF 8:00–9:20	Office Hours: M 11:00–12:30, Th 8:00–10:00
Classroom: Chandler 318	Tel: 522-9128
Office: Dept. of English and ESL, Seaver 442B	e-mail: lmchang@bxtrcc.edu

Course Description and Goals

English 110A is an academic writing course for native- and non-native speakers of English who have achieved the required score on the College Language and Critical Skills Test or who have completed the prerequisite ESL or Basic Skills courses in the Department of English and ESL. Literacy goals for English 110A include developing skills in the following areas:

1. top-down and bottom-up reading strategies
2. awareness of academic and literary genres
3. analytic and critical reasoning
4. creative self-expression.

Students should also expect to develop the following academic writing skills and strategies:

1. understanding formal writing tasks
2. investigating reader expectations
3. gathering information for writing assignments from published and online sources
4. avoiding plagiarism
5. planning academic writing assignments, including essays, reports, commentaries, and so forth
6. drafting texts under timed and untimed conditions
7. soliciting and giving peer feedback
8. revising work in progress
9. reflecting analytically on written products and composing processes.

Students will practice these skills by completing reading selections, discussing their interpretations, posting comments to the course bulletin board, sharing their work with peers, and producing formal writing assignments featuring functions such as description, narration, exposition, summary, analysis, and comparison.

Aspects of the Composing Process

Becoming a skilled academic writer usually requires more than completing assignments and turning them in on time—although these goals are essential! Writing about a topic or issue is an excellent way to measure our reading and sharpen our thinking skills. By writing and thinking about our writing, we can also discover new ideas. When we write for a genuine audience, we also broaden our perspectives and learn language conventions that make our ideas comprehensible to others. I would like you to consider this course as an opportunity to improve the quality of your writing and to strengthen the reasoning skills that will help you succeed in college. Keep in mind that writing is not always a nice, tidy process for all writers. Sometimes, a successful piece of writing (say, an essay, a take-home exam, or a research paper) does not start out with a meticulous outline or follow a clear sequence of development. Unlike the process of building a house, writing sometimes requires us to take apart what we have started and build back from the foundation. In fact, not all writing has to end up in a nice, clean, grammatically accurate package: Some writing tasks can be very messy but very useful for the writer him- or herself. For most of us, writing for academic purposes is an ongoing process that requires a lot of rethinking and plenty of revision. Writing also forces us to struggle with language, an activity that challenges nonnative and native speakers of English alike. As a result, we may sometimes need the help of others (e.g., a classmate, an instructor, a friend) who can respond to our work and offer a new perspective. And although we spend a lot of time by ourselves when we write, we often can make our writing more meaningful if we plan to share it with somebody else. We also can learn about the strengths and weaknesses of our own written expression by reading what our peers write. Because so much academic writing is public, I encourage you to use our class activities and assignments as means of becoming better readers and writers. Much of our time in this course will therefore focus on reading formal texts and working with your classmates' drafts.

Required Course Materials

1. Coleman, Bob, Rebecca Brittenham, Scott Campbell, and Stephanie Girard. *Making Sense: Constructing Knowledge in the Arts and Sciences.* Boston: Houghton Mifflin, 2002. [Note: *Making Sense* is also required in English 110B.]
2. Hacker, Diana. *The Bedford Handbook.* 6th ed. Boston: Bedford/St. Martin's, 2002. [Note: *The Bedford Handbook* is also required in English 110B.]
3. A one-inch, three-ring binder to serve as your English 110A Portfolio (see *English 110A Portfolio Guidelines, 2004* – available in handout form and on the course bulletin board).
4. An active BCCIntranet account and password for the ENG110A-F bulletin board (Passwords will be distributed on the second day of class).

Recommended Course Materials

1. Harnack, Andrew, and Eugene Kleppinger. *Online! A reference guide to using Internet resources.* Boston: Bedford/St. Martin's, 2001.
2. A current, comprehensive English dictionary (e.g., *The American Heritage Dictionary of the English Language*).

Requirements and Student Responsibilities

1. **Attendance** is mandatory. Except for officially excused absences, students are expected to attend all class sessions. Department and College policy stipulates that an excess of three hours of unexcused absence will result in automatic exclusion from the course. Two late arrivals count as a one-hour absence.
2. **Late work** is not acceptable, except under extenuating circumstances (i.e., illness, personal and family emergencies, and so forth, as defined in the *Student Handbook, 2004*).
3. **Participation** in class discussion, feedback sessions, and course bulletin board discussions is expected of all students and will be considered in the course grade.
4. **Word processing** is required for all graded writing assignments and for assignments included in the ENG110A Portfolio. All ENG110A students are required to complete the

College Computer Literacy Workshop and to hold a current Computer Lab Pass (Details of this policy appear on your registration card). At the instructor's discretion, students may submit handwritten or word-processed journal entries and assignment drafts.

(Reproduced from the *Department of English and ESL Academic Policies Statement, 2004*)

Assessment and Grading Policies

Your course grade will be determined on the basis of the following weighted scale:

1. Portfolio	80%
a. Your choice of three revised writing assignments (40%)	
b. One timed writing of your choice (10%)	
c. Two written peer responses (10%)	
d. Two additional items of your choice (e.g., journal entries, bulletin board postings) (10%)	
e. Self-assessment summary (10%)	
2. Journal entries, bulletin board postings, and peer response tasks not included in your Portfolio	10%
3. Reading and grammar quizzes	10%

1. **Portfolio:** The Department of English and ESL requires students enrolled in ENG110A and ENG110B to compile and submit a Portfolio for assessment. Directions, options, and requirements for the Portfolio are explained in the *English 110A Portfolio Guidelines, 2004,* which contains sample student writing for you to use as models.

   a. **Revised writing assignments** will count for graded credit when you submit your final version to me. The first two assignments will consist of three drafts (a first, second, and final version). For each writing assignment, you will be given a choice of topics related to a reading selection (or set of selections), along with guidelines and a model paper. You will receive a percentage grade only on the final version, unless you request a provisional grade on previous drafts. The quality of writing assignments will be assessed according to the scoring rubric in the *English 110A Portfolio Guidelines, 2004* (pp. 7–8). We will review the scoring rubric in class so that you can use the criteria to improve your writing. Assignments are assessed not only on the basis of content and form, but also on the basis of the writer's use of peer and instructor feedback in revising the text.

b. **Timed writings** will be administered two or three times during the semester to give you practice writing in-class exams. We will practice techniques for writing under timed conditions. Topics and criteria will be given at least one week in advance of each timed writing, one of which may be revised.

c. **Written peer responses** will be required at least four times during the semester. We will practice and evaluate peer review techniques periodically, and you will be given instructor feedback to help you become an effective peer reader.

d. **Journal entries** will consist of your informal, written responses to questions and topics given about once per week. Occasionally, I will ask you to post your journal entries as electronic **bulletin board postings** for the class to read and react to. You will always be given a choice of topics, and you will receive full credit for entries as long as they are long enough (usually about 100 words).

e. **Your self-assessment** will consist of a thoughtful, two-page commentary reflecting on your progress over the semester and your goals for your future academic writing (in particular, ENG110B). You will have a chance to work on your self-assessment in class before finalizing it. See the *English 110A Portfolio Guidelines, 2004* (p. 5) for suggestions and details.

As the *English 110A Portfolio Guidelines, 2004* explain, you will maintain and present your Portfolio in a one-inch, three-ring binder in which you will organize your assignment drafts and revisions, feedback worksheets, timed writings, journal entries, bulletin board postings, quizzes, and so on. Your Portfolio is an ongoing activity, so keep it in good order! If you maintain your Portfolio throughout the semester, your work at the end of the semester will be very simple.

2. **Journal entries, bulletin board postings, and peer response tasks** (oral and written) that are not included in your Portfolio will also be given credit. These short tasks are designed to encourage you to read extensively, record your thoughts in writing, and share your ideas with your fellow classmates. As long as you complete 90% of these tasks, you will receive full credit for this portion of your course grade.

3. **Reading and grammar quizzes** will cover selections from *Making Sense* and chapters from *The Bedford Handbook* that we work on in class.

Department of English and ESL **Scoring Guide**

A = 95–100%	B+ = 87–90%	B– = 80–82%
A– = 90–94%	B = 83–86%	C+ = 77–79%
C = 73–76%	D+ = 67–69%	D– = 60–62%
C– = 70–72%	D = 63–66%	E = 0–60%

Course Outline

The course outline (see attached page) lists some readings from *Making Sense* (MS) and *The Bedford Handbook* (BH) on the writing process and academic genres to get us started. We will make decisions about some of the reading selections from *Making Sense* as a class. Therefore, our outline is partly a work in progress. Nevertheless, I have included topics, tasks, and assignment deadlines to keep us on track with the course goals and our Portfolio requirements. Where topics and assignments are listed, you will be expected to come to class with the relevant work completed. Please use the blank cells in the outline chart for keeping track of homework and assignment deadlines, which I will announce in class and post on our electronic bulletin board as we move ahead.

PARTIAL COURSE OUTLINE

ENGLISH 110A, Section F

Week	Day	Topics and Activities	Assignments Due
1	M	• Introduction to the writing process • Group activities: Strategies for academic reading and writing • Course introduction	
	W	• Making sense through writing • Discuss and choose reading selections from MS • Reading about texts	• Read MS pp. 13–26 • Journal entry 1: Preview topics in MS and choose 8 to 10 selections for the semester
	F	• Reading and writing about texts • Present and analyze Assignment 1: Description and analysis	• Read BH pp. 477–491 • Read "The Owl Has Flown" by S. Birkerts (MS pp. 59–71)
2	M	CLASS MEETS IN COMPUTER LAB (Seaver 120) • Quiz 1: "The Owl Has Flown" • Discuss and critique "The Owl Has Flown" • Discuss and practice prewriting strategies	• Review "The Owl Has Flown" by S. Birkerts (MS pp. 59–71) • Journal entry 2—Response to "The Owl Has Flown"
	W	CLASS MEETS IN COMPUTER LAB (Seaver 120) • Practice prewriting techniques • Group practice: Brainstorming and planning • Begin drafting Assignment 1	• Read BH pp. 1–29: Generating ideas and sketching a plan • Review "The Owl Has Flown"
	F	CLASS MEETS IN COMPUTER LAB (Seaver 120) • Draft Assignment 1 in class • Teacher–student conferences	• Review BH pp. 30–71 • Journal entry 3—Response to BH pp. 30–71 • Partial draft of Assignment 1
3	M	• Quiz 2: BH pp. 1–71 • Peer review techniques: Discussion and practice • Peer response: Assignment 1 (Draft 1)	• Assignment 1 (Draft 1) • Preview selection from MS: _____
	W	• Group discussions of selection from MS: _____ • Explore document design for writing in academic disciplines • Introduce and discuss Assignment 2: Analysis and comparison	• **Assignment 1 (Draft 2)**: Submit for instructor feedback • Read BH pp. 101–134: Document design
	F	• Group discussions of reading selection from MS (cont'd.) • Understanding and drafting timed writing assignments; preview Timed Writing 1 • Return Assignment 1 (Draft 2); explore revision strategies	• Planning and drafting worksheet for Assignment 2 • Read text(s) for Timed Writing 1

(Continued)

Week	Day	Topics and Activities	Assignments Due
4	M	• Discussion and exercise: Exploring academic genres • Grammar and style workshop (topics to be announced)	• **Assignment 1 (Draft 3)**: Submit for instructor evaluation • Review assigned sections in BH
	W	• **Timed Writing 1** (45 min)	• Review texts assigned for Timed Writing 1
	F	• Peer review: Assignment 2 (Draft 1)	• Assignment 2 (Draft 1)
5	M	• Return and evaluate Timed Writing 1	•
	W	•	•
	F	•	•
6	M	• Begin Assignment 3: Summary and synthesis	•
	W	•	•
	F	•	•
7	M	•	• **Assignment 2 (Draft 2)**: Submit for instructor evaluation
	W	•	•
	F	•	•
8	M	•	•
	W	•	•
	F	• Begin Assignment 4: Analysis and argument	•
9	M	•	• **Assignment 3 (Draft 2)**: Submit for instructor evaluation
	W	•	•
	F	•	•
10	M	•	•
	W	•	•
	F	•	•
11	M	•	•
	W	•	•
	F	• Begin Assignment 5: Analysis and argument (basic research paper)	•
12	M	•	•
	W	•	•
	F	*HOLIDAY—NO CLASS*	•

(Continued)

Week	Day	Topics and Activities	Assignments Due
13	M	•	•
	W	•	•
	F	•	•
14	M	•	•
	W	•	•
	F	•	• **Assignment 5 (Draft 2):** Submit for instructor evaluation
15	M	• Student–teacher Portfolio conferences • Peer Portfolio conferences	•
	W	• Student–teacher Portfolio conferences • Peer Portfolio conferences • Draft Portfolio Self-Assessment	•
	F	• Final Portfolio checks • Draft Portfolio Self-Assessment • Course Evaluations	•
16	W	**FINAL EXAM WEEK—NO CLASS**	• Portfolios due 12:00: Lydia's office

APPENDIX 3B: SAMPLE LESSON PLAN

Background: This detailed, 2-hour lesson plan is designed for a lower division (freshman- and sophomore-level) university EAP course serving ESL students in the social sciences. The course syllabus emphasizes writing in academic disciplines such as linguistics, anthropology, psychology, and sociology. Course objectives focus on analyzing common academic genres (e.g., articles, essays, editorials) and producing summaries, analytic essays, and bibliographic research papers. The lesson takes place in the second week of the term, at the beginning of a thematic unit on language varieties, identity, and culture. The course meets twice per week, for a total of 4 hr.

COMP 220 LESSON PLAN	Week 02: First Meeting

LEARNING OBJECTIVES

→ Develop and consolidate students' familiarity with rhetorical features of academic writing
→ Enhance students' awareness of language-related issues to build their schemata for the first formal writing assignment.

ENABLING OBJECTIVES (TEACHING AIMS)

→ Review and practice academic reading strategies
→ Discuss language varieties, identity, and culture in the context of students' experiences as language learners and writers
→ Practice skills for understanding writing assignments and faculty expectations for student writing
→ Introduce and practice prewriting and drafting strategies while initiating first assignment.

NOTES ON PRIOR WORK

• Students (Ss) have read essays by Edite Cunha (1998)[1] and Maxine Hong Kingston (1998)[2] from course anthology.

- Ss have read and completed comprehension worksheet on a selection of three texts on language, identity, and culture from the course pack or course anthology.
- Ss have been introduced to basic principles of academic writing and bibliographic research through readings, minilectures, and exercises drawn from chapters 1 (Taking Control of Your Reading) and 3 (Strategic Reading for Topics, Subtopics, and Main Ideas) of textbook.[3]

MATERIALS

- Copies of essays and articles (see above)
- Overhead transparencies (OHTs)
- S copies of worksheet: "Understanding Academic Writing Assignments"
- S copies of assignment sheet: "Guidelines for Writing Assignment #1" (Directions and choice of prompts for first revised writing assignment)
- Annotated timed writings from week 1 to return, along with copies of model texts
- Ss' annotated reading journals.

CLASS MANAGEMENT NOTES

- Announce homework for next class period (Display on OHT; assignments also posted on electronic course bulletin board):
  1. Read *Academic Literacy*, Chapter 4;
  2. Review "Research" section (pp. 140–165) in *Easy Writer*[4] in preparation for Writing Assignment #1.
- Announcements and reminders:
  1. Class meets in multimedia computer lab next week for Inspiration demonstration and prewriting workshop.
  2. Ask Ss to complete computer lab questionnaires beforehand.

LESSON OUTLINE

1. **Attendance and Class Business** [5 min]
   → Take roll while Ss copy assignments from OHP.
   → Make announcements (see above).

2. **Review Principles of Academic Writing** [10 min]
   - → Ask Ss to report what thy recall from last week's lecture on academic writing genres, the role of research, and their readings from Chapters 1 and 3 of *Academic Literacy.*
   - → Review main points by highlighting main points of lecture, discussion, and reading on OHTs.

3. **Discussion: Language Readings and Reading Strategies** [20 min]
   - → Ask Ss to take out copies of their self-selected texts and to write at least three complete sentences summarizing each text's hypothesis or main argument. Encourage Ss to write their summary statements on OHT for plenary review and discussion. Allow about 5 min for this activity.
   - → Ask several Ss to display and read their summary statements aloud for the class. Instruct Ss to compare summary statements. Note distinct perspectives taken on OHT.
   - → Elicit Ss' input in reviewing the core issues treated in each text.
   - → Ask Ss to describe how notetaking helped them to understand the texts. On OHT, list the advantages of taking notes while and after reading. Notetaking
     - focuses attention on primary themes and main arguments
     - helps readers to identify significant details
     - aids recall processes
     - promotes comparison with other texts
     - provides a written record for research, review, and exam preparation.
   - → Draw Ss' attention to the need to practice focused reading strategies, as described in *Academic Literacy.* Remind Ss that strategic reading will help them develop their academic writing skills.

4. **Understanding Academic Writing Assignments** [45 min]
   - → Assign Ss to working groups of three.
   - → Distribute worksheet, "Understanding Academic Writing Assignments." Ask for a volunteer to read and explain worksheet directions.
   - → Assign each group to two sample assignments from the five authentic tasks provided on the worksheet.
   - → Inform Ss that we will record their ideas on OHTs as they complete the exercise.

$\rightarrow$ Allow groups to work for about 10 min. Then bring the class together for plenary discussion. Reiterate these principles (outlined and explained in *Academic Literacy*):

- Several of these academic writing assignments require analysis and complex thinking. They are therefore *unlike* the formulaic essays often assigned in English composition courses.

- Each assignment involves a specific approach to a topic or a problem. A "cookie cutter" written response (e.g., a five-paragraph essay) probably will not satisfy the instructor's expectations. We need to learn both the subject matter and the appropriate *genre conventions* for preparing an acceptable text.

- Keep these goals in mind when undertaking an academic writing assignment: (a) Prove to the instructor that you understand the course material; (b) demonstrate that you can express your knowledge objectively, and; (c) "package" the information in a style that matches the way experts in the field write.

- IDENTIFY—Look for words in the assignment guidelines that indicate what you need to do to complete the task successfully.

- SUGGEST—Try to narrow your focus so that you know what sources to use, what information to focus on, and how to present it concisely.

- WRITE—Here is where you further narrow your focus, specify the information that you will present in your writing, and assemble your documentation. Make practical decisions and plan your time to meet deadlines.

- How will you get started? Review past readings. Identify information, theories, hypotheses, and so on that emerge repeatedly. Take note of ideas and hypotheses that conflict. Review past and current readings, take notes, look at sample assignments completed by successful students, and so on. When you are ready to begin composing, try several of these prewriting techniques (see *Easy Writer* and writing strategies worksheets from class):

• Brainstorm	• Classify	• Map
• Free-write	• Cluster	• Outline
• List	• Cube	

- • GO BACK—Review the assignment guidelines now and then to make sure you are on the right track. Make sure that the text you are developing really fulfills the assignment's objectives.
- → Summarize purposes and functions of this exercise. Mention connections to exam writing.

5. **Introduce Writing Assignment #1** [20 min]
   - → Distribute "Guidelines for Writing Assignment #1." Ask Ss to preview the directions and selection of writing prompts before discussing their options.
   - → Ask Ss to take out their reading notes from the assigned texts on language varieties, identity, and culture.
   - → If time allows, ask Ss to do a 5-min free-write in their journals on an assignment option that interests them.
   - → Instruct Ss to bring the assignment sheet and their notes to class next time for our prewriting workshop in the multimedia computer lab.

6. **Return Timed Writings** [10 min]
   - → Return timed (in-class) papers from Week 1. Ask Ss to read the comments and to preview the model student text (handout attached to each timed writing).
   - → Invite Ss to consider the strengths and weaknesses of their timed writings and how they can prepare for the next one (Week 03).
   - → Refer Ss to *Academic Literacy*, Chapter 1 and class hand-outs on exam writing

---

[1]Cunha, E. (1998). Talking in the new land. In V. P. Clark, P. A. Eschholz, & A. F. Rosa (Eds.), *Language: Readings in language and culture* (6th ed., pp. 3–11). Boston: Bedford/St. Martin's.

[2]Hong Kingston, M. (1998). Finding a voice. In V. P. Clark, P. A. Eschholz, & A. F. Rosa (Eds.), *Language: Readings in language and culture* (6th ed., pp. 13–17). Boston: Bedford/St. Martin's.

[3]Lewis, J. (2001). *Academic literacy: Readings and strategies* (2nd ed.). Boston: Houghton Mifflin.

[4]Lunsford, A. A. (2002). *Easy writer: A pocket guide* (2nd ed.). Boston: Bedford/St. Martin's.

Chapter 4

Text Selection, Materials Development, and Task Construction in ESL Composition

Questions for Reflection

- *What aspects of textbooks and other instructional materials have you found particularly valuable to your learning? What elements have you found to be unhelpful or uninformative? Why?*
- *If you have had experience as a classroom teacher, identify the features that you seek and value in a course book or materials set. In your view, what distinguishes a good textbook from a poor one, and why?*
- *In what respects might the expectations for an ESL literacy or composition textbook differ from those we might have for other textbook types? Why?*
- *Under what conditions should a composition teacher augment a textbook with supplemental materials, tasks, and assignments? Justify your response.*
- *What types of in-class and out-of-class activities and exercises are most productive for inexperienced writers? For experienced writers? Why?*
- *What procedures make writing tasks engaging, productive, and successful?*

This chapter elaborates on the procedures of instructional design introduced in chapter 3. Specifically, we examine elements of materials selection, steps in supplementing textbooks, and procedures for designing classroom tasks and assignments for ESL writing courses. These crucial teaching tasks go hand in hand with designing syllabi, organizing course outlines, preparing daily lesson plans, and conducting effective classroom writing assessment.

We begin with a discussion of textbook and materials selection criteria partly because textbooks are so pervasive in educational systems throughout the world. Indeed, textbooks provide the backbone for the courses many educators teach. In this chapter, we urge literacy teachers to develop their own materials and to supplement textbooks, yet we recognize that "many teachers are required to use textbooks, a majority of teachers don't have the time or resources to prepare their own materials, and so textbooks are a necessity" (Graves, 2000, p. 173). Before exploring strategies for evaluating and using textbooks, we should consider arguments for and against basing literacy courses on published sources.

Benefits of relying on a textbook

- Because a textbook reflects the author's decisions about course goals and learning objectives, it can provide a framework for a course. Content and skills to be targeted in the course are explained and sequenced for the teacher, thereby facilitating instructional planning.
- Students often enjoy the sense of security provided by a textbook, which helps students understand what will be expected of them in the course.
- A textbook provides teachers and learners with reading material, activities, exercises, and sometimes visual aids. This "package" can save the teacher valuable time in locating and adapting authentic materials.
- Some textbooks offer assessment tools such as quizzes, tests, assignments, and projects that directly reflect the textbook's content and pedagogical aims.
- Supporting materials such as audio- and videocassettes, CD-ROM disks, companion Web sites, overhead transparencies, worksheets, scoring guides, teachers' manuals, and the like frequently accompany commercial textbooks.

[handwritten marginalia: Could be packets. online materials?]

- Textbooks can offer a common point of reference in delivering a curriculum. When used by all instructors in a program, a textbook can ensure that a course adheres to program and institutional goals across a given level of instruction. A textbook series used in a program can similarly provide continuity and coherence among levels of instruction.

Drawbacks of relying on a textbook

- A textbook's approach, content, and tasks may not be entirely relevant or appropriate to a particular cohort of students.
- Texts and tasks might not suitably match students' language proficiency, literacy skills, or educational needs.
- Textbooks often focus too much or too little on selected dimensions of language and literacy. In other words, a textbook's content and skills focus may be too narrow or too broad to serve a range of educational needs.
- The combination of task and activity types might be ill suited to a student population (e.g., too many or too few grammar-focused exercises, discovery tasks that are too open-ended).
- Some textbooks are designed according to a linear, mechanical sequence, making creative deviations difficult.
- Textbook reading selections, activities, exercises, and visual enhancements may lack authenticity and appeal, thereby boring students and decreasing their motivation.
- Textbooks may contain material (e.g., topical or thematic reading selections, journalistic texts) that quickly lose their currency.
- A textbook's prescribed timetable or syllabus may be overly ambitious or unrealistic, resulting in the teacher's failure to complete a portion of the material. (Adapted from Graves, 2000)

Given these considerations, we encourage teachers to approach textbook selection critically and with reasonable expectations in mind (Grady, 1997). First, there is no reason to presuppose that an ESL literacy course must be based on a textbook. In fact, instructors in many content-based, English for Academic Purposes (EAP) and English for Specific Purposes (ESP) contexts often manage without any textbooks at all. Second, for cases in which a textbook is required or desired, it simply cannot provide each and every feature that teachers and students would like it to offer. Therefore, we should always anticipate the need to adapt and supplement even the very best published materials (Byrd, 2001; Grant, 1987; Masuhara, 1998).

SURVEYING AND SELECTING ESL COMPOSITION MATERIALS

Because of the overwhelming quantity of published materials available for teaching ESL literacy, evaluating and selecting instructional materials can be an intimidating experience for even seasoned classroom teachers. Excellent resources for evaluating and selecting textbooks for various types of language and content courses are available (Brown, 1995, 2001; Byrd, 2001; Chambers, 1997; Dubin & Olshtain, 1986; Littlejohn, 1998; Omaggio Hadley, 2001; Ur, 1996). Nonetheless, few of these resources explicitly target L2 literacy or the specific needs of L2 writers. Therefore, in the following sections, we offer classification and evaluation procedures geared toward ESL composition instruction. We have divided our model of textbook evaluation into two broad categories: instructional needs and textbook features. When combined, the components within these categories should provide teachers with useful criteria for undertaking an efficient selection process.

Profiling Students, Instructional Needs, and Institutional Goals

Clearly, as argued in chapter 3, decisions about how and what to teach in a composition course should be directly informed by the makeup of the learner population, student needs, and institutional goals. Systematic and ongoing needs assessment should obviously be a primary source of data for both course design and materials selection, so teachers can choose materials that best accommodate goals and objectives. Before evaluating textbooks, teachers should therefore study their students' backgrounds and the requirements of their programs and institutions, perhaps by reviewing the findings of a recent needs assessment. In particular, it is invaluable for them to know about students' prior educational experiences, language proficiency, and literacy skills. Similarly, it can be extremely useful to know students' immigration status and the proportion of traditional to nontraditional students (see chapter 3).

Knowledge of demographic factors and programmatic goals is essential to a fair assessment of the level of difficulty, thematic content, classroom tasks, writing assignments, and pedagogical orientation of literacy textbooks. Equally important is a consideration of a textbook's appropriateness for use in a particular academic program or educational institution. For example, a literary reader or rhetoric, in combination with a standard reference guide or style manual, might be a suitable option for a college composition course or an advanced-level Intensive English Program (IEP) course designed to introduce nonimmigrant students to academic discourse (McKay, 2001; Ramanathan & Kaplan, 1996a, 1996b). However, these options would not be appropriate for a basic- or intermediate-level academic skills course in a community college or for a graduate-level ESP writing course. For low-level students, the material may be too difficult, because such learners may need more extensive practice reading academic prose and composing prototypical texts. In contrast, the reader and style manual combination might match the linguistic proficiency and literacy skills of graduate ESP students, but the literature-based content may be unsuitable for addressing their specialized needs as future writers of the dominant genres in their specialized disciplines (Dudley-Evans & St. John, 1998; Johns, 1997; Johns & Price-Machado, 2001). For these reasons, effective textbook selection should start with an accurate profile of the learner population and the institutional requirements.

Textbook Types and Features

Successful materials selection depends fundamentally on striking a good match between the attributes of the textbook and other course materials on the one hand and the student profile and institutional goals on the other. To some extent, we can rely on general criteria for predicting such a match, but these criteria are most effectively applied with the specific characteristics of textbook types in mind. Because of the numbing array of books and other resources aimed at both ESL and mainstream writers, we first identify several prevalent textbook genres currently available before surveying selection criteria. The following discussion is keyed to the categorized Resource List on pages 168–170.

Comprehensive Textbook, Rhetoric, Reader, Reference Guide, or Combination? Because of the rapid pace with which instructional approaches and materials have evolved, it would be misleading to represent the categories that follow as mutually exclusive or static. In fact, the textbook categories we characterize in this section overlap significantly because the boundaries distinguishing textbook genres are becoming increasingly blurred as materials writers endeavor to appeal to the diverse needs of L2 literacy instructors by producing hybrid materials. Many literacy textbooks intentionally address multiple purposes by combining the features of two or more genres into a single course book, aiming to address the complex needs of diverse learner populations. For instance, one can easily find writing process textbooks that include anthologies of literary texts and sample student writing. Our central purpose in this section is to provide a general but meaningful sketch of dominant textbook types.

• *Comprehensive textbooks* frequently aim to teach writing skills, strategies, and processes in a sequential or cyclical manner. Comprehensive textbooks designed for ESL literacy students are frequently geared toward beginning- and intermediate-level writers presumed to have little or no experience with composing processes such as prewriting, drafting, feedback, and revision. Textbooks of this genre, many of which reflect the current–traditional and process paradigms (chapter 1) include reading passages, although such textbooks are made up chiefly of tasks and activities designed to give students practice in composing increasingly substantial and complex texts (e.g., paragraphs, essays, research papers). Composing assignments, which frequently involve multidrafting, are often intended to culminate in academic essays that reflect a specific rhetorical mode (e.g., description, narration, comparison, literary analysis, argument, persuasion). Many comprehensive textbooks are intended to serve as the primary (or sole) textbook for an entire composition course or course sequence. Some comprehensive textbooks are intended exclusively for ESL writers at various levels of proficiency (see "Comprehensive, Multipurpose ESL Writing Textbooks" in the Resource List), whereas other titles are aimed at NS- and NNS-track academic writers, including those in "remedial," "developmental," and premainstream courses. A common type of comprehensive textbook is geared toward college freshman composition courses. Such a book may be indistinguishable from a rhetoric, reader, or anthology. Generally intended for NS writers, many of these books also contain sections on grammar, style, and mechanics directed explicitly at ESL writers. Such textbooks also may promote the use of technological resources (see "Readers/Anthologies for ESL Students and Comprehensive Composition Textbooks for Combined NS/NNS Courses" in the Resource List).

• *Rhetorics*, often used in conjunction with readers (anthologies) or reference guides, typically explicate selected rhetorical forms, present sample texts exemplifying those rhetorical patterns, and offer procedures for reproducing those patterns and genres in their own academic writing. Stand-alone rhetorics are rarely used in ESL composition courses, even at advanced levels, although they are sometimes used in NS composition courses, often along with a reader. Textbooks and readers for both ESL and NS writers increasingly incorporate rhetorical content into a single course book (see "Combination Rhetorics/Readers for ESL Writers and Combination Rhetorics/Readers/Handbooks for NS Writers" in the Resource List).

• *Readers*, or *anthologies*, frequently serve as the primary source content in literacy courses at various levels of language proficiency. A sizable number of readers for both NS and NNS learners include thematic collections containing short fiction, poetry, drama, personal essays, journalistic writing, editorials, political writing, humor, and various other genres. Such readers and anthologies often include excerpts from authentic sources, although those aimed at ESL learners may contain entries that are both more numerous and more extensive (see "Readers/Anthologies for ESL Students and Readers/Anthologies for NS Students" in the Resource List). An increasing number of readers and anthologies also feature student writing samples as primary content. These textbooks may contain pre- and postreading activities for treating the literary selections both in and outside of class, frequently providing writing prompts and even complete assignments. Depending on the role of literature in the curriculum, instructors may use an anthology in conjunction with a reference manual or a rhetoric.

• *Reference guides* often appear in handbook or spiral-bound volume form. Their primary content involves explanations and examples of rhetorical, grammatical, stylistic, and mechanical conventions. Many such handbooks also provide abbreviated guidelines for formatting assignments, bibliographies, and so on according to academic style sheets (e.g., APA, MLA, Chicago, and the like). As technological resources in education continue to expand, these reference guides have begun to address both the conventions for citing electronic sources and the mechanics of electronic document design (e.g., creating files in text and HTML formats, designing Web sites). Some reference guides also contain exercises for classroom use and self-study. A number of these materials are available on CD-ROM or through publishers' interactive Web sites. Whereas such materials are generally not featured as core textbooks, teachers frequently require their students to use them as resources in drafting, revising, and especially editing their writing assignments. Commonly used in mainstream NS writing courses, reference guides are sometimes built into comprehensive textbooks and even rhetorics as appendices. Reference guides often are formatted with numeric index systems that teachers can use for referring students to particular grammatical topics, rules, examples, and exercises. A growing number of reference guides also provide supplementary sections written specifically for ESL writers (see "Comprehensive Composition Textbooks for Combined NS/NNS Courses" in the Resource List).

Textbook Selection Criteria. Given the staggering range of textbooks and other resources available for teaching writing, it is easy to see why a "one-size-fits-all" approach to materials selection is not likely to produce satisfactory results. This section nonetheless describes several overarching features to consider, regardless of the type of book you are considering.[1] We then propose a more specific set of criteria to be applied selectively by considering particular students and course goals (Fig. 4.1).

It is sometimes possible to eliminate from consideration materials that fail to meet most or all of your general requirements. We suggest asking the following simple yes/no questions as part of your preliminary screening:

Does the textbook ...
- Cover topics, genres, and literacy skills targeted in your course?
- Present suitable samples of the genres and text types that you want your students to read, analyze, interpret, critique, and reproduce?
- Contain clear, well-constructed activities, tasks, exercises, and projects that will help your students develop the L2 literacy skills targeted in the curriculum plan and course objectives?

NA = Not applicable	1 = Unsatisfactory	3 = Good
0 = Totally lacking	2 = Satisfactory	4 = Excellent to outstanding

Textbook Features and Evaluation Criteria	RATING					
	NA	0	1	2	3	4
Bibliographic Features						
1 Authors' record of past accomplishment and qualifications to produce a writing textbook for your student population and institution type.						
2 Availability of accompanying materials, such as instructor's manual, workbook, sample syllabi, software, interactive Web support.						
3 Completeness: How easily can the course be taught using only the students' versions and accompanying materials?						
4 Cost-effectiveness: How reasonable is the retail price of the material, given the book's instructional benefits?						
Instructor's Manual and Supplemental Materials						
1 Completeness and explicitness of instructor's manual: Does it include sample syllabi, lesson plans, classroom activities, teaching ideas, assignments, solution keys, and so on?						
2 Flexibility and teachability: Does the manual offer guidance on how to present lessons tailored to your educational setting?						
3 Feedback and evaluation tools: Does the manual offer guidance on responding to and assessing student writing?						
4 Professional quality, appropriateness, and user-friendliness of student supplements (workbook, software, interactive Website, and so on).						
5 Fit between textbook and supplements: Are the workbook, software, and other resources designed for easy use alongside the core textbook?						
Goals, Objectives, and Approach						
1 Audience appropriateness: Does the text address your student population in terms of maturity, cultural background, educational experience, L1 and L2 literacy, and so on?						
2 Match between textbook, students, and student expectations: How well does the textbook address your students' instructional needs, as determined in your needs assessment?						
3 Match between textbook and your instructional approach: How well does the overall design of the textbook reflect your methodology, practice, and style?						
4 Match between textbook and institutional expectations: Does the textbook accommodate the learning and teaching objectives of your program, department, or institution?						
Content						
1 Appropriateness and potential appeal: Does the textbook's subject matter include topics, themes, issues, texts, tasks, and processes that will appeal to the interests and needs of your students?						
2 Motivational potential: Does the textbook's subject matter include topics, themes, issues, texts, tasks, and processes that will engage your students in the course and motivate them to develop their literacy skills?						
3 Authenticity: Does the material feature texts, genres, and discursive styles that accurately represent and expose the types of writing that students will need to read, process, and reproduce?						
4 Variety: Does the textbook offer an adequate assortment of genres and texts (e.g., literary samples, academic texts, model student writing) to sustain student interest?						
5 Flexibility and potential for adaptation: Is the book's material varied and flexible enough for you to customize your selection of texts and tasks to student and institutional needs?						
6 Editorial quality and accuracy: Are the texts and apparatus well written, academically sound, stylistically appropriate, and factually accurate?						

FIG. 4.1. Textbook assessment guide.

Textbook Features and Evaluation Criteria	RATING					
	NA	0	1	2	3	4
Design and Organization						
1 Feasibility: Can the quantity and type of material in the textbook be covered in the time frame specified in your syllabus?						
2 Sequencing and progression: Do chapters or units present topics, themes, skills, genres, text types, functions, and tasks in a logical, transparent, and coherent manner?						
3 Grading: Are the materials and tasks graded according to students' language literacy levels, general knowledge, and literacy needs?						
4 Schema-building, review, and recycling: To what extent do the text's content, tasks, and assignments facilitate practice of new literacy skills (especially composing) while offering opportunities to practice students' existing skills?						
5 Skills integration and recursion: How extensively are reading tasks interwoven with writing tasks to promote recursive phases of student writing processes?						
6 Flexibility: How easily can you sequence chapters, reading selections, activities, and so forth to fit your syllabus and your students' changing needs?						
7 Adaptability: How suitable is the book for students with disparate learning styles?						
8 Currency: How recent is the material? Does it reflect current composition theory and instructional practice?						
Apparatus (i.e., explanations, tasks, assignments, exercises, directions, glossaries, indices, and so forth)						
1 Potential for engagement and participation: Do activities, tasks, exercises, assignments, and so on lead to internalization of subject matter, genre knowledge, and composing skills by encouraging students to participate actively in reading, discussion, feedback, and composing tasks?						
2 Promotion of critical thinking: Do classroom tasks and writing assignments promote students' interpretation, application, analysis, synthesis, and evaluation skills?						
3 Promotion of independent skills development: Do literacy tasks and assignments enable students to develop autonomous skills, strategies, and tactics?						
4 Clarity of presentation: Are the instructions to activities, tasks, exercises, and assignments transparent, comprehensible, and explicit about intended outcomes?						
5 Feedback tools: Does the text offer models for peer and instructor feedback on student writing? Are they clear and easy to use?						
Layout and Physical Attributes						
1 Useful front and back matter: Are the table of contents, glossaries, indices, references, and solution keys well located, clearly organized, and easy to use?						
2 Layout and visual appeal: Are text, white space, and shadowed sections balanced to promote readability? Are margins wide enough to facilitate easy reading and note-taking? Are figures, tables, and illustrations appropriately sized, clearly reproduced, and suitably positioned?						
3 Textual attributes and enhancements: Are the font and font pitch readable and appealing? Does the textbook include highlighting or boldface type to signal key lexical items?						
4 Physical features: Do your students prefer a cloth or paper cover? Traditional or spiral binding? Are the format, dimensions, and weight of the book appropriate for the book's intended uses? Are a the paper and binding of durable quality?						
Cumulative Value						
Overall quality, suitability, and potential effectiveness: In view of student needs, teaching and learning objectives, curricular goals, time constraints, your educational beliefs, and so on, to what extent is the textbook (and its supplemental material) pedagogically sound, appropriate, and cost effective?						

FIG. 4.1.   Textbook assessment guide (Continued).

- Provide an adequate number of useful, productive, provocative, and socioculturally appropriate discussion topics, classroom activities, and composing assignments?
- Present information, explanations, procedures, strategies, and supplemental material that will help you present new material, skill incentives, and composing strategies to your students effectively?
- Appeal to you in terms of its underlying philosophy, organization, comprehensiveness, visual features, and potential ease of use?

If you are unsure about any of these issues, review the questions from your students' point of view. How confidently can you predict that the book's approach, design, content, and tasks will enable your students to achieve your learning objectives? If your answer to one or more of these questions is "no," then you might legitimately eliminate the book from further appraisal.

Once you have winnowed prospective selections to a field of two or three books, you can incorporate a more detailed, comprehensive checklist into your evaluation process. The textbook assessment guide displayed in Fig. 4.1 is designed to facilitate both analysis (i.e., systematic examination of the material's content and presentation) and judgment (i.e., a decision whether to accept or reject a source on the basis of relevant criteria). Also see Fig. 4.2 for additional ideas on textbook selection.

As with other tools and checklists in this book, this guide is designed to be adapted, abbreviated, or expanded depending on the user's individual needs and preferences. Each item also can be weighted according to your specific priorities. For example, instructors in search of self-contained materials for a content-based college ESL or EFL course may place the highest value on a textbook that provides extensive readings, discussion activities, sample syllabi, lesson plans, and writing assignments covering related contemporary themes. If their primary objective is to supply students with multiple reading and writing opportunities, teachers might thus weight content-related criteria more heavily than the instructor's manual or layout features.

Under less-than-optimal conditions, evaluating instructional materials can certainly amount to a wholly subjective and even arbitrary exercise. However, the use of simple yet systematic materials assessment tools can streamline the process of selecting

Task Types and Functions by Proficiency Level	Aims				
	Linguistic Control	Rhetorical Knowledge	Schematic Knowledge	Sociocultural Awareness	Writing Strategies
BEGINNING					
• Extract information from written text			✓		
• Basic analysis of authentic texts for rhetorical patterns		✓			
• Apply basic rhetorical metalanguage (e.g., topic, thesis) to describe and analyze genres and authentic texts		✓			
• Apply prewriting skills (e.g., brainstorm, list, cluster, cube)			✓		✓
• Practice sentence-combining	✓				
• Write on free and focused journal topics (see chapter 2)			✓		✓
• Compose simple sentences and paragraphs using models		✓			✓
• Compose deductive, expository paragraphs on self-selected topics		✓			✓
• Read and respond to other students' writing (see chapter 6)				✓	
• Revise draft material while attending to expert feedback (see chapter 7)					✓
• Practice with basic mechanical conventions (e.g., capitalization, punctuation, indentation)	✓				
• Practice basic editing (e.g., for coherence, grammar, mechanics) (see chapter 7)	✓				✓
INTERMEDIATE					
• All of the task and functions listed under the Beginning heading	(✓)	(✓)	(✓)	(✓)	(✓)
• Practice drafting based on the outcomes of prewriting tasks					✓
• Reproduce multiple genres and text types (e.g., summaries, letters, portions of academic texts)		✓	✓		✓
• Reproduce paragraph- and essay-length texts that replicate specified genres and rhetorical patterns (e.g., narration, description, comparison, process analysis)		✓			✓
• Predict the needs and expectations of an academic reader				✓	
• Develop independent prewriting and drafting skills					✓
• Respond meaningfully to other students' writing (see chapter 6)				✓	
• Practice with more extensive revision processes (i.e., multidrafting)					✓
• Practice with self-checks for producing revised texts (see chapter 7)	✓	✓			✓
• Practice with more finely tuned editing for a range of rhetorical, grammatical, and mechanical conventions (see chapter 7)	✓	✓			✓
ADVANCED					
• All of the tasks and functions listed under the Intermediate heading	(✓)	(✓)	(✓)	(✓)	(✓)
• Identify, analyze, critique, and replicate multiple written genres	✓	✓	✓	✓	✓
• Deepen awareness of audience and reader expectations				✓	✓
• Draft and revise complex texts designed for specific purposes and audiences		✓	✓	✓	✓
• Reproduce novel text types that reflect authentic genre categories		✓	✓		✓
• Practice with inductive writing and other rhetorical approaches as complements to deductive text structure		✓			✓
• Develop confidence and personal voice					✓
• Read and review other students' writing; practice applying this experience to one's own writing (see chapter 6)				✓	✓
• Use self-selected and self-generated checklists for independent revision and editing (see chapter 7)	✓	✓			✓

FIG. 4.2.   Task types and functions for the ESL writing class.

resources that best meet the needs of students, teachers, and institutions. A final point to be made in this discussion is that effective materials assessment is an ongoing process, one that should take place both while the materials are being used and after the instructional period has ended (Brown, 1995; Graves, 2000).

SUPPLEMENTING COURSE TEXTS WITH ORIGINAL MATERIALS AND TASKS

Many composition teachers seek textbooks or materials packages that meet all of their instructional needs. Unfortunately, few find exactly what they want. A textbook and its accompanying materials can rarely meet all of a teacher's criteria, simply because the needs of students, teachers, and institutions vary so widely. Prevailing wisdom in the field holds that "there is no such thing as a perfect textbook" (Brown, 1995, p. 166). Moreover, teachers often want and need to adapt supplemental instructional materials to evolving student learning needs and individual interests. For these reasons, it is essential for teachers to develop basic skills in supplementing and adapting published course texts and in devising techniques for deploying these materials effectively in the classroom.

Locating and Adapting Supporting Materials

The process of supplementing a core textbook or materials package typically begins when an instructor inevitably notices a gap in existing course materials or perceives a mismatch between those materials and student needs and capabilities—or between materials and course goals (Byrd, 2001).

Consider the case of an intermediate-level community college or IEP literacy course (i.e., a prerequisite to an advanced writing course, which in turn would be a prerequisite to mainstream or NS freshman composition). The assigned text is a course book with short, thematically organized reading selections and literary texts 1,000 to 5,000 words in length. Writing practice tasks and assignments lead students through multiple drafts of paragraphs exemplifying common academic rhetorical modes and genre patterns (e.g., description, exposition, comparison, text analysis, argument).

After teaching the students fundamental techniques of description and reading their descriptive paragraphs, the instructor determines that they need more sustained work with descriptive genres, in addition to further practice using descriptive discursive functions in their own writing. No further models in the course book provide additional practice assignments. Instead of moving on to another rhetorical pattern, the instructor opts to present a descriptive passage from a popular novel, using it for textual analysis in class and as a departure point for an elaborated, multidraft composing assignment. Without compromising the syllabus or course objectives, the instructor integrates this additional practice into lesson planning, treating the supplemental descriptive text as an extension of the corresponding activities in the textbook (see chapter 2).

Discerning such gaps or mismatches in the coursebook may necessitate locating alternative materials and evaluating them via a process similar to (although perhaps simpler than) the one described in the preceding sections. To fill a gap or to reconcile a mismatch, teachers can turn to obvious and almost innumerable sources of authentic genres and text samples, including those in the following list:

- Competing materials and their supplements (i.e., literacy course books, resource materials, software, and companion Web sites designed for equivalent courses and similar students)
- Textbooks from disciplines other than ESL, literacy, composition, and language education but related to the topics and themes addressed in the writing course (i.e., coursebooks used in academic disciplines, such as the humanities, sciences, social sciences, and business)
- Academic texts (e.g., monographs, dissertations, scholarly articles, research reports, essays, reviews, newsletters, editorials)
- Professional and technical texts (e.g., business and administrative memos, correspondence, reports, policy documents, procedural and instructional manuals)
- Literature (e.g., fiction and nonfiction prose, biography, essays, poetry, drama, folk tales, essays, reviews)
- Journalistic and periodical literature (e.g., articles and reviews from newspapers, newsmagazines, literary and artistic periodicals, special interest magazines, Web sites)
- Sample student writing representing a range of genres
- Popular media (e.g., film and music recordings, television and radio broadcasts)
- Recordings and transcriptions of planned and unplanned oral discourse (e.g., Webcasts, radio and television interviews, speeches, lectures, debates, discussions, conversations)
- Digital resources such as audio, video, and text excerpts found on carefully screened Web sites.

Formerly, teachers might have had to conduct searches in libraries, bookstores, newsstands, and departmental resource files. Thanks to the availability of electronic media, of course, a growing number of university, college, and secondary school instructors and students have access to the Internet and CD-ROM disks in their offices, campus computer labs, libraries, classrooms, student centers, coffee houses, homes, and dormitories. Locating supplemental material is thus much less of a challenge than selecting and presenting it in a pedagogically sound way.

Features of Task Design: Balancing Process and Product, Content and Form

This section outlines principles and procedures for constructing effective tasks for writing instruction, some of which incorporate authentic text types listed in the preceding section (see also chapter 2). According to Skehan (1996), "a task is taken to be an activity in which meaning is primary; there is some sort of relationship to the real world; task completion has some priority" (p. 38). For Nunan (1989), a task consists of "the smallest unit of classroom work" that engages learners in "comprehending, manipulating, producing, or interacting in the target language." In addition, tasks minimally "contain some form of data or input" and embed "a goal and roles for teachers and learners" (p. 5).

Referring more specifically to components related to literacy learning processes and their outcomes, Doyle (1983) defined a *task* in terms of

> (a) the products students are to formulate, such as an original essay or answers to a set of test questions (i.e., target tasks), (b) the operations (or processes) that are necessary to produce these products, such as memorizing and classifying (i.e., learner tasks), and (c) the givens, the resources available to students while they are generating the product, such as a model essay. (p. 162)

For Doyle, then, academic tasks reflect "the answers students are required to produce and the routes that can be used to obtain these answers" (p. 162). This view of the task as a procedural unit not only parallels social constructionist views of academic and disciplinary literacies (Coe, 1987; Johns, 1997, 2003), but also incorporates essential learning and composing processes (see chapters 1 and 2). Doyle's (1983) definition of task thus integrates process and product, enabling us to avoid a misleading, artificial separation of these two crucial elements of academic apprenticeship.

From an analytic perspective, a task minimally contains verbal input data (e.g., a reading passage from one of the multiple sources listed earlier, a dialogue) or a nonverbal stimulus (e.g., a picture sequence), along with an activity related to the input. A task likewise exposes "what learners are to do in relation to the input," the task's purposes, and participants' roles (Nunan, 1989, p. 10). McKay (1994) outlined four global aims that teachers can use to identify, adapt, and develop meaningful tasks for the composition classroom. These aims include developing students' schemata, their social awareness, their knowledge of rhetorical patterns, and their control of the conventions of written language. We have added a process element to this list: writing strategies. The items shown in Fig. 4.2, categorized according to the principal learning and strategic objectives they are intended to achieve, are designed to offer ideas for constructing tasks appropriate for beginning-, intermediate-, and advanced-level ESL writers. Specific sample tasks are presented later. Underlying these task types and functions is the purpose of equipping students with both learning and composing strategies that will enable them to undertake "real academic assignments" (Horowitz, 1986a) in disciplinary contexts outside an ESL, EAP, or ESP literacy course (see chapter 2).

The Mechanics of Task Design and Implementation

Before constructing and integrating a new task or assignment into a lesson or unit, the teacher should first consider the extent to which the exercise will enable students to practice one or more aspects of the composing process (i.e., prewriting, drafting, revision, editing, and so forth) and to test their developing composing strategies (Skehan, 1996; White, 1999). The checklist items in Fig. 4.3 target both general and specific features to consider in selecting content matter, narrowing pedagogical expectations, writing directions and procedures, and operationalizing the task. Elements of this checklist can be used selectively for devising day-to-day in-class and out-of-class tasks as well as more formal writing assignments (i.e., those that will require extensive advance planning or undergo formal assessment).

Do the assignment guidelines include the following components?

1. Practical, procedural, and mechanical requirements

☐ A timetable or list of deadlines for drafts, feedback, self-evaluation, final submission, and so on
☐ Explicit reference to the genre category or rhetorical form (e.g., essay, editorial, summary, lab report, critical review, memorandum, research paper)
☐ Succinct, unambiguous, and easy-to-follow directions and procedural descriptions (i.e., step-by-step descriptions of the multiple stages entailed in completing the assignment successfully)
☐ Notes concerning recommended or required length
☐ A description of presentation requirements (e.g., text format and document design, preferred style sheet, mechanical conventions)
☐ A description of required documentation, if applicable (e.g., use of bibliographic sources, primary data)

2. Socioliterate context and core content

☐ A task that fairly and authentically represents (or approximates) the genre knowledge and skills that students will be required to display in the educational context, their academic disciplines, or the workplace
☐ A characterization of the text's intended audience and audience expectations (i.e., a portrayal of the socioliterate context for the assignment)
☐ An explanation of the text's purposes (i.e., why writers of that genre and text type compose such texts)
☐ A topic, theme, subject, or range of options that will interest, motivate, and appeal to student writers at all proficiency levels in the course
☐ A topic, theme, subject, or range of options that covers a wide enough band of content and literacy skills to engage all students without unfairly privileging some writers over others (i.e., a topic, issue, question, or problem that can be written about with equal ease by using resources presented and practiced in the course)
☐ A task that necessitates the production of connected written discourse and presents options leading to comparable written products (i.e., writing samples that can be fairly compared in terms of complexity, length, rhetorical control, linguistic fluency, grammatical accuracy, and so on)
☐ A task that requires cognitive and linguistic skills that tap into writers' current schemata and competencies, takes them beyond their current level of expertise, and diversifies their rhetorical and stylistic repertoires
☐ A description of the assignment's purpose, as well as the skills that writers will develop and demonstrate by completing the assignment
☐ A rationale for the task as a tool for addressing student writers' literacy and educational needs and goals

3. Resources

☐ Notes concerning the texts that students should consult for ideas, inspiration, and assistance
☐ Explicit reference to relevant class discussions, workshops, lectures, project work, and so on
☐ Description of helpful and relevant prewriting, drafting, revision, and editing strategies
☐ Suggestions and guidelines governing outside help such as peers, writing center tutors, librarians, word-processing and composing software, online tools, and so on
☐ Description of roles to be played by instructor and peer feedback in the revision process
☐ Notes concerning how writers should manage their time to complete the assignment in a timely manner

4. Assessment criteria

☐ An account of specific elements and criteria that will determine writers' success in completing the assignment (e.g., topical focus, essential content, adherence to prespecified rhetorical conventions, grammatical and stylistic features, length; see chapter 8)
☐ Standards to be applied in evaluating the product and the process (e.g., extent of feedback incorporation, departmental or program-wide presentation requirements, grammatical accuracy; see chapter 8)

FIG. 4.3.   Writing assignment checklist.

Admittedly, it would be difficult to ensure that all our classroom tasks and activities meet each of these expectations. However, it is crucial for teachers to realize that meaningful writing assignments—even day-to-day practice activities—should not be devised haphazardly and often are more difficult for students to undertake than teachers think (Carson, 2001; Gottschalk & Hjortshoj, 2004; Hamp-Lyons & Mathias, 1994; Leki, 1995b; Way, Joiner, & Seaman, 2000; Weigle, 2002). In summary, composing tasks that engage students and lead to the enhancement of their writing skills rely fundamentally on thoughtful planning and contextualization, in addition to concrete, accessible, and engaging content (Johns, 1997; Raimes, 1983; Reid & Kroll, 1995).

The sample tasks and assignments described next are aimed at various writing proficiency levels and correspond to one or more components of a potentially iterative writing cycle. Models are designed to reflect the basic properties of sound pedagogical tasks, and to serve as departure points for devising your own materials, exercises, assignments, and projects.

Developing Materials and Tasks Using Models and Other Authentic Texts

Chapter 2 underscores the essential role played by extensive and intensive reading in the development of ESL writing proficiency, suggesting tools for building instruction upon authentic texts, genre analysis, and reading techniques. This section focuses more specifically on the use of such texts as the basis for writing exercises and more complex composing assignments. We begin with a brief description of model texts as pedagogical tools and their possible roles in materials development. Models can take the form of published "professional" texts (or excerpts thereof) as well as sample texts written by students and other novice writers (cf. the so-called "product" approaches discussed in chapter 1). Another variety of model is the schematic drawing or diagram of a particular text type, sometimes used in combination with a sample text, to illustrate topic and discourse structure in a visual medium. The linear structure of a deductively organized expository paragraph, for example, can be sketched out, discussed, and compared with other samples.

The study of models has not been a primary feature of process-oriented or postprocess approaches, for important reasons that we address before considering their use in an L2 literacy course.

A serious and justifiable objection to the use of models is that they can lead students to attend mainly, if not exclusively, to rhetorical and grammatical form far too early in the composing process, thereby short-circuiting productive invention, drafting, and revision processes (Spack, 1984). If not used judiciously as a complement to a range of reading and composing activities, models, even when used occasionally, can perpetuate the misleading impression that writing involves following simple rhetorical formulas or merely pouring content and ideas into a prefabricated mold, in much the same way that a baker pours batter into a tin to produce muffins of uniform size and shape (Cope & Kalantzis, 1993; Kroll, 2003b; Raimes, 1983). More serious is the very real danger that the imitation of models can inhibit writers, preventing them from developing their own voices and productive compositional skills. It is thus essential to avoid using models mechanically or prematurely. Instead, we should incorporate them into our teaching as "a resource rather than an ideal" (Watson-Reekie, 1982, p. 12). When thoughtfully presented, carefully constructed model-based exercises involving textual analysis can measurably enhance ESL writers' awareness of how rhetorical, lexical, grammatical, and mechanical features are used effectively by NS and NNS writers in authentic discursive contexts (Frodesen, 2001).

In beginning-level literacy courses, model-based tasks tend to be tightly controlled (Olshtain, 2001). Although such control may offer limited advantages, process-oriented and socioliterate approaches to writing instruction are in some ways incompatible with the extensive use of expert- and student-generated models. Therefore, we suggest that when teachers include model-based tasks in their literacy courses, these activities should be used as a springboard for tasks that generate authentically situated written production.

Watson-Reekie (1982) categorized model-based tasks according to focus and emphasis. Focus may consist of formal features represented in the model (e.g., verb tenses, aspectual markers, relative clauses, pronoun use), its dominant rhetorical patterns (e.g., deductive, inductive, descriptive, analytic, argumentative), and its communicative functions (to report, describe, explain, narrate, convince, admonish, and so on). Paragraph-length exercises are intended to activate learners' awareness by directing their attention to sentence- and paragraph-level features of written discourse during prewriting and drafting activities. We caution, however, that many professionals reject such highly controlled, paragraph-level tasks because they tend to reduce text analysis activities to mechanical, grammar-based practice. Such activities should be used sparingly, if at all. We recommend instead that teachers construct tasks aimed at comprehension and analysis of model texts for the purpose of initiating the production process, albeit under restricted conditions.

A basic form of this task type involves requiring students to imitate and reproduce model forms by undertaking some kind of structural manipulation. The instructional aim of such exercises (sometimes termed "controlled compositions") is to enhance students' confidence and fluency in the use of word-, sentence-, and paragraph-level patterns and conventions (e.g., novel lexical items, the use of pronouns as referring expressions for full noun phrases introduced earlier in the discourse, or verb tense inflection). Controlled compositions, and variations thereof, were once widespread in ESL instruction and still tend to be common task types in EFL settings. In such contexts, student writing assignments often are designed primarily to provide learners with language practice. This task type should be used judiciously to avoid boredom and to prevent excessive attention to discrete-level textual features when the development of global fluency is of much greater concern to both students and teachers (MacGowan-Gilhooly, 1991).

Completion exercises based on similar authentic passages may be more helpful and pedagogically sound if designed to guide rather than to control students' reasoning and writing production (Freedman, 1993, 1994; Frodesen, 2001). That is, text-based tasks requiring learners to comprehend and also to perform a meaningful and authentic activity are more likely to promote awareness of linguistic and discursive patterns (Feez, 1998; Johns, 2003). Often referred to as "guided compositions" (Raimes, 1983), or structured process tasks, these exercises simultaneously challenge and reassure learners as they generalize the lexical, morphosyntactic, stylistic, and rhetorical features apparent in a model text. For example, a model-based exercise might require students to answer focus questions or prompts about an explicitly defined topic or a photo image, or to complete individual sentences that combine to form a coherent narrative or summary congruent with the model (as in Fig. 4.4). Alternatively, students can be given the first sentence (or sentences) of a model text (as in Fig. 4.5), a paraphrase, or a summary, and then be instructed to draft the rest of the parallel text individually, in pairs, or in small groups (Frodesen, 2001). A more sophisticated approach to model-based instruction, exemplified in Appendix 4, entails text analysis, explicit treatment

Guided Composition Exercise

Purpose: To give students guided practice with basic descriptive writing techniques and conventions
Target proficiency levels: Beginning to intermediate
Materials:
- Model text drawn from published materials or an appropriate student-generated sample
- Corresponding photo, drawing, or sketch (optional)

Procedure: Introduce, analyze, and discuss model paragraph as appropriate. See directions to students.

Directions to students. Please read the following paragraph, which was written by an ESL student about a teacher who was nominated for a community service award. In the paragraph, the writer describes her teacher and explains why she respects and admires her; she sums up by noting how her teacher has influenced her life. In this assignment, you will compose and revise a similar paragraph about a person you know, respect, and admire.

A teacher who earned my respect and admiration

One of the people I most respect and admire is Eliana Todorov. I met Eliana soon after I arrived in the United States and began my junior year of high school. Eliana was my English teacher. Because of her background as an immigrant and her teaching style, she impressed me very much. First, even though I could understand very little English and speak only a few words at first, Eliana was always patient and encouraging. For example, she promised me and the other students that she would help us speak, read, and write English well as long as we worked hard in class and at home. She fulfilled her promise by speaking slowly and clearly, by repeating things when we couldn't understand her, by giving us plenty of practice, and by inspiring us to learn. Second, in our English classes, she led lively and interesting discussions about the stories we read. Often, the students did the talking, while she smiled and listened carefully. Usually, we didn't even realize we were learning so much because we were so interested in the stories and what they meant. Third, Eliana never corrected our mistakes in class; instead, she held private conferences with us to let us know about our progress and how we could improve our speaking and writing skills. Her words were always positive, and she told us often that she was proud of our improvement and hard work. Finally, I admire Eliana because she showed us every day how important it was to believe in our abilities, even when we were discouraged. She told us of her experience as an immigrant from Russia who struggled with English through high school and then the university in the United States. She found English very difficult at first and couldn't speak it at all, but she learned the language so well that she was able to become an English teacher. In fact, she is the best English teacher I have ever had. Even though I am now in college, I remember her inspiring words and actions because they give me confidence that I will continue to improve my skills and enjoy my learning. (Edited and reprinted with permission.)

Now, think of a person who has influenced you in a similarly positive way. Imagine that this person has been nominated for a special award and that you have been asked by a committee to write a statement of support for him or her. The committee has sent you a list of items to mention and questions to answer. Draft a paragraph in which you respond to these items in the order in which they appear. In preparing your second draft, you may wish to rearrange the information.

1. Name one of the people you most respect and admire.
2. When and where did you meet this person?
3. What was this person's profession or job at the time you met him or her? What was your relationship to him or her?
4. Describe at least two reasons for which you respect and admire this person. Try to give specific details or examples.
5. State one of this person's qualities that you try to imitate in your life. Describe why this person is still influential in your life.

FIG. 4.4. Sample task based on a model paragraph.

Variation: Picture-Based Guided Composition

Purpose:	To give students guided practice with basic descriptive writing and speculative techniques based on a visual stimulus
Target proficiency levels:	Beginning to intermediate
Materials:	• Photo, drawing, or sketch with easily identifiable images, objects, or characters
	• Corresponding model text drawn from published materials or an appropriate student-generated sample (optional)
Procedure:	Give students copies of a photo, drawing, or sketch. After a discussion of the image, ask students to write their answers in paragraph form to a set of factual and speculative questions. Consider the image presented below. Suitable questions and prompts might include the following:

1. Where is this event taking place?
2. Who are the men holding the stretcher?
3. What are they wearing?
4. Who is lying in the stretcher?
5. What do you think has happened?
6. What do you think the men are about to do with the person in the stretcher?
7. Where do you think they will travel in the helicopter?

FIG. 4.4.   Sample task based on a model paragraph (Continued).

of genre features, and guided production of complex written discourse, including summaries, paraphrases, and passages that integrate quoted material.

Promoting Fluency with Prewriting Tasks

Controlled and guided tasks such as those presented in the preceding section are geared primarily toward beginning- to intermediate-level L2 writers for whom a degree of structure and focus are useful for framing and initiating a writing process. Involving learners in such simple, narrowly-defined activities can break down barriers to putting pen to paper or applying one's fingers to the keyboard. Guided and open-ended tasks also can offer students practice in the mechanics of writing, easing their sometimes inevitable fear of getting started (Elbow, 1973, 1981b; Jones, 1985; Raimes, 1983). Eventually, of course, most writers need to develop strategies and skills for composing fluently (Kroll, 2001; MacGowan-Gilhooly, 1991).

In this section, we examine several types of tasks and exercises aimed at building the fluency of writers at the beginning, intermediate, and advanced levels of ESL literacy. Of course,

Descriptive Message

Purpose:	To offer students practice with techniques and descriptive conventions for giving directions
Target proficiency levels:	Beginning to low-intermediate
Materials:	• Partially completed sentences presented in sequence (see below)
	• A model text following the format sketched in the partially completed sentences
	• A corresponding picture or map (optional)

Directions to students: You have arranged with a classmate to study for an upcoming exam at your home. Your classmate, a new stud ent, is unfamiliar with your campus and the surrounding neighborhood. He or she asks you to write detailed directions in an e-mail message. Your friend asks for specific directions and landmarks because you can't easily recreate a map on e-mail. Complete sentences 1 to 5; then put them together in paragraph form in a note to your classmate, like the one shown below. Remember to mention details and landmarks that will help your classmate find your home easily.

1. My house/apartment/dormitory room is _____ from campus.
2. You can reach it easily by _____ (walking, cycling, driving).
3. From _____ (point of origin), you'll first _____ (give directions).
4. Look for _____ (give the address) on the _____ side of the street.
5. The house/building _____ (give a description of the building and how to gain access).
6. In case you get tied up or have trouble finding it, _____.

> **Example: Directions from campus to home**
>
> Sam — I'm glad we decided to get ready for the physics exam together. My apartment is about $1\frac{1}{2}$ miles from campus. Since it's so close, you can walk or ride your bike. From campus, take University Boulevard north six blocks; then turn right on 17th Avenue (just past the convenience store). After you turn right on 17th Avenue, go two blocks up the hill to Hannum Lane. Turn left next to a two-story house with a hedge in front. Look for 1726 on the left side of Hannum. It's on the right-hand side of a one-story white house. My building is a three-story brick house with a center door. There's a stairway on the right side leading to my apartment (#4). Just in case, my number is 555-6214. (Edited and reprinted with permission.)

Variation: Paragraph Completion

Purpose:	To give students practice composing focused, open-ended texts
Target proficiency levels:	Beginning to intermediate
Materials:	• A prompt consisting of a topic sentence or thesis statement such as those listed below
	• Model texts drawn from published materials or an appropriate student-generated sample (optional)
Procedure:	Instruct students to begin writing based on a single prompt or a selection of two or three after studying one or more models that represent a similar rhetorical pattern.
	Alternatively, delay analysis of a model until after students have composed a first draft; then use selected samples of students' texts for analysis, expansion, and revision.

Directions to students. You have begun corresponding with an e-mail penpal on another campus. She or he has just sent you a message telling you something about him- or herself and has requested a reply from you. Draft a one-paragraph, 100- to 200-word response that begins with one of the following sentences:

• The wisest/most foolish decision I ever made was...
• The most rewarding experience I ever had as a student was...
• I have chosen to pursue a college degree because...
• The most serious problem facing this campus/city/state/country is...
• As a writer, I feel that my greatest strengths/weaknesses include...

FIG. 4.5. Sample paragraph completion exercises.

these tasks should not be viewed as isolated from one another or as representative of a single, normative approach to teaching composition. Rather, as we emphasized in chapter 3, effective writing units and lessons are made up of multiple tasks representing a range of functions, modalities, and formats. This diversity is essential for building options for recursion into a writing cycle that involves one or more iterations of reading, thinking, invention, drafting, feedback, revision, editing, publishing, and so forth (Fig. 3.5). Variety also ensures that instruction includes tasks and interactional patterns that accommodate students' multiple learning styles, strategies, and preferences (Cohen, 1998; Reid, 1995b).

Unstructured Prewriting. Unstructured prewriting tasks such as freewriting, brainstorming, and listing are hallmarks of process-oriented approaches to writing instruction. Now familiar to many teachers and student writers at the K–12 and postsecondary levels, these teaching and learning tools aim to build writing fluency and creativity by stimulating thought and invention under uninhibited conditions (Glenn et al., 2003; Spack, 1984). When teachers use such unstructured activities to help students develop new knowledge or to organize existing knowledge in novel ways, these strategies can "become gateways to open competencies and to better writing" (Tarvers, 1993, p. 78).

For example, *freewriting* (sometimes termed "speed writing") has been recommended as a means of releasing students from the compulsion to write "correctly" (Macrorie, 1984). Elbow (1973), a well-known proponent of cultivating uninhibited writing processes, offered the following description of the freewriting technique:

> The idea is simply to write for ten minutes (later on, perhaps fifteen or twenty). Don't stop for anything. Go quickly without rushing. Never stop to look back, to cross something out, to wonder how to spell something, to wonder what word or thought to use, or to think about what you are doing. If you can't think of a word or a spelling, just use a squiggle or else write, "I can't think of it." Just put down something. The easiest thing is just to put down whatever is in your mind. If you get stuck it's fine to write "I can't think of what to say," "I can't think of what to say" as many times as you want: Or repeat the last word you wrote over and over again; or anything else. The only requirement is that you never stop. (p. 3)

If you elect to try freewriting with your students, we suggest much shorter sessions (of 3 to 5 min) in which freewriting is focused on a relevant theme or topic and leads directly into a goal-oriented activity such as responding to a reading selection, brainstorming, discussing, or planning a more formal writing assignment. Using freewriting productively in ESL writing instruction requires planning, practice, and patience.

Because freewriting tasks are "designed to stimulate thoughts and ideas" (Williams, 1996, p. 40), many teachers do not even collect or review students' freewriting samples. The process is intended mainly as a private activity in which students envision themselves as the primary audience for these very preliminary texts. Clearly, it is inappropriate for teachers to evaluate freewriting. Many literacy teachers also incorporate freewriting into pair and group sharing sessions geared toward probing more deeply into the ideas generated and expanding on them in discussion and writing (Clarke, 2003d; Glenn et al., 2004).

Many NNS writers are uncomfortable with freewriting, and some resist the procedure entirely because it contradicts their innate predispositions as planners, as well as their prior literacy training (Cohen, 1998; Koffolt & Holt, 1997; Manchón-Ruiz, 1997; Raimes, 1987; Reid, 1995a). Furthermore, despite its popularity and widespread use in L1 composition and L2 literacy education (particularly in the North American context), freewriting is perhaps "not a particularly effective technique" for developing formal writing skills (Williams, 1996, p. 41). Reliable research on the usefulness of prewriting is surprisingly sparse, although the outcomes of several L1 studies (Gauntlett, 1978; Hillocks, 1986; Olson & DiStephano, 1980) have suggested that freewriting and related prewriting techniques favorably influence writing performance and proficiency only marginally, if at all. We thus suggest that teachers avoid the temptation to allow freewriting to become mechanized or entrenched in composition pedagogy, particularly in the ESL context. Instead, teachers should observe and respect their students' divergent learning styles by deploying freewriting as one of numerous options for building writing fluency.

Brainstorming, a related invention technique, aims to allow writers to explore different facets of a topic, issue, or text— privately or collectively (Brisk & Harrington, 2000; Kroll, 2001). Quite simply, brainstorming consists of "producing words, phrases, ideas as rapidly as possible, just as they occur to us, without concern for appropriateness, order, or accuracy" (Raimes, 1983, p. 10). As writers freely associate, they generate ideas and establish connections among them. The process can take place orally in class, in small groups, or individually in writing.

The fundamental technique for brainstorming is straightforward: "The writer decides on a subject, sits down in a quiet place with pen and paper or computer, and writes down everything that comes to mind about the subject" (Glenn et al., 2003, p. 220). In many cases, classroom brainstorming sessions can precede or immediately follow a freewriting exercise. Prompts can derive from the reading of sample texts or models, lead toward responding to a preplanned writing prompt, or be directed at constructing a new topic for writing.

During classwide and group brainstorming sessions, the teacher assumes the role of facilitator and scribe. That is, he or she prompts and probes by asking questions such as "What do you mean?" "Can you give an example?" or "How are these ideas related?"—recording these ideas on the board, an overhead transparency, or an electronic display. Notwithstanding the short-term objective of the brainstorming or the stimulus (e.g., a reading passage, a textbook topic, a picture, a personal experience, a formal writing prompt, an online chat), the teacher can encourage students to produce relevant vocabulary, make comments, ask questions, and make free associations at a rapid pace (Clark, 2003d; Raimes, 1983; Soven, 1999). "The ideas should come quickly and the suggesters shouldn't worry about grammar, spelling, or syntactic completeness. Those come at a much later stage" (Tarvers, 1993, p. 79). Recorded on the board, on a transparency, in students' handwritten notes, or on a computer, the outcomes of a brainstorming session can subsequently be used as a resource for further freewriting, listing, or more structured prewriting activities.

Like brainstorming, *listing* involves the unmonitored generation of words, phrases, and ideas. Listing offers another way of producing concepts and sources for further thought, exploration, and speculation. Listing is distinct from freewriting and brainstorming in that students generate only words and phrases, which can be classified and organized, if only in a sketchy way. Consider the case of a postsecondary academic ESL writing course in which students are first asked to develop a topic related to modern college life and then to compose a letter or editorial piece on the subject. One of the broad topics that emerged in freewriting and brainstorming sessions was "The Benefits and Challenges of Being a College Student." This simple stimulus generated the following list:

Benefits	*Challenges*
independence	*financial and social responsibilities*
living away from home	*paying bills*
freedom to come and go	*managing time*
learning responsibility	*making new friends*
new friends	*practicing good study habits*

The items in this preliminary list overlap considerably. Nonetheless, such a list can offer students concrete ideas for narrowing a broad topic to a manageable scope and for selecting a meaningful direction for their writing.

Structured Prewriting. Like their less-structured counterparts, structured prewriting tasks help students explore topics, generate ideas, gather information, relate new knowledge to existing knowledge, and develop strategies. Structured tasks, however, tend to be more systematic and heuristic in design. They often are aimed at focusing students' attention and preparing them to undertake planning. That is, structured prewriting activities scaffold processes and procedures without specifying sequences, contents, or outcomes in an a priori fashion (Hayes & Nash, 1996; Hughey, Wormuth, Hartfiel, & Jacobs, 1983; Sharples, 1999). Many structured prewriting tools thus lend themselves particularly well to procedures leading to drafting and the composition of genre-oriented writing assignments, which may be intensive or extensive. Although we characterize these techniques in terms of how they can be deployed in the classroom, most are also designed to be incorporated into the reflective writing that students do outside class, namely, in journals, reading logs, and the like (see chapter 2).

Loop-writing, a somewhat overlooked technique, piggybacks directly on the freewriting techniques introduced earlier, although it involves more focus and systematic recycling. Elbow (1981b) described the looping process as "a way to get the best of both worlds: both control and creativity" (p. 59). In loop-writing, writers are given a broad or narrow subject related to the theme at hand (e.g., tradition, education, social values, multiculturalism, globalization). They are then instructed to keep this topic in mind as they freewrite. If their writing goes off track, they are encouraged to write what comes to their minds until their thinking returns to the focus topic. After the freewriting session, students read their texts, then summarize them in a single sentence. In some cases, students can merely extract a sentence they have already written. At other times, they have to construct a new one. This summary sentence constitutes the first loop in the process.

To begin the second loop, the teacher asks the students to freewrite again, this time focusing on the summary sentence as the departure point. Next, the students are instructed to complete another iteration of freewriting and to summarize the new writing in a single sentence, which subsequently becomes the stimulus for a third loop, and so on. The summary sentences can be compared, expanded, or even discarded. This reflection and winnowing process provides a means of capturing the gist of the writer's thoughts and ideas on the topic. As with any invention or prewriting task, loop-writing must be modeled so students can practice the procedure on their own and use it independently (Spack, 1984). Furthermore, the effectiveness and appeal of loop-writing should be monitored because, like freewriting, looping may not be suitable for all, or even most, novice ESL writers, particularly those unaccustomed to process-oriented instructional practices.

Clustering (sometimes also known as "branching" or "mapping") is a structured technique based on the same associative principles as brainstorming and listing. Clustering is distinct, however, because it involves a slightly more developed heuristic (Buzan & Buzan, 1993; Glenn et al., 2003; Sharples, 1999; Soven, 1999). Clustering procedures vary considerably, although the fundamental objective is to equip students with tools for arranging the words, phrases, concepts, memories, and propositions triggered by a single stimulus (i.e., a piece of information, a topic, a provocative question, a metaphor, a visual image). As with the other techniques described so far, clustering should first be modeled and practiced in class so students can eventually incorporate the tool into their own repertoire of invention and planning strategies. The procedure itself is simple, although its self-defining steps can result in a complex representation of relationships, mediated connections, and networks.

Figure 4.6 shows part of a cluster diagram generated by a pair of ESL students in a mainstream composition course in which they had been asked to plan and draft a collaborative essay. After leading the students through a thematic unit on the role of technology in modern society and its institutions, the instructor, with the students, developed the prompt for a revised argumentative essay that would include library research.

Although the sample in Fig. 4.6 was sketched by a pair of students working together, similar diagrams can just as easily be developed by individual writers and entire classes. An advantage of a cluster diagram is that it provides a visual medium in which students can classify and cluster ideas, concepts, and abstractions captured in words and phrases. Cluster diagrams also stimulate thought and problem-solving processes revolving around relationships among elements in a cluster and the

<u>Assignment</u>. To conclude our readings, discussions, and debates on technology and its impact on society, you will compose a four- to five-page position paper aimed at your classmates, whose points of view may differ significantly from your own. Based on the required course readings and sources you have gathered in your own research, explain and justify your position concerning the contributions of technology (preferably, a specific kind of technology) to a culture, community, or institution that you know well. Express your views by stating whether you think the role of technology has been primarily positive or negative. Instead of assuming a "middle-of-the-road" stance, you should formulate a decisive opinion, taking steps to persuade your audience that your view is supported by convincing evidence. Outline your proposition by providing convincing facts, research findings, expert opinions, examples, and so on, and by addressing plausible counterarguments.

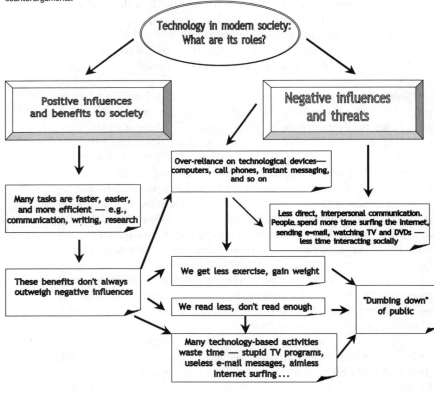

FIG. 4.6.   Sample cluster diagram.

connections between clusters, sometimes leading to more formalized planning procedures.

Cubing similarly provides a tool allowing writers to select an effective and appropriate way of approaching a topic, or to combine methods of understanding and developing a topic. In procedural terms, cubing requires students to examine an idea or proposition from six perspectives, each corresponding to one of

CUBING EXERCISE

Directions. Envision the topic (subject, theme, or object) that you will write about as a cube, like the one below. Each of the six sides of your cube represents a particular way of understanding your topic. Imagine, for example, that the bottom side of the cube represents description. What is the topic? What does it consist of? How would you describe it? Use the stimulus questions in the chart below to discuss or write about all six sides of your cube.

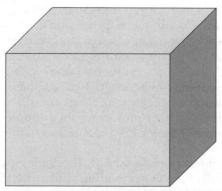

Side	Function	Stimulus Questions
1	DESCRIBE	What is it? What does it consist of? How would you describe it?
2	COMPARE	What is it similar to? What is it different from?
3	ANALYZE	What are its constituent elements? How do these elements fit together?
4	ASSOCIATE	What do you associate it with? What does it remind you of?
5	APPLY	How can you use it? What can you do with it?
6	ARGUE	What positions can be argued in favor of it? Against it?

FIG. 4.7. Cubing diagram.

the six sides of a cube. In cubing, writers are encouraged to look quickly at their topic and to construct a statement or position corresponding to each side, or rhetorical perspective, so they generate multiple approaches from which to choose before undertaking planning or drafting. As Fig. 4.7 shows, each side of the cube corresponds to a rhetorical angle and set of focus questions, which are not unlike the classic "journalists' questions" (i.e., who, what, why, where, when, and how) (Tarvers, 1993, p. 83).

To illustrate the use of cubing, consider how the technique could be applied to a topic such as bilingualism. We could *describe* bilingualism as a state of linguistic and sociocultural knowledge that is doubly rich when compared with monolingualism. We could further *compare* bilingualism to monolingualism by noting the particular intellectual and social advantages of knowing two or more languages and cultures. To *analyze* bilingualism, we could point out that it consists of two sets of linguistic and cultural skills, as well as expertise in how and when to use them. We could *associate* bilingualism with a talent such as knowing how to play a musical instrument (i.e., bilingualism can expand the ways in which one can express oneself). Likewise, we could *apply* bilingual skills in any social, professional, or educational setting in which knowing a single language is not enough. Finally, we could *argue* that bilingualism is a desirable state of knowledge because it doubles (or multiplies) one's prospects for communicating, granting one access to two or more linguistic and cultural communities. Clearly, thinking carefully and systematically about a single issue or problem from multiple angles offers the writer a range of rhetorical directions to follow before planning a piece of writing.

A related technique aimed at developing perceptual and expressive skills involves providing students with stimuli that induce them to "break out of old patterns and find new ways of viewing their subjects" (Tarvers, 1993, p. 80). Topics and foci for such perspective-taking activities can range from the wholly concrete and pedestrian to the highly abstract. Consider the following tasks and prompts, that might be used effectively at nearly any proficiency level:

- Write a detailed, one-paragraph description of a familiar object such as the dashboard display in your car, your computer keyboard, a radio alarm clock, or the control panel on your microwave oven. Compare your description with the real thing and record the differences. What did you miss? Why?
- In a single paragraph, describe from memory a familiar place such as a room in your house, a coffee shop that you frequent, the supermarket, or the classroom in which your English class meets. Afterward, visit the place you described and add salient details that you missed. Next, revise your paragraph as though you were writing it for a blind person.
- Select a familiar place such as your kitchen, your bedroom, or your favorite place to study in the campus library. Describe the location from the point of view of an insect that has landed on a light fixture.

- Select a place that you frequent but where you do not spend extended periods, such as a local convenience store, a department store, your gym, or a doctor's office. Describe this place from the perspective of the person behind the counter.
- "Ask students to write two papers: one explaining a topic to a young member of the family and the other explaining the same topic to an unfamiliar faculty member" (Johns, 1997, p. 123).

For assignments requiring rhetorical patterns more sophisticated than description, teachers can ask students to play the devil's advocate by arguing against a position they have elected to defend, by contrasting their position to that of a classmate, or by identifying the precedents for their own points of view. These tasks can be undertaken in freewriting sessions, in students' writing journals, or even in formal writing assignments that students will submit for assessment.

Planning and Drafting Heuristics

Both planning and drafting are addressed in this section because, as research on composing processes has consistently shown, planning does not necessarily precede drafting, nor does drafting begin only after a definitive "plan" for a piece of writing has been formalized (see chapter 1). Many effective L1 and L2 writers plan as they move through the numerous stages that comprise their drafting processes (Bamberg, 2003; Clark, 2003d; Emig, 1971; Flower & Hayes, 1980, 1981; Glenn et al., 2003; Hayes & Nash, 1996; Perl, 1979; Rose, 1980; Zamel, 1983). To enhance discovery processes entailed in making and revising plans as a text evolves, we recommend that preliminary planning take shape flexibly, with reference to whatever structural frameworks or strategies are most effective for individual writers and specific writing tasks. We therefore discourage teachers from imposing the formal outlining processes that once characterized both L1 and L2 composition teaching, particularly in traditional and current–traditional pedagogies.

Teachers and novice writers should understand that successful planning processes can take many forms. They should thus experiment with an array of heuristics and techniques, some of which are better matched to particular composing tasks than others.

For example, the planning and decision making entailed in composing a timed essay examination are necessarily compressed, as compared with the extended and involved planning required to develop a bibliographic research assignment or an action research project. We therefore suggest that teachers offer students generous opportunities for experimenting with planning tools, some of which may actually involve drafting, a process that in itself can further systematize subsequent planning (Clark, 2003; Murray, 1978).

This is not to say that outlines and variations on them are not productive for many writers, experienced and inexperienced. In fact, observational and experimental research has often shown that skilled writers tend to plan their texts, and that outlining can serve as an effective prewriting and planning tool for some writers. Kellogg (1993), for example, compared the 200- to 300-word essays of student writers subjected to four distinct prewriting conditions: no explicit instructions for planning, listing, graphic clustering, and structured outlining. The listing group produced significantly better essays than did the control and clustering groups, but the outlining group produced essays that were significantly better than all the rest. Kellogg's (1993) results suggested not only that outlining works, but also that it can be more effective than other prewriting strategies.

Experimental outcomes such as these need to be interpreted cautiously, however. We could fairly speculate, for instance, that the outlining group performed best because the students had had more experience with outlining in school. Indeed, according to textbooks reflecting traditional and current–traditional paradigms, generations of academic writers might certainly have been led to believe that the only acceptable kind of planning (or prewriting, for that matter) consisted of the formal outline, with Roman and Arabic numerals neatly aligned and headings spelled out in complete sentences. In some educational settings, students still are required to produce and submit such traditional outlines with lengthy essays and research papers. Teachers who find themselves in this situation may find it useful to present the formal outline as a distinct rhetorical form that can actually follow a complete piece of prose rather than a linear structure that must necessarily precede it (Glenn et al., 2003).

We offer this suggestion for both practical and pedagogical reasons. Practically speaking, student writers may need to supply outlines along with the writing they do outside the composition course. Moreover, a post hoc outline can serve as a useful advance organizer for readers. Lengthy texts in many disciplines, for example, require a table of contents. Meanwhile, the exercise of preparing an outline can give the writer a sense of the hierarchical and linear structure of the themes, propositional content, and rhetorical links that bind the prose text on which the outline is based. Our point is not to discourage the use of written outlines, but to situate them more broadly as rhetorical and analytic tools to be applied after drafting, not necessarily as indispensable prewriting heuristics or planning devices. Moreover, as Sharples (1999) pointed out, for school-based genres such as essays and summaries, "making an outline or list in the head may be just as successful as doing it on paper" (p. 88). On the other hand, writers planning more extensive and complex texts (e.g., novels, business reports, research articles, theses, dissertations) are much more likely to need and use a hierarchically structured, formal outline.

Informal outlining (i.e., taking notes and sketching out a rough plan for a piece of writing) derives from the classic outline and naturally flows from prewriting and invention procedures. After a brainstorming, listing, clustering, or cubing session, for example, students may have developed enough raw material to lay out a rough plan for a piece of extended written discourse. By the process of making a list, cluster, or cube diagram, writers can be shown how to exclude extraneous or unrelated ideas, to narrow elements that cohere and can be explicitly linked, and to arrange them in ways that exhibit some sort of logic (e.g., chronological, spatial, thematic, categorical). What emerges from this process may amount to a simple, sketchy list of topics and subtopics that make sense only to the writer. However, as a preliminary scaffold for a developing text, this list or network is all that the writer may need to begin the composing process, although significant changes to this plan are likely to occur once he or she begins to produce sentences and paragraphs.

Whether formal and structured or informal and flexible, planning clearly promotes the fluid production of meaningful text. Sharples (1999), referring to empirical studies as well as instructional experience, summarized the observable benefits of prewriting and planning:

> Making a writing plan organises thought and it guides the production of a text. A plan needs to satisfy both of these purposes. If it is illogical and fails to organise ideas then it will not form the basis for a coherent argument. If it does not offer a coherent

rhetorical structure, then the resulting text is likely to be shapeless and rambling.... At the very least, time devoted to planning is time well spent. It gives an opportunity to reflect on the content and structure of the text, and this appears to pay dividends in improved quality. (pp. 88–89)

The sample plan shown in Fig. 4.8 illustrates how one student writer structured a written draft in which he would compare university studies in the United States with those in Japan, his home country. The symmetrical plan shown in Fig. 4.8 evolved from a list that included subtopics, each with specific notes about examples. Obviously, this plan could be rearranged and expanded with further details, although many details might come to the writer's mind during the composing phase. Furthermore, the writer has

---

University Studies in the United States

✓ In general: Rigorous
✓ Application and admission: Personal essay, high school grades, SATs, teachers' recommendations
✓ Professors' expectations: Generally high (students given assignments, papers, tests, etc. throughout the semester)
✓ Student attitudes: Generally mature and serious
✓ Other points: Tuition can be costly, and high school studies may not be too difficult, so students have to study hard

University Studies in Japan

✓ In general: Rigorous only for some students
✓ Application and admission: By entrance examination
✓ Professors' expectations: Generally low (students may only have to take one exam at the end of the year)
✓ Student attitudes: Generally not very serious
✓ Other points: Public universities are not expensive; university entrance exams are very competitive, so getting accepted may be the hardest part

(Edited and reprinted with permission.)

FIG. 4.8. Sample student essay plan.

noted "other points" that seem important to him, but that he has not yet fit squarely into his dualistic plan. In drafting the essay, however, he discovered a way to unify his "other points" as an informative organizing principle that reflected his thesis concerning the characteristics distinguishing university studies in the United States from those in Japan.

A variation on this approach to planning, *zero-drafting,* involves creating more text material and reorganizing it. Murray (1985, 1986) recommended this planning technique as a way of reducing students' inhibitions about generating extended prose. Zero-drafting essentially consists of extended freewriting done in multiple iterations, much as with loop-writing. In contrast to loop-writing, however, each iteration of zero-drafting may focus on a distinct subtopic or rhetorical angle (see the descriptions of cubing and perspective-taking procedures described earlier in this chapter). According to Tarvers (1993), "the goal is simply to get a couple of sheets of writing together, so that the writer can begin working; they're private, safe places to put down ideas" (p. 87). After several focused freewriting sessions, the writer has assembled multiple "chunks" of text that he or she can shuffle or discard according to the topic and purpose of the writing task. The resulting series of roughly hewn texts may be disjointed and far from what the writer anticipates even as a preliminary product. Nevertheless, these sketchy writings can allow him or her to formulate a structure or work plan that emerges from extended discourse rather than a series of key words and phrases (as in the informal planning process described earlier).

Whereas some writers are comfortable with idea development and planning strategies, others may find them unnecessary or unsuitable for their individual drafting styles, or inappropriate to the task. That is, not all writers need to execute direct planning strategies by writing ideas, plans, or outlines on paper or a computer screen (Matsuda, 2003). Some students may, in fact, have developed internal planning skills that enable them to begin drafting confidently without a written plan (Carrell & Monroe, 1995). In keeping with the insights of postprocess proponents, planning techniques should therefore be presented and practiced as options, but they should not be forced—nor should they become obligatory elements of a writing cycle or syllabus (see chapters 1 and 3).

Regardless whether our students are extensive or minimal planners, they may need many opportunities for drafting in class and in the computer writing lab. By promoting the drafting process, we can model planning and other processes that might reasonably take place as writers draft and redraft their texts. For many writers, revision and feedback incorporation may be part of the drafting and redrafting processes (see chapters 5, 6, and 7). We have already suggested tasks and procedures for drafting using journals (see chapter 2). Class time also can be used productively for more focused and structured types of assignments, such as developing multidraft texts and timed writings. Designating time for in-class drafting is especially valuable for inexperienced writers, who may have an especially difficult time getting started or maintaining momentum on their own (Rose, 1985). The social context of the classroom can provide the motivation necessary to overcome these obstacles. In-class writing also enables writers to avail themselves of their peers and the instructor if they need a reader, help, inspiration, or moral support (Elbow, 1981b; Elbow & Belanoff, 1989).

Some composition specialists recommend leading inexperienced writers through one or more drafting sequences, the phases of which are conducted primarily in class (Flowerdew, 1993; Koffolt & Holt, 1997; Kroll, 2001; Zamel, 1982). The purposes of such an extended exercise include providing students with concrete practice and dramatizing how expert writers can benefit from multidrafting. It has often been reported, for example, that Ernest Hemingway rewrote the final page of *A Farewell to Arms* nearly 40 times before he was satisfied with the passage. Clearly, few composition teachers or students have this amount of time available to them. However, it is possible to compress a drafting sequence into manageable stages. Tarvers (1993), for example, suggested planning five drafting sessions:

1. Zero draft
2. Shaping draft (students focus on organization, audience, and voice)
3. Style draft (students focus on paragraphing, syntax, and diction)
4. Editing draft (students focus on grammatical, mechanical, and formatting features; see chapters 6 and 7)
5. Final draft (students submit the text for inclusion in their portfolios or for the instructor's evaluation).

Of course, a multistage drafting sequence such as this should not be seen as a prescription for rigid sequencing (see chapter 3). This plan, for example, can be reduced or expanded according to students' proficiency levels, features of the writing task, and amount of class time available. These tasks also lend themselves to the incorporation of teacher and peer feedback (see chapters 5 and 6), in addition to the introduction of new reading selections and model texts.

Finally, to stimulate the production of more precise or complex ideas, and to encourage students to expand and sharpen their drafting skills, teachers can incorporate focusing and elaboration tasks based on existing drafts. The tasks outlined in Fig. 4.9, inspired by what Murray (1986) called "messing around with texts," can help writers to see their drafts and the written

---

Imitation and Incorporation

Ask students to select a brief passage from the draft of a peer or a related course reading that they particularly like (five sentences, a paragraph). Help them identify why they like the passage by analyzing its content and form. Next, instruct them to apply one or more of these techniques or stylistic features into the draft they are currently developing. Optionally, suggest that students include a note to you about what they have done when they submit the draft for your comments.

Text Expansion

Ask students to imagine that their editor was very pleased with one or more aspects of their latest piece of writing (e.g., a forceful argument, an appealing set of details, a compelling narrative). The editor has asked them to expand on these strengths and insists on a new draft in which these strengths are enriched. Help students think of sources for enhancing these qualities (e.g., a thesaurus for improving word choice and clarity, metaphors to make details and images more vivid).

Text Compression

Instruct students to cut their texts or a particular passage by a significant proportion (e.g., 25%, 50%, 70%) to balance them more appropriately or to meet space restrictions. Assist students with techniques for preserving their original meaning, structure, and voice while conforming to a fiercely enforced limitation. Remind students that writers in many fields (e.g., journalists, editors, academic authors) are required to meet such demands.

Rhetorical Reorganization

Ask students to reorganize major or minor elements of their current drafts. For example, they might rearrange the supporting points of an argument, present its weaknesses before its strengths, or describe objections before introducing solutions. Help students to decide on a structure that works most effectively.

In-Progress Rhetorical Analysis

After a brief incubation period (e.g., one or several days), instruct students to sketch a strategy diagram or informal outline of their drafts. Ask students to analyze these skeletal representations of their texts and to examine how well they express their original intentions. This exercise can highlight gaps that students might not have seen otherwise. To expand on this activity, ask students to share their diagrams or outlines with a peer, who evaluates them for logic, clarity, completeness, or other relevant criteria.

Recasting

Specify a new audience for your students; then ask them to recast their drafts (or a portion thereof) to accommodate this different group of readers. For example, whereas their original draft may have been directed at an audience of their peers, suggest that they recast their texts to appeal to a group of professionals in their field, a university admissions committee, or a scholarship panel. Discuss appropriate changes in perspective, register, tone, and voice.

(Sources: Murray, 1986; Tarvers, 1993)

FIG. 4.9.   Focus and elaboration tasks.

products of others as fluid and evolving, rather than as mechanical and confining. These mid- and between-draft tasks can give students practice in devising alternative ways of moving through the drafting process toward a product that meets their expectations, satisfies reader expectations, and conforms to the rhetorical conventions of the genre under study. Clearly, not all of these tasks will effect changes in what students eventually submit for evaluation, but they offer teachers and students versatile methods for working with drafts.

Constructing and Evaluating Formal Tasks and Assignments

This final section addresses issues related to the design and implementation of formal writing tasks, which may differ from the task types covered so far in one or more respects. We use the term "formal" to refer to tasks and assignments designed explicitly to elicit writing that will be used to evaluate students' performance and progress. Formal assignments may likewise involve one or more of the subtasks introduced in the preceding sections, as well as one or more cycles of revision (including feedback incorporation). Clearly, all of the elements presented in the Writing Assignment Checklist (Fig. 4.3) apply as well to formal assignments as they do to those that lead up to them. Because formal assignments may require substantial forethought, however, several additional points concerning their planning and presentation are worth treating in detail.

Issues of topic and scope are obviously of eminent importance in developing writing tasks, planning composition instruction, and evaluating student performance (Gottschalk & Hjortshoj, 2004; Graves, 1990; Hamp-Lyons, 2003; Kroll, 2001; Lippman, 2003; Nelson & Burns, 2000; White, 1999; Williams, 1996). A well-designed assignment can stimulate a range of varied and productive classroom activities, writing tasks, and feedback techniques. To bring about these desirable outcomes, however, the task needs to stimulate thought and scaffold procedures that writers can use to carry it out. It also should establish guidelines that writers can use to compare their emergent texts with the assignment's demands. On the basis of their extensive analyses of processes leading to the design and assessment of effective writing prompts, Kroll and Reid (1994) and Reid and Kroll (1995) proposed several straightforward categories for teachers and evaluators to use in developing fair and meaningful assignments. They suggested addressing the following questions to shape the composition assignments we give in our courses:

- For what *reason(s)/purpose(s)* will the writing be assigned?
- How will the assignment fit into the *immediate context,* and in the *overall objectives* of the class? That is, how *authentic* is the prompt?
- In what ways will the content of the prompt be *accessible* to students as it *integrates* classroom learning with long-term goals?
- Who are the *students* who will be responding to the assignment, and what are their *needs*?
- How will the writing processes *engage* the students and *further their knowledge* of the content and skills being taught?
- What knowledge should the students be *"demonstrating"* in their written products?

(Reid & Kroll, 1995, p. 21)

It is also worth reiterating the importance of targeting the rhetorical approaches, structures, and modes that are most logical and appropriate for engaging with a given topic or prompt. As McKay (1994) urged, writing assignments should collectively, if not individually, "reflect a range of rhetorical development so that students can experiment with different patterns" (p. 201). In addition to developing assignments that are explicitly identified with relevant genres, Johns (1997) pointed out that student writers also need to gain experience writing in and for diverse contexts:

[Students] can be asked to write down observations as they sit in the school cafeteria; they can be asked to write (and discuss) class notes in a lecture; they can be required to assess a literacy context in one of their classes and reflect upon that experience. Perhaps most important for student flexibility is the opportunity to read or write under various time constraints. For some assignments, students should go through the writing process: first draft, peer review, second draft, editing, and so on; in others, students should be asked to read or write quickly, under pressure....

> When considering contexts and constraints, we should also
> consider the type of assignment that is made. Students should
> have the opportunity to experience open-ended assignments
> ("Write about your previous semester") or assignments of their
> own choosing, but they should also experience . . . assignments
> that are very tightly written. (p. 123)

Related to the issues of topical focus, genre, and rhetorical
range is the question of choice. In other words, teachers designing writing assignments need to weigh the advantages of giving
students a single prompt or offering them two or more options. A
convincing argument can be made for assigning a single prompt
because it gives students practice with tasks that approximate
the academic assignment genres that are common outside ESL
and English departments. Designing genre-oriented tasks is also
a viable pedagogical choice when the teacher is working with
beginning- and intermediate-level writers who may work best
with a confined topical area and a limited set of rhetorical and
grammatical patterns. A single question or prompt also is appropriate for introducing intermediate- and advanced-level writers
to unfamiliar genres and rhetorical forms, particularly when the
course syllabus involves unfamiliar content.

On the other hand, providing students with a choice offers
notable advantages. The first and most obvious advantage is
that students may be more interested in, and motivated by, a
prompt they have selected from a short menu. A related benefit for both teacher and students is that the texts produced by
students are likely to represent a wider variety, making peer feedback more appealing and teacher response a bit less monotonous.
At the same time, it is worth recalling one of the criteria listed
in the checklist in Fig. 4.3: When students are presented with
two or more options, the prompts should be written so that student texts can be fairly compared on the basis of context, content,
genre, complexity, and so on.

As most experienced writing teachers know, designing tasks
that guide writers toward the achievement of their goals is time-
consuming. Furthermore, skill and experience are required to
construct assignments that capitalize on students' strengths and
help them develop strategies for overcoming their weaknesses.
Nonetheless, we can alert ourselves to common pitfalls and
take steps to avoid them. According to Reid and Kroll (1995),
a common pitfall is posing a task that is "too broadly focused
for successful student writing within the classroom context" in

Directions
Please read the information on this sheet carefully.

Topic
Immigration Policy Reform

Background Information

Our recent readings and discussions have revealed that immigration policy has become an urgent concern of many governments around the world, notably those of countries in North America and the European Union. In some of these countries, efforts to reform immigration policy and the agencies that enforce it have ignited spirited debates. According to a number of public officials, analysts, and journalists, anti-immigrant sentiment has simultaneously erupted, alarming immigrants and raising public worries about nationalistic fervor and racism. In the United States, for example, controversy continues to surround the Immigration Reform Bill, while restructuring at the Immigration and Naturalization Service (INS) has largely failed to satisfy Congress, lobbyists, or immigrant applicants for legal resident status and citizenship. In addition, several state governments have proposed initiatives to crack down on illegal immigration and to reduce even legal migration across their borders. For example, California's Proposition 187, approved by voters in November 1994, officially discourages illegal immigration by denying undocumented immigrants access to health care and public education. Because of the significant political, social, and educational implications of controlling the flow of legal and illegal immigrants across international borders, policies such as Proposition 187 have presented significant dilemmas for government lawmakers, legal analysts, enforcement agencies, and especially immigrants.

Policy Analysis and Advisory Assignment

On the basis of our course readings and your developing knowledge concerning the immigration issues we have explored, analyze the current immigration policy of the government of your choice. In your eight- to ten-page advisory assignment, you will consider how this policy might change in the near or distant future. Because many societies are currently grappling with immigration issues, you may wish to refer to the official policies of other governments, although you are not required to make extensive comparisons. In your analysis, you will identify a salient problem (or set of problems) in the policy or proposed legislation that you analyze. You then will propose a plausible solution to that problem, outlining recommended steps leading to its implementation. In describing your solution, you will discuss how your solution would ameliorate the problem(s) you have examined.

Suggestions for Getting Started

You have already begun to explore this topic in the course readings. You also have written several Journal entries related to this issue. Review the material you have read as well as your personal reflections; then begin collecting data for your research. As soon as possible, look very carefully at some of the sample policy analysis and advisory papers that I have left

FIG. 4.10. Sample formal essay assignment for an advanced EAP course.

at the Reserve Desk at the Library. We will compare and evaluate two of these papers in class to help you understand the key components of successful advisory papers.

Reading Materials and Resources

First, check the course Webpage for an updated bibliography, to which several of you have already added. I also encourage you to check *The Economist, The New Republic, The New York Times,* and your political science Websites for recent news items related to immigration policy and reform in your region of specialization. Print-only resources in the EAP 2170 binder at the Reserve Desk will be updated twice per week. Please contribute to the binder yourselves and update the online bibliography when you do so!

Timeline

25 January   Bring your readings and reading notes to class for brainstorming session. Begin draft in class.
30 January   Exchange first advisory draft with classmates; bring one photocopy of your paper to class
1 February   After reviewing your classmate's paper carefully and preparing written comments, present your suggestions in class
6 February   Submit first revision of advisory to me for written feedback
8 February   Attend individual conferences with me.
13 February Bring newly revised advisory (second revision) to class for proofreading in peer groups
15 February Submit edited, proofread second revision for evaluation (along with your self-analysis checklist and the first two drafts)

Evaluation Criteria

The "Evaluation criteria for revised writing assignments" will be used to assess the final version of Writing Assignment #1. Special attention will be paid to the following features:

➢ A title that reflects key elements of your advisory position.
➢ An introductory section that previews your entire paper.
➢ A methodical, point-by-point policy analysis following the format in your *Style Book.*
➢ A concise problem statement followed by logically ordered explanatory paragraphs, each developed with specific, empirical evidence from reliable policy sources (at least five print sources and one online policy memo).
➢ Clear distinctions between your ideas and those of the authors you cite.
➢ A step-by-step exposition of your proposed solution (try following the "action plan" approach described in the *Style Book*)
➢ A concluding section summarizing main elements of your analysis, the policy problem or problems, and your solution
➢ A complete bibliography that follows the conventions of the *Style Book.*
➢ Adherence to formal conventions of grammar, diction, spelling, and mechanics, as detailed in the *Style Book.*

FIG. 4.10.   Sample formal essay assignment for an advanced EAP course (Continued).

which it is assigned (p. 29). A related danger concerns flawed and underspecified content, whereas another concerns problematic, ambiguous, or opaque language (Glenn et al., 2003; Gottschalk & Hjortshoj, 2004). The authentic sample assignments shown in Figs. 4.10 and 4.11 are designed to avoid the pitfalls identified by Reid and Kroll (1995) and to exemplify the criteria listed in Fig. 4.3.[2]

Linguistics 120 — Introduction to Linguistics
Essay Assignment 2: Due October 7

<u>Directions</u>. Identify one of the principal findings or concepts from chapter 7 on language typology that most intrigued or surprised you (e.g., pronoun marking systems across languages, the noun phrase accessibility hierarchy (NPAH), cross-linguistic differences in color terminology). Consider how and why your learning about this research might affect your future learning about language, culture, cognition, and education.

In an essay of 1,500 to 2,000 words, please

1. Describe how your understanding of your selected finding, concept, or hypothesis has helped you to understand linguistics as a field of inquiry
2. Explain the discovery process that has led to your new understanding, noting key steps that have deepened your personal theory of language
3. Discuss your reaction to that learning and its application to your current and future learning (in linguistics as well as other fields).

Focus on one finding or concept only, and resist the temptation to review and summarize typological research. Although this assignment certainly will require you to explore linguistic typology and its applications, remember that the task is *not* to prepare a bibliographic essay. Therefore, avoid excessive quoting of and overreliance on the textbook and reading selections (Remember, I know these sources pretty well!). The collection of sample essays on Reserve at the Library will give you a sense of how other students have successfully narrowed their topics, organized their reflections, and expressed their thoughts.

<u>Assessment criteria</u>. Per the syllabus, I will assign numeric grades based on how completely you address the assignment. Here are my specific expectations:

1. Demonstration of your awareness of the linguistic principle under study
2. Accurate characterization of the findings and the guiding theory
3. Clear, explicit connections between the linguistic facts and your personal learning process
4. Adherence to conventional standards of academic English, including grammatical and readable prose, accurate spelling, and mechanics
5. APA-style document design and bibliographic format.

<u>Essay presentation</u>. Your text should be word-processed, double-spaced (with $1^1/_2$" margins), spell-checked, and headed with your name, section number, and essay title in the upper left hand corner (no cover sheets, please).

FIG. 4.11. Sample formal essay assignment from an undergraduate linguistics course.

SUMMARY

This chapter explores principles of textbook selection and supplementation, materials development, and task design, with specific reference to practical approaches and techniques. Congruent with the theme of flexibility introduced in chapter 3, we outline specific recommendations for designing materials and tasks in ways that recognize the diverse needs of ESL writers, teachers, and educational institutions. Although we emphasize the importance of systematic planning and execution, we also attempt to illustrate the value of offering students abundant variety and opportunities for carrying out diverse writing processes in the composition classroom. Our major precepts can be summarized in the following brief list of generalizations:

* As with syllabus design and lesson planning, decisions concerning materials selection and task construction need to be grounded in the teacher's assessment of student needs and abilities, the purposes and socioliterate contexts for writing, target genres, and the teacher's particular approach to writing instruction.
* Textbook evaluation and selection are facilitated by applying both coarsely grained and finely tuned criteria that address textbook type.
* Textbooks almost invariably require supplementation and adaptation, which are processes requiring a careful balance of process and product, content and form.
* Meaningful and productive prewriting tasks and composing assignments can derive from a wide range of authentic models and instructional procedures, none of which should be applied rigidly or dogmatically.

RESOURCE LIST[3]

ESL Literacy Textbooks by Category

Comprehensive, Multipurpose ESL Writing Textbooks: Beginning to Low-Intermediate

Blanchard, K., & Root, C. (1998). *Get ready to write: A beginning writing text.* Reading, MA: Addison-Wesley.

Cobb, C. (1998). *Process and pattern: Controlled composition for ESL students.* Belmont, CA: Wadsworth.

Fellag, L. R. (2003). *Write ahead: Skills for academic success.* Upper Saddle River, NJ: Pearson.

Folse, K. S., Mahnke, M. K., Solomon, E. V., & Williams, L. (2003). *Blueprints 1: Composition skills for academic writing.* Boston: Houghton Mifflin.

Huizenga, J. (1999). *Basic composition for ESL: An expository workbook* (3rd ed.). Boston: Heinle.

Miller, J. L., & Cohen, R. F. (2001). *Reason to write: Strategies for success in academic writing—Low intermediate.* New York: Oxford University Press.

Shoemaker, C., & Larson, D. (1998). *Write in the middle: A guide to writing for the ESL student* (2nd ed.). Boston: Heinle.

Comprehensive, Multipurpose ESL Writing Textbooks: Intermediate

Folse, K. S., Muchmore-Vokoun, A., & Solomon, E. V. (1999). *Great essays.* Boston: Houghton Mifflin.

Frank, M. (2003). *Writing from experience: Grammar and language skills for intermediate ESL/EFL students* (Rev. ed.). Ann Arbor: University of Michigan Press.

Haber, S. B. (1998). *In our own words: A guide with readings for student writers* (2nd ed.). New York: Cambridge University Press.

Smoke, T. (1999). *A writer's workbook: An interactive writing text for ESL students* (3rd ed.). New York: Cambridge University Press.

Tickle, A. (1997). *The writing process: A guide for ESL students.* Reading, MA: Addison-Wesley.

Winkler, A. C., & McCuen-Metherell, J. R. (2003). *Writing talk: Paragraphs and short essays with readings* (3rd ed.). Upper Saddle River, NJ: Prentice-Hall.

Comprehensive, Multipurpose ESL Writing Textbooks: Advanced

Hall, E., & Jung, C. S. Y. (2000). *Reflecting on writing: Composing in English for ESL students.* Ann Arbor: University of Michigan Press.

Leki, I. (1995a). *Academic writing: Exploring processes and strategies* (2nd ed.). New York: St. Martin's Press.

Raimes, A. (1999). *Exploring through writing: A process approach to ESL composition.* New York: Cambridge University Press.

Smalzer, W. R. (1996). *Write to be read: Reading, reflection, and writing.* New York: Cambridge University Press.

Spack, R. (1999). *Guidelines: A cross-cultural reading/writing text* (2nd ed.). New York: St. Martin's Press.

Swales, J., & Feak, C. (1994). *Academic writing for graduate students.* Ann Arbor: University of Michigan Press.

Readers/Anthologies for ESL Students

Brooks, E., & Fox, L. (1995). *Making peace: A reading/writing/thinking text on global community.* New York: St. Martin's Press.

Spack, R. (1994). *The international story: An anthology with guidelines for reading and writing about fiction.* New York: St. Martin's Press.

Combination Rhetoric/Reader for ESL Writers

Smalley, R. L., & Ruetten, M. K., & Kozyrev, J. (2000). *Refining composition skills: Rhetoric and grammar* (5th ed.). Boston: Heinle.

Combined Mainstream/ESL Resources by Category

Comprehensive Composition Textbooks for Combined NS/NNS Courses

Axelrod, R. B., & Cooper, C. C. (2001). *The St. Martin's guide to writing* (Short 6th ed.). Boston: Bedford/St. Martin's.

Bazerman, C., & Wiener, H. S. (2003). *Writing skills handbook.* Boston: Houghton Mifflin.

Hacker, D. (2002a). *The Bedford handbook* (6th ed.). Boston: Bedford/St. Martin's.

Hacker, D. (2002b). *Research and documentation in the electronic age.* Boston: Bedford/St. Martin's Press.

Lunsford, A. A. (2003). *St. Martin's handbook* (5th ed.). Boston: Bedford/ St. Martin's.

Palmquist, M. (2003). *Bedford researcher: An integrated text, CD-ROM, and Web site.* Boston: Bedford/St. Martin's.

Raimes, A. (2002). *Keys for writers: A brief handbook* (3rd ed.). Boston: Houghton Mifflin.

Raimes, A. (2004). *Universal keys for writers.* Boston: Houghton Mifflin.

Multipurpose Developmental Textbook for Combined NS/NNS Courses

Biays, J. S., & Wershoven, C. (2004). *Along these lines: Writing paragraphs and essays* (3rd ed.). Upper Saddle River, NJ: Pearson/Prentice-Hall.

NS Literacy Resources by Category

Combination Rhetorics/Readers/Handbooks for NS Writers

Barnet, S., & Bedau, H. (2002). *Critical thinking, reading, and writing: A brief guide to argument* (4th ed.). Boston: Bedford/St. Martin's.

Rottenberg, A. T. (2003). *Elements of argument: A text and reader* (7th ed.). Boston: Bedford/St. Martin's.

Readers/Anthologies for NS Students

Bartholomae, D., & Petrosky, A. (2003). *Ways of reading: Words and images.* Boston: Bedford/St. Martin's.

Colombo, G. (2002). *Mind readings: An anthology for writers.* Boston: Bedford/ St. Martin's.

Kennedy, X. J., Kennedy, D. M., & Aaron, J. E. (2003). *Bedford reader* (8th ed.). Boston: Bedford/St. Martin's.

Mainstream (NS) Reference Guides

Oliu, W. E., Brusaw, C. T., & Alred, G. J. (2001). *Writing that works: Communicating effectively on the job* (7th ed.). Boston: Bedford/St. Martin's.

Perrin, R. (2003). *Beacon handbook and desk reference* (6th ed.). Boston: Houghton Mifflin.

Spatt, B. (2003). *Writing from sources* (6th ed.). Boston: Bedford/St. Martin's.

Weidenborner, S., & Caruso, D. (2001). *Writing research papers: A guide to the process* (6th ed.). Boston: Bedford/St. Martin's.

REFLECTION AND REVIEW

1. Compare the foci of the textbook genres described in this chapter (i.e., comprehensive textbook, rhetoric, reader, reference guide). Which of these genres are most suitable for your current or future students? Why?
2. Discuss the practical and pedagogical justifications for supplementing and adapting a course textbook.

3. Identify the pedagogical and cognitive benefits of incorporating diverse genres, task types, and tasks into the ESL composition curriculum. What do students gain from undertaking varied literacy processes and procedures?
4. Assess the benefits and drawbacks of using model texts.
5. Why have the boundaries between prewriting and writing, process and product, fluency and accuracy, and so on become blurred? Why should composition teachers understand these relationships?

Application Activity 4.1: Practice Textbook Evaluation

Directions. Select a course book or materials set being used in an ESL or EFL literacy course at your institution or at an institution in your community. On the basis of what you know about the institution and its population of writers, decide which of the criteria in Fig. 4.1 you would apply to construct a manageable textbook evaluation instrument. In consultation with a teacher in the program or a classmate, assemble an appropriate set of criteria, then apply these to the textbook or textbooks in question. Substantiate your evaluation with a written prose commentary of one to two pages in which you describe particular features not covered in the evaluation instrument.

Application Activity 4.2: Writing Task Analysis and Assessment

Directions. Request samples of authentic instructional tasks and exercises from your instructor, a colleague, or a literacy instructor at an institution near you. Analyze a task in terms of the functions outlined in Fig. 4.2 and the checklist components listed in Fig. 4.3. You may also wish to use the materials in Figs. 4.4, 4.5, 4.10, and 4.11 as reference points. If you think the task merits revision or further development, modify it according to the outcomes of your analysis. Justify your proposed revisions in a brief prose commentary.

Application Activity 4.3: Writing Task Adaptation

The tasks and prompts shown for this activity, all aimed at composing notes or letters, are designed for both ESL and NS writers. Although they are clearly not designed to serve as academic writing assignments, the tasks might serve as exercises for practicing functions that could be part of more extensive academic tasks (e.g., spatial description, narration in the past, composing observations and requests).

Directions. Individually, in groups, or as a class, examine the sample writing tasks below by addressing the focus questions given. Next, select a prompt and revise it for a specific population of writers with which you are familiar. You may elect to rewrite the directions so that the task addresses a particular audience, genre, rhetorical design, or grammatical function. Finally, devise an in-class or out-of-class task of a similar nature that would be appropriate for your target group of ESL writers.

Focus Questions

1. For what population of writers would the task or prompt be most appropriate? Why?
2. What writing skills and strategies do you think the task or prompt targets?
3. Given the type of writers you have identified, assess the potential effectiveness of the task or prompt.

Tasks and Prompts

- Compose a brief e-mail message to a friend from whom you have not heard in several months. Give him or her an update on recent events and describe your daily routine of classes, work, study, exercise, and so on. Ask him or her about recent events in his or her life and request a reply.
- Write a handwritten or e-mail message to a professor requesting an appointment to discuss an assignment.
- Imagine that your housemate or spouse has displayed some unpleasant and messy habits lately, including leaving food and personal effects around your house. Draft a note explaining how you feel about this behavior and ask him or her to show more consideration.

Application Activity 4.4: Writing Assignment Critique

The sample writing assignments in this activity were drawn from a variety of authentic sources, some of which include high school, college, and university courses in disciplines other than English or ESL.

Directions. Individually or with a classmate examine the sample prompts and questions, identifying their flaws and weaknesses on the basis of the criteria presented in this chapter (especially Fig. 4.3). Decide which of the assignments you think could be salvaged after careful revision. Then rewrite two or more of the prompts so they conform to guidelines that you find acceptable.

1. Out-of-class essay assignment for an undergraduate freshman composition course:

   ```
   Critique the College's affirmative action
   policy.
   ```

2. Timed essay exam item for an undergraduate geology course:

   ```
   Describe tectonic plate movement. (Do not
   exceed 500 words.)
   ```

3. In-class paragraph topic for an intermediate-level IEP reading and writing course:

   ```
   Define friendship.
   ```

4. Overnight essay assignment for a university undergraduate course in comparative philosophy:

   ```
   Do you believe in fate or free will?
   Explain.
   ```

5. Take-home examination item for a community college U.S. history course:

   ```
   Using a contemporary federal political
   issue, demonstrate in one to two word-
   processed pages what aspects (if any) of
   the separation of powers doctrine should be
   changed.
   ```

6. Library research assignment for a history of science course at a liberal arts college:

   ```
   Write a five- to six-page biographical
   report on a 20th century chemist,
   physicist, or astronomer who has strongly
   influenced an applied science such as
   genetics, engineering, computer science,
   atmospheric science, and so forth. Use at
   least three separate sources. Be sure that
   your paper is adequately researched and
   well-written.
   ```

Application Activity 4.5: Constructing a Writing Assignment

Directions

1. Individually or with a partner, select a topic or content stimulus from each of the four ESL proficiency levels listed in this activity.
2. Compose a writing assignment or prompt centered on that topic or content stimulus. Please be specific about procedures, techniques, and apparatus (see Figs. 4.2–4.3).
3. Explain the functions and genre(s) that your task would help learners to explore and practice. Specify the goal(s) that your task would achieve.
   a. Low ESL proficiency topics/stimuli
      * Objects in the classroom
      * Numbers
      * Dates
      * Weather or seasons
      * Colors
      * Biographic data
      * Family relationships
   b. Low-intermediate ESL proficiency topics/stimuli
      * Class demographic information
      * Personal preferences (e.g., foods, films, fashion)
      * Health
      * Travel/transportation
      * Leisure activities
      * Career goals
      * Popular culture
      * Reasons for studying English
      * A strange or humorous event
   c. High-intermediate ESL proficiency topics/stimuli
      * An admired person/role model
      * Topics related to personal interests
      * Current events
      * A pivotal or momentous event
      * Reactions to an academic or nonacademic reading
   d. Advanced ESL proficiency topics/stimuli
      * Social problems
      * Position on a controversial issue
      * Comparison of opposing points of view

(Sources: Glenn et al., 2003; Omaggio Hadley, 2001; Tarvers, 1993)

NOTES

[1]Textbook reviews regularly appear in *College Composition and Communication,* the *Journal of English for Academic Purposes, English for Specific Purposes, Essential Teacher, Research in the Teaching of English,* and *TESOL Quarterly.* The journal *Writing Program Administration* annually publishes an annotated guide to recently published materials (mainly texts for NSs, but ESL and developmental titles are also now included). In addition to reading textbook evaluations in leading periodicals, teachers seeking course materials also can contact publishers directly to request catalogues and desk copies, which often are offered on a complimentary basis.

[2]Additional resources for designing writing assignments include Glenn et al. (2003); Gottschalk and Hjortshoj (2004); Hadfield and Hadfield (2000); Johns (1997); Jordan (1997); Lippman (2003); Weigle (2002); and White (1999).

[3]This list reflects neither a comprehensive bibliography nor an endorsement of any titles included therein.

APPENDIX 4: SAMPLE SUMMARY, PARAPHRASE, AND QUOTATION EXERCISE FOR AN ADVANCED EAP WRITING COURSE

Background: The following series of exercises is adapted for an advanced-level EAP writing course and keyed to the course's primary textbook. The sample materials and analysis tasks aim to help novice writers understand and distinguish the purposes of summary, paraphrase, and quotation. The worksheet requires students not only to analyze conventions, but also to practice incorporating these conventions into their own academic writing.

> *Summary, Paraphrase, and Quotation Worksheet:*
> *Using Sources and Avoiding Plagiarism*
> ENGL 0320 — English for Academic Purposes II

This worksheet supplements *Keys for Writers*, Sections 7c–8e and 51 (pp. 58–68; 332–336). Please consult these pages for explanations and examples.

SUMMARY

Directions: *Please review the following information individually or with a partner. Then complete the exercise at the end of the section.*

A **summary** is "a significantly shortened version of a passage, a section, or even a whole chapter or work that *captures main ideas in your own words*"(Lunsford, A., & Connors, R. [1992]. *The St. Martin's handbook* [2nd ed.]. New York: St. Martin's Press, p. 574).

Principal Features of a Summary

1. A summary should represent the original text in a balanced way. Summary writers sometimes devote more coverage to earlier parts of the main source, but this tendency should be avoided. A summary should represent a fair sampling of the information presented in the original.

2. A summary should characterize the original material neutrally (i.e., without critique or evaluation).
3. A summary should condense the original information and be cast in the summary writer's own words. Summaries that consist partly or largely of quotations rarely succeed.
4. A summary must acknowledge its original source.

Steps Toward Composing a Successful Summary

1. Read *Keys for Writers*, Section 7d (pp. 59–60).
2. Skim the original text. Make a note of headings and subheadings, if any. If there are no headings, divide the text into thematic sections. Examine the text and identify its purpose and audience. These techniques will help you focus on the most essential information.
3. As you reread the text more carefully, highlight important passages or take notes.
4. Paraphrase the main point of each of the sections you identified in step 1 (above). Draft a one-sentence summary of each section.
5. Write out the supporting points for the main topic or argument, but avoid including minor details.
6. Check that you have not copied more than three or four words from the original text.
7. Go through this process again to make appropriate changes.

Summary Language

Summaries may open with a sentence in the present tense that contains two elements: the source and the main idea. Here are some examples of how first sentences may begin:

a. In Anthony Tyson's article, "Mapping Dark Matter with Gravitational Lenses," ...
b. According to Yvonne Boskin's article, "Blue Whale Population May be Increasing off California," ...
c. In his book *Capital Idea*, Bernstein asserts that ...

Here are some introductory statements that students have written for a summary of a research article:

a. Author Steven Goodman in "Transformation of the Nile River Basin" states that the Nile Basin has changed as a result of continuous irrigation.

b. In "Transformation of the Nile River Basin," author Steven Goodman suggests that the Nile River basin has changed mainly as a result of continuous irrigation.

Although summaries usually are supposed to be "objective," summary writers may use a wide range of reporting verbs, some of which may convey evaluative meaning. That is, some reporting verbs are more objective than others, indirectly reflecting the summary writer's biases and personal opinions. Evaluative verbs should be used sparingly. The following list presents just a few examples of these useful verbs:

OBJECTIVE			EVALUATIVE	
argue	describe	maintain	allege	insist
assert	discuss	present	assume	presume
claim	examine	reveal	believe	suppose
conclude	explain	state	contend	
define	hold	suggest	imply	
demonstrate	indicate		insinuate	

Adapted from Swales, J., & Feak, C. (1994). *Academic writing for graduate students.* Ann Arbor: Univ. of Michigan Press.

Exercise

Read the following passage from a popular psychology textbook; then draft a one- to two-sentence summary. Use the suggestions in the preceding sections to select the most important information from the text and to develop an informative, accurate summary.

Intelligence has been defined in many different ways. Some have defined it as the sum total of everything you know; others have defined it as the ability to learn and profit from experience. Still others define it as the ability to solve problems. Of course, there is nothing wrong with any of these definitions of intelligence. The problem is that not one of them alone seems to say it all. We use the term *intelligence* so often as a general label for so many abilities, that it is now almost impossible to give it a specific definition. (Gerow, J. R. (1989). *Psychology: An introduction* (2nd. ed). New York: Scott, Foresman.)

PARAPHRASE

Directions: *Please review the following information individually or with a partner; then complete the exercise at the end of the section.*

A **paraphrase** "accurately states all the relevant information from a passage *in your own words and phrasing,* without any additional comments or elaborations" (Lunsford, A., & Connors, R. [1992]. *The St. Martin's handbook* [2nd ed.]. New York: St. Martin's Press, p. 570).

Principal Features of a Paraphrase

1. A paraphrase is most useful when the main points of the original passage (and their order of presentation) are important but are not worth quoting (see below).
2. Unlike a summary, a paraphrase restates all the main points of the original passage in the same order.
3. A paraphrase is often the same length as the original passage.
4. A successful paraphrase does not simply substitute synonyms from the original, nor does it imitate the author's writing style.
5. Paraphrases must acknowledge their original sources.

Steps Toward Composing a Successful Paraphrase

1. Read *Keys for Writers,* Section 7d–8c (pp. 59–64).
2. Skim the original text. Make a note of headings and subheadings, if any. Highlight main ideas, supporting evidence, and conclusions.
3. As you compose your paraphrase, try to capture the meaning of the entire passage. Avoid paraphrasing a word or a phrase at a time.
4. If you wish to include some of the author's words within the paraphrase, enclose them in quotation marks (see the final section on using quotations).
5. To ensure your originality, try to paraphrase without looking at the original.
6. Check to see that your paraphrase accurately presents the author's meaning *in your own words.*

Exercise 1

Examine the original text and the paraphrase that follows. Explain why the paraphrase is unacceptable.

ORIGINAL

Frida's outlook was vastly different from that of the surrealists. Her art was not the product of a disillusioned European culture searching for an escape from the limits of logic by plumbing the subconscious. Instead, her fantasy was a product of her temperament, life, and place; it was a way of coming to terms with reality, not of passing beyond reality into another realm. (Herrera, H. (1991). *Frida: A biography of Frida Kahlo.* New York : HarperCollins, p. 258)

PARAPHRASE

As Herrera explains, Frida's vision differed vastly from the surrealists' outlook, which grew out of a disillusioned European culture hoping to escape the confines of logic. Her fantasy was due to her own personality and life, including her Mexican roots, and she used it to come to terms with reality rather than to move beyond reality.

The paraphrase needs improvement because...

Exercise 2

Draft a paraphrase of the following passage from a university communications textbook.

Even small movements are extremely important in interpersonal relationships. We can often tell, for example, when two people genuinely like each other and when they are merely being polite. If we had to state how we know this, we would probably have considerable difficulty. These inferences, many of which are correct, are based primarily on these small nonverbal behaviors of the participants—the muscles around the eyes, the degree of eye contact, the way in which the individuals face each other, and so on. All nonverbal behavior, however small or transitory, is significant; all of it communicates.   (De Vito, J. A. [1989]. *The interpersonal communication book* [5th ed.]. New York: Harper-Collins.)

QUOTATION

Directions: *Review the following information individually or with a partner; then complete the exercise at the end of the section.*

A **quotation** "involves noting down a source's *exact words*" (Lunsford, A., & Connors, R. [1992]. *The St. Martin's handbook* [2nd ed.]. New York: St. Martin's Press, p. 570).

Features and Uses of Quotations

1. A quotation is an *exact duplication* of the original.
2. Quotations can be particularly helpful when you wish to demonstrate fairness. That is, when you need to criticize or argue against an author's ideas or findings, you allow the author to speak for him- or herself.
3. Quotations are most useful when the words of the original are particularly striking or attention-grabbing. A quotation from a respected authority also can lend credibility to your research.
4. Quotations should be used selectively and sparingly. Too many quotations in a text distract the reader and interrupt the flow of your own writing.
5. For the same reasons, quotations should not be too lengthy and should be integrated into your own text with appropriate transitions (see below).
   (Herrera, H. (1991). *Frida: A biography of Frida Kahlo.* New York: HarperCollins, p. 258)

Steps Toward Successful Integration of Quotations

1. Read *Keys for Writers,* Sections 7d–8e (pp. 59–68).
2. Skim the original text, noting passages that you find particularly clear, forceful, eloquent, succinct, or informative.
3. As you select quotations to include in your own writing, try to grasp the author's meaning so that you avoid quoting material out of context.
4. Copy quotations *carefully*, with punctuation, capitalization, and spelling as in the original.
5. Use brackets if you introduce words of your own or omit material (see *Keys for Writers for*, p. 65).

6. Enclose the quotation in quotation marks and include the appropriate parenthetical citation or footnote (see *Keys for Writers*, Sections 14–18).

7. Make sure you have a corresponding working bibliography entry with complete publication information.

Exercise 1

Examine the text below, which contains quoted material as well as paraphrased material. Explain why you think the writer, Ruth Conniff, chose to quote Kaus, another author.

Kaus . . . remind[s] me of nothing so much as [a] precocious sophomore, dominating the class discussion, eager to sound off about the lives and motivations of people [he has] never met. . . .

Kaus (1991) wants to create a massive "neo-WPA" program, with guaranteed jobs for everyone. But the jobs, he says, should be "authoritarian, even a little militaristic" (p. 167), and they should pay less than the minimum wage. The program would not raise anyone out of poverty, since there would be no opportunity for advancement within it. We can't have a class of workers dependent on the state for permanent employment, Kaus reasons. Instead, once people have gained work "skills" through his jobs program, Kaus says, the transition to a job in the private sector will "take care of itself" (p. 178). Never mind the recession, the thousands of former middle-class workers who are now out of work, or the fact that even in the best of times we do not have a full-employment economy. [Reproduced from Conniff, R. (1992). The culture of cruelty. *The Progressive*, September, p. 315. The Kaus work cited is from: Kaus, M. (1991). *Rethinking social policy: Race, poverty, and the underclass*. New York: Random House.]

This passage contains quoted material because. . .

Exercise 2

Compose at least two sentences that incorporate quoted material from the following sample passages. Try to use one or more of the suggested phrases.

The essential problem with this form of affirmative action is the way it leaps over the hard business of developing a formerly oppressed people to the point where they can achieve proportionate representation on their own (given equal opportunity) and goes straight for the proportionate representation. This may satisfy some whites of their innocence and some blacks of their power, but it does very little to truly uplift blacks. (Steele, S. (1990). *Content of our character: A new vision of race in America.* New York: St. Martin's Press.)

We have a qualified "yes" and a qualified "no" as answers to our questions about age and IQ so far. Probably the best answer is "It depends." Some studies of cognitive abilities seem to demonstrate that we should ask about specific intellectual skills, because they do not all decline at the same rate, and some do not decline at all. For example, tests of vocabulary often show no drop in scores with increasing age whatsoever, while tests of verbal fluency often show steep declines beginning at age 30. (Gerow, J. R. (1989). *Psychology: An introduction* (2nd ed.). New York: Scott, Foresman.)

Sample phrases for incorporating quoted material (also see *Keys for Writers*, Section 51, pp. 332–336)

- As XXX states/notes/observes/maintains/points out/holds/argues/reports, "..."
- XXX states/notes/observes/maintains/points out/holds/argues/reports that "..."
- According to XXX, "..."
- In XXX's view/opinion/model, "..."

Sentences incorporating quoted material...

Chapter 5

Teacher Response to Student Writing: Issues in Oral and Written Feedback

Questions for Reflection

- *From your own experiences as a student writer, what memories do you have of teacher responses to your texts?*
- *What types of feedback have you as a writer found most helpful? Most problematic?*
- *Do you feel that the types of responses that you have received would also be appropriate for ESL student writers? Why or why not?*
- *As you think about responding to student writing in your present or future teaching, what questions and concerns come to mind? What do you feel you need to know or do to be able to give your students effective feedback?*

PERSPECTIVES ON TEACHER RESPONSE

As discussed in chapter 1, approaches to teaching composition (whether to native speaker [NS] or ESL writers) have changed dramatically over the past quarter century. Despite all these changes, however, one element has remained constant: Both teachers and students feel that teacher feedback on student writing is a critical, nonnegotiable aspect of writing instruction. In most instances, teacher response represents the single largest investment of teacher time and energy, much more than time spent preparing for or conducting classroom sessions. Teacher feedback also provides the opportunity for instruction to be tailored to the needs of individual students through face-to-face dialogue in teacher–student writing conferences and through the draft–response–revision cycle, during which teachers assist students through their written commentary at various points.

Teachers' awareness of the time they spend responding to student writing and of the potential benefits of their commentary raises the stakes of this complex and challenging endeavor. Novice teachers can be paralyzed with anxiety over providing feedback to student writers, not knowing where to start or how to make comments that are clear and constructive without conveying messages that are too discouraging or directive. More experienced instructors can be overwhelmed by the time it takes to respond effectively to student writing and can find themselves wondering if, at the end of the day, their feedback is helpful and has really done their students any good. When we have made conference presentations or conducted workshops on this topic, one of the most frequently asked questions is, "I am drowning in the paper load. How can I make this go more quickly?"[1]

This chapter addresses the concerns of both novice teachers who may feel they do not know where to start and veteran teachers who would like to improve the effectiveness and the efficiency of their commentary. We first outline what L1 and L2 composition researchers have discovered about teacher feedback and then move to some principles and practical guidelines for optimal responding practices.

RESEARCH ON TEACHER FEEDBACK

Although researchers have examined error correction in ESL writing quite extensively (see chapter 7 and Ferris, 2002b, 2003b), surprisingly little research has investigated other sorts of teacher commentary in L2 writing. A number of articles suggest procedures and techniques for responding to ESL compositions, but most of these appear to be based largely on L1 research or on individual teachers' experience and intuitions. Many L1 studies suffer from serious methodological flaws and are not directly applicable to L2 writing instruction. Notably, in a mid-1990s collection of articles on second language writing (Leeds, 1996), the only article on teachers' written response to ESL writing was one published more than a decade earlier (Zamel, 1985). However, since the first edition of this book was published, the research base on this topic has grown steadily.

Empirical studies of teacher feedback have typically represented three major categories: (a) descriptive studies of what teachers actually do when responding to student writing, (b) research on the short- and long-term effects of teacher commentary, and (c) surveys of student opinions about and reactions to instructor feedback. Although the research base on these issues is far from comprehensive or even adequate, enough studies have been undertaken in both L1 and L2 composition settings to allow speculation based on patterns and trends that emerge from the literature to date.[2]

Descriptive Studies on the Nature of Teacher Feedback

In attempting to describe and categorize teacher commentary, researchers have looked at two major issues: what teacher feedback is focused on and how teacher comments are constructed. Early reviewers of L1 and L2 research on the nature of teacher feedback were sharply critical of instructors' responding behaviors, variably describing them as ineffective and as an "exercise in futility" (Knoblauch & Brannon, 1981, p. 1); as "arbitrary and idiosyncratic" if not mean-spirited (Sommers, 1982, p. 149); as overly directive, removing "students' rights to their own texts" (Brannon & Knoblauch, 1982; Connors & Lunsford, 1993; Sommers, 1982; Straub, 1996); and as consisting primarily of "short, careless, exhausted, or insensitive comments" (Connors & Lunsford, 1993, p. 215). Zamel (1985) noted that L2 research findings agreed with the major conclusions drawn concerning the response patterns of L1 writing teachers.

In considering such negative reports, however, we should recognize that most of them arose from earlier instructional paradigms in which instructors read only one draft of student papers. Their feedback was provided primarily to explain and justify a grade, perhaps including some general suggestions for the student writer to consider "next time." Recent L1 and L2 research, focused on process-oriented models of instruction, have yielded far more encouraging and informative results. As teachers have adopted a multiple-draft response-and-revision approach to composition instruction, they have begun to intervene at earlier stages of the process (e.g., as students generate preliminary drafts), and to provide commentary on a broader range of issues.

Whereas it is fairly straightforward to observe that teachers should and do provide feedback at various stages of the writing process (not just at the end) and about a range of issues (not just grammar), how such commentary is constructed poses a question of greater complexity and practical interest to most teachers. Text-analytic descriptions of teacher commentary, whether written or oral, have been rare in the literature, no doubt, because such investigations are labor-intensive. Nonetheless, several recent studies have provided a promising start to this research base, yielding valuable and replicable analytic models (Conrad & Goldstein, 1999; Ferris 1997, 2001a; Ferris, Pezone, Tade, & Tinti, 1997; Hyland & Hyland, 2002; Straub & Lunsford, 1995).

Effects of Teacher Commentary

Quantitative descriptions of teacher commentary are interesting and illustrative, yet perhaps the most pressing question for writing instructors is whether the feedback over which they labor so diligently actually helps their students' writing development. Studies that explicitly link teacher commentary to student revision have been scarce, indeed, and longitudinal research on student improvement as a result of teacher feedback has been virtually nonexistent. Part of the problem, perhaps, is that it can be difficult to trace the effects of specific teacher comments on revision, to measure "improvement," and to isolate the effects of teacher feedback from other aspects of the writing instruction, including composing practice, reading, and so on, that likely also affect literacy development.

That said, the few studies conducted along these lines have yielded results that are helpful in assessing the effectiveness of teacher commentary and certainly in identifying areas for future empirical investigations. One important and clear finding is that L2 student writers are very likely to incorporate teacher commentary into their subsequent revisions. For instance, Ferris (1997) found that 76% of a teacher's suggestions were observably incorporated into students' next-draft revisions. Such findings should be simultaneously heartening and sobering. On the one hand, it certainly is encouraging to find that the commentary on which we work so hard is taken seriously by our student writers. On the other, it is daunting to realize that, because our students likely will not ignore our comments, the burden is on us to make sure that our feedback is helpful, or at least does no harm!

Thus, assuming that students do indeed pay attention to teacher commentary and try to use it in revision, the next question is whether such teacher-influenced revisions actually are beneficial to the quality of student texts and to the students' development as writers over time. Again, evidence on this point is scarce, but in the few attempts to trace the influence of teacher commentary on student writing, it appears that whereas most changes made by students in response to teacher feedback have a positive impact on their revised texts, at least some teacher comments lead students to make changes that actually weaken their papers (Conrad & Goldstein, 1999; Ferris, 1997, 2001; Goldstein & Conrad, 1990; Hyland & Hyland, 2002; Patthey-Chavez & Ferris, 1997).

Student Views on Teacher Feedback

Studies on the nature of teacher feedback and its effects on student writers have been rare. Nonetheless, a more substantial body of work in both L1 and L2 composition examines student reactions to teacher response (Arndt, 1993; Brice, 1995; Cohen, 1987; Cohen & Cavalcanti, 1990; Enginarlar, 1993; Ferris, 1995b; Hedgcock & Lefkowitz, 1994, 1996; Radecki & Swales, 1988; Saito, 1994; Straub, 1997; see also Ferris, 2003b, chapter 5, for a review). Findings across these studies are surprisingly consistent and include the following insights:

1. Students greatly appreciate and value teacher feedback, considering teacher commentary extremely important and helpful to their writing development.
2. Students see value in teacher feedback on a variety of issues, not just language errors.[3]
3. Students are frustrated by teacher feedback when it is illegible, cryptic (e.g., consisting of symbols, circles, single-word questions, comments), or confusing

(e.g., consisting of questions that are unclear, suggestions that are difficult to incorporate into emergent drafts).
4. Students value a mix of encouragement and constructive criticism and are generally not offended or hurt by thoughtful suggestions for improvement.

Research on Teacher Commentary: Summary and Critique

Whereas research on teacher feedback still is in its preliminary stages (although certainly more evolved than when the first edition of this text was published!), we can offer the following suggestions based on the existing research findings:

- Feedback is most effective when provided at intermediate stages of the writing process.[4]
- Teachers should provide feedback on a range of writing issues (i.e., not just "language" or not just "ideas").
- Teachers should pay attention to the formal characteristics of their feedback (scope, pragmatic form, and so on) so that students can understand it and use it effectively.

Finally, we should add that contextual issues also need to be considered in evaluating the effectiveness of various feedback types (Conrad & Goldstein, 1999; Knoblauch & Brannon, 1981; Leki, 1990a; Reid, 1994). These issues include individual differences and predispositions (educational, cultural, and linguistic backgrounds; L2 writing proficiency levels; motivation for writing; see chapters 1 and 3); types of writing being considered (e.g., genres and text types, journal entries, speed-writes); and classroom context (class size, teacher–student rapport, instructional style); and other types of feedback provided (peer response, self-evaluation, and so forth). In other words, we cannot simply look at teachers' written comments or transcripts of their oral feedback as well as students' revisions and conclude that we know everything we need to know about a particular teacher, student, or class.

PRINCIPLES FOR PROVIDING WRITTEN FEEDBACK

Considering our own experiences with the feedback we have received on our own writing as well as feedback we have offered as teachers, together with what the literature suggests about teacher commentary in L2 writing, we present the following guiding principles (summarized in Fig. 5.1 and discussed briefly here) for approaching the delicate and arduous process of constructing written feedback for L2 student writers:

1. *The teacher is not the only respondent.* Depending on their ability and experience with writing, students also can benefit greatly from peer response and guided self-evaluation. Chapter 6 focuses extensively on peer response, touching briefly on self-evaluation. Many students will benefit further from working individually with private tutors in a campus writing center, or interacting with peers or experts in an online context (see chapter 9).

2. *Written commentary is not the only option.* For some writing issues and for some individual writers' temperaments and learning styles, in-person writing conferences may be a superior option to written commentary. We provide

Guiding Principles of Written Teacher Commentary	
1.	The teacher is not the only respondent.
2.	Written commentary is not the only option.
3.	Teachers do not need to respond to every single problem on every single student draft.
4.	Feedback should focus on the issues presented by an individual student and his or her paper, not on rigid prescriptions.
5.	Teachers should take care to avoid "appropriating," or taking over, a student's text. Final decisions about content or revisions should be left in the control of the writer.
6.	Teachers should provide both encouragement and constructive criticism through their feedback.
7.	Teachers should treat their students as individuals and consider their written feedback as part of an ongoing conversation between themselves and each student.

FIG. 5.1. Guiding principles.

guidelines for effective teacher–student conferences later in this chapter. Some teachers also use alternative delivery modes such as audiotaped feedback and commentary sent to students electronically.

3. *Teachers need not respond to every single problem on every single student draft.* Many instructors prefer to focus primarily or even exclusively on the development of student ideas in early drafts, saving language or editing issues for the penultimate draft. In any case, experienced teachers prioritize issues on individual student papers and selectively respond to the most important issues. Attempting to address all student problems on every paper can exhaust teachers and overwhelm students with commentary that, in some cases, may exceed the amount of text they themselves produced!

4. *Feedback should focus on the issues presented by an individual student and his or her paper, not on rigid prescriptions.* Many instructors have been taught that they should never mark errors on early drafts or address content issues on final drafts. However, if a student's initial version is solid in terms of idea development and organization yet replete with frequent and serious grammatical errors, it could be counterproductive to ignore these problems and struggle to find something "content-related" to say. Conversely, if a penultimate or final draft shows inadequate development or ineffective organization, it would not serve the student's needs simply to mark grammatical errors and ignore the major rhetorical issues.

5. *Teachers should take care to avoid "appropriating," or taking over, a student's text. Final decisions about content or revisions should be left in the control of the writer.* A great deal has been written about teacher "appropriation" of student writing, a serious concern. As Brannon and Knoblauch (1982) argued, if a student feels that his or her text belongs to the teacher rather than to him or herself, the student may lose the motivation to write and revise. Students may resent overly controlling teacher responses. With L2 writers, however, the more serious risk is that they will make every attempt to please the teacher. However, if the teacher has misunderstood the student's purposes, or if the student has misunderstood the teacher's chief message, the writer's rigor in trying to give the teacher exactly what he or she asked for may well lead to

an inferior revised product. All that said, in efforts to avoid such appropriative behavior (e.g., through questioning, indirectness, hedging) teachers also may fail to communicate suggestions and advice that student writers truly need.

6. *Teachers should provide both encouragement and constructive criticism through their feedback.* Most students recognize that teacher feedback is intended to help them and will not feel offended if we provide suggestions for improvement. However, it is human nature to desire and appreciate positive responses as well to the work we have done. Some teachers, reticent to discourage or offend students, may lavish praise through their written commentary while making few revision suggestions. Other teachers may be so dismayed at the problems they see that they jump right into extensive critiques without ever stopping to consider what the student writer might have done well. An important part of our job as L2 writing instructors is to build students' motivation, especially their confidence in expressing their ideas in English. Although it is not strictly necessary to strive for a 50/50 distribution of praise and criticism, teachers should recognize that both types of feedback are needed for the overall development of the writer and discipline themselves to provide written feedback at both ends of the spectrum on a regular basis.

7. *Teachers should treat their students as individuals, considering their written feedback as part of an ongoing conversation between themselves and each student writer.* Some authors urge teachers to provide "personalized" feedback, by writing summary endnotes like a letter, addressing the student by name and signing their own. Whereas providing personalized feedback is a good goal—and one that we strive toward—treating students as individuals additionally means following their development from draft to draft and assignment to assignment, pointing out persistent areas of weakness and encouraging them for the progress we observe. To accomplish all this, we will need to become acquainted with our students in class, during conferences, and through their writing (whether graded or not). We also must collect and read ongoing writing assignments (not just individual drafts) to trace and comment on student progress (or lack thereof, in some cases!).

GUIDELINES FOR WRITTEN TEACHER COMMENTARY

With some guiding principles in mind, we can turn to practical suggestions for constructing responses that are helpful, clear, personalized, and appropriately encouraging. This discussion is divided into three general "stages": approach (knowing what to look for and prioritization), response (providing the commentary itself), and follow-up (helping students maximize feedback and holding them accountable for considering it) (Fig. 5.2).

Approach

Preservice and novice teachers in our courses often articulate their greatest fear and struggle in responding to student papers as "Knowing where to start." Teachers may find themselves at one of two extremes: not knowing what to look for or how to analyze student work critically on the one hand, or being so overwhelmed

Suggestions for Teacher Commentary
1. Clarify your own principles and strategies for responding and share them with students.
2. Read through the entire paper before making any comments.
3. Use a scoring rubric, checklist, specific writing assignments, and prior in-class instruction to identify possible feedback points.
4. Select two to four high-priority feedback points for that particular student and writing task.
5. Compose a summary endnote that highlights both strengths and weaknesses of the paper.
6. Add marginal commentary that further illustrates the specific points raised in the endnote.
7. Check your comments to make certain that they are clear and effective; avoid jargon and questions.
8. Give students opportunities in class to pose questions about your feedback.
9. Ask students to write a cover memo that they submit with revisions, explaining how they have considered and addressed comments they received, or why they chose not to address them.

FIG. 5.2. Suggestions for teacher commentary.

with the amount and severity of students' writing problems that they are paralyzed with indecision about where to begin.

Instructors who are not sure what to look for can use institutional grading criteria to identify possible areas of weakness or student need (see chapter 8). A rubric or checklist that outlines the qualities of passing or excellent papers for that specific context can help us to articulate questions that we might ask ourselves as we read student papers. For example, one checklist includes the following point: "Opposing viewpoints have been considered and responded to clearly and effectively" (Ferris, 2003b, p. 135). Thus, a question that the teacher might consider while reading could be "Is this a one-sided argument, or have possible counterarguments been anticipated and addressed in the paper?"

A second lens through which teachers can look at student writing is the assignment or task type as well as the task's genre category (see chapters 4 and 8). For example, a prototypical freshman composition assignment requires writers to describe a personal experience and analyze its significance in their lives (Spack, 1990/1996). This assignment raises two possible heuristic questions that teachers could ask as they review student papers: (a) Has the experience or event been described clearly and effectively with adequate but not extraneous detail? and (b) Has the writer analyzed the importance of the experience and how it has shaped his or her life?

A third way in which teachers can approach written commentary is to consider specific issues that have been covered in the syllabus and to look carefully at student papers to see the extent to which they have grasped and applied those concepts to their writing. Class time may have been spent on writing effective introductory sections and using systematic connectors (transitional expressions, repetition, synonyms, pronouns, and so on) to achieve better textual cohesion and coherence. Instruction may have focused on using summary, paraphrase, and quotation to incorporate ideas from another author into one's text, shifting verb tense and aspect accurately in telling personal narratives, and so forth. Under such conditions, the teacher may wish to comment on those specific issues to remind the students of what they have studied and practiced in class.

Once an instructor has examined a writing sample and identified strengths, weaknesses, and "feedback points," he or she then needs to consider how to prioritize these features and select which ones to address in written commentary. As suggested by principle 3 earlier, it can be counterproductive for the teacher to comment on every possible problem that he or she sees. Although prioritization decisions are highly variable and by definition subjective, in selecting feedback points to address, teachers should take into consideration: the point in the term and what has been covered in class; where students are in the drafting and composing cycle (first draft, penultimate draft); the needs of individual student writers including issues that have been covered in prior feedback cycles, persistent problems, and encouraging signs of progress; and the teacher's own judgments concerning the relative urgency of the possible feedback points in a particular paper, which again can and should vary from student to student. Considering all of these concerns, we have found that two to four major feedback points usually is about optimal.

The final point about an instructor's "approach" to writing comments on student papers is that he or she should have a philosophy or theory of commentary, such as the "guiding principles" discussed in chapter 1, and a strategy for commentary, whether it be using a checklist, writing a letter, highlighting language errors, or a combination of these options. The teacher should strive to be consistent in adhering to his or her own philosophy and strategy. We also would recommend explaining our own approach to students: Doing so forces teachers to articulate their approaches and attempts to follow them!

Response

Having selected feedback points for response, the instructor next has specific practical choices to make in providing commentary.

The Mechanics of Feedback. As teachers have become more conscious of developing effective response procedures, a variety of techniques have been proposed for providing feedback to students. These techniques include audiotaped oral feedback (in contrast to written comments on papers), comments inserted into students' word-processing files, and comments sent via e-mail.

Clearly, all of these techniques have their advantages. In the case of audiotaped commentary, students are provided with listening comprehension practice. In addition, student writers who are more comfortable processing information via auditory modes may find such feedback more helpful than written commentary (Reid, 1993b). However, some students may find oral responses frustrating and confusing because of weak aural skills or a more visually oriented learning style. Teacher feedback provided via computer, whether via floppy disk or e-mail attachment, has the same visual advantages as handwritten commentary, with the added benefit that the teacher's handwriting will not interfere with students' mental processing of the written message (Ferris, 1995b). Further, feedback provided on the computer can encourage students to become comfortable with technology that can help them improve their writing (see chapter 9).

Although all these alternative response techniques have their appeal, convenience and the availability of technology may be the deciding issues for many classroom teachers. Some teachers find it easier to take a stack of papers with them wherever they go, working on them as they have time. Because of the time and space limitations associated with audiotape and computerized formats, many teachers may find these options to be practical for only a small proportion of their students' assignments. Teachers' decisions about whether to use these tools likely will rest on student preferences and learning styles (i.e., for oral vs. written feedback) and on teachers' preferences and needs.

The Tools of Handwritten Feedback. For the aforementioned reasons, a majority of teacher response is likely to be of the pen-and-paper variety. Even with this more traditional mode of response, teachers have several choices to make: Will they use pen or pencil—and what color pen? Will they use a separate response sheet or write directly on the student's paper? Will they use some sort of rubric, coding sheet, or checklist for responses, or will they provide only verbal comments? Again, research findings do not point to an advantage of a single method over another. Some practitioners insist that using a red pen seems punitive and can inhibit students or make them anxious. Others argue that the tone and substance of the response (and the relationship between teacher and student) is far more significant than the color of ink used (Hedgcock & Lefkowitz, 1994).

Regarding response sheets, rubrics, and checklists, it can be argued that such forms provide teachers and students with a consistent framework and terminology for providing and processing feedback. However, it also can be argued that response checklists can limit and inhibit teachers from providing personalized responses appropriate to the student and the assignment given. In Ferris et al. (1997), when a teacher switched from writing endnotes directly on the student paper to using a response form, she produced significantly fewer (and shorter) comments (although not necessarily less effective ones). Perhaps more important, if students do not understand the checklist or rubric, the forms can actually be distracting and counterproductive.

Beyond the mechanics of feedback, a number of other practical questions should be considered.

Preliminary Drafts or Final Drafts? Most scholars agree that teacher feedback is most effective and most likely to be used when it is provided on preliminary drafts that will be revised subsequently (Ferris, 1995b; Krashen, 1984; Zamel, 1985). However, does this precept mean that feedback on a final draft is wasted energy? Perhaps not, but the process probably could be handled differently. Whereas feedback on earlier drafts is formative, helping students to see where their developing text can be improved, final-draft feedback tends to be evaluative and summative, informing students about what they did well, explaining the basis for a grade or a score (if one is given), and perhaps offering general suggestions for consideration in subsequent assignments (e.g., "Great job adding more support for your arguments in your body paragraphs! The conclusion is still underdeveloped, and you need to stay aware of the errors you make in article usage. Let's see if we can work on those things on the next paper").

In one study that asked students about the degree to which they read and paid attention to teacher comments on first drafts versus final drafts, the students clearly indicated that they valued feedback at both stages of the process (Ferris, 1995b). Finally, with many instructors using a portfolio approach to assess student writing (see chapter 8), even "final draft feedback" may not truly be final if the student chooses to revise that paper further. Therefore, it can be worth the instructor's effort to let the writer know where the paper stands and what still could be done to improve its quality.

Endnotes or marginal comments? Arguments can be made on both sides of this issue. Endnotes enable the teacher to summarize his or her reactions to the entire paper. Also, because endnotes are not subject to the space limitations of marginal notes, they can be longer, clearer, less cryptic, and easier to read. Marginal comments, on the other hand, offer immediacy in that they are clearly keyed by proximity to specific ideas in the text. Moreover, marginal notes communicate to the writer the sense of an involved, interested reader engaged in a dialogue with the creator of the text.

We have found that the ideal solution is a combination of both marginal and endnotes. We recommend that instructors, after reading through a student text carefully and selecting feedback points as described earlier, next construct a summary endnote, perhaps in the form of a personal letter to the student (Fig. 5.3). Teachers then can go back through the text making marginal comments that highlight or illustrate the points raised in the endnote, offering praise and other "interested reader" comments. However, if time is short, we recommend privileging the summary endnote over the marginal comments, simply because it provides a comprehensive overview of the paper that tends to be clearer and easier to read.

Praise or Criticism? As noted previously, solid arguments can be posited for incorporating both comments of encouragement and suggestions or constructive criticism into our written commentary. Many teachers like to use the "sandwich" approach to writing endnotes: beginning and ending the note

---

Julia,

You did a nice job with this essay. I liked your examples about listening to music and observing nature. You did a great job of discussing Sarton's essay, too.

A couple of suggestions for your next draft:

1. The paragraph about "sightseeing" is shorter than the other body paragraphs. You might try developing it more fully by including summary and quotation from Sarton's essay that might support or frame your personal experience.
2. The paragraph about "College" needs to be more closely connected with the rest of the essay, maybe by specifically mentioning Sarton's essay, and how Yezierska's experience shows "The Rewards of Living a Solitary Life."
3. There are a lot of language errors, too. I've highlighted them for you. Be sure to edit carefully!

Good work! I'll look forward to seeing your next draft!

Best wishes,

Dr. Ferris

FIG. 5.3.   Sample summary endnote (letter) to student.

with encouraging remarks (the "bread") and making the two to four feedback points or suggestions in the middle (the "filling"). Figure. 5.3 illustrates this style of commentary. Most instructors also like to write positive comments in the margins of student texts to communicate that they are interested, engaged readers.

Questions or Statements? The literature reflects some debate about the formal characteristics of teacher commentary and even about whether such considerations are important (Conrad & Goldstein, 1999). Following strongly worded cautions in the L1 response literature about the danger of appropriating student texts through overly directive teacher commentary (Brannon & Knoblauch, 1982; Sommers, 1982; Sperling & Freedman, 1987), both L1 and L2 composition professionals have, since the 1980s, been explicitly trained to use questions rather than imperatives or statements in responding to student writers, both to encourage students to think more clearly and critically about their ideas (or, as Sommers [1982] put it, "forcing students back into the chaos" [p. 154]) and to communicate through the form of their comments that authority and ownership of the paper still belong to the student writer.

For some ESL writers, particularly those educated in their home countries, teacher questions can cause both pragmatic and cultural confusion. Whereas NS writers can easily recognize an indirect comment such as "Can you give an example here?" as a politely phrased teacher request rather than a "real" question (akin to "Can you shut the door?"), students less experienced with English pragmatic phenomena or North American teachers' desire to assume a nonappropriative stance may either misinterpret the question as a real yes/no question (possibly answering "no"!) or wonder if the teacher's wishy-washiness is a sign of incompetence or insecurity. The writer may consequently ignore feedback from a teacher for whom they have lost respect. This unfortunate outcome could, in turn, lead to frustration when the teacher receives a revised assignment in which it appears that the student completely ignored a clear, reasonable suggestion.

We are not suggesting by this discussion that instructors should abandon questioning as a commenting strategy. On the contrary, we use questions consistently in feedback on our own students' writing. However, we believe that writing teachers should perhaps reexamine their questioning techniques. First, they should not assume that questions are the only or always the best approach for all types of feedback. When writing comments in the form of questions, teachers might ask themselves three questions: (a) If the student answers this question, will it really improve the effectiveness of the paper? (b) Will the student be able to understand this question's intent and form? (c) On a rhetorical level, will the student know how to incorporate the answer to this question into his or her evolving draft? One practical approach to this final issue is to pair questions with statements explicitly suggesting revision, but perhaps hedging the suggestion ("Maybe you could...").

Content or Form?   Another area of disagreement in the literature concerns whether L2 writing teachers should avoid mixing commentary on students' ideas and content with feedback on their errors or the linguistic form of their texts. As we have already discussed, it is neither necessary nor desirable for a teacher to respond to every problem on every draft of a student essay. Chapter 7 discusses in detail how teachers might approach the challenging task of error correction and how they might effectively combine feedback on form with explicit grammar instruction and strategy training to build independent self-editing skills.

Although the chapter division in this volume explicitly separates the issues of responding to student content and responding to lexical and syntactic problems (as does most research), it is important to note that the oft-cited dichotomy between content and form is largely artificial. For instance, consistent errors in verb tense and aspect inflection (form) can cause confusion for the reader about the time frame or immediacy of the action (content). Inaccurate lexical choices (form) can cause major problems in the overall comprehensibility of a text, causing the reader to be unsure of what the writer intended to express (content). Nonetheless, because teachers' strategies for detecting and marking lexical and syntactic errors tend to be different from their strategies for responding to content issues, the techniques that can be used warrant a separate discussion.

It is also important to acknowledge that in the available L2 research to date, no empirical evidence suggests that L2 writers will ignore teacher feedback on content if errors are also addressed in the same draft of an assignment, or that they cannot simultaneously make successful revisions in both content and formal accuracy. On the contrary, we can cite evidence that student writers who received feedback on both content and form improved in both areas during revision (Ashwell, 2000; Fathman & Whalley,

1990; Ferris, 1997). In any case, the principle of personalized or in-dividualized feedback (Fig. 5.1, principle 7) should guide teach-ers here: Teachers should give each student what he or she most needs on a particular assignment at a specific point in time, rather than follow prescriptions such as "Never mix feedback on con-tent with feedback on form."

Follow-Up

An aspect of the response cycle that teachers may neglect to incor-porate is follow-up. That is, we should ensure that students un-derstand the feedback we have given them, helping students with revision strategies after receiving feedback and holding students accountable through the writing process and marking scheme. These strategies and tools should explicitly guide students in reading and understanding the feedback they have been given (see chapter 6 for further discussion of techniques for holding stu-dents accountable for peer response). Regrettably, teachers often simply return marked papers to students at the end of class or via e-mail, saying "The next draft is due 1 week from today." This lack of attention to follow-up is unfortunate because it fails to recognize that students may not understand the comments we have made despite our best attempts to be clear, that students may not know how to revise skillfully even if they understand our feedback, and that students may not be highly motivated to exert themselves during revision, preferring instead to make minor microlevel changes that can be done at the computer in a matter of minutes.

The first step in ensuring that students understand our written feedback is, of course, to do a careful job of constructing it. If we are so hasty, careless, or exhausted that students cannot under-stand what we are trying to tell them, we might as well not bother responding at all. It should be obvious that feedback that is in-comprehensible to students cannot help them. Nonetheless, even when we are careful and systematic, all human communication can and does misfire at times, particularly when participants in the exchange include novice writers composing in their second language. We should also make the humbling observation that writing teachers, no matter how experienced, can misunderstand their students' intentions and purposes. Consequently, they may write comments that are off the point, inaccurate, or unhelpful. With these inevitable communication pitfalls in mind, we should allow students time in class to read over our feedback and to ask questions about it immediately, or we should ask them to write a one- to two-paragraph response to our feedback articulating what they think the main points of our feedback might be.

Students should also receive explicit classroom instruction on revision strategies, both in general and specifically on how to take suggestions from an expert or peer reader and to use them to make effective changes in their evolving texts. At the same time, writers should be assured that they are the authors of their work, and that the final decisions about revisions should remain in their hands. In other words, they should be given explicit permission to disregard suggestions that they find unhelpful or with which they disagree.

We recommend several ways to hold students accountable for taking feedback seriously. One method requires that students include with revisions a cover memo explaining how they have or have not incorporated their teacher's suggestions and why. Another requires students to turn in folders or miniportfolios of ongoing writing projects so that teachers can compare earlier drafts with later drafts (and be reminded of their own previous suggestions). Teachers can choose to make comments about the quality and effort demonstrated in student revisions or actually make such good-faith effort part of the course grading scheme.

Written Commentary: Summary

Research on written teacher commentary has helped us identify issues to consider and possible strategies for providing feedback that is transparent, helpful, encouraging, and constructive. To summarize, insights from research and practice include the following:

- Teachers should identify and articulate—to themselves and to their students—their purposes for and philosophies (or theories) of response to student writing.
- Teachers can use different sources of information (course grading rubric, assignment specifications, prior classroom instruction, individual student needs) to examine student writing and then select and prioritize feedback points about which to write comments.

- The ideal approach to commentary involves a thoughtful mix of a summary endnote and marginal comments. However, if teachers have time for only one mode of response, they should opt for endnotes.
- Feedback should optimally include a fair balance of praise and constructive criticism.
- Especially for L2 writers, teachers should consider the formal characteristics of their comments (questions, jargon, and so forth) to ensure that their comments are clear and comprehensible.
- Teachers may wish to prioritize comments about content over feedback concerning language errors on different drafts of student papers, or they may choose to provide a combination of both feedback types on all drafts.
- Teachers should also be intentional in making sure that students understand their feedback and that they use it effectively in revision and future writing tasks.

TEACHER–STUDENT WRITING CONFERENCES

Another important means of giving feedback and instruction to writing students is through one-to-one writing conferences. Over the past several decades, the writing conference has achieved widespread popularity as a teaching tool for several reasons. One concerns the perception that writing conferences save teachers time and energy that would otherwise be spent marking student papers. Another is the immediacy and potential for interaction and negotiation that the conferencing event offers, allowing for on-the-spot clarification of difficult issues (Conrad & Goldstein, 1999) and helping teachers to avoid appropriating student texts (Brannon & Knoblauch, 1982; Sommers, 1982; Zamel, 1985). Finally, with the consideration given in recent years to students' learning styles (Reid, 1995b; see chapter 1), it is argued that writing conferences offer a more effective means for communicating with students who are auditory rather than visual learners. Some writing instructors feel so strongly about the value of writing conferences that they have suggested doing away with all other forms of in-class instruction to make time for them (Carnicelli, 1980; Garrison, 1974).

Research on Teacher–Student Writing Conferences: Empirical Trends

A number of researchers have described various aspects of conferencing, including attitudes toward and advantages of teacher–student writing conferences, the discourse of writing conferences, the outcomes and effects of the conferences, and the differing roles and behaviors of teachers and students during conferences. Early researchers (Arndt, 1993; Carnicelli, 1980; Sokmen, 1988; Zamel, 1985) examined students' or teachers' attitudes toward conferencing, concluding with strong endorsements of writing conferences as pedagogical tools because students can ask for on-the-spot clarification, and because "dynamic interchange and negotiation" can take place (Zamel, 1985, p. 97). Arndt (1993) also found that students wanted both written comments and conferences, whereas their teachers preferred conferences.

Conferencing Techniques: Suggestions and Criticisms

Early process-oriented concerns, particularly the desire to avoid appropriating students' texts or dictating the terms of the revisions, led to specific suggestions and guidelines for conducting teacher–student writing conferences. For instance, Murray (1985) encouraged teachers to allow students to take the lead in conferences by eliciting student writers' responses to their own writing before offering any feedback or evaluation, a procedure characterized by Newkirk (1995) as indirect. Similarly, Harris (1986) presented a list of nondirective strategies to guide teachers in their one-to-one interactions with students.

However, some composition theorists have expressed concern that in empowering students to retain ownership of their writing, we force them into roles for which they are not prepared and with which they are not comfortable (Arndt, 1993; Bartholomae & Petrosky, 1986; Delpit, 1988; Newkirk, 1995; Silva, 1997). In ESL writing research, scholars have argued that nondirective approaches to teaching and responding to student writing leave L2 writers ill-prepared to deal with the demands for either linguistic accuracy or the literate and critical skills expected by subject matter faculty in the disciplines (Eskey, 1983; Ferris, 1995b, 1997; Horowitz, 1986c; Johns, 1995a).

Most previous research on response to ESL student writing has examined teachers' written feedback, but it is safe to assume that some students may have problems adequately comprehending oral feedback, even though the conference format allows them increased opportunities to request clarification. Goldstein and Conrad (1990) pointed out that "ESL students bring with them diverse cultures and languages that potentially affect how students conference [and] how their teachers respond to them" (p. 459). For instance, some students may have strong inhibitions against questioning or challenging a teacher in any situation, especially a one-to-one conference. Meanwhile, others may feel that teachers' comments or corrections are to be incorporated verbatim into their texts because of instructors' presumed superior knowledge and authority. Arndt (1993), who compared teachers' and English as a foreign language (EFL) students' reactions to written commentary and conferences, noted that the potential for miscommunication existed in both modes, and that not all students were naturals at "the art of conferencing" (p. 100).

Implementing Writing Conferences: Issues and Options

If a teacher wishes to incorporate writing conferences into a composition or literacy course, several practical issues are worth considering. The first is whether to provide feedback to all students in this manner. Some students would no doubt enjoy the opportunity to discuss their writing in person with their teacher, both to get individual attention and to clear up any problems. Meanwhile, others might prefer written feedback because they find one-to-one discussions with their instructor intimidating, because they prefer seeing feedback in writing, or because they might forget what they have discussed with the teacher during the conference.

Several options are available for addressing these challenges. A teacher can ask students at the beginning of the term whether they prefer written or oral feedback or some combination of both (e.g., in a needs assessment; see chapter 3). For students who are unsure, the teacher can provide written feedback on one assignment and oral feedback on the next. For students who feel nervous about conference dynamics, ideas to relieve their anxieties include conferencing with pairs of students (also adding a peer feedback dynamic to the mix) and allowing students to audiotape or take notes during the conference.

Logistics: When, Where, and How Often?

Along with the question of whom to involve in conferences, a teacher must decide when, where, and how often to hold such conferences. Options range from holding conferences every week or at every class session (the "Garrison Method," in which students write during class and come up to the teacher's desk for a conference whenever they feel the need) to holding them at regular intervals (e.g., seeing each student during office hours on a 3- to 4-week rotation) to requiring students to come in at least once during class sessions for a conference to making conferences completely optional and holding them only at the student's request.

Decisions about frequency and time frames depend on logistical constraints such as scheduling and office space. If a teacher has an office and holds regular office hours, scheduled office time can be the best way to hold conferences. Some instructors occasionally cancel classes to hold conferences with hard-to-schedule students. However, many part-time ESL literacy instructors have neither an office nor office hours. If teachers in this situation wish to hold one-to-one conferences, they most likely have to do so during class time, a situation that requires careful planning because the other students need to be productively engaged while the teacher holds individual discussions. Alternatively, as discussed in chapter 9, the computer writing lab can be an ideal setting for one-to-one teacher–student interaction because students work at individual terminals, and the teacher can move around the room to hold brief conferences as the need arises and inclination leads.

What Topics Should Conferences Cover?

Once the teacher has overcome the logistical obstacles, it is important to prepare and plan for conferences. What to discuss during conferences will vary according to the context of the conference. For instance, if the conference is student-initiated, the student may well have a particular question to discuss or problem to resolve. If the teacher has scheduled a conference, the options for topics to discuss range from a holistic reaction to the student's latest draft to a specific discussion of a particular writing problem or a teaching point covered in class. If the teacher has an opportunity to prepare ahead of time for a conference, he or she might make notes on particular issues that have arisen during class or that he or she has noted in previous papers. Alternatively, if discussing a particular assignment, the teacher may want to read through the text and make a few notes or check marks in the margins as reminders of items to discuss.

How Should Conference Dynamics Be Shaped?

Another pedagogical issue concerns the dynamics of teacher–student writing conferences, specifically, the relative proportion of talk by teacher and student as well as instructor directiveness (or lack thereof). Studies focusing on this issue have suggested that teacher–student conferences are most successful (with "success" not always operationally defined) when the writer makes a significant contribution to the conference, meaning that he or she participates fully in the discussion instead of sitting passively as the teacher dispenses criticism and advice. Moreover, researchers have suggested that when teachers avoid being overly directive in the conference setting, students can participate more fully, negotiate meaning more effectively, and ultimately produce texts that result from their own thought processes (presumably influenced by the teacher's input) rather than from verbatim reflections of the teacher's oral feedback. Specific ways to encourage students to participate and avoid being overly directive include asking questions (e.g., "What do you think about this paper?" and "Can you explain in another way what you were trying to say here?"), actively eliciting student participation ("Do you have any questions or issues to bring up?"), and allowing occasional silences so the student can formulate and articulate his or her thoughts.

SUMMARY

In L1 and L2 studies of teachers' feedback on student writing, a range of theoretical and practical questions have been examined:

- At what point or points in the writing process should a teacher intervene (if at all)?
- What are the differences between appropriation and intervention in responding to student writing?

- Should feedback related to content and organization be given separately from comments and corrections on form (grammar, spelling, punctuation, and so on)?
- To what extent is written or oral feedback more effective in a given context?
- How should teachers identify, select, and prioritize feedback points for their commentary?
- What is the appropriate balance between praise and constructive criticism?
- Are marginal comments more helpful than end comments, or are both necessary?
- How can teachers write clear, helpful comments and conduct effective conferences?
- What problems do ESL students experience in understanding teacher feedback, and how should teachers endeavor to mitigate these problems?

Teacher response to student writing is important at all levels and in all instructional contexts. However, responding effectively to student writing is a skill that can elude even experienced teachers. Like any other form of interpersonal communication, teachers' written responses to their students' writing vary considerably according to the needs, personalities, and abilities of the participants (i.e., the teacher and student) and according to the context (i.e., the course, institutional goals, constraints of the particular assignment, point in the course at which the feedback is being given, and so forth). Because of this variation, we must understand the underlying issues and considerations that constrain our responses. Providing written feedback on student writing is a skill that can improve with practice and reflection. To gauge our effectiveness, of course, we must rely on information from our students and on continuous assessment of ultimate outcomes.

REFLECTION AND REVIEW

1. If you were planning a composition course syllabus, what are some of the options that you might consider about when and how students should receive feedback? How might

you balance some of these alternatives over the course of a quarter- or semester-long course?

2. What aspects of teacher feedback might be unique to (or at least more pronounced for) L2 writers? How might you adapt your feedback strategies between a mainstream (L1) composition course and an ESL course—or a course that serves both L1 and L2 student writers?

3. To what extent is the issue of teacher appropriation of student writing a serious one for the teaching of ESL writing? Why do you think so?

4. What are your evolving views on the question of whether to separate content-focused feedback and form-focused feedback or not?

5. What are the advantages of using a rubric or checklist as part of your system for giving feedback to your students? Are there any potential drawbacks or dangers in doing so, and what might be some ways to mitigate these risks?

6. What are the advantages of written commentary over one-on-one conferences? At this stage in your teaching career, do you have a preference or a mode that you prefer? Why?

Application Activity 5.1: Analyzing a Rubric and Creating a Checklist

Directions. Appendix 5A presents a holistic scoring rubric and an essay feedback checklist that was derived from it. Examine the content and the format of the checklist, looking for explicit connections between it and the rubric. Then, using the paragraph rubric in Fig. 8.1, or other rubrics you might have available to you, design a checklist that you might use for identifying feedback points in a student writing sample as you give commentary.

Application Activity 5.2: Examining a Student Paper, Selecting Feedback Points, and Constructing An Endnote

Directions. A student first draft appears in Appendix 5B. Read the writing sample carefully. Using the rubric and checklist in Appendix 5A and the assignment prompt as a starting point, identify one to two strengths and two to four feedback points (suggestions or constructive criticisms to facilitate revision). Then, following the example shown in Fig. 5.2, write a summary endnote to the student.

Application Activity 5.3: Constructing Commentary

Directions. Appendix 5C presents one student paper with teacher commentary, followed by three unmarked student papers. Read the samples carefully, and then construct commentary for each of the three unmarked papers using a combination of marginal comments and endnotes. (You may wish to make extra "scratch" copies of the papers.) Compose an analysis of your experience, considering the following questions:

- What principles guided you as you read and responded to the student papers?
- What practical decisions did you make (use of checklist, questions, comments about language errors, and so forth) and why?
- What struggles, if any, did you have in responding to the student papers?
- What questions or concerns do you have about responding effectively to student writing in the future?

NOTES

[1] One of the authors (Ferris) was recently asked to give a workshop on the assigned topic of "Giving Meaningful Feedback Without Increasing Teacher Workload." In a nutshell, this title expresses the desire of most writing teachers: They truly want to help their students improve through their feedback, but they do not want to become "composition slaves" (Hairston, 1986).

[2] For a detailed review and critique of this body of studies, see Ferris (2003b), especially Chapter 2.

[3] However, in all cases, students reported that they see language-related feedback as critical, in addition to comments on other aspects of their writing. See chapter 7 for more discussion of this point. Also see Ferris (2003b, Chapter 5) for a more in-depth review of this student survey research.

[4] One could argue, however, for also providing summative feedback on a final draft if such feedback is intended to help the writer reflect on lessons learned that can be applied to future writing projects.

APPENDIX 5A: COURSE RUBRIC AND ESSAY CHECKLIST

SCORES	CHARACTERISTICS OF PAPER RECEIVING THIS SCORE
6	**Demonstrates clear competence in development, organization and sentence structure.**

- clearly addresses assignment with thoughtful thesis
- is well organized and developed, using appropriate and effective details and analysis to support the thesis
- demonstrates thorough understanding of the issues presented in the reading; documents sources of ideas and quotations
- consistently uses language well: varied sentences and precise word choice
- grammatical errors are rare and do not interfere with effectiveness of paper

5	**Demonstrates competence in development, organization, and sentence structure, but will have errors.**

- addresses assignment with clear thesis
- is generally well organized and developed, using effective details and analysis to support thesis
- demonstrates competent understanding of the issues presented in the reading; documents sources of ideas and quotations
- generally uses language well: varied sentences and clear and appropriate word choice
- grammatical errors may occur throughout but are not serious and do not interfere with understanding

4	**Demonstrates minimal competence in development, organization, and sentence structure, but will probably have weaknesses in one or more areas.**

- addresses assignment adequately with thesis, though it may be imprecisely worded or insufficiently focused

(Continued)

SCORES	CHARACTERISTICS OF PAPER RECEIVING THIS SCORE

- is adequately organized and developed using details and analysis, though development may be thin at times
- demonstrates adequate understanding of the issues presented in the reading; documents sources of ideas or quotations
- uses language adequately: reasonable command of sentence structure and word choice
- may contain varied grammatical errors, but not to the point of interfering with understanding

3   **Demonstrates developing competence in writing, but remains flawed in development, organization, or language.**

- may not respond adequately to the topic or be sufficiently focused
- may not be adequately organized or developed, be illogical, or have insufficient or inappropriate support for thesis
- may demonstrate lack of understanding of the issues presented in the reading; may fail to document sources of ideas or quotations
- may have an accumulation of errors in sentence structure and word choice and form, may have an accumulation of grammatical errors; errors may interfere with understanding.

2   **Demonstrates serious problems in writing.**

- does not deal adequately with topic; may be off the point, unclear, or poorly focused
- may have serious problems with organization and development, use little or no detail, or have irrelevant specifics or unsupported generalizations
- may demonstrate serious misunderstanding of the issues presented in reading; may fail to document sources of ideas or quotations
- may have serious and frequent errors in sentence structure and word choice and form
- may have an accumulation of serious grammatical errors that interfere with understanding

(Continued)

SCORES	CHARACTERISTICS OF PAPER RECEIVING THIS SCORE

1   **Demonstrates incompetence in writing.**

- may be unfocused, confusing, or incoherent or completely misunderstand the issues presented in the reading
- may be severely underdeveloped
- may contain severe and persistent errors that interfere with understanding

Source: California State University, Sacramento, Dept. of English: Course Grading Rubric for English 109E: Writing for Proficiency. See also Ferris, 2001b.

Sample Essay Feedback Checklist

I. Response to Prompt/Assignment
____ The paper responds clearly and completely to the specific instructions in the prompt or assignment.
____ The essay stays clearly focused on the topic throughout.

II. Content (Ideas)
____ The essay has a clear main idea or thesis.
____ The thesis is well supported with several major points or arguments.
____ The supporting points are developed with ideas from the readings, facts, or other examples from the writer's own experiences or observations.
____ The arguments or examples are clear and logical.
____ Opposing viewpoints have been considered and responded to clearly and effectively.

III. Use of Readings
____ The writer has incorporated other texts into his/her essay.
____ The ideas in the readings have been reported accurately.
____ The writer has used summary, paraphrase, and quotations from the readings to strengthen his/her paper.

(Continued)

_____ The writer has mastered the mechanics of incorporating ideas from other texts, including accurate use of quotation marks and other punctuation, accurate verb tenses, appropriate identification of the author and title, and effective integration of quotations into the writer's own text.

IV. Organization

_____ There is a clear beginning (introduction), middle (body), and end (conclusion) to the essay.

_____ The beginning introduces the topic and clearly expresses the main idea.

_____ The body paragraphs include topic sentences that are directly tied to the main idea (thesis).

_____ Each body paragraph is well organized and includes a topic sentence, supporting details, and a summary of the ideas.

_____ Coherence devices (transitions, repetition, synonyms, pronoun reference, etc.) are used effectively within and between paragraphs.

_____ The conclusion ties the ideas in the body back to the thesis and summarizes why the issue is interesting or important.

V. Language & Mechanics

_____ The paper is spell-checked (typed essays only).

_____ The paper is proof-read and does not have serious and frequent errors in grammar, spelling, typing, or punctuation.

_____ The paper is double-spaced and has appropriate margins all around.

_____ The paper is legible (handwritten papers).

ADDITIONAL COMMENTS:

Source: Ferris (2003, FIG. 6.3, p. 120).

APPENDIX 5B: SAMPLE STUDENT PAPER

> ### *Assignment: Relating a Reading to Personal Experience*
>
> For your essay assignment, you will *compare and contrast the ideas in one (or more) of the readings in your textbook with your own ideas or experiences.*
>
> To do this, you will need to BOTH clearly summarize what the author(s) say in their text(s) AND clearly describe your own personal experience, explaining how it is similar to or different from what the author(s) discuss(es).

My Adaptation to a New Culture

My thoughts, feelings, and attitudes had adjusted to the United States culture. It was difficult at the very beginning when I first stepped foot in the United States. I expected to meet many new friends, but I also ran into some difficulties which made me realized that there were some barriers I need to adjust. These barriers, discussed in LaRay M. Barna's essay, "Intercultural Communication Stumbling Blocks," are experiences related to me which I will share.

One of the Vietnamese student mentioned in Barna's essay that Americans are superficial and they smile and talk too much. Not only do they smile and talk too much, they also express their feelings emotionally. Truly, I observed and experienced how one American overly express her feelings and emotions toward one simple, ordinary conversation. I did not know what triggered her to express so emotionally, but I did not want to be rude by just staring at her with my mouth open, so I respond by smiling.

There are many more barriers to face when adapting to a new culture. For instance, according to Barna's essay, "the lack of comprehension of obvious nonverbal signs and symbols such as gestures, postures, and vocalizations" (Paragraph 2) are even more difficult to comprehend than facing the questionable feelings why Americans laugh so emotionally and why some treat others so friendly. A thumb sticking up could mean "alright" or "way to go," but what does a toss of a hair mean? I constantly watched one of my American classmate toss her hair back every time she walked by me. I didn't understand what it meant, but one of my

American friends told me that a toss of a hair back means a sign of jealousy and hatred. Could it be that once I accidently placed my legs out too far from under the table, and she tripped over it? Since then, I still didn't understand why she felt that way and I didn't ask.

Another barrier Barna had mentioned is language. The American slangs and dialects that cause difficulty for international students to relate with American students. International students like to stick together because they could communicate with one another better. If an American student use slang words like "word up" or "chill" in their conversations with a foreigner, that could end up with misscommunication or no communication at all. I agree with Barna in his essay when he mentioned that English is impossible to cope with and that's why some foreign students waved it aside. That's how I coped with English when I first arrived to the United States. I didn't understand the American's dialect and slangs and I try possibly to avoid the

Adapting to a new culture is a new experience. We do not have to act or be like the Americans, but to adjust and be familiar with the culture. I agree with Barna in his essay that "each person's culture, his own way of life, always seems right, proper, and natural." (Paragraph 13) We can stick with our own believes, values, and traditions. We can also stick to the new culture's. What I belive is when we adapt to a new culture, we are not losing our own culture, but we are gaining new experiences and other people's way of living. When I lived here in the United States, I've learned a lot. I've adapted to their culture and I met many new friends. I will still be adapting to the culture because there will always be something new.

APPENDIX 5C: SAMPLE STUDENT ESSAYS AND TEACHER COMMENTARY

Note: The four papers following were written for a university ESL writing course titled "Writing for Proficiency" (see Ferris, 2001b). See also Appendix 5A for the grading rubric for this course; the prompt is reproduced in the box below. The essays were written in 50 minutes in class during the first week of the semester. Students had been given the reading and some prewriting questions to consider in advance.

Please read the attached article by Terry Lee Goodrich [en]titled "Lies are so commonplace, they almost seem like the truth." Then write a clear, well-organized essay that responds to the following question:

Is lying always wrong? Why or why not?

Be sure to consider both sides of the issue as you explain your opinion. References to the article — facts, quotations, summary, and so on — are required.

Note: The first essay has been marked by a teacher with marginal and end comments; it is followed by a brief analysis. The remaining three essays are for responding practice (see Application Activity 5.3).

Lying is not always wrong, if it is used for good intentions. Lying can be very manipulative, yet that particular quality, Goodrich mentioned, "is also exciting". Instead of using it for evil, lying can be a vital source for good, whether it from sparing a child feelings or doing it just to get something out of it. There are numerous explanations why people would create white lies. One reason why people lie is to surprise or distract a love one. Another reason why people do it is to create a diversion, in order to escape the difficulties that may take place by telling the truth.

Who is Goodrich?

Good clear response to the essay question

Nice example of a "white lie"

There is no greater rush than getting away with a good, harmless lie. For example, on one occasion, I have used lies for good intention. My close friend birthday was coming up. My friends and I were planning a surprise birthday. We did not want the birthday girl to know of this, so we manipulated her into thinking that we did not remember her birthday. Making up stories that we were busy on that day, to convince her so. Seeing the hurt in her eyes further greaten our smile. Like Goodrich said, "even though people lie for good reason, lying can be harmful". My friends and I knew that by lying to her, the surprise party would be a total success. Yes, our way of springing the party on her was wrong, but when the surprise was successful, seeing the joy on her face gave everyone involve a great rush, and that is exciting

When Goodrich said that, "everyone lie" it could very well be the truth. People lie constantly to avoid difficult situation by telling the truth. For instant, I was at my friends' house for dinner. His mother was cooking her best dish that took hours to make. During the course of the meal she asked me how was it. The truth is that I didn't like it, maybe is because I hate shrimp, but to avoid being an unwanted guess, I bit my lips and told her that the meal was excellent. Besides my stomach hurting from the shrimp, no feelings got hurt.

To conclude, small, harmless lies can be exciting and fun. Not knowing if you will get caught in a lie, or knowing that you just got away with a lie is a great thrill. The truth is, some lies can be damaging when it is discovered, but if done properly, lies can be very benificial. No one really likes to lie, but not everyone is aware that they are lying. Lying is not always wrong.

is getting a "great rush" good if it hurts someone's feelings?

What might you do differently next time?

When might lies be "damaging"?

Good example of lying to spare someone from hurt feelings!

Lies are "exciting, fun, and a great thrill"—but "no one really liks to lie"? This is conflusing.

Lucy,
    You did a nice job of taking a clear stand on the essay question by saying that "lying is not always wrong." Your two examples—the surprise party and the shrimp dish—were both effective in illustrating times when a lie may be harmless and even beneficial.

There are a couple of issues you need to think about as you write your next draft:

(1) You need to consider also times when lying is harmful. You hint at this a couple of times in your introduction and conclusion by saying that lying can be "manipulative" and "damaging," but the rest of your essay presents a very positive view of lying. I'd suggest adding a paragraph or two that defines the types of lies that are harmful and provides an example or two. You should also look carefully at the article, which discusses both the positive and negative aspects of lying, and see if there are ideas, examples, or quotations that might help you present a more two-sided argument.

(2) The story about your friend's birthday is a bit confusing. You are honest about the fact that your lying caused her pain, and you even describe it as "wrong," yet you present it as an example of when lying can be beneficial. See if you can make this clearer by explaining ei￭ *￭ (a) what you might have done differently or better; or (b) why you think the positive aspects of the surprise "erased" the hurt she felt when she thought you had forgotten her birthday.*

(3) You need to use Goodrich's article more in your essay. Be sure to introduce it clearly at the beginning—author's full name, article title, and a brief summary of the main idea(s)—and see if you can use facts, examples, or specific quotations to support your own arguments and examples throughout the paper.

You are off to a great start with clear organization and nice examples. I will look forward to reading your next draft! Be sure to e-mail me, talk to me in class, or come by my office if you need any help as you revise!

Good luck!

Teacher

STUDENT ESSAYS 2–4 (Provided for Responding Practice)

Essay 2

In an everyday going, many people lie all the time. There are many reasons why people lie. They lie to protect themselves, to protect others, to get attention, to get things they desire or want. In my opinion, lying is a part of everybody's daily routine, such as waking up in the morning, eating, going to work or school, and sleeping. A daily routine of lying can be simple as telling your mom that you are not able to go home early due to a group study, but instead you're going out with your friends to a perty. This is the type of lie that many people often do everyday of there lives, and it is normal. I believe that lies are not always harmful, and it is appropriate sometimes. However, everybody should set limits and boundaries to determine whether a lie should be acceptable or not.

In the article,"Lies Are So Commonplace, They Almost Seem Like The Truth" Goodrich states that many people lie for good reasons, but lying can be hurtful and risky if the lies are discovered and it can destroy the trust and the relationship with the peson. I agree with this statement because everybody should know the consequences from lying, even if the lie is simple or serious. For example, I was in a relationship for five and a half years. At the last year of our relationship, he constantly made excuses that he was busy and could not spend time with me.

Afterward, I had found out that all the times that he had refused to go out with me, he was out with my best friend. They had been seeing each other for several months. I was very devistated and hurt. I couldn't believe it. They've been lying to me for so long that I felt so stupied. In this type of situation, the lie will soon be discovered. I believe that this type of lie is unacceptable and it should not be a daily routine.

Overall, lying is something that everybody will do as a part of growing up. A harmful lie or an appropriate lie depends on how an individual use it.

Essay 3

In my past experiences I have come across so many people that lie for so many different reasons. Their are certain lies that does not have major consequences, but their are some that could destroy you, or a relationship. Their are lies that are very harmful, their are appropriate lies, and their are lies that do not effect either party.

Most lies can be very harmful, whether its on your body or to someone else. "But even hough people lie for good reasons, lying can be harmful." Lies can destroy the trust between people. Their are people who would for a close friend or family member to protect them, but this can have very serious consequences. It could put you in prison. Also Goodrich said that "lying is hard on the brain because one lie leads to another and we always have to remember our false story." (Lies are so commonplace, Goodrich)

Although, most lies can have really bad consequences, their are times when lying is appropriate. "We fudge on how old we are, how much we weigh, what we are paid. Some people tell their children that Santa Claus will com on Christmas eve." Like Goodrich said these lies do not have serious consequences. People to get out of going out with them. This is not justified, but we all do it at one point or another, sometimes what out even noticing it. Parents lie to their kids all the time in order to scare them or protect them. Kids constently lie to their parents, sometimes it because thay want to get out of explaining their selves. Their have been many time if I was going to movies with a friend, I would tell my parents that I was goung to study so I didn't have explain my self. People call in sick to work because something came up and they rather be their than at work, so they call and make up a story about why they cant be at work. (lies are so commonplace, they almost seem like the truth, Goodrich).

Their are people who would lie for any given reason. They do it because its exciting, its dangerous. I have a friend who lies to make her interesting. She will change her stories to make people listen. Their are times that said lied about thing that do not effect me or relate to me in any way. "We also lie to make people agree with us without really realizing that we're doing so." I think lying comes naturally to certain people, they do not have to think about it. (lies are so common place, thy almost seem like the truth, David Welsh).

Whatever the motivation, people lie on every day basis. Some do it to protect themselves. Some do it to protect other, whether their children or friend. And their are some that do it for the excitement, or to be important.

Essay 4

Sometime lie can be appropiated because, if a person had to lie for a good reason then its alright. A good reason to lie may also be harmful. In this case, lies are harmful.

Lying to someone can be harmful at the same time it can be appropriated. Sometime people have to lie because they dont want to get in trouble. Lying is appropriated when a person is lying in a good way. When I ask a friend to have lunch with me tomorrow, and she responded by saying I have to work late tomorrow, but she actually got out of work early. She lied because she did not want to hurt my feeling by saying she have other plan. This way of lying can be appropriated because it's used in a way of not wanting to hurt a friend feeling. Lies can be appropriated when using it for a good reason, but lying is always is going to be harmful to everyone, even when using it as a good reason.

When or where a person may lie the truth may be still known, when the truth comes out lies may be harmful. Lying is harmful, it may add excitment to a person life, but at the same time it can destroy a person life.

Some time people tell the storie about Santa Clause coming down the chimney on Christmas eve and give present to good little boys and girls. Children around the world probably heard this stories about old St. Nick. The stories is just to make children believe in old St. Nick, when when children are grown to a certain age and realize that the stories was a lie, then it break their heart. Lying can be misleading. I think that lies are so common that people don't realized that people are telling the truth sometime.

I remember that my sister lies to my parent about going to the store to get some vegetable, and would be back in 30 min. My parent waited for the vegetable for an hours. She would never show up with the vegetable intill two hour later.

She lied to my parent. My parent would not trust het to go grocery shopping again.

By lying to my parent she causes my parent not to trust her again.

Lying is harmful because it lead others to think of you in a different way. It makes other people judge your trust.

Lying is bad because its misleading you into a wrong decision, making wrong mistake and causing problem when the truth is known.

Chapter **6**

Building a Community of Writers: Principles of Peer Response

Questions for Reflection

- *Beyond the specific context of composition courses, what types of experiences have you had with peer feedback and collaboration, whether in academic or nonacademic settings?*
- *Do you enjoy collaboration with peers? Do you find it helpful? Why or why not?*
- *Considering your own previous experiences with peer feedback (if any), what are the potential benefits of implementing it in an ESL literacy course? What are the possible drawbacks? In what ways (if any) do you think these considerations might differ for L2 students?*

PEER RESPONSE: KUDOS AND CRITICISMS

The brief history of peer response in L2 writing instruction, both as a pedagogical technique and as a research domain, has been somewhat tumultuous. In the 1970s and 1980s, L1 composition

223

scholars were almost lyrical in their praise of peer response, citing many advantages and benefits of varied forms of peer review (Brannon & Knoblauch, 1981; Elbow, 1973; Hairston, 1986; Knoblauch & Brannon, 1982; Moxley, 1989; Sommers, 1982; Sperling & Freedman, 1987). This fervor contrasted strikingly with critiques of teacher feedback. Many experts saw teacher commentary as fraught with problems (such as teacher appropriation) and as possibly an "exercise in futility" (Marzano & Arthur, 1977, cited in Brannon & Knoblauch, 1981, p. 1). Early proponents of process-oriented pedagogies in L2 composition (Zamel, 1982, 1985) similarly endorsed peer response as both an alternative to teacher feedback and as a means of facilitating second language development through interaction (Long & Porter, 1985).

However, other L2 researchers have urged caution, stressing that techniques appropriate for L1 writers should not be transferred uncritically to L2 writing contexts (Silva, 1988, 1993, 1997; Zhang, 1995). It has been observed that peer response, in particular, presents unique challenges to L2 writers as well as potential culture conflicts, resulting in classroom procedures that are less successful than teachers might hope, because of language and affective barriers. Critics of peer response in L2 writing instruction claim that peer feedback activities are, at best, limited in their influence on student writing (Connor & Asenavage, 1994). At worst, they are potentially harmful to students because of novice writers' ineptitude in providing useful responses and because of L2 students' lukewarm, if not downright hostile, feelings toward peer feedback (Carson & Nelson, 1994; Leki, 1990b; Zhang, 1995).

In this regard, the history of research and pedagogy in peer response in L2 writing is more comparable to that of computer-assisted writing instruction (see chapter 9) than to that of discussions of teacher feedback (see chapter 5). As discussed in chapter 5, written teacher feedback has most typically been regarded by L1 and L2 researchers as a necessary evil, burdensome to writing teachers and limited in its effectiveness for helping student writers improve their literacy skills. Enthusiastic scholarly proponents of written teacher response are few in number, although recent surveys of ESL student opinions on teacher feedback have found that L2 writers feel that instructor feedback is both necessary and helpful (Ferris, 1995b; Hedgcock & Lefkowitz, 1994; Zhang, 1995).

Furthermore, as previously discussed, surprisingly few detailed examinations of written teacher feedback have appeared (Ferris, Pezone, Tade, & Tinti, 1997). In contrast, peer response, like computer-assisted writing instruction, has forceful, vocal proponents and detractors as well as a rapidly increasing number of detailed studies on its nature and influence.

Benefits of Peer Response

Theoretical Frameworks.   Arguments in favor of peer response have been based on several related schools of thought. First, because peer response activities can take place at various stages of the writing process (prewriting/discovery/invention, between-draft revision, and editing), they fit well with the increased emphasis on cognitive processes and social constructionism in composition teaching (Connor & Asenavage, 1994; Emig, 1971; Flower & Hayes, 1981; Zamel, 1982, 1985, 1987).

A second theoretical basis for peer response "is the notion of collaborative learning which derives from the social constructionist view ... that knowledge is essentially a socially justified belief" (Carson & Nelson, 1994, pp. 17–18). According to social constructionists, new ideas or paradigms are "constructs generated by communities of like-minded peers" (Bruffee, 1986, p. 774). Support for collaborative learning and social constructionism is derived, in turn, from the Vygotskyan view that "cognitive development results from social interaction" (Carson & Nelson, 1994, p. 18; Mendonça & Johnson, 1994; Vygotsky, 1962/1986). Finally, in the L2 context, group work in general and writing response groups in particular have support from second language acquisition claims about the importance of interaction for L2 development (Duff, 1986; Ellis, 1991; Gass & Selinker, 2001; Long & Porter, 1985; Mangelsdorf, 1989; Mittan, 1989; Pica, 1984; Pica, Young, & Doughty, 1987). Liu and Hansen (2002) presented a detailed discussion of the "benefits and constraints in using peer response" (p. 8) (see also Ferris, 2003a; 2003b).

Practical Benefits.   Both L1 and L2 teachers and researchers have claimed that peer feedback activities in the classroom offer numerous advantages. For novice writers in general, whether native speakers (NSs) or non-native speakers (NNSs), the following benefits have been suggested:

- Students can take active roles in their own learning (Hirvela, 1999; Mendonça & Johnson, 1994).
- Students can "reconceptualize their ideas in light of their peers' reactions" (Mendonça & Johnson, 1994, p. 746).
- Students can engage in unrehearsed, low-risk, exploratory talk that is less feasible in classroom and teacher–student interactions.
- Students receive "reactions, questions, and responses from authentic readers" (Mittan, 1989, p. 209; but see Leki, 1990b; Newkirk, 1984, for counterarguments to this assertion).
- Students receive feedback from multiple sources (Chaudron, 1983; Mittan, 1989).
- Students gain a clearer understanding of reader expectations by receiving feedback on what they have done well and on what remains unclear (Mittan, 1989; Moore, 1986; Witbeck, 1976).
- Responding to peers' writing builds the critical skills needed to analyze and revise one's own writing (Leki, 1990b; Mittan, 1989).
- Students gain confidence and reduce apprehension by seeing peers' strengths and weaknesses in writing (Leki, 1990b; Mittan, 1989).
- Peer response activities build classroom community (Ferris, 2003b; Hirvela, 1999; Liu & Hansen, 2002; Mendonça & Johnson, 1994).

In addition to the benefits of peer feedback for all student writers, Mangelsdorf (1989) highlighted specific benefits of peer response for L2 students' linguistic development, noting that peer interactions build communication skills and provide important opportunities for students to test and revise their L2 hypotheses.

Finally, it has been suggested that peer response activities can reduce the writing teacher's workload and can impart to the teacher important information about individual students' literacy skills and their understanding of what constitutes good writing (but see Mittan, 1989, p. 211 for a counterassertion). Mittan (1989) called this latter point

> the ultimate benefit of the peer review process for the teacher. Regardless of how I judge the quality of [a student's] finished essays, [the] peer review can show me some of her knowledge about

good writing. . . . Indeed, I have found that students whose writing is consistently average or even poor very often write the most thoughtful and helpful peer reviews. This is true empowerment: encouraging students to demonstrate and use their knowledge and expertise rather than punishing them for their as-yet unpolished performance. (p. 212)

Criticisms of Peer Response

Practical Limitations. In discussing the topic of peer response in ESL writing classes with other teachers and with conference audiences, we have many times heard the comment, "I tried peer feedback in my class, and it didn't work. I don't think it's appropriate for ESL writers." As previously noted, peer response as a pedagogical tool is not without its detractors. Leki (1990b) noted several potential problems with peer feedback, derived both from the comments of 20 ESL students and from her own and other writing teachers' experiences (see also: Ferris, 2003a, 2003b; Liu & Hansen, 2002):

- Students sometimes focus too heavily on "surface concerns" (p. 9) or editing, neglecting larger revising issues.
- Students can provide vague, unhelpful comments.
- Students may be hostile, sarcastic, overly critical, or unkind in their criticisms of their classmates' writing.
- Students feel uncertain about the validity of their classmates' responses.
- In peer group discussions, students may struggle with their own listening comprehension skills or with the peer's accent.
- Lack of L2 formal (rhetorical) schemata may lead to inappropriate expectations about the content and structure of peers' texts, which can then result in counterproductive feedback that leads writers further away from U.S. academic expectations.

Cultural Issues. In addition to the practical concerns outlined by Leki and others, Carson and Nelson (1994) raised questions about peer response and writing groups based on broader cultural issues rather than specific pedagogical problems (see also Allaei & Connor, 1990). Drawing a distinction between collectivist cultures (e.g., Chinese and Japanese) and individualist cultures (e.g., United States), Carson and Nelson (1994) pointed out that whereas both collectivist and individualist cultures use collaborative learning, they typically do so for opposing purposes. In collectivist cultures, "a primary goal of the group is to maintain the relationships that constitute the group, to maintain cohesion and group harmony among group members" (Carson & Nelson, 1994, p. 20). However, "writing groups, as they are frequently implemented in composition classes in the United States, function more often for the benefit of the individual writer than for the benefit of the group" (p. 22).

The result of these differing cultural expectations for group work may be that for students from collectivist cultures, "the impetus/motivation behind their responses is likely to come from a need for a positive group climate rather than a need to help an individual writer" (p. 23). In a subsequent study investigating the interactions of several Chinese ESL students in a writing group, Carson and Nelson (1996) found that "the Chinese students were reluctant to initiate comments and, when they did, monitored themselves carefully so as not to precipitate conflict within the group" (p. 1). In a similar vein, Allaei and Connor (1990) cautioned that culturally mixed writing groups may experience problems attributable to differing expectations and communication patterns.

Affective Factors.   Zhang (1995) took a critical look at the so-called affective advantage of peer feedback for ESL students. In a survey of 81 college and university ESL writers, he found that respondents overwhelmingly preferred teacher feedback over peer or self-feedback. On the basis of these results, he argued that L2 practitioners should exercise caution in applying the findings and recommendations of L1 composition researchers and teachers to the teaching of ESL composition pedagogy, noting that "the L2 student and the L1 student may enter the writing process with distinctly different conceptualizations and priorities about input or intervention at the revision stage" (p. 218; see also Silva, 1993, 1997). Although a subsequent study (Jacobs, Curtis, Braine, & Huang, 1998) led to somewhat different findings (see Ferris, 2003b, pp. 111–112 for a detailed discussion), all researchers concerned appeared to agree that "it is not advisable to either use peer feedback exclusively or to abolish it altogether" (Ferris, 2003b, p. 112; Zhang, 1999).

RESEARCH ON PEER RESPONSE

Studies on peer response in L2 writing over the past 15 years or so have focused on three general areas of concern:[1]

1. Descriptive studies of what actually takes place during peer review sessions (including both what is discussed [e.g., ideas, language] and how students collaborate)
2. Text-analytic studies of the effects of peer response on subsequent student revisions and their progress as writers over time
3. Survey studies investigating student views of or responses to peer response, either by itself or compared with teacher feedback or self-evaluation.

Before discussing these studies, we observe that, to evaluate the research findings fairly, a range of questions must be asked about participants and setting, peer feedback procedures deployed, and research methods (see Ferris, 2003b, pp. 71–73, especially Fig. 4.2, for a detailed discussion). That said, the empirical research base on the nature and effects of peer feedback is growing, and has led to a fairly consistent set of findings, discussed briefly in the sections that follow.

Descriptions of Student Interactions in Peer Response Sessions

Several researchers have undertaken discourse-analytic descriptions of the types of communicative moves and stances used and adopted by students during peer feedback activities (Lockhart & Ng, 1995a, 1995b; Mangelsdorf & Schlumberger, 1992; Mendonça & Johnson, 1994; Nelson & Murphy, 1992; Villamil & de Guerrero, 1996). In the earliest study, Mangelsdorf and Schlumberger (1992) found that students' stances during peer review sessions fell into three categories with some overlap: interpretive (23%), prescriptive (45%), and collaborative (32%). The researchers also evaluated the types of comments made by the student reviewers on content and found five distinct categories of response: no comment, generic comment, critical evaluation, critical evaluations and suggestions (the largest category, comprising 41% of the comments), and critical evaluations and extended suggestions.

In a later analysis of peer review negotiations, Mendonça and Johnson (1994) identified five major categories of interactions (with related subtypes): question, explanation, restatement, suggestion, and grammar correction. Studies by Lockhart and Ng (1995a; 1995b), Nelson and Murphy (1992) and Villamil and de Guerrero (1996), further examined the types of roles, stances, and social dynamics present in ESL peer response groups. Although these studies focused on different aspects of student–student interaction, all concluded that peer review is "an extremely complex interactive process" (Villamil & deGuerrero, 1996, p. 51) and that many different factors influence this process (Lockhart & Ng, 1995a; 1995b). As noted by Ferris (2003b), these studies "further suggest how important social dynamics and reader stances may be in predicting the success and failure, in both practical and affective terms, of peer response activities" (p. 75).

The Effects of Peer Feedback on Student Revision

Several studies have examined the relationship between peer feedback and subsequent revision. Research questions have included whether students consider and act on their peers' comments when revising (Connor & Asenavage, 1994; Mendonça & Johnson, 1994; Nelson & Murphy, 1992, 1992/1993, 1993; Paulus, 1999; Schmid, 1999; Stanley, 1992), the sorts of revisions students make after receiving peer feedback (Berg, 1999; Berger, 1990; Connor & Asenavage, 1994; Huang, 1994; Paulus, 1999; Resh, 1994), and whether peer feedback leads to high-quality end products (Hedgcock & Lefkowitz, 1992; Resh, 1994; Schmid, 1999).

Studies examining the extent to which writers address peer feedback in their revisions report conflicting findings. For instance, in a study of two peer response groups (N = 8), Connor and Asenavage (1994) indicated that few of their students' revisions (about 5% of the total changes) responded to peer commentary, and that the vast majority of the revisions derived from other sources (teacher feedback and the writer's own textual adjustments). In contrast, Mendonça and Johnson (1994) reported that their 12 participants used peer feedback in 53% of their revisions. Nelson and Murphy (1993) reported a mixed finding. Their analyses of the responses given and the revisions made by four intermediate ESL students in an ongoing (10-week) response group determined that students sometimes, but not always, used peer comments in revising their drafts. Findings also showed that the extent to which they did so appeared to be based on group dynamics. Two recent studies (Paulus, 1999, similar to Connor & Asenavage, 1994; Schmid, 1999, modeled after Mendonça & Johnson, 1994) both found much stronger effects of peer feedback on revision than did the earlier authors.

Several researchers have examined the types of revisions made by student writers in response to peer commentary. Berg (1999), Berger (1990), Connor and Asenavage (1994), and Paulus (1999) all used Faigley and Witte's (1981) taxonomy of revisions to categorize the types of revisions made in response to feedback from various sources (peers and self in the earlier study, and peers, teacher, and self/other in the later report). Berger (1990) found that the majority (more than 65%) of her 46 participants' revisions fell into the broad subcategory of surface changes, regardless of feedback source (peer or self-evaluation). Connor and Asenavage (1994) found that one of their two groups made more surface changes, whereas the other made more text-based changes. However, the two more recent studies (Berg, 1999; Paulus, 1999), found that writers made both meaning and surface changes. The effects of these changes on essay quality were positive, and in Berg's (1999) study, the students' prior training in peer response had a measurable impact on the types and on the effects of the revisions made.

Other researchers have examined the effects of peer response activities on writers and their written products. In a dissertation case study, Resh (1994) examined the effects of responding to other students' texts on three student writers, concluding that the activity of responding to peers' papers predicts and influences the writers' own future revision behaviors. In an experimental study of college French L2 students, Hedgcock and Lefkowitz (1992) found that texts written by students who revised collaboratively received higher scores than those of students who revised after receiving teacher feedback instead. Finally, Schmid (1999) found that revisions made in response to peer feedback had positive effects on essay quality in 57% of the cases (see Ferris, 2003b, Fig. 4.6, p. 79).

Student Opinions About Peer Feedback

A major portion of the debate over the appropriateness of peer feedback activities in ESL writing instruction centers on students' reactions to them. As noted by Zhang (1995), L1 researchers made strong claims about not only the appropriateness of peer response, but also about its superiority over teacher feedback. Researchers investigating L1 asserted that that teachers tended to "take over," or "appropriate" student writing with their comments, that student writers resented such interference, and that students could instead receive the benefits of a real audience by engaging in peer response, without the drawbacks of being judged by an authority. In contrast, as already noted, ESL writing specialists have wondered whether their students would resist peer feedback for both practical and cultural reasons (Ferris, 2003a, 2003b; Leki, 1990b; Liu & Hansen, 2002).

Given this debate, it is interesting to observe that studies of L2 writers' reactions to peer response have yielded almost uniformly positive results (Arndt, 1993; Jacobs, Curtis, Braine, & Huang, 1998; Leki, 1990b; Mangelsdorf, 1992; Mendonça & Johnson, 1994; Schmid, 1999). Although students did raise complaints about peer response in such studies, the overwhelming sense is that they enjoy such collaboration and find it helpful. Even apparent counterevidence (Leki, 1990b; Zhang, 1995) to this claim, when scrutinized closely, does not truly contradict this trend. In other words, whereas ESL writers likely would never be comfortable with the wholesale substitution of peer feedback for teacher commentary, they do not appear to have strong objections to peer feedback itself.[2]

Summary of Research

In our view, inquiry into the nature and effects of peer feedback provides a great deal of positive evidence for incorporating it as a regular component of L2 literacy education. Only one study (Connor & Asenavage, 1994) reported truly discouraging findings concerning peer response in ESL composition courses. In contrast, the trends of the other studies clearly indicate that students value peer feedback, that they pay attention to it when they revise, and that that revisions made in response to thoughtful peer comments lead to improved essay quality. Furthermore, evidence is strong that novice writers enjoy positive affective benefits by engaging in systematic peer feedback activities. For the most part, students report that they enjoy such activities.

Why, then, do so many ESL writing teachers resist this collaborative practice? We suspect that the answer lies in the practical implementation of peer feedback in the classroom. When teachers report implementing peer response processes in their literacy courses with unsatisfactory results, we wonder if the procedures

Principles for Effective Peer Response
1. Make peer response an integral part of the course.
2. Model the process.
3. Build peer response skills progressively throughout the term.
4. Structure the peer response task.
5. Vary peer response activities.
6. Hold students accountable for giving feedback and for considering any feedback they receive.
7. Consider individual student needs.
8. Consider logistical issues, including ☞ the size and composition of groups ☞ the mechanics of exchanging papers ☞ time management and crowd control.

FIG. 6.1.   Principles for effective peer response.

were given a fair trial and if the conditions for effective peer response were truly present. We believe strongly that peer feedback can and does "work," provided it is planned and implemented thoughtfully, carefully, and consistently (Fig. 6.1). It is to these practical issues that we turn next.

PRINCIPLES OF EFFECTIVE PEER RESPONSE ACTIVITIES

Making Peer Response an Integral Part of the Course

Mittan (1989) provided one of the earliest comprehensive discussions of techniques for using peer response in L2 writing, presenting a number of arguments in favor of peer review and guiding principles for its implementation. Mittan's (1989) first principle entails integrating and weaving peer review throughout a writing course, rather than treating the process as a peripheral or isolated pedagogical practice. We can achieve successful integration in several ways: by making clear to the students from the beginning of the course that peer response will be required, even noting in the syllabus (where applicable) when peer group activities will take place, by using peer review frequently and consistently throughout the term, by using peer review to accomplish a variety of goals, and by holding students accountable (through formal assessment and feedback) for their responses and for serious consideration of peer feedback in writing and revising their own papers.

Such considerations are important for two reasons. First, by communicating to students that peer response is a regular, expected part of the literacy course, we validate its importance in the writing process. Second, like teacher commentary, peer response constitutes a skill that develops and improves with practice and with increasing confidence on the part of student respondents.

Modeling the Process

Most advocates of peer response in L2 writing stress the importance of teacher input and modeling before initial peer response sessions (Carson & Nelson, 1996; Leki, 1990b; Liu & Hansen, 2002; Lockhart & Ng, 1995a, 1995b; Mittan, 1989; Nelson & Murphy, 1992/1993, 1993). Studies involving trained peer respondents have consistently found that students' performance and attitudes improve if they are carefully prepared for such collaborative activities (Berg, 1999; Rothschild & Klingenberg, 1990; Stanley, 1992). Typical suggestions include discussing with students the rationale for peer response, furnishing them with guidelines for acceptable responses (i.e., specifying expectations for substance and tone), and instructing learners to practice the process through role-plays and simulations, as well as reading and discussing sample essays not written by class members during teacher-led class sessions.

For the more ambitious teacher, Carson and Nelson (1996) suggested asking students to view videotaped recordings of response sessions from previous semesters to analyze the types of oral comments made and the language used to express opinions and suggestions for revision. Similarly, Lockhart and Ng (1995a; 1995b) suggested giving students transcripts of peer review sessions to examine and critique. It also is important to point out that teachers implicitly and indirectly (and sometimes unconsciously) model feedback patterns for their students through their own oral and written responses to student papers (Connor & Asenavage, 1994; Lockhart & Ng, 1995a, 1995; Stanley, 1992). If a teacher focuses intensively on surface errors or writes brief, cryptic comments on student texts, students are also likely to adopt those priorities and behaviors in responding to the writing of their counterparts. However, if the teacher assumes a collegial, interested, collaborative stance in responding to student papers, students will similarly tend to follow this collaborative lead.

In their recent book on effective peer response in L2 writing instruction, Liu and Hansen (2002) devoted an entire chapter to the topic of "instructing" students in the finer points of peer response. They pointed out that peer response (and training for peer response) is "four-dimensional: affective, cognitive, socio-cultural, and linguistic" (p. 155), recommending that teachers consider writers' backgrounds and motivations before engaging in peer response training. Liu and Hansen (2002) likewise recommended that classroom procedures feature modeling and explicit instruction in what to look for and how to frame responses that are sensitive yet constructive and substantive. This chapter provides numerous suggestions and examples of training materials, including "task-specific peer response sheets and concrete examples from previous students' drafts, completed peer response sheets, and revisions based on peers' comments" (Liu & Hansen, 2002, p. 155).

Liu and Hansen (2002) also encourage teachers to provide their own oral and written responses to sample student texts during training as a model for comparison. Finally, they underscore the need to provide some fixed expressions or formulas for response and to stress concern for "open-mindedness, politeness, [and] turn-taking strategies" (p. 156). Figure 6.2 provides a sample peer review training activity that exemplifies these precepts.

Building Peer Response Skills Progressively Throughout the Term

Mittan (1989) suggested that the basic format of peer review should remain consistent throughout the writing course (Koch, 1982). That is, the reader should offer a positive, encouraging response to the writer, identify the purpose or main point or points of the sample being reviewed, direct questions to the writer, and offer concrete suggestions for revising or expanding the text. However, Mittan (1989) suggested that as the term progresses, teachers should "raise the ante slightly, asking students to detail why they find a particular passage effective or to explain how a suggested revision will improve the writing" (p. 213). We can build students' competence in reading and responding to peers' papers by carefully structuring peer review tasks and by gradually increasing their difficulty.

Peer Review Exercise

Note: This exercise is based on a personal narrative essay assignment in which students are asked to describe an event or experience and analyze its significance (see Spack, 1996). This entire exercise takes 30 to 45 minutes.

1. Explain to students that they will be reviewing classmates' first drafts to give each other suggestions for revision. Elicit from students some possible reasons for or benefits of peer response. Write them on a board if available.
2. Review the course grading criteria or Essay Feedback Checklist.
3. Distribute a sample essay first draft. Give students 10 minutes to read it carefully and to complete the checklist.
4. Give students a handout with the peer response form they will use to respond to each other's essay drafts. Put a copy up on the overhead, if possible.
5. Lead the students through discussion of the sample essay by using the questions on the peer response form. Conclude the discussion by identifying 1–2 positive comments and 1–2 suggestions to give the student writer.
6. Then ask the students to pretend that the student writer is actually in the room. (You might ask for a volunteer to come to the front of the room and sit facing the rest of the class.) Ask the class to role-play how they might deliver the feedback points they agreed upon in step 5. As a class, evaluate the language used in the comments. Is it clear? Specific? Encouraging? Respectful? Too negative? Elicit possible rephrasings of any problematic comments.
7. Now or later: Examine the revision of the paper (if available). Discuss with the students whether the writer revised effectively. Were the concerns raised in your class discussion addressed by the revision? What further suggestions might they give the writer?

[For further suggestions on peer review training, see Berg (1999) and Liu and Hansen (2002).]

FIG. 6.2. Sample peer review training exercise.

Of course, along with the aim of building students' skills in peer feedback comes the presupposition that teachers are committed to the process and willing to set reasonable expectations for the activity—and to be patient as students' responding skills develop over time. Teachers should not expect students to assume full responsibility for providing feedback to one another or to exempt themselves from giving comments, if for no other reason than that students will not be capable of providing adequate feedback, particularly at the beginning of a course. Instructors should therefore remember that effective response is a skill that develops with practice and coaching over time (Huang, 1994; Mittan, 1989). Even if students initially do not provide effective feedback to peers, they still will benefit from reading one another's papers and from the relationships and classroom community that grow through peer review activities (Leki, 1990b; Mangelsdorf, 1992; Mittan, 1989; Resh, 1994; Stanley, 1992).

Structuring the Peer Response Task

Although peer response enthusiasts agree that providing students with guidance for the peer review sessions is critical, some proponents disagree about the extent to which teachers should structure peer review activities. Advocates of a less structured approach have argued that if the teacher establishes an overly directive or prescriptive position concerning the substance or form of peer feedback, students' interactions will reflect the instructor's intentions and priorities rather than their own independent thoughts and reactions—another form of teacher appropriation of the writing process (Elbow, 1973; Lockhart & Ng, 1995a, 1995b; Nelson & Murphy, 1992/1993; see also chapter 5 for discussion of feedback and appropriation). The student guidelines proposed by Nelson and Murphy (1992/1993), for instance, simply advise students to "describe [their] reactions to the paper" and to "be specific—point to particular items in the paper" (p. 25). Lockhart and Ng (1995a, 1995b) suggested that "guiding questions may help provide a direction and a focus to the interaction," but that once students become comfortable with the process, "they should be allowed greater autonomy to respond according to the needs of the text and the writer" (p. 648).

Other experts, however, have suggested that teachers should carefully structure writing group sessions to build responding skills, vary peer review tasks, and provide indirect instruction. Even within this faction, we find divergent opinions. For example, Moore (1986) advocated using the same peer response form throughout the course so that students feel comfortable with the task and response process. In contrast, Mittan (1989) suggested that teachers should "design a peer review sheet specifically for each peer review session" (p. 215), claiming that tailoring the process to the task allows a teacher to build on previous peer response sessions, vary the task according to the specifications of the assignment, and respond to students' needs, strengths, or weaknesses.

Commenting on the theme of teacher appropriation in response to student writing, Reid (1994) noted that "the teacher's primary responsibility is to provide opportunities for change in the classroom" (p. 277) and that "teachers must intervene to provide adequate schemata ... that will serve as a scaffolding for writing" (p. 286). In the current context, when peer response tasks are carefully structured to meet pedagogical goals, they can

---

Peer Review Form—Completed Essay Draft

Writer's Name: _____

Reviewer's Name: _____

Your purpose in answering these questions is to provide an honest and helpful response to your partner's draft and to suggest ways to make his/her writing better. *Be sure to read the entire paper carefully before writing any responses.* Be as specific as possible, referring to particular parts of the paper in your answers.

1. What do you like most about the paper? Choose the most interesting idea and explain why it captured your attention.

2. In your own words, state what you think the paper is about.

3. What parts of the paper need to have more detail added so that readers can understand it better?

4. Choose the statement with which you most agree:

   ❏ Each of your paragraphs discusses only one idea, and everything in the paragraph is related to that specific idea.

   ❏ Some of your paragraphs are confusing because they seem to be about more than one idea. I marked them with an X.

   ❏ Your writing seems to be all in one paragraph. I cannot tell where you start discussing a new idea. Please help!

5. On the back of this page, write a short letter to your partner explaining how his or her writing can be improved. Be very specific and explain *why* you think these changes will help readers. Begin your letter with your partner's name and sign your own name.

FIG. 6.3.   Sample peer response form.

serve as a form of modeling and instruction that is qualitatively different from traditional, teacher-fronted instruction and even direct oral feedback from the instructor. Liu and Hansen (2002) provided numerous examples to show the different foci of peer response (content, rhetorical structure, grammatical form, and so on) and how peer feedback activities can be structured to focus on diverse aspects of a text, at different points of the writing process, and in response to different genres and assignment types.

Figure. 6.3 illustrates a sample peer response form, the advantages of which are explained by Mittan (1989):

1. It begins with clear instructions as to the purpose, audience, and procedure for completing the form.
2. It is limited to one page.
3. It follows a format of encouragement, identification of purpose, questions, and suggestions, which can be used for all peer response activities and also for teacher

feedback, thus providing an integrated and consistent framework for response throughout the writing course.

4. The question types and tasks vary from open-ended comments (questions 1 and 3) to reformulation of the writer's main idea (question 2) to selecting the most appropriate response from several choices (Question 4), to writing a letter (which Mittan calls "mini-essays in themselves") to the writer. Question 5, the letter-writing task, "stipulates a particular genre and indicates the role of the participants, both of which are familiar and informal" (Mittan, 1989, p. 217).

We have found that designing effective peer response tasks can be harder than it might first appear. Common mistakes or problems, which we have seen in both commercial textbooks and classroom materials, include prompts and questions that are not engaging enough. For example, the question "Did the writer provide enough support for his or her thesis?" is problematic because of its yes/no format and the vagueness of the word "enough." Questions such as "How did the writer's introduction make you want to keep reading?" can prove to be too abstract for peer respondents to grapple with: This question, of course, begs the [probably unspoken] answer, "I didn't want to, but I had to anyway because the teacher told us to read each other's papers!" Our best advice for designing peer response forms includes the following suggestions:

1. Avoid yes/no questions entirely, if possible. If selected yes/no prompts are required, pair them with a question or imperative requiring specific information. For example, the aforementioned yes/no question could be rephrased as follows: "Examine the body of the paper. List in note form the support for the main arguments (facts, ideas from the reading, examples from personal experience) used by the writer."

2. Cast questions and prompts as concretely as possible, sending students back into the peer's text or into source material. For instance, the abstract question about the introduction could be revised in the following manner: "Review the ideas for writing an interesting introduction

on p.__ of your textbook. Which option did the writer choose? If you think another option might have worked better, state which one and why you think so."

3. Instruct students to analyze the scoring rubric or the assignment guidelines as a means of reviewing and evaluating their peers' work (see chapters 4 and 8).

Varying Peer Response Activities

A commonplace version of peer response occurs when students exchange completed drafts and provide one another feedback before undertaking a subsequent revision. Naturally, peer interaction need not be limited to comments on completed drafts. Writing groups can function to perform a variety of tasks. For instance, students can engage in idea generation or prewriting activities and then collaborate before even beginning a draft. Sample activities are shown in Figs. 6.4 to 6.6, which show scaffolded peer review tasks for the prewriting stage and the editing stages. Figure 6.4 displays two common idea generation activities (listing and freewriting) and shows how peers can help each other find ideas (strategy 1) and focus them more clearly (strategy 2). The activity shown in Fig. 6.5 encourages students to clarify their ideas before committing themselves to an entire completed draft by listing ideas, preparing an informal outline, and drafting an introductory passage. They then are to show their introductions to a peer to assess how clearly they have expressed their initial ideas. (see also Ferris, 2003b, Fig. 8.2, p.166, and Liu & Hansen, 2002, especially Chapters 5 and 6).

Peers also can engage in the writing process at the editing stage, helping classmates to detect grammatical and mechanical errors before finalizing a ratable version (see Ferris, 1995c; 2002b, pp. 102–105; 2003b, p. 180 for discussion and examples). Critics of peer response—both teachers and ESL students—have wondered whether peer-editing tasks (i.e., peer feedback on linguistic and mechanical features) are appropriate in L2 literacy courses, given students' understandable lack of familiarity with the forms and rules of written discourse. Obviously, the effectiveness of such activities depends to some extent on the background, L2 proficiency levels, and literacy skills of the students, but these tasks can be useful for helping students develop self-editing skills and metalinguistic awareness (see chapter 7).

~~~~~~

Peer Collaboration: Brainstorming
STRATEGY 1: MAKING A LIST

To begin, you can list several experiences and concepts that might be good topics for a personal writing task. Here are some examples:

Experiences	Concepts
Leaving home	Loneliness
Starting at a new school	Self-respect
Learning a new language	Fear

Activity. **Working in a small group,** add five topics to the lists of experiences and concepts. Share your lists with the other groups in the class.

Follow-up. Make a list of topics you might want to write about in your own personal essay. Star the topics that seem most promising.

STRATEGY 2: FREEWRITING

Sometimes writing quickly on a topic will stimulate your ideas and help you identify things to include in your essay.

Guidelines for Freewriting

1. Write quickly and steadily for a brief period of time (5–10 minutes is ideal).
2. Do not worry about mistakes, word choice, style, and so on.
3. Whatever you do, <u>do not stop writing</u>. If your mind goes blank, write "I don't know what to write. I don't know" until a new thought develops.

Activity

1. Choose one of the topics you starred in the "making a list" activity. Freewrite for 5 minutes on that topic.
2. **Exchange freewrites with a partner. Have that partner underline a word, phrase, or idea from your freewrite that particularly interests her or him.**
3. Now take the word/phrase/concept **that your partner identified** and freewrite on that for 5 minutes.

(Adapted from Spack, 1990, pp. 38–40)

[Note: Collaborative portions of the activities are **highlighted.**]

~~~~~~

FIG. 6.4. Peer collaboration during brainstorming activities.

Teachers who use peer editing workshops need to structure and monitor these sessions carefully and set realistic expectations for them. Editing workshops will not relieve teachers of the need to provide error feedback at some stage of a multidrafting cycle. It is helpful, for example, to ask peer editors simply to underline in pencil any errors that they perceive rather than offer corrections. Reviewers can look for specific error patterns rather than follow vague instructions such as "Go through your partner's paper and circle all the errors you find." Classroom follow-up work should require students to ask questions of their peer editors and their teacher, leading students to chart their own errors (i.e., malformations that their peers helped them identify as well as errors that they discovered on their own).

PEER RESPONSE WORKSHEET
PREWRITING ACTIVITIES

1. What reading(s) have you selected to comment on?
2. Write a two- to three-sentence reaction to the essay.
3. Make a list of details, examples, or experiences you might use to support or contradict the ideas in the reading. Write your list below.
   List of possible examples . . .
4. Following the example of Doxis (p. 107), organize your list into an informal outline.
5. Read p. 109 on "The introduction." Draft an introduction for your essay. Be sure to include the three steps listed on p. 109!

✳ ◆ ✳ ◆ ✳ ◆ ✳ ◆ ✳ ◆ ✳ ◆ ✳ ◆ ✳ ◆ ✳ ◆ ✳ ◆ ✳ ◆ ✳

PREWRITING: PEER RESPONSE

Your Name: _____   **Writer's Name:** _____

Directions. *Read your group member's introduction draft and write down **brief** answers to the following questions:*

1. Which essay(s) has your classmate selected to respond to?
2. What is your classmate's reaction to the essay? How do you know?
3. What ideas or examples from his or her own experience might your classmate be planning to include in his or her paper?

After you have written your responses, compare them with the worksheet that your group member completed. This should give both of you an idea of how clear the introduction is and what still needs to be improved!

[Note: These activities are based on an essay assignment in that students had to select a reading from their textbook (Spack, 1990) and relate the ideas in the reading to their own experience. Page numbers in the instructions refer to the textbook.]

FIG. 6.5. Peer response during the early drafting phase.

After an assignment has been completed and polished, many teachers complete the process with a publication or celebration stage in which writers share their finished products with their writing groups or the entire class. The sharing of papers with a group is perhaps more feasible with primary and secondary writers because they spend more time in class. Nonetheless, students in adult, college, and university settings can share their final papers with their writing groups. Alternatively, papers can be compiled into a booklet, on a CD, or a course web page to be reproduced and shared with classmates.

Finally, numerous other activities can be completed in pairs or groups in a literacy course. For instance, pairs or groups of students can discuss course readings, take turns preparing questions and leading discussions of assigned reading selections, collaborate on oral presentations related to course readings and essay topics, and conduct library research together to find sources for a research assignment. None of these activities deals specifically with the students' own writing. However, used in conjunction

FEEDBACK LOG: PEER EDITING WORKSHOP

Your Name:	Writer's Name:

Instructions. *Read your partner's essay drafts looking for any errors in grammar, vocabulary, punctuation, or spelling. Use the chart below as a guide to what to look for.* Underline *any errors you find, but* **DO NOT** *write any corrections!*

NOTE to WRITERS: Go through your essay and try to correct any errors your partner marked. Also correct any you notice yourself that your partner might have missed! When you have finished, complete the chart below.

	Error Type	*Number of Errors Found*
Spelling		
Incorrect word or word form		
Noun endings and determiner errors		
Verb tense and form errors		
Sentence structure errors (missing words, unnecessary words, run-ons, fragments, and so on)		
Mechanical errors (punctuation, capitalization, and so forth)		

FIG. 6.6. Peer editing workshop.

with peer response sessions, these alternatives can help build relationships among students, leading to a greater sense of classroom community. Moreover, guided collaborative tasks can give students valuable experience working on both written and oral assignments with their classmates, an important skill that is increasingly needed across the disciplines in university courses (Ferris & Tagg, 1996) and in the workplace. Collaborative tasks are especially useful for accommodating students from collectivist cultures who expect group work to benefit the group as a whole, not just individual writers (Carson & Nelson, 1994, 1996). In addition, cooperative activities allow for the integration of language skills (listening, speaking, reading, writing), all of which are crucial for L2 literacy development and L2 acquisition in general (Mangelsdorf, 1989).

Holding Students Accountable for Giving Feedback and Considering Peer Responses

Mittan (1989) and Leki (1990b) encouraged teachers to read and respond to peer feedback. Mittan (1989) went a step further by suggesting that students actually be assigned grades on their peer response sheets. Both authors stressed that writers and respondents need access to teacher feedback on the peer responses (e.g., by receiving photocopies of the response form with the teacher's feedback) "so that both may know what is expected" of respondents (Leki, 1990b, p. 17). In addition to providing feedback and marks on the quality and substance of peer feedback, teachers can ask writers to write a brief summary of, and reaction to, the feedback they have received from peers (e.g., in a journal entry). Alternatively, students can compose a letter in which they explain how they incorporated peer feedback into their revisions (or discuss why they chose not to do so) when they submit their revised work for the instructor to assess. All of these techniques help students take the peer review process seriously, consider the peer feedback they give carefully, and think critically about the responses they have received from classmates. See Fig. 6.7 for sample follow-up activities to peer response.

Considering Individual Students' Needs

Most of the principles and suggestions outlined so far assume a relatively advanced level of linguistic and writing proficiency. Mittan (1989) claimed that peer review activities could be incorporated at all levels and for all age groups. Along similar lines, Berger (1990) suggested that "teachers should adjust their expectations and the amount of guidance they give to [students'] proficiency level, maturity, and backgrounds ... [and] teach much simpler and more specific feedback techniques with a lower level writing class" (p. 30). Nelson and Murphy (1992/1993) reported that peer response activities worked well with intermediate-level students in a university-level intensive English program. Huang (1994) found that weaker writers benefited even more than stronger writers from peer review. Several popular entry-level academic writing textbooks (Benesch, Rakijas, & Rorschach, 1987; Reid & Lindstrom, 1985; Rooks, 1988) offer a variety of simple, focused peer response activities for students with low levels of English proficiency and limited English writing experience

---

PEER EDITING FOLLOW-UP TASKS

1. ***In-Class Activity.*** Immediately after a peer response session, give students 5 to 10 minutes to freewrite on the following questions:

   a. What did you learn from reading your classmates' papers?
   b. Can you summarize your group members' suggestions about your papers in 1–2 sentences?
   c. Do you agree with their comments? Do you find them helpful (clear, specific)? Do you think you will use them in your revision? Why or why not?

2. ***Homework Activity.*** Ask students to complete the following task for homework after a peer response session:

   > In class on Tuesday, two of your peers read and responded to your essay. Read your essay over again. Now read and think about your peers' comments using the peer feedback forms you received from them and your own notes on your group discussion.

   > Write 1–2 paragraphs (about half a page) in which you explain (a) which of your classmates' comments you found most helpful and why, (b) any comments you did *not* find helpful and with which you disagree and why, (c) your own ideas (from your own rereading and from your peers' comments) about what you need to change when you write Draft 2.

3. ***Revision Cover Memo.*** When students submit a revised essay following peer feedback, ask them to write a one-page cover memo that goes through the revision suggestions given by peers one by one. For each suggestion, ask students to explain either (a) how they addressed the suggestion, referring to specific points in their text; or (b) why they chose not to address it.

FIG. 6.7. Peer response follow-up activities.

(Fig. 6.8). Liu and Hansen (2002) also discussed this issue extensively, devoting an entire chapter to the "contexts" of response (i.e., ESL/EFL, institutions, student characteristics, and so forth).

As we have noted, students' prior experiences with collaborative learning and with English-language literacy courses also may affect their reactions toward, and behaviors in, writing groups (Allaei & Connor, 1990; Carson & Nelson, 1994, 1996). Leki (1990b) noted that, ironically, students with limited literacy experience in their primary languages (i.e., immigrant students) may have a relatively easier time with peer review because their judgments of peers' texts may not be colored by L1-based rhetorical schemata. Furthermore, lower-level writers may have attended schools in North America or other English-speaking environments for a number of years and may have become familiar and comfortable with group work. International students, particularly those who are highly educated and have strong L1 literacy skills, may require some preparatory contrastive rhetoric consciousness-raising (during the modeling phase of the peer

PEER RESPONSE WORKSHEET

Sharing information before writing

Directions. Get into a group with two or three classmates. Read your personal information forms out loud to each other. You may ask each other for more information. Then write the information about you and your group members in the chart below. Use the information in the chart to write a paragraph called "About My Group."

Name:	
Home Country:	
Home Language(s):	
Hobbies:	
Major:	
Other:	

(Adapted from Benesch et al., 1987, pp. 19–21)

Sharing a Paragraph Draft (General)

Directions, Read your paragraph about you to a small group of classmates or to a partner. You may read it more than once or you may give it to them to read. Ask them what they think about your paragraph. Do they understand everything? Ask them for at least one more piece of information that they would like to see in your paragraph. Then read your paragraph again. Is there anything you want to change? How can you write your ideas more clearly?

(Adapted from Rooks, 1988, p. 4)

Sharing a Paragraph Draft (Specific)

Directions, Write a paragraph describing one thing about your country. Your reader will be a classmate who is from a different country. Then exchange paragraphs with that classmate, read your partner's paragraph, and answer the following questions:

1. What questions did the writer answer (Who? What? etc.). Underline the answers to the questions in the paragraph.
2. What did you find most interesting about this paragraph?
3. What other interesting information could the writer add to this paragraph?

(Adapted from Reid & Lindstrom, 1985, pp. 52–53)

FIG. 6.8.   **Peer response activities for students at lower proficiency levels.**

response process) before attempting to review other students' work (see chapter 1).

Some students may object to peer response activities on personal or cultural grounds. Learning style research indicates that some students learn best through working individually. Such students may be frustrated and resentful if forced to spend class time in group work and to share their writing with others (Reid, 1995a). Other students, influenced by sociocultural expectations, may feel that the teacher is the only legitimate critic of student writing, and that it is inappropriate to offer opinions about or critique other students' work (Carson & Nelson, 1994, 1996). Teachers certainly should be aware of and sensitive to students' feelings, but they can dispel some student objections through careful preparation and modeling, thoughtful matching of participants to pairs and groups, and acquainting students with the advantages of peer feedback. Not only can peer feedback promote writing development (e.g., many professional writers depend on writers' groups), but it also builds relationships and enables learners to work with peers. All of these activities that become especially crucial for writers who need to develop proficient academic literacy skills (Ferris & Tagg, 1996; chapters 1 and 2). A compromise approach would be to have students work collaboratively during the first half of the term, then allow them to opt out of peer response sessions later on, in which case they should complete self-evaluation activities while others are working collaboratively.

Logistical Concerns

As Mittan (1989) noted, successful peer review sessions require more than "simply telling students to exchange their papers and comment on them" (p. 212). Before beginning collaborative work in the writing class, teachers must consider several practical questions:

How Big Should Peer Response Groups Be and How Should They Be Formed? Although writing teachers vary in their preferred group size, the optimal number of students working together is probably between two and four. The advantage of dyads is that students have time to engage in thoughtful consideration of peers' papers and substantive in-class interaction. The benefit of having three or four students in a group is a wider range of opinions and perspectives. A group larger than four may be unable to give adequate time to reading and discussing each participant's paper. Larger groups also diminish individuals' opportunities to contribute and participate in discussions because of reduced floor time.

Some practitioners argue that students should be able to select their own peer groups. Nonetheless, we can cite compelling reasons why teachers should assign learners to specific groups and maintain consistent groups throughout the course. Because some evidence suggests that peer response is most beneficial when writing abilities vary widely, teachers can take students' strengths and weaknesses into account when placing students into groups. Teachers also should consider students' first language backgrounds, genders, and personalities in forming groups. We should acknowledge that working in either homogeneous or heterogeneous L1 groups entails both advantages and disadvantages. Moreover, if group composition remains constant over time, students have the advantage of becoming familiar with group members' work and seeing development over successive drafts, enabling respondents to give more specific and helpful feedback. However, if it becomes clear that a particular dyad or group is not working well together, teachers may need to consider some reconfiguration later in the term. (see also Liu & Hansen, 2002, Chapter 3, for a detailed discussion of grouping students for peer response).

How Will Students Exchange Papers? The simplest way for students to read one another's papers (or sections of papers) is to exchange them in class and read them on the spot. However, problems can occur if students fail to bring their drafts to class on peer-review day. In-class reading of drafts can also be time consuming. Although the standard L1 peer review practice is for the writer to read his or her paper aloud to a partner or group, this practice is problematic for some ESL students because of listening comprehension and pronunciation difficulties. A possible solution to these problems involves asking writers to bring a photocopy of their drafts to class the day before the peer review session so that group members can read the papers at home and be prepared to discuss them. Another option that is rapidly becoming easier and more widely available is for students to exchange and comment on drafts electronically (see chapter 9).

Should Peer Feedback Be Oral or Written? Giving students specific questions to answer and requiring them to write their responses emphasizes the importance of the activity, enabling the teacher to hold students accountable for their efforts. However, ESL students may sit silently in class, write out answers to the feedback prompts, exchange forms with their partners, and never engage in any sustained discussion. This problem can be avoided by requiring students to read drafts and write responses before coming to class. Both of these aims can be accomplished electronically. By requiring advance preparation, teachers can ensure that valuable class time is used for oral interaction focused on student writing. If advance preparation is not possible or practical, the teacher should monitor peer groups carefully during response sessions to ensure that students are talking as well as writing. We recommend that teachers specify how much time students will be given to read their peers' samples, write reactions on the peer response forms, and discuss their reactions.

What About Time Management and Crowd Control? Any time a teacher assigns group work, he or she relinquishes a degree of control over class time and student participation. Teachers should allot time in the syllabus and lesson plans for peer review and carefully plan adequate time for the activity, especially if students read drafts for the first time in class (see chapter 3). As we mentioned, it is also helpful to give students time parameters at the beginning of peer review sessions and then remind them when to move along in the responding process (e.g., "It's time to switch and talk about your partner's paper now"). Another risk inherent in collaborative work is that some groups may work more quickly or slowly than others. Instructors should be prepared with follow-up activities for group members who finish early and should check in with slower groups to help them to stay on task and pick up their pace if necessary. Structuring peer response tasks clearly, arranging the groups carefully, and monitoring group progress should minimize the noise level and keep students on track.

SUMMARY

Our overview of research on peer response activities leaves us with some encouraging evidence in favor of implementing peer response as a regular component of L2 literacy courses. Studies of student opinion generally indicate that ESL writers enjoy peer feedback and find it helpful, especially if it is offered in conjunction with instructor feedback—but at different stages of the drafting-and-composing cycle (e.g., peer feedback on first drafts, teacher feedback on revisions). Recent studies investigating the influence of teacher feedback on student revision, with few exceptions, suggest that student writers use peer feedback in their revisions, and that such revisions improve overall text quality.

Despite some of the potential problems and concerns that have been raised, carefully designed peer response activities can be extremely beneficial to individual student writers and to the classroom climate. Teachers who dismiss peer feedback because the practice "doesn't work" or wastes time, or because students react negatively, may have inappropriate expectations concerning the procedure. Teachers should not assume that peer response, even when implemented effectively, can (or should) replace or drastically reduce the need for teacher response. Before anticipating favorable outcomes, teachers must prepare students adequately and structure peer review sessions appropriately. Although the cost of peer response as an integrated part of a writing course is high—it takes a great deal of time not easily spared from the typically crowded course syllabus—the potential benefits are enormous. The principles and practical suggestions outlined in this chapter should help ESL writing teachers to implement this valuable technique more successfully.

REFLECTION AND REVIEW

1. Identify some hypothetical arguments in favor of using peer response instead of teacher response or vice versa. What arguments favor implementing both?
2. After reflecting on your own experience and reading the principles presented in this chapter, determine the single greatest potential benefit for students who participate in peer feedback activities. Consider conditions and circumstances that could prevent this advantage from being realized in an authentic classroom context.
3. On the basis of your own experience and your reading of this chapter, what do you think is the single greatest potential drawback for students who participate in peer feedback activities? What steps might teachers take either to avoid or to solve this problem?
4. Do you agree with those who favor a more open-ended approach to peer response or those who advocate tighter teacher control? This chapter clearly favors the latter position. Justify your opinion.
5. Identify the advantages and disadvantages of allowing students to choose their own partners or groups, as opposed to teacher assignment of groups. Although this chapter clearly favors the latter position, persuasive arguments can be made for both positions.
6. What are the benefits and drawbacks of peer feedback groups consisting of homogeneous L1 groups? What could be done to optimize the advantages and mitigate the disadvantages?

Application Activity 6.1: Comparing Studies on the Effects of Peer Feedback

Directions. Obtain and read the studies by Connor and Asenavage (1994) and Paulus (1999), both published in the *Journal of Second Language Writing*. Read both studies carefully, taking notes on the questions outlined in the chart below.

Evaluation Questions for Peer Response Studies

Participants and Setting

- How many students and teachers were involved?
- If the students were divided into treatment groups, what were the group sizes?
- What was the instructional context?
- What were the proficiency and literacy levels of the students?

Peer Feedback Procedures

- Was any modeling or training given before peer review sessions?
- How were peer review sessions structured?
- How were peer groups or dyads formed?
- How consistently was peer review used?
- What did the students do after receiving peer feedback?

Research Design Issues

- What specific research questions did the studies explore (e.g., nature of interactions, student attitudes, effects on revision)?
- How were effects measured?
- Were multiple raters or coders used, and were interrater reliabilities calculated and reported?

(Source: Ferris, 2003b, Fig. 4.2, p. 72.)

After reading and critically evaluating the two studies, discuss the following questions:

1. What do you think accounts for the different results reported in the two studies?
2. Do you find either study more convincing? If so, which one, and why?

3. What are the practical implications of the two studies for the use of peer response in the L2 writing classroom?

(Source: Ferris, 1997, p. 322)

Application Activity 6.2: Designing Peer Response Forms

Directions. Imagine you are teaching high-intermediate to advanced ESL students in a secondary or college English class. Their first-week, in-class, diagnostic writing assignment was an argumentative essay based on a newspaper article entitled "Violent Essay Lands Boy in Jail." (see Appendix 6B for the prompt and a sample student essay).

Considering the peer response principles and suggestions discussed in this chapter, imagine that you are designing a peer feedback activity based on this assignment. For this exercise, assume that your students have written Draft 1 in class and are going to revise it at least twice before it is finalized.

1. Create a worksheet that you would give students to structure the peer response activity. This worksheet can take a variety of forms, but it must have clear instructions for the students to follow.
2. Be prepared to explain (a) the procedures you would use (in or out of class) to implement this activity and (b) the philosophies or principles of response that guided you (see chapters 1, 5, and 6).
3. When you have completed this activity, examine the three peer response forms designed by pre-service writing instructors in a MATESOL program for this assignment in Appendix 6A. How is your activity similar to or different from the samples? How are they different from one another?

Application Activity 6.3: Giving and Receiving Peer Feedback

Directions

1. Select a writing or teaching project you have worked on recently (e.g., a paper for a graduate course or conference presentation, a lesson plan or syllabus, a set of class materials).

Find a partner who is working on the same project or something similar.

2. Using the precepts and examples discussed in this chapter, design a peer response form appropriate for critiquing the paper or project.
3. Exchange materials with your partner. Before meeting, read your partner's materials carefully and write answers to the peer response questions you constructed in step 2.
4. Meet with your partner and discuss your responses to each other's papers. Take notes on or audiotape your discussion.
5. Compose a reflective essay in which you discuss
   - the experience of designing response questions for a professional project
   - the experience of reading and responding to your peer's work
   - what you thought about your partner's responses (written and oral) to your work. Did you agree with him or her? Find the responses valuable? Why or why not?
   - insights you gained about the peer response process from participating in the discussion, and from your notes or tape of the discussion
   - how this experience relates to your own teaching and to the students with whom you work (or hope to work).

NOTES

[1] We can observe overlap between categories among these studies. For example, Mendonça and Johnson (1994) addressed all three of these areas. Moreover, some "combination studies" (Arndt, 1993) have looked intensively at both teacher and peer feedback.

[2] Studies by Carson and Nelson (1996) and Nelson and Carson (1998) reported on videotaped analyses of peer response sessions with three ESL students. The authors noted that the Chinese students in particular were uncomfortable with their sessions. However, in our view, these case studies, being so small, highlight practical issues important for making peer response more successful instead of providing strong evidence contradicting the larger survey studies of student views about peer feedback.

APPENDIX 6A: SAMPLE PEER RESPONSE TASKS

Sample 1

Purpose: The purpose of this exercise is to enhance your skills in critical analysis and further your familiarization with American academic writing. You will assist your classmates by helping them analyze their essays, and you will also be able to recognize areas of weakness with regard to focus and organization in your own writing.

Workshop Instructions: *Before reading your peer's essay, please reread the attached assignment prompt and recall the objectives of the essay task. After you have read through your peer's essay, please use this form to record information from your analysis. Refer back to your peer's essay as needed.*

Your Name: _____
Writer's Name: _____

1. In your own words, state the main idea of the author's essay.
2. How does the writer's main idea relate back to the assignment prompt?
3. Complete the following chart:

	What arguments did the writer present?	What information cited from readings relates to the arguments?	What examples did the writer provide for each argument?	What information appears insignificant to the arguments?
a.				
b.				
c.				

4. What difficulties, if any, did you encounter in locating the information you needed for the chart?

5. How does each argument relate back to the writer's main idea?
6. What did you find in the writer's essay that you do or may apply in your own writing?
7. In a brief paragraph addressed to the writer, please comment on the positive aspects of the essay, and provide suggestions that might guide your peer to improve in a revision of the essay.

Source: Suzie Dollesin, 2003. California State University, Sacramento, Department of English: English 215B assignment. Used with student permission.

Sample 2
Student Response Form

Name: _____
Student Reviewer: _____

Activity: *Thoroughly read your classmate's draft essay. Using the course feedback checklist, choose two or three aspects from each category that you think are especially good or need some additional work.* **Note them in the chart below with specific comments.**

Discussion: *Circle what you think are the three strongest and three weakest areas in each essay. Be prepared to discuss these with your team, and take notes on the discussion of your own paper!*

	What I like...	*What needs work...*
Response to Prompt		
Content/ Ideas		
Use of Readings		
Organization		
Language and Mechanics		

Additional Comments:

Source: Patricia Doris, 2003. California State University, Sacramento, Department of English: English 215B assignment. Used with student permission.

Sample 3

Peer Response for Draft 1

Reader's Name: _____

Writer's Name: _____

Directions: *Exchange your first draft with a partner. Read the paper from beginning to end. Then, read the following questions and reread the essay with these questions in mind. Write your response in the space provided. Discuss your response with your group members. Remember to "sandwich" any suggestions with positive comments!*

Positive comment
Suggestion
Positive comment

1. What was the writer's answer to the question in the prompt: "Should a student be punished for something he or she writes in a school assignment?"
2. What do you think the main idea or thesis is?
3. What evidence or examples did the writer use as support?
4. What do you like best about this essay?
5. What do you think could use more work?
6. Do you have any suggestions, considering our class grading criteria?

Source: Sarah Oettle, 2003. California State University, Sacramento, Department of English: English 215B assignment. Used with student permission.

APPENDIX 6B: MATERIALS (PROMPT, AND STUDENT ESSAY) FOR APPLICATION ACTIVITY 6.5: DESIGNING A PEER RESPONSE FORM

DIAGNOSTIC ESSAY

Directions: *Please read the article, "Violent Essay Lands Boy in Jail." Then respond to the writing prompt below.*

BACKGROUND

School violence has been a major problem in recent years. Due to the fear of violence, many schools have adopted a "zero tolerance" policy toward students who carry weapons, make threats, or commit violent acts. These students are suspended or expelled by the school, and often they also are arrested by the police. In the article, "Violent Essay Lands Boy in Jail," a student is suspended and arrested for writing a scary Halloween essay.

TASK

Write an essay giving your opinion: *Should a student be punished for something he or she writes for a school assignment?* Support your position with facts from the article or other news stories of which you are aware. You also may use your personal experience or that of your friends. Be sure to state your opinion clearly and include specific references to the reading text.

STUDENT ESSAY: "Violent Essay Lands Boy in Jail"

Have you ever heard that a student was punished as a criminal because of writing an essay for the school assignment. You have probably not heard about it, but I have. According to the article, "Violent Essay Lands Boy in Jail," the author Ponder, Texas,* writes that a student in seventh grade, Christopher, was arrested "for writing a story about shooting two classmates and a teacher." It was very strange, but it was true. Students like me do not feel secure when we read this story. To me, punishing students for writing an essay for the school assignment is extremely wrong.

Young people have imagination. They like to think about adventure and share that adventure with other people. I also did the same thing when I was a teenager. For example, when I was in eighth grade, I dreamed to become superman in "The Superman Show" so I could hurt bad people who intend to do bad things. And I shared this dream with my mom, but she did not react because she knew that I would not do what I was interested to, hurt bad people. When I read the article "Violent Essay Lands Boy in Jail," Christopher and I had something in common. We were both interested in adventure and hormor to share our interests. I told my mom what my dream was about. As the same as Christopher, he wanted to share his interested essay to his teacher and classmates. However, we did not act what we were interested in. Christopher did not kill any classmate or teacher, according to the information in the article. Likewise, many times many authors write about violent stories such as killing people, but most of them are not killers at all. As a result, imagination and acting are very different. When people imagine something, it does not mean that they are going to act the same as their imagination. Therefore, punishing students for writing essays is a very terrible idea.

Also, the acts of writing should not be limited. If the acts of writing is limited, students face more difficulties. For example, I may know well about fighting steak, I believe that I am going to write well about the topic. However, my teacher does not allow me to write about that topic for class assignment. Then I have to chose another topic that I might not know about. This can give me trouble. As a result, I believe that the school system should let students create or have a freedom to write essays for the school assignment. That is why writing should not be limited and students should not be punished as criminal for something.

In conclusion, I believe that punishing students for writing essays for the school assignment is not a good idea. The school system should allow students to chose a good topic to write about.

---

*Ponder, Texas is the city, not the author.

Chapter 7

Improving Accuracy in Student Writing: Error Treatment in the Composition Class

Questions for Reflection

- *Think about your own writing processes. At what point in your writing do you focus on the linguistic accuracy of your work?*
- *Of what strategies are you aware when you edit your own writing?*
- *How and where did you acquire the grammatical knowledge that you use to edit your work?*
- *How effective is your approach to editing your own writing? If it is effective, why do you think so? If it does not always work, what might improve it?*
- *What do you find most challenging about giving students feedback on their language errors (grammar, word choice, spelling, mechanics, and so on)?*
- *What ideas do you have about the best way or ways to help ESL students focus on editing their written work? Are these ideas congruent with your own editing process? Why or why not?*

A BRIEF HISTORY OF ERROR CORRECTION AND GRAMMAR TEACHING IN THE WRITING CLASS

Most writing theorists and instructors would agree that process-oriented pedagogies have greatly enhanced the outcomes of both L1 and L2 composition instruction. However, although students may be much better at idea generation and revision than they once were, ESL student papers may nonetheless contain excessive grammatical and lexical inaccuracies by the standards of English-speaking academic readers. Among ESL professionals it is understood that L2 acquisition is a process that takes time and that an expectation of perfect papers, even from advanced students, is unrealistic. Other readers of ESL student writing, however, often demand a high level of formal accuracy. Because of these realities and because ESL teachers will not always be there to assist their students, writing instructors need to help their students develop and improve their editing skills.

Before the advent of process-oriented instruction in ESL literacy instruction, teacher feedback to second language writing students often was excessively concerned with eradicating student errors (Applebee, 1981; Zamel, 1985). Often, that feedback was notably unsuccessful in helping to reduce error frequency in subsequent student writing (see Truscott, 1996, for a review). However, as process-oriented practices, with their emphasis on student writers' ideas and individual writing processes, achieved widespread acceptance, some instructors swung to the opposite extreme, giving little or no attention to the morphosyntactic or lexical accuracy of students' final products (Horowitz, 1986a). Zamel (1982) has reminded us that

> engaging students in the process of composing [does not eliminate] our obligation to upgrade their linguistic competencies. . . . If, however, students learn that writing is a process through which they can explore and discover their thoughts and ideas, then product is likely to improve as well. (p. 207)

Some L2 scholars (Eskey, 1983; Horowitz, 1986a) immediately raised questions about whether fervent adherence to process approaches would meet the needs of L2 writers, who are grappling simultaneously with second language acquisition and the development of their literacy skills. Those ESL writing teachers trained in process pedagogies also found that students' errors "were not magically disappearing as the sure result of a more enlightened process and view of writing" (Ferris, 2002b, p. xi). Worse, they "helplessly watched some of [their] own students fail the course exit exam and the university's writing proficiency exam" (Ferris, 2002a, p. 6). Thus, instructors in the late 1980s and early 1990s began seeking better answers about techniques and strategies to help students improve the accuracy of their writing while working within a process-oriented paradigm (see chapter 1). These questions led to the publication of various "how-to" articles, books, and chapters for teachers (Bates, Lane, & Lange, 1993; Ferris, 1995c, 2002b; Frodesen, 1991; Frodesen & Holten, 2003; Reid, 1998b), editing handbooks specifically authored for ESL writers (Ascher, 1993; Fox, 1992; Lane & Lange, 1999; Raimes, 1992), and novel primary research on the effects of error correction, grammar instruction, and strategy training (see Ferris, 2002b; 2003b for reviews).

A new era in the debate surrounding error treatment in the larger process–product conversation was ushered in by a review essay published in *Language Learning* by Truscott (1996). In his article, Truscott argued strongly for the abolition of grammar correction in L2 writing courses. The appearance of Truscott's article led to a published debate in 1999 in the *Journal of Second Language Writing* (Ferris, 1999a; Truscott, 1999; see also Ferris, 2004), spurring new research efforts that are ongoing.

Still, for most teachers, students, and readers of L2 writing, the "debate" is, quite literally, academic. They know that L2 student writers have gaps in morphological, syntactic, and lexical knowledge that are more pronounced than those of L1 writers. They also know that most L2 students have not had enough exposure to the language (especially written English) to have developed intuitions that match those of their native speaker (NS) counterparts. They know that the resulting errors students make in their writing may be serious (interfering with the message) and stigmatizing (irritating to a NS academic audience). In short, they know that ESL student writers need expert help in improving the linguistic accuracy of their texts. The remainder of this chapter is therefore devoted to reviewing the questions concerning error treatment, grammar instruction, and strategy training for L2 writers. We also aim to offer practical suggestions based on our best guesses about how to approach these challenging tasks derived from the existing research base and from our own experiences as teachers. However, because we definitely do not wish to argue that error treatment should be the only or the primary concern of an L2 writing course, we conclude this chapter by proposing ways of integrating these concerns with other dimensions of literacy education.

ERROR CORRECTION: QUESTIONS, ISSUES, AND OPTIONS

The following section addresses eight core questions that reflect the concerns of researchers and teachers regarding the practice of formal error treatment. Figure 7.1 encapsulates these questions.

Does Error Feedback Help Students At All?

The most pressing question to ask of the research base is the one raised by Truscott (1996): Is error feedback harmful or helpful? In his review, Truscott argued that: the existing research base provides no evidence that "grammar correction"[1] ever helps any students, that a number of "practical problems" (teacher incompetence, student inattention, and so on) render error correction a futile exercise, and that time spent on error correction is actually harmful because it takes energy and attention away from more important issues (i.e., student ideas) in writing courses.

1. Does error feedback help students at all?

2. What is an error? Should we mark for "errors" or "style"?

3. What kinds of errors do ESL writers most typically make?

4. Should error feedback be *selective* or *comprehensive*?

5. Should error feedback focus on *larger* or smaller *categories* or types?

6. Should feedback be *direct* or *indirect*?

7. Should errors be *labeled* or *located*?

8. *Where in the text* should error feedback be given?

FIG. 7.1. Questions about error feedback.

However, contrary to Truscott's (1996) assertion, empirical evidence strongly suggests that error feedback can help students, both in the short and long term. In the second language acquisition (SLA) literature, for instance, findings show that adult acquirers in particular need their errors made salient and explicit to them so they can avoid fossilization and continue developing their target language competence (Doughty & Varela, 1998; Doughty & Williams, 1998; Ellis, 1998; Ellis et al., 2001; James, 1998; Lightbown, 1998; Lyster & Ranta, 1997; Tomasello & Herron, 1989). In studies of error correction in L2 writing, we find evidence favorable to systematic error treatment in two strands of research: (a) studies that compare the accuracy of texts generated by students who received error correction with that of the texts of students who did not (Fathman & Whalley, 1990; Ferris & Roberts, 2001; Kepner, 1991)[2] and (b) studies that measure increases in linguistic accuracy in student texts over time (Ferris, 1995a, 1997; Lalande, 1982; Robb, Ross, & Shortreed, 1986).[3] (See Ferris, 2004, for an in-depth analysis of this issue; see also Ferris, 2002b; 2003b)

What Is an Error? Should Teachers Mark for "Errors" or "Style"?

Disputes concerning errors have often centered on the question of whether it is fair or accurate to label the non–target-like production of L2 learners as "errors," or whether such forms should more properly be considered natural consequences of the evolving stages of learner interlanguage (Corder, 1967; James, 1998; Truscott, 1996). Nevertheless, many teachers would likely be comfortable with a working definition of errors such as the following: Errors consist of morphological, syntactic, and lexical deviations from the grammatical rules of a language that violate the intuitions of NSs.[4] Issues of "style," on the other hand, relate more to the teacher's sense that a particular word or phrase might flow more smoothly or idiomatically in a text than to any violation of underlying or universal grammatical patterns. With the exception of very advanced, highly proficient L2 writers, it probably is both more urgent and more productive to focus on errors rather than style, and specifically to focus on patterned and rule-governed errors that can be addressed constructively through instruction and strategy training.

What Kinds of Errors Do ESL Writers Most Typically Make?

Whereas NS composition students also produce errors in their texts, the errors produced by L2 writers tend to be distinct from those of their NS counterparts. For instance, ESL writers frequently struggle with a range of issues related to verbs, (e.g., errors in verb tense, errors in form including target-like formation of tenses, passive constructions, modal constructions, and so forth) and subject–verb agreement. Rarely if ever do NS students make analogous verb errors, with the exception perhaps of inappropriate use (or avoidance) of relatively obscure verb inflections such as the future perfect progressive. Typically, L2 writers also wrestle with understanding the properties of English nouns. Specifically, they may not grasp distinctions between the various subclasses of nouns (count/noncount, abstract, collective, and so on) or their implications for plural or possessive endings, use of articles and other determiners, or subject-verb agreement.[5]

It is important to note that ESL students produce a range of errors depending on the structure of their L1s and the extent and nature of their previous exposure to and instruction in English (Ferris, 1999b, 2003a; Leki, 1992; Reid, 1998a). Particularly in heterogeneous ESL classrooms in English-speaking countries, a teacher may encounter one group of students that makes frequent verb tense errors, another that struggles with the English determiner system, and still another that has trouble with word order. There may be no overlap across groups. It is thus extremely important for L2 writing teachers to take time to analyze the error patterns and needs of individual students and of each new group of student writers, instead of making assumptions about what "all ESL writers need."[6]

Should Error Feedback Be Selective or Comprehensive?

The next question to consider in providing error feedback is whether to mark only some errors or all of them. Arguments in favor of the former approach (selective correction) are compelling. It is less overwhelming to teachers and students and allows for prioritization of the most serious, frequent patterns of errors made by individual students. This option is thought to facilitate progress toward the development of successful self-editing strategies (Bates, et al., 1993; Ferris, 1995c; Hendrick-son, 1980; Lane & Lange, 1999; Reid, 1998a, 2002). Arguments against this position come from students themselves. Survey reports indicate that students prefer all of their errors to be identified so that they do not "miss anything" (Komura, 1999; Leki, 1991a; Rennie, 2000). Some indicators have been supplied by SLA researchers, who have suggested that leaving errors uncorrected can lead to fossilization (Scarcella, 1996).

The question of selective versus comprehensive error correction may also rest on the stage of the writing process at which the feedback is given. For some composition researchers and many instructors, it is axiomatic that editing for language errors should be postponed until the end of the writing process (Sommers, 1982; Zamel, 1985). As a corollary, proponents of multidrafting maintain that teachers should withhold error feedback until the penultimate or final drafts. The concern is that students will prematurely attend to form instead of continuing to develop their ideas, and "that students cannot attend to multiple concerns at the same time" (Frodesen & Holten, 2003, p. 145). However, the empirical evidence available actually suggests otherwise (Fathman & Whalley, 1990; Ferris, 1997), namely, that students are capable of addressing language and content issues simultaneously. One researcher has even argued that an excessively hands-off approach to error feedback may be harmful to students' progress (Shih, 1998).

According to Frodesen and Holten (2003), "research . . . suggests that it is in the best interest of L2 writers to attend to language issues consistently throughout the drafting process" (p. 145). They are careful to note, however, that their conclusion does not necessarily imply that teachers should mark errors on every single paper, but rather that the teacher may wish to use a range of strategies through a multidraft process to focus students appropriately on selected forms. For example, an instructor may wish to mark or comment selectively on several major patterns of error in a preliminary student draft, knowing that the content of the paper still may change a great deal, but wanting nonetheless to give some language-related advice. On a final draft of a paper, one that has been graded or will not be further revised, the instructor may wish to mark all remaining errors so the writer has that information available for charting (discussed later in this chapter) or simply for future reference.

If an instructor opts for selective error feedback, the question of which errors to mark then arises. Experts have suggested that teachers focus on patterns of error that are global or serious (interfering with the comprehensibility of a text), frequent (relative to other error types and considering percentages of correct and incorrect forms in obligatory contexts), and stigmatizing (more typical of ESL writers than of NS students and potentially more offensive to NS academic audiences). Take, for instance, a hypothetical student paper with 30 obligatory contexts for verbs to be marked morphologically for tense, aspect, or voice. The writer either omits the required morpheme or uses an incorrect form in 10 of the 30 contexts. This frequency of ungrammaticality would exemplify an error that is both frequent and stigmatizing. Whether or not errors are serious or global depends on the coherence of the paper and whether the writer successfully indicates time frame, active/passive voice, and completion of actions and states (aspect) in other ways.

Should Error Feedback Focus on Larger or Smaller Categories or Types?

With the general features that are troublesome for ESL writers identified as well as principles for prioritizing errors on which to focus, another question arises: Is it most helpful to student writers to give feedback on discrete categories of error (e.g., verb tense vs. verb form), or simply to indicate that there is a problem within a broad category (verbs). On this issue, ESL writing textbooks and editing handbooks are split. Some focus on 15 to 20 smaller categories (Lane & Lange, 1999; Raimes, 1992), whereas others select 5 or 6 (Ascher, 1993; Fox, 1992).

The argument in favor of narrower categories maintains that students can be provided with a more learnable, "bite-sized" set of rules to master, topics that can be covered more easily in classroom minilessons, and practice exercises that can be integrated into a literacy course syllabus. On the other hand, we often detect overlap among these narrower categories, and even experienced teachers disagree about whether an error should be classified as "verb tense" or "verb form," whether a noun phrase is ill-formed because it needs a plural ending or an article, or whether a lexical error reflects a problem of spelling or word choice. Thus, an elaborate marking system of 15 to 20 error types or codes may lead to instructor errors, may overwhelm teachers, and may confuse and discourage students. Figure 7.2 provides examples of student errors marked for micro- and macrolevel error types.

The student text excerpt below has been marked in two ways: (1) Errors in five larger categories marked; (2) Errors in smaller, more discrete categories.

Option A (Larger)

Lying is considered dishonest, cheating, or not telling the *[WW]* **true**, but can anyone *[V/WW]* **tells** that he or she never *[V]* ever **lie**? *[SS]* Of **course not,** "everyone lies." I used to lie, and I cannot guarantee that I will not lie again in the future. Many people lie because they want to *[WW]* **make** fun while others lie to take advantage of someone else. However, lying is harmful *[WW]* **while** the person we lie to discovers that we are telling a lie. *[SS]* Despite **of** *[WW]* that, all lies are not **necessary** bad or wrong.

    We sometimes lie because we want to make people happy. I lied to a girl, *[WW]* **for** she *[SS]* **would** get mad. I met a girl four years ago. She *[V]* **is** very *[WW]* **quite**, but her friend, Mindy, *[V]* **likes** to talk a lot. I liked Mindy because she and I had a *[WW]* very good conversation. **While** Mindy left, I told that girl that I liked her more than Mindy because Mindy talked too much. I also told her that most *[WW]* **quite** girls are polite and honest, so *[SS]* so she must be a very good girl. Although I really **didn't her,** I lied to make her happy.

KEY: *V* = verb errors; *WW* = word choice/form errors; *SS* = sentence structure errors.

Option B (Smaller)

Lying is considered dishonest, cheating, or not telling the **true**, *[WF]* but can anyone **tells** *[VF/WW]* that he or she never *[VF]* ever **lie**? *[RO]* Of **course not,** "everyone lies." I used to lie, and I cannot guarantee that I will not lie again in the future. Many people lie because they want to *[WW]* **make** fun while others lie to take advantage of someone else. However, lying is harmful *[WW]* **while** the person we lie to discovers that we are telling a lie. *[SS]* Despite **of** *[WF]* that, all lies are not **necessary** bad or wrong.

    We sometimes lie because we want to make people happy. I lied to a girl, *[WW]* **for** she *[SS]* **would** get mad. I met a girl four years ago. She *[VT]* **is** very *[SP]* **quite**, but her friend, Mindy, *[VT]* **likes** to talk a lot. I liked Mindy because she and I had a *[WW]* very good conversation. **While** Mindy left, I told that girl that I liked her more *[SP]* that I liked her more than Mindy because Mindy talked too much. I also told her that most **quite** girls are *[SS]* polite and honest, so she must be a very good girl. Although I really **didn't her,** I lied to make her happy.

KEY: *VT* = verb tense; *VF* = verb form; *WW* = word choice; *WF* = word form errors;
SS = sentence structure errors; *SP* = spelling.

FIG. 7.2.   Error marking strategies: Larger and smaller categories.

Should Feedback Be Direct or Indirect?

One of the most important decisions in error correction is whether teachers should provide direct or indirect feedback. With direct feedback, the teacher simply provides a target-like form for the student writer (or a suggested correction, if more than one is possible or if it is not entirely clear what the student intended to express). Indirect feedback, on the other hand, provides students with an indication that an error has been made, but requires the student to self-correct.

Most experts agree that indirect feedback clearly has the most potential for helping students to continue developing their L2 proficiency and metalinguistic knowledge. Students themselves, when asked about error feedback preferences, seem to realize that they will learn more from indirect feedback (Ferris & Roberts, 2001; Komura, 1999; Leki, 1991a; Rennie, 2000). However, we suggest that direct correction can play a productive role among lower-level students who are unable to self-edit even when an error is called to their attention. Direct correction also is appropriate for selected idiomatic lexical errors (e.g., collocations involving wrongly selected prepositions) and perhaps when a student text will not be further revised and the teacher wishes to call students' attention to remaining errors. Figure 7.3 presents samples of direct and indirect feedback supplied by a teacher on a brief piece of student writing.

If a teacher opts for indirect feedback as the "default" mechanism, a further correction option to consider is whether the errors should be labeled as to error type (with verbal labels or correction codes) or whether they should simply be located, with the error circled or highlighted but no further information provided. The argument in favor of the labeling option is that an indication of error type might elicit for students previously learned rules that they can then apply to the self-editing task. The opposite argument is that the less explicit option (locating) requires even more effort on the part of the student writer, who must not only figure out the correct form, but also determine what is ill-formed in the first place.

In deciding about labeling or locating, teachers have several questions to consider. First, what are the students' backgrounds? Are they "eye learners" (e.g., international students educated in their home countries who learned English grammar through formal instruction) or "ear learners" (long-term immigrants or even U.S.-born bilinguals who have never undergone formal

---

Option A: Direct Feedback

Lying is considered dishonest, cheating, or not telling the **true** *[truth]*, but can anyone **tells** *[say]* that he or she never ever **lie** *[lies]*? Of **course not,** "everyone lies." I used to lie, and I cannot guarantee that I will not lie again in the future. Many people lie because they want to **make** *[have]* fun while others lie to take advantage of someone else. However, lying is harmful **while** *[when]* the person we lie to discovers that we are telling a lie. Despite **of** that, all lies are not **necessary** *[necessarily]* bad or wrong.

We sometimes lie because we want to make people happy. I lied to a girl **for** *[so]* she **would** *[not]* get mad. I met a girl four years ago. She **is** *[was]* very **quite** *[quiet]*, but her friend, Mindy, **likes** *[liked]* to talk a lot. I liked Mindy because she and I had a very good conversation. **While** *[After/When]* Mindy left, I told that girl that I liked her more than Mindy because Mindy talked too much. I also told her that most **quite** *[quiet]* girls are polite and honest, so she must be a very good girl. Although I really **didn't her** *[like]*, I lied to make her happy.

Option B: Indirect Feedback (error location)

Lying is considered dishonest, cheating, or not telling the **true**, but can anyone **tells** that he or she never ever **lie**? Of **course not,** "everyone lies." I used to lie, and I cannot guarantee that I will not lie again in the future. Many people lie because they want to **make** fun while others lie to take advantage of someone else. However, lying is harmful **while** the person we lie to discovers that we are telling a lie. Despite **of** that, all lies are not **necessary** bad or wrong.

We sometimes lie because we want to make people happy. I lied to a girl, **for** she **would** get mad. I met a girl four years ago. She **is** very **quite**, but her friend, Mindy, **likes** to talk a lot. I liked Mindy because she and I had a very good conversation. **While** Mindy left, I told that girl that I liked her more than Mindy because Mindy talked too much. I also told her that most **quite** girls are polite and honest, so she must be a very good girl. Although I really **didn't her**, I lied to make her happy.

Option C: Indirect Feedback (Verbal End Note)

*As you revise, be sure to check your **verbs** to see if they are in the right tense (past or present) and check your **word choice.** I've highlighted some examples of errors in the first two paragraphs to show you what I mean, but there are others throughout your paper.*

FIG. 7.3. Direct and indirect feedback.

instruction in English outside an English-speaking country and whose exposure to the language has been more naturalistic than classroom based)? The former group might benefit from rule reminders or codes that will jog their memories of formal grammar instruction. Simple location of errors might not provide enough information or elicit enough implicit knowledge for them to self-correct successfully. In contrast, the latter group may have a much stronger "felt sense" of the language, much like NSs, but very little grasp of metalinguistic terminology or access to learned rules. To put the problem another way, "whereas an international student may access a language rule to identify and explain an ungrammatical form, an immigrant ESL student intuits that the form 'sounds wrong' much as a native English speaker might" (Frodesen & Holten, 2003, p. 150).

A related concern involves where to provide corrections. Although many teachers provide direct or indirect in-text feedback at the error location, some opt for check marks in the margin (i. e., "There's an error somewhere in this line, but you have to find it yourself"), or even for verbal end comments about patterns of error, with or without some in-text errors underlined for illustrative purposes (e.g., "You have a lot of missing verb tense endings. I've underlined some examples on the first page, but there are others throughout the essay.") Students tend to prefer point-of-error feedback, but if a teacher is purposefully moving students toward becoming autonomous self-editors, providing less explicit feedback may be an appropriate instructional strategy in some cases (Ferris, 1995c, 1997; Robb et al., 1986).

In short, the task of providing error feedback on student writing is complex, involving teacher decisions about what constitutes an "error," which errors to mark and how, what specific groups and individuals need most, and how error correction fits in with other classroom instructional choices. Furthermore, it is important for teachers not only to consider these "what, how, who, and why" questions, but also to make sure that they are adequately prepared themselves to assess the accuracy of student writing and to provide meaningful guidance for their students. Finally, in addition to providing error feedback on student texts, the "treatment of error" in L2 student writing also may involve in-class grammar instruction and certainly should incorporate strategy training to help students move toward autonomy in editing their own work. It is to these latter two topics that we turn next.

GRAMMAR INSTRUCTION: RESEARCH AND SUGGESTIONS

Disagreement exists among L1 and L2 composition specialists about whether formal grammar instruction is necessary or effective for improving the accuracy of student writing. Over the past several decades, L1 researchers have consistently challenged the practice of teaching grammar and punctuation rules in composition courses. The basic argument is that student writers already have an intuitive sense of the rules of their language. What is needed, rather, are opportunities to put them into practice: "Language cannot be learned in isolation but only by manipulating it in meaningful contexts" (Frodesen & Holten, 2003, p. 143; see also Hartwell, 1985; Shaughnessy, 1977).

In addition, L2 scholars and teachers have questioned the efficacy of grammar instruction, noting that "the return on grammar instruction is often disappointing. Teachers find that even when a grammatical feature has been covered and practiced, students may not use it accurately in their own writing" (Frodesen & Holten, 2003, p. 142). It also has been noted that L2 writers do not have the same "felt sense" of correctness nor intuitive grasp of the grammatical rules of English, so formal instruction may be more important for them (Frodesen & Holten, 2003). Moreover, SLA researchers have increasingly argued that, particularly for adult L2 learners, focus on form is not only beneficial but necessary (Doughty & Williams, 1998; Ellis, 2002). Finally, limited empirical evidence points to a positive role for supplemental grammar instruction in L2 writing instruction, which can work in tandem with error correction to facilitate increased accuracy over time (see Ferris, 2003b, Ch. 3, for a review). To summarize,

> in light of both new research findings and the inherent differences in L1 and L2 writers' literacy development, it is clear that ESL writing instructors have a role to play in making writers aware of language form. Overt and systematic grammar instruction can help students access the grammar rules that they know and use their intuitions about the language judiciously. (Frodesen & Holten, 2003, p. 144)

Principles for Grammar Instruction in an L2 Writing Class

From the evolving scholarship in composition studies and SLA, it is clear that traditional, decontextualized grammar instruction (learning rules deductively, engaging in practice with exercises, and so on) is not effective in promoting long-term development in written accuracy. Rather, supplemental grammar instruction should be carefully integrated with other elements of the literacy syllabus, responsive to specific student needs, meaningful, and contextualized. With these criteria in mind, we offer principles and practices for teachers who wish to provide grammar instruction for their L2 writing students.

A Writing Class Is Not a Grammar Class. It is critical for teachers not to lose perspective on the relative importance of grammar instruction. A teacher can easily become overwhelmed by the range, depth, and urgency of student needs as to accuracy and attention to form. Many high-quality, in-depth ESL grammar textbooks are available, and it can be tempting to start teaching through one of these. Nonetheless, we must remember that many other important aims and processes must be incorporated into effective literacy instruction (Figs. 3.3–3.5). We must also avoid the temptation to neglect those priorities in favor of intensive grammar instruction. Grammar instruction should be thoughtfully integrated with other phases of the writing and editing process, as we argue later (see also Ferris, 1995c).

Grammar Instruction Should Start With Awareness of Student Needs. It can be tempting to address grammar issues by consulting lists of "common ESL errors" or by working through the topics in an editing or grammar handbook (see Ferris, 1995c; 2002b for examples and discussion). However, students' needs for grammar instruction vary dramatically depending on their level of L2 proficiency, their L1 background, and especially the formal or informal nature of their prior exposure to English. Therefore, it is essential for teachers to spend time at the beginning of a course assessing students' knowledge and linguistic gaps. Teachers can undertake this task by conducting a error analysis based on an initial writing sample, perhaps paired with a grammar knowledge pretest or questionnaire about what students already know (see Ferris, 2002b, pp. 117–122 for sample materials). The teacher then should target areas for explicit instruction based on awareness of individual and collective needs.

Grammar Instruction Should Be Brief and Narrowly Focused. Most L1 and L2 composition experts advocate the use of the minilesson for classroom grammar presentations, as well as other types of writing instruction (Atwell, 1998; Ferris, 2002b; Weaver, 1996). As their name implies, minilessons are brief (thus addressing the first principle of not allowing grammar teaching to overshadow other priorities) and can be developed to target specific areas of student need. Minilessons also are beneficial because they focus intensively on restricted areas of grammatical knowledge, allowing students to grasp, practice, and apply manageable chunks of material. For instance, a minilesson on verb tenses might focus on shifts between past and present tense in narrative discourse or between the functions of the past simple and the present perfect, rather than present all 12 tense-aspect combinations in English (some of which are rarely used in written discourse).

In addition to being short (say between 10 and 30 minutes, including practice or application activities) and narrowly focused, effective grammar minilessons typically include the following components in some form:

Discovery Activity: Identifying Modal Auxiliaries and Modal Verb Phrases
Directions

1. Highlight each modal or modal verb phrase in the passage below.
2. Use the table below to make a list of the modals and modal verb phrases.
3. Beside each modal, write down the type of modal being used. The first one is done for you.

Modal	Modal Verb Phrase	Modal Type
1. *Should*	*Should have seen*	*Advice*
2.		
3.		
4.		
5.		
6.		
7.		
8.		
9.		

(1) Visitors should have seen the fabulous views of the Grand Canyon National Park last summer. (2) It's not too late to go. (3) Will you consider going there this summer? (4) Visitors should see the fabulous view of the canyon, and its beautifully colored walls. (5) The headquarters and Visitor Center is at the South Rim where visitors can find information about the park. (6) Visitors may drive along parts of the rim or hike down into the canyon on various trails. (7) Hikers must be sure to drink plenty of water to avoid dehydration as the weather can be extremely hot. (8) They also might carry extra food in case they become hungry while hiking on the trail. (9) Perhaps the best way to see the canyon is to float down the Colorado River on a rubber raft. (10) Seeing the canyon from this perspective is spectacular, but people who are afraid of whitewater should not take this trip since some of the Colorado River rapids are among the biggest in the world.

(Paragraph adapted from Lane & Lange, 1993, *Writing Clearly*, p. 61. Boston: Heinle.)

Note: This activity assumes prior knowledge of modal auxiliaries and their types. See Fig. 7.5.

FIG. 7.4. Sample discovery activity: Identifying modal auxiliaries and modal verb phrases.

- *Text analysis and discovery activities.* These activities allow students to observe and analyze how the target structure is used in natural discourse. Teachers often use authentic texts (professionally written literary or expository texts) and well-executed student texts as models for analysis.[7] For example, for a minilesson on article usage, a teacher might ask students to analyze a couple of paragraphs from a sample text by first identifying all the nouns; determining whether definite, indefinite, or zero articles are used in the noun phrases; and then discussing why those choices were made. Figure 7.4 provides an example of a text analysis exercise.
- *Brief deductive explanations of important terms and rules.* Whereas some instructors move students directly from inductive discovery activities to practice and application, it is important to remember that many students have more deductive, field-dependent learning styles and can become frustrated if they are not provided with a straightforward presentation of important terms and applicable rules. Narrowing down the information and presenting it in a way that students can quickly grasp is perhaps the most challenging aspect of developing a minilesson. We recommend keeping such presentations simple, introducing only a few rules, and perhaps including an "editing guide" offering a series of heuristic questions students can use to evaluate their own writing or the writing of peers. See Figure 7.5 for an example.
- *Practice and application activities.* An effective minilesson also includes opportunities for students to apply what they have learned through editing for errors in sample student texts, participating in peer editing workshops, and scrutinizing their own in-progress work. Probably the most overlooked application type is the minilesson focused on students' own writing, but this is arguably the most important. After all, if students are not expected to make a hands-on connection between what they have been taught and the writing they are producing, we would be, in a very real sense, repeating the mistakes of the earlier era of decontextualized grammar instruction, which never carried over to real-world language production. (See Fig. 7.6 for an example.)

Modal Auxiliaries

A. Basic Definitions and Introduction to Modal Auxiliaries

1. **Types of Auxiliaries.** As you have already learned, verb phrases are formed by using auxiliaries: words which "help" the verb. Auxiliaries come before verbs in the verb phrase. There are two types of auxiliaries: auxiliary verbs and modal auxiliaries.

Auxiliaries	Modals
be, do, have	can could
	may might
	will would
	shall should (ought to)
	must (have to, need to)

2. **Past vs. Present Form of Modal Verb Phrases:**

EXAMPLE: *You should stop.* = Advice; in the present→talking about future

EXAMPLE: *You should have stopped.* = Advice; in the present→talking about past

3. **Categories of Modals:**

Request: *Will/would/can/could you open the door?*

Permission: *May/might/can/could you open the door?*

Advice/Obligation: *You must(have to,need to)/should (ought to) open the door.*

Ability: *Can (be able to). She can (is able to) play the piano.*

B. Editing Guide. Four basic rules govern the use of modal auxiliaries:

Rule 1: Modal auxiliaries never take subject–verb agreement

Incorrect: *She may walks to the store.*

Correct: *She may walk to the store.*

Strategy: Make sure there's no -s attached to the verb in a modal verb phrase.

RULE 2: The next verb after a modal is always in its base form.

Incorrect: *I could taking the job.*

Correct: *I could take the job.*

Strategy: Make sure each verb is in its base form after the modal.

RULE 3: If a modal is used, it is always the first element in the verb phrase.

Incorrect: *She like would to go to the store.*

Correct: *She would like to go to the store.*

Strategy: Double-check the sequence in your verb phrase.

RULE 4: Standard English allows only one modal auxiliary per clause.

Incorrect: *They must could go out at night.*

Correct: *They must go out at night.*

Strategy: Pick the modal verb that makes the most sense for what idea you are trying to convey. For instance, the sentence, "they must go out at night," is a command; however, "they could go out at night" means they had permission to go out at night or they were able to go out at night.

FIG. 7.5. Sample deductive presentation: Modal auxiliaries.

Although the development of grammar minilessons can be challenging and time-consuming for a teacher, they can be highly effective in presenting important language content in ways that students can instantly grasp and apply. In addition, mini-lessons can be built on in two distinct ways. First, teachers may wish to take important form-focused topics (e.g., verb tenses,

Modal Auxiliary Application Activities

Practice Exercise 1

Directions. *In each sentence, decide if the modal auxiliary is correct (C) or incorrect (I). Cross out the incorrect part of the modal auxiliary verb phrase and write the correct word. The first one is done for you.*

1. ____ I must need to be home by midnight. (**correction: Use** *must* **OR** *need,* **but not both!)**
2. ____ She should walks more carefully.
3. ____ You should be more careful.
4. ____ Should you please take off your hat?
5. ____ You can should see the view from here.
6. ____ He might watching the game tonight.
7. ____ Did you answered the question?
8. ____ He should notices what the sign says.
9. ____ May you open the door, please?
10. ____ How could I helped you?

Practice Exercise

Directions. *Read the following paragraph and cross out any incorrect modal auxiliaries or verb forms used with modal auxiliaries. Write the correct answer in its place.*

```
Life was hard for me when I first came to this country. I was a new
bride and had to adapted to my new environment. I know I should being
more adventurous, but I didn't want to go outside by myself. I expect
life might be better for you. You should taking my advice and be more
open to the world around you. You not might think that this is
original advice, but you must follow your dreams. You are the only
person who can finds your dreams.
```

[Exercise adapted from Raimes (1993), *How English Works*, p. 122. New York: St. Martin's.]

Practice Exercise

Directions. *Read through the latest draft of your essay, and complete the following three tasks:*

1. Highlight *all* verb phrases.
2. Circle any phrases that contain *modal auxiliaries.*
3. Using the Editing Guide (see Fig. 7.5), check to see if there are any errors in your verb phrases that contain modals. If you find any, try to correct them.
4. Now look again at the verb phrases you highlighted and see if any might be *improved or strengthened* by adding a modal auxiliary. Rewrite the sentences to include the modal you have chosen. (Don't forget to change any verb tense endings, if needed!)

FIG. 7.6. Sample application activities: Modal auxiliaries.

article usage, clause boundaries, subject–verb agreement, and so forth) and break them down in a continuing series of minilessons that uses earlier lessons as scaffolding for new material. Second, teachers can tie the minilessons to other aspects of the feedback and revision process by marking student papers for specific structures covered in minilessons, and by requiring students to chart their progress in mastering these rules and structures.

Individualized or Small Group Instruction Should Be Considered for Specific Topics That Do Not Apply to the Whole Class. Depending on the demographics of a particular writing class, a teacher may well find that not all grammar topics are relevant to the entire group. We often find this diversity of needs in secondary and postsecondary ESL courses in an English-speaking setting, which may include students from a wide range of L1 backgrounds. Such courses also may serve traditional ESL students (international students and recent immigrants), as well as long-term residents. For example, one of the authors, while teaching a recent ESL freshman composition course, found through a diagnostic error analysis that the average number of "verb" errors (including errors in both tense and form) was four, and that the range was 0 to 7. In other words, verbs were the most serious problem for some students, whereas other students had no need for instruction on verbs at all.

A teacher encountering this dynamic has several choices. One is to design and deliver minilessons for the whole group by identifying the most prevalent areas of collective need, recognizing that these lessons may be more relevant for some students than for others. However, as the lessons are "mini," they will not tax the students' patience excessively. Another option is to provide minilessons to smaller groups of students, outside class time or while the rest of the students work on something else. Finally, a teacher may opt entirely or partially for individualized "instruction" by providing each student with personalized feedback on his or her most significant patterns of error, and by referring students to specific sections of a grammar or editing handbook or to handouts and exercises provided by the teacher (see Ferris, 1995c, and Ferris, 2002b, pp. 101–102 for ideas on selecting resources for self-study). Obviously, a "one-size-fits-all" approach to these challenges is out of the question. Teachers must determine for themselves what model of delivery works best for a particular group of students.

To summarize, we believe that in most instances, ESL literacy teachers should carefully consider providing classroom instruction on language issues, in addition to giving students feedback on their errors. Whereas such instruction need not, and should not, consume extensive amounts of class time, judicious selection, presentation, and application of grammar points may be extremely important for students' continued language and literacy development.

STRATEGY TRAINING FOR SELF-EDITING

We previously alluded to the controversy among teachers and researchers concerning whether teacher error correction and overt grammar instruction offer measurable benefits for L2 student writers. In contrast, experts agree[8] that L2 writers need strategy training for the purpose of becoming independent, autonomous self-editors. We all recognize that linguistic accuracy is, in fact, one essential component (among many) of effective writing. Furthermore, because they lack native-speaker intuition and have less had extensive exposure to the language, L2 writers may struggle with accurate written production more than NS writers do. The errors of L2 writers also may be stigmatizing and thus harmful to them, at least with some academic and professional audiences. Finally, we, their writing instructors, will not always be there to guide them. Thus, we need to help these students learn to help themselves.

Techniques for Teaching Editing Skills in the Writing Class

Most modern researchers advocate an indirect discovery approach for teaching editing skills to ESL students. Although the goal of teaching students to become "independent self-editors" (Lane & Lange, 1993, p. xix) is clearly a crucial one, students at beginning to intermediate levels of English proficiency may not have the linguistic skills to monitor their own written products successfully (Jones, 1985). In a general discussion of error production and correction in second language acquisition, Brown (2000) suggested that learners pass through successive stages in developing an ability to recognize and correct their own errors, ranging from the "random error stage," in which learners have no systematic idea about a given structure, to the "stabilization stage," in which learners make relatively few errors and can self-correct. Many ESL writing students find themselves at an in-between stage where their errors are systematic, and where they can self-correct some errors, but not all—if they are pointed

Editing Activities

A. Controlled Writing Exercise
Instructions. *Change the paragraph into past tense. The first sentence is done for you.*

My wife gets up early in the morning. She hates to get up in the morning. She has to get dressed quickly to catch an early bus to work. I go to work later, and I drive my car. She doesn't have much time for breakfast, so she just has a cup of coffee when she gets to work. I have a bowl of cereal and fruit before I go to work. I understand why my wife doesn't like mornings? (Adapted from Fox, 1992)

Beginning of Past tense Paragraph:
My wife got up earlier in the morning than I did.

B. Guided Writing Exercise
Instructions. *You just read a paragraph about a man and his wife getting ready for work in the morning. Now write a paragraph about what **you** did this morning. Answer the questions to get ideas for your paragraph.*

- Did you get up early or late?
- Did you have a lot of time or did you have to hurry?
- How did you get to school? Did you walk, ride a bike, drive a car, or ride a bus?
- Did you eat breakfast? Where (at home or at school)?
- What did you eat for breakfast?
- Do you usually enjoy mornings?

Follow-up. *Now change your paragraph about this morning into one about your usual morning.*

C. Dictocomp
Procedure. *Use a paragraph like the one in Part A. Read the paragraph aloud several times at normal speed. Then write the key words on the board in sequence (see following list for an example) and ask the students to rewrite the paragraph as they remember it, using the words on the board.*

KEY WORDS

hates	bus	breakfast	understand
get up	later	coffee	
get dressed	car	cereal	

(Activities developed from suggestions in Brown, 2001)

FIG. 7.7.   Sample exercises for beginning L2 writers.

out by someone else. It is a rare student in an L2 writing course who can find and correct his or her own errors without any assistance from a teacher or other more expert source (see Fathman & Whalley, 1990, and Ferris & Roberts, 2001, for empirical evidence on this question).

Students with an emergent ability to recognize and correct their errors most likely need types of intervention that differ from those needed by more proficient students. Brown (2001) and Frodesen (1991) suggested that the types of writing within the capability of low-level students include copying (of model texts and their own teacher-corrected compositions), controlled and guided writing exercises involving manipulation of various syntactic structures, and dictocomps (Fig. 7.7).

As students progress in their acquisition of English syntax, morphology, and lexis, as well as their formal learning of more complex discursive conventions, they can be given more responsibility for correcting their own errors. An error correction system such as the one advocated in two companion volumes on editing (Bates et al.,1993; Lane & Lange, 1993, 1999) may be useful for this intermediate level of editing proficiency. In these texts, teachers and students learn a system of marking papers for different types of errors and are encouraged to prioritize and keep track of their error patterns. However, depending on students' prior educational experience, especially their English language development, systems such as these may need to be adapted to accommodate students' relative knowledge of formal grammar terminology.

Once students have progressed to a point at which they can either correct a variety of errors when they are pointed out or find and correct errors themselves, teachers can take several steps to help them move further toward autonomy. With this approach, advanced ESL students can be taught over several phases during the writing course to become self-sufficient as editors (Fig. 7.8).

Teaching Editing Over a 15-Week Semester

Phase 1 (Weeks 1–3): *FOCUSING STUDENTS ON FORM*
  Goals
  - Students learn to recognize the importance of improving editing skills
  - Students begin to identify their own "sources of error."
  Activities
  - Students write a diagnostic essay; teacher prepares a report of major weaknesses and indicates what sort of grade the student is likely to receive if such problems persist to the end of the term;
  - Students examine sample sentences and essays for the purpose of noting what comprehensibility problems are rooted in sentence–level errors.

Phase 2 (Weeks 4–10): *TRAINING STUDENTS TO RECOGNIZE MAJOR ERROR TYPES*
  Goals and Activities
  - Students understand and identify major error types in sample essays
  - Students "peer edit"
  - Students keep written records of the major types of errors they make, turned in with writing projects
  - Instruction on major sources of error is given in class, lab, or through independent study, as necessary.

Phase 3 (Weeks 11–15): *HELPING STUDENTS TO FIND AND CORRECT THEIR OWN ERRORS*
  Goals and Activities
  - Students edit their own essays and chart their progress
  - Instruction on major sources of error continues.

(Source: Ferris, 1995c, p. 46)

FIG. 7.8. Student self-editing process.

Phase 1: Focusing Students on Form. The intent of this stage is to help students realize the importance of improving their editing skills. According to Ferris (1995c), some teachers assume that ESL writers focus excessively on grammatical form at the expense of developing and organizing their ideas. However, many ESL students have little interest in editing their written production. Such writers may find editing tedious, may not see it as important, or may have become overly dependent on experts (i.e., teachers, tutors, and so on) to correct their work for them. "Thus, a crucial step in teaching students to become good editors is to convince them of the necessity of doing so" (Ferris, 1995c, p. 18).

We recommend several strategies for raising students' awareness of the importance of editing in general, and of addressing the expectations of a socioliterate audience (see chapters 1 through 4). The first strategy involves setting classroom tasks in which writers look at sentences or a short student text containing a variety of editing problems (Fig. 7.9). Another useful strategy for convincing students of the necessity to develop editing skills is to give them a diagnostic essay assignment early in the term and provide them with comprehensive feedback about their writing, including detailed information about their editing weaknesses, so that they have specific grammatical features on which to focus throughout the semester (see Ferris, 2002b, pp. 78–85 for a more detailed discussion of this "consciousness-raising" stage).

Phase 2: Providing Strategy Training. Once the importance of accuracy and the development of self-editing strategies has been established, the teacher should share with students

---

Editing Exercise

Instructions. *Read a sample student paper and look at the course grading criteria (especially the criteria for a "4" [passing] paper and a "3" [failing] paper). Discuss the following questions with your instructor and classmates:*

1. Considering *errors only*, if this paper were written for the final, do you think the student would pass the class? Why or why not?
2. What are the most frequent *types* of errors you see in this essay?

   Note: This exercise is adapted from Ferris (2002b, pp. 133–134).

FIG. 7.9. Consciousness-raising exercise with sample student paper.

both general principles of SLA and specific strategies for self-editing. As to the former, students should be relieved to hear that adult language learning takes time and occurs in stages, that errors are a normal part of the acquisition process (comparisons with child language acquisition are helpful here), that aspects of English grammar are idiosyncratic and full of troublesome exceptions (thus lightening some guilt they may feel about "carelessness" or inability to master certain structures), and that it is neither possible nor necessary to expect that they will produce perfect, error-free papers by the end of a writing course.

Many ESL literacy materials and resources for teachers provide lists of strategies that students should consider in editing their texts. These include recommendations such as "read your paper aloud," "run the spell-check" (but see chapter 9 for some caveats and warnings about this practice), and so forth. One of the most important editing strategies that students can learn, however, involves making separate, narrowly focused passes through texts to look for targeted error types or patterns. These categories may vary depending on the teacher's perception of student needs. However, these error forms should be selected from frequent, serious, and stigmatizing error types. Students are sensitized to these error patterns by reviewing the targeted categories, identifying them in sample student essays, and looking for these errors in peer editing exercises (Fig. 7.10; see also Ferris, 2002b, pp. 85–91). Such activities can also "lead students away from the frustrating and often counterproductive notion that they can or should attempt to correct every single error in a given essay draft" (Ferris, 1995c, p. 19).

Exercise: Identifying Error Patterns

Directions. *Read through a sample student essay and highlight every verb or verb phrase. Examine each one carefully to see if there are any errors in verb tense or form. If you find any errors, see if you can suggest a correction. Then, using a different color highlighter, highlight all of the nouns and noun phrases. Check each one to see if it needs a plural or possessive ending, has an incorrect ending, or has an ending that is unnecessary. For any errors you find, suggest a correction. Be prepared to discuss with your classmates and teacher what errors you found, why you think they are wrong, and why you corrected them in the way that you did.*

Note: This exercise is adapted from Ferris, 2002b, p. 89.

FIG. 7.10.   Exercise for identifying error patterns.

ERROR LOG

Essay Draft	Verb Errors	Noun Ending Errors	Article Errors	Word Choice Errors	Sentence Structure Errors	Other Errors
1A						
1B						
1C						
2A						
2B						
2C						
3A						
3B						
3C						
4A						
4B						
4C						

Source: Ferris, 2003b, Fig. 7.9, p. 156.

FIG. 7.11. Sample error log.

Phase 3: Students Finding and Correcting Their Own Errors. After students have been made aware of their unique weaknesses in editing through teacher and peer feedback and have practiced identifying error patterns on model student essays and peers' drafts, they should be instructed to locate and correct errors in their own essay drafts. In addition, throughout the semester, the students can keep a log of error frequencies in the different categories to observe their improvement and build their confidence as editors (see Fig. 7.11 and Ferris, 2002b, pp. 91–93 for examples and further discussion). Several researchers have reported that students who consistently maintained error logs made significant progress in reducing their frequency of targeted errors over time (Ferris, Chaney, Komura, Roberts, & McKee, 2000; Lalande, 1982; Roberts, 1999). As the semester progresses and students accumulate more and more editing practice, the amount of editing feedback provided by the teacher should gradually decrease, with the editing task turned over first to peer editors and then to the writers themselves.

Many instructors find it extremely helpful to conduct "error conferences" with their students or to encourage students to meet with a tutor for such conferences (Fig. 7.12). Error conferences can occur during at least two distinct stages of the writing process. First, the teacher can walk with the student through an unmarked

Preliminary (Unmarked) Drafts

1. Ask the student to read the paper aloud while you follow along on a separate copy. Instruct the student to stop and verbalize comments about any errors or corrections she or he notices. Note the errors caught by the student and suggested corrections on your copy of the paper.

2. Then go through the paper again, this time reading it aloud yourself. For any remaining errors not caught by the student during step 1, stop and ask an indirect question ("What about this?" or simply repeat the erroneou s form or phrase). See if the student can suggest a correction for errors you call to his or her attention. Take notes on your copy using a different color of ink.

3. Show the student your paper, marked with two pen colors—one representing errors she or he found and attempted to correct independently, the other representing errors you pointed out. Discuss your findings, pointing out (a) what the student did well in terms of finding and correcting errors, and (b) problematic error types that you notice (either frequent or types resistant to self-editing). Ask the student to take notes on his or her paper, including correct forms that you provide for him or her.

4. Keep your copy of the paper on file for future reference about the student's progress, and for identifying topics for class minilessons.

Marked Drafts

1. Read and provide indirect feedback (error location only) on the student's essay draft. Then ask the student, in class, to attempt corrections for all errors that you marked. Ask the student to number each marked error consecutively and complete an error analysis chart (see following example). Ask the student to produce a revised essay draft (including both corrections and responses to feedback on other issues) before your error conference.

Error Type	Total Number of Errors
Verb tense/form	
Noun endings	
Determiners	
Word choice/word form	
Sentence structure: Missing or unnecessary words, word order	
Sentence structure: Fragments, run-ons, or comma Splices	
Spelling, punctuation, and capitalization	
Other	

Source: Ferris, 2003b, Appendix 7A, p. 161.

2. Use the marked essay draft, the chart, and the new revision as data sources for your conference. First, walk through the in-class corrections made by the student, discussing (a) whether the student categorized the errors correctly on the chart, and (b) whether the corrections suggested by the student are accurate. Next, compare that draft with the subsequent out-of-class revision. Note where the student did or did not make edits from the previous draft and discuss why (lack of understanding, carelessness, larger text revision, and so on) Take notes on your discussion. Ask the student to summarize what she or he has learned about his or her patterns of error, points of confusion, and editing and revision strategies.

3. Take copies of all the student drafts and attach the notes from your conference. Keep them on file for future reference and lesson planning.

FIG. 7.12. Suggested procedures for error conferences.

student draft, asking the student to read it aloud and noting what structural errors the student can notice by doing so. The teacher can call to the student's attention any errors missed through indirect questioning ("What about this one?") to determine whether the student can recognize the problem when pointed out and suggest a solution.

At a later stage, the teacher and student can look together at a preliminary draft with teacher (or peer or self) error feedback marked, plus the student's edited text. The student should go point-by-point through the marked and edited texts, explaining how and why specific corrections were made (or not made). Similar to miscue analyses in assessing reading comprehension, error conferences can be extremely informative for the teacher, helping him or her to understand students' points of confusion both with error feedback they have received and with the grammatical patterns themselves. Such knowledge can help teachers to refine their own feedback practices and to design minilessons based on firsthand awareness of what students already know or do not know. For students, such focused, contextualized attention to formal errors can be invaluable, especially if they articulate what they think the "rule" is and what their source of knowledge about the language forms might be ("It just doesn't sound right" vs. "I learned it in a grammar class in high school"). Error conferences can also be used for peer editing sessions, allowing students to pool their collective knowledge and intuitions about the language, but with the caveat that the information they share as learners may sometimes be incomplete or even erroneous.

CONCLUSION: PUTTING IT ALL TOGETHER

We have covered three major themes in this chapter under the rubric of helping to promote accuracy in student writing: expert error feedback, grammar instruction, and strategy training. Nonetheless, L2 writing teachers must balance a range of priorities in designing a literacy course that features written production (see chapter 3). Dealing with student errors is only one of these priorities and arguably not even the most important. How, then, do we integrate the "treatment of error" into a comprehensive plan for a particular course? Whereas the specific answer to this question will vary according to the length and

nature of a course, we offer the following summary suggestions for tying error treatment processes into an overall course
plan:

1. *Begin each writing course with a diagnostic needs analysis.*
   This exercise could include student background questionnaires (see Figs. 3.1 and 3.2 for samples), a specific
   grammar knowledge pretest, and a diagnostic error analysis based on student-produced texts.
2. *As part of teaching students about writing processes, discuss
   the importance of editing and introduce self-editing strategies.*
   In our own ESL literacy courses, we tend to move systematically and recursively through the stages of drafting,
   revision, and editing with each new writing assignment,
   for example, by teaching idea-generation strategies before first-draft production, revision strategies after the
   completion of a draft, working with editing strategies
   after at least one revision, and so on.
3. *Give students individual feedback on essay drafts at various
   stages of the process.* As discussed earlier in this chapter,
   this strategy does not necessarily mean marking errors
   on every single assignment that students produce. It does
   mean that students should receive feedback regularly
   from the teacher as well as through peer-editing workshops. (See also chapter 6 for more discussion of peer
   response.)
4. *Give students time in class to self-edit marked drafts and to
   chart their errors.* It is tempting simply to return papers
   to students at the end of class and let them revise and
   edit on their own time. However, allowing students 10
   to 20 minutes in class to review teacher corrections, ask
   questions of the teacher and peers, and self-correct on the
   spot can be a very productive use of class time, catching
   students at a "teachable moment" and allowing them to
   obtain clarification about problems.
5. *Design and deliver a series of minilessons on grammar and
   error strategies.* Minilessons should come directly from
   the initial needs analysis. Teachers may wish to deliver
   minilessons once a week, every other week, or every time
   an essay draft is submitted or returned.
6. *Intentionally move students toward autonomy throughout the writing course.* This goal is accomplished by

> systematically reducing the amount of error feedback given by the teacher, providing structured in-class and out-of-class opportunities for peer- and self-editing, and requiring students to analyze, chart, and reflect on their progress.

SUMMARY

Over the past two decades, ESL writing instruction has swung from one extreme (attempting to eradicate every single student error) to another (primary attention given to writers' ideas and individual writing processes, with linguistic concerns basically left to "take care of themselves") to a middle ground (combining the best of process-oriented approaches with increased but selective attention to linguistic accuracy). Teachers and students of ESL writing as well as faculty in the disciplines generally agree on the importance of accuracy in student writing and of teaching students to become self-sufficient as editors. As the English-language proficiency of learners' increases, more and more responsibility for editing their own writing can and should be turned over to them. Techniques such as guided writing exercises, identification of error patterns, text analysis, and grammar minilessons can be used to build students' editing skills as they become more proficient in terms of their linguistic and literacy skills. The goal of such a discovery approach should not be perfect written products, but rather ESL writers who gradually reduce the frequency of error in their written production and become increasingly autonomous as editors. It is also extremely important that teachers take students' mother tongue knowledge, L2 skills, and academic backgrounds (especially prior English language instruction) into account in planning instruction, selecting materials, and providing feedback.

REFLECTION AND REVIEW

1. Summarize the arguments in favor of providing feedback only on ideas and organization on preliminary drafts of student papers. What are the arguments in favor of also

providing grammar feedback on early drafts? Which set of arguments do you find more persuasive and why?

2. This chapter maintains that neither teachers nor students should attempt to correct all the errors in a given piece of writing. What are some arguments against this position?

3. To what extent can or should student preferences affect teachers' decisions regarding error correction and explicit grammar instruction? What are the benefits and drawbacks of varying feedback strategies to accommodate individual students' preferences and perceived needs?

4. After arguing that there is no theoretical justification for error correction in L2 writing and that the practical problems with doing so are virtually insurmountable, Truscott (1996) asserted that error correction is worse than useless. He maintained that it is actually harmful because it consumes so much teacher and student energy and attention, taking time away from activities that could promote genuine learning. Imagine that you are a writing teacher who agrees with Truscott's arguments and have therefore decided not to correct students' written errors any longer. You need to write a memo to your supervisor explaining your new position. What would you say? What counterarguments might your supervisor offer in response?

5. The discussion of Truscott's (1996) arguments against error correction in this chapter raises a broader issue: If research evidence contradicts common sense or intuitions, on which should a teacher rely? What if the research evidence is scarce, conflicting, or incomplete (as for many issues in L2 teaching)? While we are waiting for researchers to come up with conclusive answers (if such answers are, indeed, forthcoming), what should teachers do in the meantime?

6. This chapter holds that under certain conditions, supplemental grammar instruction may be necessary and helpful for L2 writing students. What are the potential pitfalls and practical constraints entailed in pursuing this advice, and what should ESL literacy educators do to address or mitigate these problems?

7. Peer feedback and self-evaluation are mentioned at various points in this chapter as mechanisms for helping students improve the accuracy of their written texts and for developing self-editing strategies. Does the idea of learners providing feedback to themselves and others on their errors set off any alarm bells for you? If so, what are they, and

what might you do either to "disconnect the alarm" or to "lower the volume" (i.e., counterarguments or mitigating strategies)?

Application Activity 7.1: Analyzing a Research Review

Directions. Truscott (1996) and Ferris (2003b, Ch. 3) both reviewed numerous studies of L2 error correction. Obtain and carefully read the listed studies and then answer the questions that follow.

Studies: Cohen & Robbins (1976), Fathman & Whalley (1990), Kepner (1991), Lalande (1982), Robb, Ross, & Shortreed (1986), Semke (1984).

Note: Bibliographic information for all the preceding studies is provided in the References section of this volume.

---

1. For each study, note the following research elements carefully:

   a. How many participants were involved?
   b. In what pedagogical context were the data collected?
   c. What was the duration of the data collection?
   d. If the design was experimental, was a control group used?
   e. What methods were used to collect and analyze data?

2. Now compare your notes on each study. Do you think this body of research is consistent in either research design or body of findings? To what extent can the findings from any one of these studies be generalized to all L2 writers? Are all the studies, taken as a group, generalizable? Why or why not?

3. For each study, note the findings reported and the conclusions drawn by the authors. Compare these conclusions with the summaries of that particular study in the two reviews. In your opinion, are the reviewers' presentations fair and accurate? Was there any other way to interpret the authors' data?

4. Now that you have read both reviews and examined the primary sources carefully, you probably have noticed that

the two reviewers (Truscott and Ferris) arrive at dramatically different conclusions. Considering your own analysis, which reviewer's presentation do you find more convincing, and why?

Application Activity 7.2: Analyzing Errors in a Student Text

Directions. Appendix 7 contains a student paper written for an advanced university ESL course. Perform the following steps to complete an error analysis for this writing sample.

1. Make an extra copy of this paper before marking it in any way. Go through the paper carefully, highlighting all the instances of errors you find for each of the categories in the chart below.

	Error Catagories
Verb errors	All errors in verb tense or form, including relevant subject–verb agreement errors.
Noun-ending errors	Plural or possessive ending incorrect, omitted, or unnecessary; includes relevant subject–verb agreement errors.
Article errors	Article or other determiner incorrect, omitted, or unnecessary.
Wrong word	All specific lexical errors in word choice or word form, including preposition and pronoun errors. Spelling errors included only if the (apparent) misspelling resulted in an actual English word.
Sentence structure	Errors in sentence/clause boundaries (run-ons, fragments, comma splices), word order, omitted words or phrases, unnecessary words or phrases, other unidiomatic sentence construction.
Spelling	Errors in spelling (other than those already classified as word choice)
Other	Errors that do not fit into previous categories (may include capitalization, punctuation not already included in the aforementioned types, and so on)

2. Now number each error you highlighted consecutively and complete the following error chart.

Error Number	Noun Ending	Verb	Article	Word Choice	Sentence Structure	Spelling	Other
1							
2							
3							
4							
5							
6							
7							
8							
9							
10							
11							
12							
13							
14							
15							
16							
17							
18							
19							
20							
21							
22							
23							
24							
25							
26							
27							
28							
29							
30							
Totals							

3. Compare your findings with those of your classmates and instructor. What problems did you encounter, and with what did you struggle as you completed this exercise? What has it taught you about the processes involved in responding to student errors?

Application Activity 7.3: Responding to a Student's Language Errors

Directions. Use the results of the error analysis completed for Application Activity 7.2 to complete this exercise.

1. Choose an error feedback method (or combination of methods) discussed in this chapter—providing direct correction, highlighting or underlining errors, marking errors with codes or verbal rule reminders, making check marks in the margins, providing verbal end comment—and provide feedback as if you were going to return it to the student writer for further editing.
2. Reflect on and discuss the following questions:
   a. What did you see as the student's chief problems or needs, and why?
   b. Did you opt for comprehensive or selective error correction, and why?
   c. Why did you select the feedback method(s) that you did (consider both student needs as identified by your error analysis, error type, and arguments about effective feedback types)?
   d. Now that you have analyzed and responded to a student's language errors, what do you think you still need to learn or practice to provide error feedback successfully on your own students' written assignments?

Application Activity 7.4: Comparing Reference Sources on a Particular Grammar Point

Directions. Imagine you are teaching an ESL writing course and have selected a particular grammar point on which to present a 20- to 30-minute minilesson to the class. Consult several sources for information on this grammar point (e.g., a reference grammar book for teachers, an ESL grammar book, or an editing handbook). After you have examined the sources, decide how you will address the following questions:

1. Is one source clearer or more appropriate for this point and group of students than the others? Why?
2. What basic information (terms, definitions, examples) will you need to present? Which sources were the most helpful in providing these?
3. What rules and strategies for avoiding errors might you include? Which sources were the most helpful in identifying these?
4. Did you find any discovery activities or editing exercises that might be helpful for your lesson? How might you need to adapt these to accommodate your own students' needs?

Application Activity 7.5: Developing Grammar/Editing Lessons

Directions. Examine the two student papers in Appendix 7. Imagine that you are teaching a writing course and that these papers are representative of your students' abilities and grammatical skills. Following the principles discussed in this chapter and the examples shown in Figs. 7.4–7.6, design a 20- to 30-minute minilesson on a specific grammar point that might address these students' needs. This minilesson must include the following components: (a) discovery (text analysis) activity, (b) deductive explanation of important terms and rules, (c) practice and application activities (some can be assigned as homework so that you can meet time constraints). Begin your lesson with a brief overview of the procedures you would use to teach this lesson. This overview should include any prior knowledge or previous instruction assumed as background for the lesson.

NOTES

[1] Truscott (1999) insisted on making a distinction between the terms "error correction" and "grammar correction." However, we use the terms interchangeably in this chapter.

[2] A study by Polio, Fleck, and Leder (1998) provided counterevidence to these studies. Their article was, of course, published after Truscott's (1996) review

essay. Another study cited by Truscott and others as negative evidence on error correction is that of Semke (1984), but the study's lack of methodologic clarity makes her results hard to interpret (see Ferris, 2003b; 2004 for discussion).

[3]Critics of error correction research have dismissed the first line of (quasi-experimental) research because it is not longitudinal, asserting that the fact that students could successfully edit their texts in the short term does not demonstrate that any such progress would stand up over time. However, we counterargue that improved products are a legitimate end in themselves, and that the cognitive investment of editing one's text after receiving error feedback is likely a necessary step on the road to long-term improvement in accuracy. The same critics similarly dismiss the second line of (longitudinal) research because, typically, no control group (i.e., a no-error-correction cohort) is included. These critics claim that measured improvements in accuracy over time could result from factors other than error correction. Although we grant this point, we observe that if error correction were truly useless or even harmful, we would see no progress and perhaps even regression in the texts of students receiving it. The research base on this issue is remarkably consistent in finding measurable, often statistically significant, improvement. See Ferris (2004) for further discussion.

[4]We do not address here the distinction made in the literature between "errors" (reflecting a gap in the learner's competence) and "mistakes" (reflecting a temporary lapse in the learner's performance).

[5]It is only fair to ESL writers to point out that some of these distinctions can seem arbitrary and idiosyncratic (Why can we say "I bought several chairs," but not "*several furnitures"?), and that even NSs do not use them systematically: We do not say "*I drank three *coffees*," but a restaurant server, taking orders, might say, "OK, that's three coffees."

[6]As an example, many ESL writing and grammar textbooks focus on helping students master the English determiner system or on understanding sentence boundaries (i.e., how to avoid run-ons, fragments, and comma splices). Yet in a recent study of nearly 100 university ESL writers in which more than 5,700 errors were classified, it was found that article errors and clause boundary errors comprised a relatively small percentage of the total: articles (6.6%), run-ons (2.9%), and fragments (1.8%). (Chaney, 1999; Ferris et al., 2000)

[7]Ferris (2002b, pp. 99–100) provided guidelines for the selection and adaptation of student text models for minilessons. These include considerations of whether to use papers written by students currently in the class, whether to correct errors, and whether the use of "good" or "bad" student models is more effective.

[8]Even Truscott (1999), the most outspoken opponent of grammar correction, acknowledges that teaching students self-editing strategies may have value.

APPENDIX 7: SAMPLE STUDENT ESSAYS

Note: These essay samples accompany Application Activities 7.2, 7.3, and 7.5. They were written by college seniors during the first week of a course entitled "Writing for Proficiency" (Ferris, 2001b). Students had 50 minutes to write in class on the topic, "Are lies always harmful or are they sometimes helpful?"

Sample Essay A

Today, in people's daily life, they often lie to protect themselves, to fit into a specific group, to make others feel better, or to help others in a different way. Yet, no matter what reason that cause people tell untruthful information, their purpose id to more on their living. However, no all lies are harmful. They can be helpful in some appropriate situations. It all depends how people view them.

It is true that sometimes lies are harmful. They can cause broken relationships, such as friendship, husband and wife, or parents and children. According to Goodrich, "if one promise to do lunch when this person knew that they will never get together." If later on the other person discovered the teller's purpose, their relationship would not go along well. Also, Goodrich states that many parents tell their children that Santa Claus will come on Christmas Eve. In this situation, although parents say that is to make the Christmas more enjoyable and make their children happier, as the children grow up and find out the true on their own, they may not very happy their parents' attitude. Although the result may not terrible till broken their parents and children relationship it may bring some negative parent's value in children's mind. In this situation, lying is harmful to both parents and children.

However, sometimes, tell a lie can be helpful if people deal with it appropriate. I remember two friends of mine Jack and John were best friends. They grew up together and went to school together. Yet, during their college year, Jack was Major in accounting because he like business very much. On the other hand, John was not interested in business much. He was having difficult time to chose his major. At the same time, he still wants to be with Jack all of the time. Once, when Jack asked John to major in business so they can still go to classes together, John responded by saying "OK", even though he did not like business classes, John found out he enjoy being manager after his college. John's lie did not hurt him and Jack. In fact, it helps him to choose his major while he did not know what to do. On the other hand, Jack also got some help from John while their studying. Therefore lies can be beneficial sometimes.

As a result, not all lies are wrong. Some are harmful while others are helpful.

Sample Essay B

I believe sometimes lies can be harmful or not appropriate. We have to lie because we do not want to hurt anybody's feelings. We lie, because we want to look good in front of some people. We lie because sometimes we want to get away from something. Sometimes we lie because we want to get caught. It's all dependent on the situation or how bad the circumstances will get if we lie.

I think the definition of "a lie" is being dishonest to others. When people lie to each other they are not true to themselves. They are simply playing with other people. Some people lie because sometimes truth can hurt someone.

"Lying is also exciting" (Margaret Summy) I believe in her statement. When people lie about stories or make up stories, they may be want to make them more interesting. For example, if a man tries to impress a woman by telling her lies, by all means do it. But the the end the result is she's going to find out sooner or later. It goes back and forth with men and women.

Some people lies to save their relationships. I believe in order to keep my family together if I have to lie I would not hesitate. I think relationships are far more important than a little or big lies. Sometimes people lie for good reasons, lying can be harmful if we act on a untrue information, we can be hurt physically or emotionally it can put a friction between a one strong relationship. Lying is bad for our body too. One lies leads to another which means we always have to keep our false story in our brain.

"Lying is hard on us physically. We breathe faster, our hearts beat harder, and our blood pressure goes up." (Terry Lee Goodrich) In our armies, we trained our soldiers to be good liars if they get caught, with a good lie they can save their lives. An expert can always pinpoint a liar. Most of us are not very good liars.

We can get caught very easily. We need to work on our breathing and heart beat in order to be a good liar.

People says everyone lies, does not matter if it is a little lie or big lie. I believe in and think this statement is true. Most of the time, when people lie they do not want to hurt no one. We lie because it's part of our lives.

Source. Ferris, Kennedy, and Senna, Spring, 2003 research corpus (Texts 18 and 19). Used with student permission.

Chapter 8

Classroom Approaches to ESL Writing Assessment

Questions for Reflection

- *In your experience as an academic writer, what procedures have your instructors used to assess and score your writing performance? To what extent were these procedures explicit and appropriate?*
- *In what ways have the scores or grades you have received on your writing helped you to improve the quality of your written products? How have scores enhanced (or inhibited) your learning and mastery of composing skills?*
- *If you have had experience as a composition instructor, what do you feel are your greatest challenges in evaluating student writing? If you are a preservice teacher, what are your most significant apprehensions regarding the assessment of student writing? Why?*
- *What should be the roles of formal assessment in the teaching of composition?*
- *Are you familiar with alternative assessment options such as portfolios? If so, under what circumstances? What benefits do you associate with alternative forms of assessment?*

This chapter approaches practices in ESL writing assessment from the viewpoint that meaningful performance evaluation is an ongoing process involving both teachers and students, not merely a procedure for assigning a quantitative score to a single product or series of performances. As a formative and inherently pedagogical endeavor, therefore, the assessment of students' writing processes and products is a central responsibility that should be tightly linked to syllabus design, lesson planning, task and assignment development, and feedback processes. Writing assessment is pedagogical in that, when reliable and valid, its outcomes inform writers in ways that directly and indirectly promote their progress as independent writers. Scores, grades, and evaluative feedback should consistently contribute to writers' learning processes and to the improvement of their measurable writing skills. As an extension of this pedagogical function, assessment, when performed responsibly, informs teachers of their own effectiveness, as reflected in their students' increasing proficiency and their achievement of programmatic and individual writing goals.

This concept is sometimes called "washback," which Weigle (2002) described as "the impact of tests on curricula and instruction" (p. 54). She defined *positive washback* as "any effect of a testing procedure that encourages teachers to adopt practices that are in line with the current best thinking in the field with respect to pedagogy" (p. 54). In contrast, *negative washback* entails "any effect of testing that leads teachers to practices which they feel are counterproductive, in terms of student learning, or which do not reflect the current thinking in the field" (Weigle, 2002, p. 54). Given the potential for influential washback effects, assessment is an essential teaching task: "We need to know what students do as writers, for both planning and the evaluation of our own teaching. Further, we need to track progress over the course of our teaching" (Hillocks, 1995, p. 132).

PROSPECTS AND PITFALLS IN L2 WRITING ASSESSMENT: MEASUREMENT TOOLS AND PARTICIPANT ROLES

Before examining the fundamentals of L2 writing assessment and their related procedures, we should first acknowledge the contradictions facing teachers when they evaluate their students' work. Educational assessment practices are frequently (if not predominantly) framed in terms of institutionalized writing tests such as the essay component of the Test of English as a Foreign

Language (TOEFL) (formerly the Test of Written English [TWE]) (Cumming, Kantor, Powers, Santos, & Taylor, 2000; Educational Testing Service, 1996; Hamp-Lyons & Kroll, 1997). Formalized tools for evaluating student writing such as those introduced later are unfortunately (and sometimes notoriously) associated with product-centered scoring that fails to assess or value student writing processes (Hamp-Lyons, 1991a; Kroll, 1998). We refer to these formalized instruments because they offer teachers systematicity, rigor, and a theoretical foundation. Our primary emphasis in this discussion is on their classroom applications, in contrast to their role in large-scale diagnostic, placement, and exit testing.[1] We likewise acknowledge the need to judge writers' products, particularly in academic settings, provided such judgments entail meaningful feedback on writers' processes and progress (see chapter 5). Thus, we view learners' written products as reflections of their ongoing development, a perspective that is particularly appropriate in the context of a socioliterate, or constructionist, approach to L2 writing instruction.

A contradiction inherent in teaching composition concerns the instructor's dual identity as respondent (i.e., audience and coach) and evaluator (Leki, 1990a). Teachers simultaneously provide formative feedback while assigning summative scores or grades, and these two objectives "may operate at cross-purposes" (Hedgcock & Lefkowitz, 1996, p. 288). Classroom evaluation is thus nearly always problematic because "the audience is usually limited to the person (the teacher) who also **designs, assigns,** and **assesses** that writing" (Reid & Kroll, 1995, p. 18). Teachers can most productively cope with this all too common situation by acknowledging the contradiction overtly, rather than by overlooking or ignoring it. To acknowledge and relieve this inherent tension, we can devote explicit attention to assessment issues in the classroom, integrate assessment mechanisms into instructional processes, and implement various methods to identify those that are most appropriate and valid for a specific population of writers.

PRINCIPLES OF TASK RELIABILITY AND VALIDITY

Whenever student performance is evaluated for the purposes of diagnosis, placement, or advancement, the classroom teacher's responsibilities may be no less important than those of a tester or administrator, in the sense that he or she may be making decisions that could affect students' further training and possibly their careers. For these reasons, it is essential that composition teachers understand the weight of their responsibilities and develop the knowledge and skills to execute them fairly and confidently. As Weigle (2002) emphasized, "designing a good test of writing involves much more than simply thinking of a topic for test takers to write about and then using our own judgment to rank order the resulting writing samples" (p. 2). She therefore proposed a list of key questions to guide the design of assessment tasks and scoring procedures, an adapted version of which follows:

- What are we trying to elicit or test? How do we define writing proficiency or performance relative to a composing task? For example, are we concerned with learning how effectively writers can perform a particular discursive function (e.g., reporting, persuasion) in written English?
- "Why do we want to test writing ability?" How will we use the output resulting from the writing task?
- Who are the writers whose performance we wish to measure? What do we need to know about our population of novice writers to construct assignments that elicit their best performances?
- Who will evaluate writers' production, and what standards will apply? What measures can be taken to guarantee consistency across scorers' evaluations?
- Who will use the data that the writing task produces, and in what form will those data be most useful?
- To what extent do practical constraints (e.g., time, materials, funding, human labor) limit the information that a composing task or test can generate about writers' abilities?
- "What do we need to know about testing to make our test valid and reliable?"

(Adapted from Weigle, 2002, p. 2)

Although we are concerned chiefly with ongoing classroom assessment, principles of educational measurement (and language testing, in particular) provide us with a framework for selecting and implementing assessment methods for everyday use (Glenn et al., 2003).

In teaching composition, an obvious precept holds that an artifact of student performance undergoing formal measurement must have been produced "through the production of writing" (Hamp-Lyons, 1991b, p. 5). When we measure or score student writing performance or proficiency, the outcome must be based on a student-generated text. This text should consist of 100 words or more and be based on a prompt that gives the writer "considerable room" in which to generate extended discourse (Hamp-Lyons, 1991b, p. 5). This type of measurement is known as "direct assessment," which contrasts with "indirect" or "objective" measurement (Camp, 1993; Cohen, 2001; McNamara, 1996, 2000; Weigle, 2002). An indirect measure may evaluate writing ability by testing verbal reasoning, error recognition, or grammatical accuracy, all of which may be related to writing performance in some way, but only indirectly. Not only are direct measures "far more credible" than indirect measures; they also "make human writers actually perform the skill on which they are being assessed, and . . . give human readers that performance to judge" (Hamp-Lyons & Condon, 2000, p. 11).

Admittedly, fair scoring of student writing requires considerably more effort and training than the scoring of indirect instruments: Raters must be trained to use scoring scales and to apply standards in a consistent, equitable manner. There is no question, however, that direct methods are the most appropriate and potentially valid form of assessment in the writing classroom. Maintaining reliability is a consistent challenge for classroom teachers, administrators, and professionals concerned with evaluating writing performance at programmatic, institutional, and governmental levels.

As we have noted, reliability in writing assessment refers to the consistency with which a writing sample is assigned the same rank or score after multiple ratings by trained evaluators (Henning, 1991). In daily practice, achieving this ideal is no easy task, because most teachers are the sole evaluators of their students' written work. Research has revealed that even seasoned raters can exhibit inconsistency in their scoring behaviors (Chiang, 1999; Cumming, 1990; Cumming, Kantor, & Powers, 2002; Erdosy, 2001; Hamp-Lyons & Mathias, 1994; Haswell, 1998; Smith, 2000; Vaughan, 1991; Weigle, 1999, 2002). Nonetheless, the systematic application of clear, specific, and level-appropriate scoring criteria can enhance an instructor's reliability in evaluating student work by focusing his or her attention on specific textual features as reflected in course objectives and task goals.

Consistent use of such criteria and tools can likewise provide an instructor with practice that, over time, will enable him or her to assign scores and offer feedback with confidence (Glenn et al., 2003).

Validity refers to a reciprocal measurement precept crucial to successful writing assessment. Validity describes the extent to which an instrument "actually measures what it purports to measure" (Cohen, 1994, p. 38). Demonstrating validity is as essential to equitable writing assessment as establishing reliability. In fact, measurement experts argue that reliability is a prerequisite to validity, for no measure "can be valid without first being reliable" (Hamp-Lyons, 1991c, p. 252). However, as Hamp-Lyons and Kroll (1996) pointed out, reliability and validity are interdependent. "The psychometric wisdom," they wrote, "is that no test can be more valid than it is reliable." Scores that lack consistency "are essentially meaningless and cannot be valid. But the knife cuts both ways: If a test is not valid, there is no point in its being reliable since it is not testing any behavior of interest" (p. 65). Because a thorough treatment of reliability and validity verification is beyond the scope of this book, this discussion focuses on testing constructs that apply specifically to the ongoing assessment activities of L2 literacy teachers.

The design and rating of valid measures of L2 writing in the classroom context often requires considerable practice and expertise. Perhaps one of the most relevant categories of validity to be understood is *face validity,* sometimes termed "surface credibility" (Bachman, 1990). If an instrument has face validity, then both teachers and students perceive it to measure what it purports to measure. A writing prompt that aims to elicit writers' argumentative skills, for example, has little or no face validity if the prompt implicitly or explicitly elicits a genre or rhetorical format other than argumentation (although other genres such as description or exposition may be used as part of a writer's argument). Because of the need to demonstrate to students that tasks are not designed to favor any writer or text, ensuring face validity is perhaps one of the teacher's most salient responsibilities. Effective assessment instruments also aim to provide writers with an awareness of their performance on the task (Bailey, 1998; Hamp-Lyons, 2003).

Criterion validity, a more complex type of validity with which classroom teachers should be familiar, can be most practicably measured in large-scale testing situations over extended periods. Criterion validity globally refers to how well an instrument matches other comparable instruments or accepted standards, encompassing both *concurrent* and *predictive validity*. If an instrument has concurrent validity, it generates the same rank order of individual performances as another previously validated instrument administered under comparable conditions at the same time (Bachman, 1990; Bachman & Palmer, 1996; Hamp-Lyons, 1991b; McNamara, 2000; White, Lutz, & Kamusikiri, 1996). An instrument that has predictive validity conversely produces the same results (again, in terms of rank order of individual performances) at future points in time. The classroom setting is rarely amenable to generating the comparability required to measure criterion validity. However, to ensure the construction of fair, informative assessment tools, teachers must consider how consistently their tasks and instruments match up with prior and future instruments, how closely they parallel those administered by their peers in other courses, and how well they fit with the genres and literacy skills targeted in the syllabus (see chapters 3 and 4).

Related to criterion validity is *content validity*, which reflects how effectively an instrument activates cognitive, rhetorical, and linguistic processes (i.e., shaping explicit knowledge, personal experiences, ideas, attitudes, and so forth into a text that is rhetorically and grammatically acceptable). As Hamp-Lyons (1991a) argued, when we claim that a writing instrument has content validity, "we are talking about whether it elicits writing that allows the reader—the judge—to see a sufficient and accurate sample of what the writer can do with the key ideas and skills to be mastered" (p. 11). Content validity therefore implies that a task should not isolate knowledge domains or skills. Rather, the task should elicit writing that requires students to bring together components that constitute the composing process (i.e., knowledge, skills, and strategies).

In this sense, content validity is intertwined with *construct validity* in the domain of writing assessment. We can claim that a task has construct validity only if we can demonstrate that it measures an underlying capacity (Bachman & Palmer, 1996; Hamp-Lyons, 1991b). Tied closely to face and content validity, construct validity is essential in direct assessment, the normative approach applied in classroom assessment. We establish construct validity by demonstrating that an instrument actually tests the skills, subskills, and associated constructs it is designed to elicit and measure (Allaei & Connor, 1991; Weigle, 2002).

Admittedly, the constructs that most concern us—writing proficiency, process, and progress—cannot always be observed directly (Byrd & Nelson, 1995). We may consequently be forced to make inferences about these constructs based on students' composing performances alone (Hamp-Lyons & Kroll, 1996; Henning, 1991). Textual features that can be used to make fair and accurate inferences include communicative effectiveness, persuasiveness, linguistic accuracy, rhetorical organization, referencing, appropriateness, and reader appeal, among others. We can enhance our evaluation of these components by examining students' processes, a procedure facilitated by portfolio assessment. Regardless of the components emphasized for assessment in a writing course, teachers should have a working knowledge of the fundamental precepts of validity (particularly face, content, and construct validity) as they design instruments and make decisions about scoring procedures. Without valid instruments, it is difficult if not impossible to ensure that the assessment process will produce the desired washback effects.

APPROACHES TO SCORING IN ESL WRITING

Evaluative response to student writing can take various forms, each offering unique advantages and challenges. In this section, we describe three general approaches to scoring that are appropriate and practical for use in the classroom context: holistic, analytic, and trait-based scoring. These summative methods are also used in large-scale testing models informed by psychometric theory (Kunnan, 2000; Weigle, 2002). Our central focus in this discussion will again be on ways in which classroom teachers can apply these methods to their educational settings and writer populations.

Because writing assessment always takes place in a particular context, its implementation can vary widely. We present our approach to scoring as options from which teachers can select rather than as preferred or prescribed methods. Just as lesson plans, materials, and assignments must be designed and administered in light of key contextual factors, scoring procedures should be selected and adjusted as a function of the following critical variables:

- The knowledge and skills being elicited and evaluated
- A working definition of the writing skill(s) to be assessed
- The purposes for eliciting student writing performance
- The uses to which the test's scores will be put
- The writers who will take the test
- The maximum skill level of the writers
- The scorers
- The scoring criteria
- The methods for controlling consistency in scoring
- The decision-makers who will use the scores
- The form in which the scores will be reported
- The practical constraints governing scoring and reporting
- The expertise required to ensure validity and reliability

(Adapted from Bachman, 1990; Bailey, 1998; Weigle, 2002)

Fair, informative writing assessment practices take into account students' needs and competencies, social and institutional expectations regarding writing performance, target genres, the teacher's readiness to deploy assessment tools, and the quality of the assessment instruments themselves.

It is worthwhile to recall that the assignments, topics, and prompts used to generate student writing for assessment purposes should be devised with the same care that we apply to developing any composing task. The principles of task construction outlined in chapter 4 apply to the development of tasks and prompts used in the evaluation process. We do not make a distinction between task construction for teaching and task construction for assessment, because one of our primary operating principles is that responsible assessment is also a fundamental part of the teaching process. In this sense, summative methods of assessing student writing can also be used formatively (Hirvela & Pierson, 2000). The following characteristics offer a useful checklist for developing routine prompts for both formative and summative writing assessment.

1. *Clarity.* A clearly worded prompt does not require students to waste time understanding what the assignment requires, but offers brief and succinct directions that allow them to begin writing quickly and easily (Glenn et al., 2003).

2. *Validity.* A valid prompt generates written products whose scores reflect the range of writing proficiencies represented in the class. In other words, highly skilled writers receive higher scores than less skilled writers. Moreover, the range of outcomes does not show an excessively high proportion of scores in the middle range. A good prompt thus allows weaker writers to compose comfortably at their level while challenging the most advanced writers to perform at their best (Reid & Kroll, 1995).

3. *Reliability.* The scoring rubric (scoring guide) is transparent and succinct enough to apply consistently across all writing samples to be assessed, and multiple readings of the same papers by different raters produce similar, if not identical, scores.

4. *Interest.* The prompt is interesting and engaging enough to encourage students to write about it with genuine concern, leading to the production of texts that likewise engage the reader or evaluator. In this way, potential boredom on the part of the reader or evaluator will not unfairly bias scoring.

(Adapted from White, 1994)

Holistic Scoring

An efficient approach to writing assessment is holistic (or global) scoring, which rates or ranks writing proficiency as reflected in a given sample. Holistic scoring rubrics may comprise 4 to 10 levels or *bands*, each corresponding to a score, a set of descriptors, and "benchmark" writing samples.[2] These descriptors can be general (as in Fig. 8.1) or detailed (as in Fig. 8.2). A chief advantage of holistic scoring is that the procedure requires readers to respond to a text as a whole, rather than to a dimension that may stand out to an individual reader as particularly weak or strong (e.g., originality of ideas, grammatical accuracy). The method likewise emphasizes what the writer has done skillfully, as opposed to the text's perceived deficiencies (Cohen, 1994; Hamp-Lyons, 2003). The holistic approach has found favor with process writing proponents, because the technique stresses strengths and works effectively in multidraft instruction.

On the other hand, holistic scoring presents disadvantages that teachers should bear in mind. First, a holistic score cannot effectively provide diagnostic information. It does not explicitly reflect components that refer to specific traits of a student text (e.g., richness of content, coherence, morphosyntactic accuracy, lexical diversity). A single-value score also reduces reliability, although this problem can be addressed when two or more trained raters score each writing sample paper (Camp, 1993; Hamp-Lyons, 1991c; Sakyi, 2000). In addition, a single score may be difficult to interpret for students and teachers alike unless they share the same understanding of the descriptors in the rubric's bands, as we discuss later. Moreover, even if raters' scores reflect a strict and consistent application of a single rubric, the same score assigned to two different texts may reflect judgments of two entirely distinct sets of characteristics related to raters' cultural or disciplinary backgrounds (Connor-Linton, 1995; Kobayashi & Rinnert, 1996; Robinson, 2000; Shi, 2001; Song & Caruso, 1996).

Divergent evaluations also can result when a holistic score compresses interconnected judgments about all dimensions of a sample text (i.e., topic, genre, style, linguistic form, and so on). Conversely, raters may not apply the same weighting to certain text features, resulting in uneven, unfair scores (Casanave, 2004; DeRemer, 1998; Lumley & McNamara, 1995; Milanovic, Saville, & Shuhong, 1996). For example, research has shown that raters tend to assign higher holistic scores to longer samples, even when writing quality is comparable with that of shorter versions (Cohen, 1994; Huot, 1993). Finally, holistic scoring may produce negative washback by penalizing students' efforts to take risks, because "writers may display only novice ability with more complex forms, while those using simpler forms get higher ratings" (Cohen, 1994, p. 315). Classroom teachers can avoid a number of these pitfalls by developing clear rubrics, monitoring reliability with the help of peers, reviewing student writing in portfolios, and using consistent, explicit marking practices (see chapter 5).

Historically, scoring rubrics have been designed to aid raters, yet rubrics should also be viewed as valuable teaching tools when presented to students and used by instructors during the assessment process. Hamp-Lyons (1991c) forcefully argued that any method of writing assessment that "fails to utilize the educative potential" of the instrument itself "permits a disjunction between teaching and assessment, a disjunction we have suffered under for all too long, and need suffer no longer" (p. 244). We similarly maintain that a scoring rubric should reflect the expectations of the writer's intended audience, whether real or simulated, as well as the genre of the writing under scrutiny (Brindley & Ross, 2001; Casanave, 2004; Douglas, 2000). When given to students early in a course, a rubric can enable writers

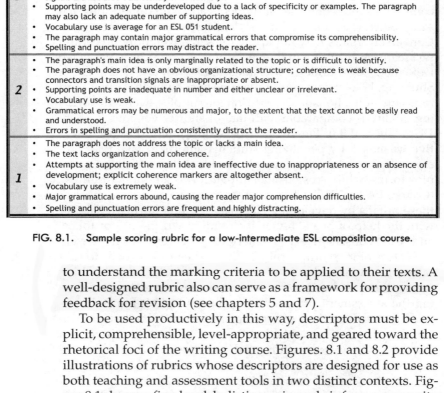

	ESL 051 Paragraph-Rating Scale
5	• The paragraph's main idea directly addresses the topic and is stated clearly and succinctly. • The paragraph is logically organized, its coherence marked by explicit transitions. • The paragraph contains specific supporting ideas, examples, and explanations explicitly connected to the main idea. • Choice of vocabulary is excellent. • Grammatical errors are minor and infrequent. • Spelling and punctuation are generally accurate.
4	• The paragraph's main idea is related to the topic and is reasonably clear. • The paragraph shows solid organization and use of coherence markers. • The paragraph contains at least two supporting ideas, examples, or explanations clearly related to the paragraph's main idea. • Vocabulary use is above average. • There may be minor grammatical errors that do not interfere with the main idea. • Errors in spelling and punctuation occur but do not distract the reader.
3	• The paragraph indicates a main idea related to the topic, but in ways that could be clearer and more explicit. • The paragraph's organization may lack logic or coherence because connectors and transition signals are not used consistently or effectively. • Supporting points may be underdeveloped due to a lack of specificity or examples. The paragraph may also lack an adequate number of supporting ideas. • Vocabulary use is average for an ESL 051 student. • The paragraph may contain major grammatical errors that compromise its comprehensibility. • Spelling and punctuation errors may distract the reader.
2	• The paragraph's main idea is only marginally related to the topic or is difficult to identify. • The paragraph does not have an obvious organizational structure; coherence is weak because connectors and transition signals are inappropriate or absent. • Supporting points are inadequate in number and either unclear or irrelevant. • Vocabulary use is weak. • Grammatical errors may be numerous and major, to the extent that the text cannot be easily read and understood. • Errors in spelling and punctuation consistently distract the reader.
1	• The paragraph does not address the topic or lacks a main idea. • The text lacks organization and coherence. • Attempts at supporting the main idea are ineffective due to inappropriateness or an absence of development; explicit coherence markers are altogether absent. • Vocabulary use is extremely weak. • Major grammatical errors abound, causing the reader major comprehension difficulties. • Spelling and punctuation errors are frequent and highly distracting.

FIG. 8.1.   Sample scoring rubric for a low-intermediate ESL composition course.

to understand the marking criteria to be applied to their texts. A well-designed rubric also can serve as a framework for providing feedback for revision (see chapters 5 and 7).

To be used productively in this way, descriptors must be explicit, comprehensible, level-appropriate, and geared toward the rhetorical foci of the writing course. Figures. 8.1 and 8.2 provide illustrations of rubrics whose descriptors are designed for use as both teaching and assessment tools in two distinct contexts. Figure 8.1 shows a five-level, holistic scoring rubric for a community college composition course aimed at traditional paragraph writing. The rubric in Figure. 8.2, meanwhile, is designed for use in a more highly specialized environment: an advanced-level English

ENSL 1405 — Advanced English Writing for the Social Science
Evaluation Criteria for Revised Writing Assignments
Characteristics of an *A Paper*
(90–100% of specified point value)

An A paper is admirably thorough and complete. Explicit and clear, the position is strongly and substantially argued with abundant reference to published works. The central issues and their complexity are treated seriously, with alternative viewpoints taken into account. The paper shows rhetorical control at the highest level and displays unity and subtle management. Ideas are balanced, with support that is organized according to the content. Textual elements are connected through explicit logical and linguistic transitions. Repetition and redundancy are minimal. The paper shows excellent language control, accurate diction, stylistic precision, and meticulous adherence to mechanical conventions.

Characteristics of a B Paper
(80–89% of specified point value)

A B paper is thorough and complete. The text deals effectively with the issues, presenting the position clearly and articulating arguments substantively. References made to published works are ample and appropriate. Alternative perspectives are also addressed competently. The paper shows strong rhetorical control and is well managed. Ideas are generally balanced with support; the whole text shows strong control of organization that is appropriate to the content. Textual elements are generally well connected, although rhetorical fluency may at times need improvement. Occasional repetitions, redundancies, and missing transitions may occur, but the paper reflects strong language control and reads smoothly. Grammatical well-formedness and accurate diction are apparent, although minor errors might be present. Stylistic and mechanical errors are minor and do not distract the reader.

Characteristics of a C Paper
(70–79% of specified point value)

Possibly lacking in thoroughness, a C paper is nonetheless complete. The text discusses the issues but requires more focus, development or synthesis of published works. The position, while thoughtful, needs to be clarified; arguments may require further substantiation. Repetition, redundancy, and inconsistency sometimes compromise the paper's focus and direction. Alternative viewpoints are minimally addressed and developed. Although the essay shows acceptable rhetorical control, competent management, and appropriate organization, ideas may not be balanced with support. The text shows evidence of planning, although a lack of connectors sometimes interferes with rhetorical fluency. Language is grammatical but may lack fluidity. Whereas the grammatical structures and lexical choices express the writer's intended meanings, more appropriate choices could have been made. Morphosyntactic, stylistic, and mechanical errors sometimes interfere with the reader's comprehension. Papers assigned a mark of C should be revised and resubmitted.

Characteristics of a D Paper
(60–69% of specified point value)

A D paper lacks both completeness and thoroughness. Although the text may consider the issues, it relies heavily on opinions or claims that lack substantial evidence, sometimes leading the reader to wonder if the writer has come to grips with the complexity of the topic. Synthesis of published works is clearly deficient. Superficial or inconsistent argumentation, along with inadequate development, seriously compromise the text's ability to convince the reader. Alternative perspectives are given little or no serious attention. Lacking rhetorical control much or most of the time, the paper's overall shape is difficult to discern. The organization suggests a lack of balance of support that leads to noticeable breakdowns in rhetorical fluency. Transitions within and across sentences and paragraphs are attempted, with only partial success. Displaying weak linguistic control, the text contains grammatical, lexical, and mechanical errors that are a serious threat to the reader's comprehension. Papers assigned a mark of D must be revised and re-submitted.

Characteristics of an F Paper
(0–59% of specified point value)

An F paper is unsuccessful because it is clearly incomplete and fails to develop and support an argument related to the topic. Although the topic may be mentioned, the text digresses or does not treat issues of relevance to the assignment. Superficial and inaccurate treatment of published works suggests a failure to read sources carefully and extensively. Demonstrating little rhetorical control, the paper shows virtually no evidence of planning or organization, as exemplified in underdeveloped or nonexistent connections and transitions. The text demonstrates inadequate linguistic control, with morphosyntactic, lexical, and mechanical errors seriously marring the writer's intended meaning. Papers assigned a mark of F must be revised and resubmitted.

FIG. 8.2. Sample scoring rubric for an advanced-level social science EAP course.

for Academic Purposes (EAP) course requiring sophisticated and extensive social science writing involving synthesis of empirical data. Its five-level scale is intended to parallel the traditional letter grade marking system.

In holistic scoring, the rater reads each sample quickly, assigning a single rating to a text based on an overall impression as described in the rubric (Figs. 8.1 and 8.2). In standardized writing assessment, two or more raters assign scores to ensure reliability, particularly if marking is done on a department- or institution-wide basis. In the classroom, however, the instructor may assign a holistic numeric or letter grade to an assignment after one or more readings. He or she also may provide the student with written or oral feedback to supplement the holistic rating. In day-to-day classroom scoring, teachers sometimes prefer a more finely tuned instrument or a more flexible tool for assigning "borderline" marks (i.e., those that fall between bands). This need arises when an assignment displays most of the characteristics of one band but simultaneously exhibits features of another band. Consider how the rubric in Fig. 8.2 might be applied to a "thorough and complete" sample that "deals with the issues" and competently addresses "alternative perspectives." These are obviously all *B* features. At the same time, ideas may not be "balanced with support"; a lack of connectors may interfere with "rhetorical fluency"; and the language may lack "fluidity." Furthermore, "morphosyntactic, stylistic and mechanical errors...interfere with...comprehension." These *C* characteristics suggest that neither a mark of *B* or *C* would be appropriate. A fairer alternative would be to assign a *B*− or a *C*+, depending on the extent to which the *B* features override the *C* features. Whereas the +/− option might not be practicable in large-scale assessment, it provides a reasonable tool for teachers who do not wish to be confined to band-specific scores that may not accurately reflect all dimensions of a writing sample.

Analytic Scoring

Analytic scoring offers advantages similar to those associated with using "+" and "−" marks in conjunction with a holistic rubric. Unlike holistic scoring, analytic scoring relies on a rating guide that separates and weights textual components a priori: Criteria are prioritized before scoring begins. Thus, components such as content, organization, cohesion, style, register, vocabulary, grammar, spelling, mechanics, and so forth, are preassigned a maximum numeric value, with decreasing step scales or bands described within each component. In the widely known "ESL Composition Profile" (Jacobs, Zingraf, Wormuth, Hartfiel, & Hughey, 1981), for example, each of the five components has a descending, multilevel scoring scale with its own descriptors. The sample Essay Rating Profile in Fig. 8.3, an adaptation of the Jacobs et al. (1981) model, illustrates the structure of such a scoring guide. The scheme in Fig. 8.3 is designed for use in a freshman composition course for both mainstream and non-native speaker (NNS) writers. Its scale allows for assigning letter

RHET 105A – Composition I
Essay Rating Profile

NAME: | EssayTitle:
INSTRUCTOR: | Date:

Record Score Here	Grade	Score Range	
			Content
	A	24–27	Superior understanding of topic and writing context; valuable central purpose/thesis defined and supported with sound generalizations and substantial, specific, and relevant details; rich, distinctive content that is original, perceptive, and/or persuasive; strong reader interest
	B	22–23	Accurate grasp of topic and writing context; worthwhile central purpose/thesis clearly defined and supported with sound generalizations and relevant details; substantial reader interest
	C	19–21	Acceptable but cursory understanding of topic and writing context; routine purpose/thesis supported with adequate generalizations and relevant details; suitable but predictable content that is somewhat sketchy or overly general; occasional repetitive or irrelevant material; one or two unsound generalizations; average reader interest
	D/F	5–18	Little or no grasp of the topic or writing context; central purpose/thesis not apparent, weak, or irrelevant to assigned task; inadequate supporting points or details; irrelevant material, numerous unsound generalizations, or needless repetition of ideas; insufficient, unsuitable, unclear, vague, or weak content; minimal or no reader interest; less than specified length
			Rhetorical Structure
	A	21–23	Exceptionally clear plan connected to thesis/purpose; plan developed with consistent attention to proportion, emphasis, logical order, flow, and synthesis of ideas; paragraphs coherent, unified, and effectively developed; striking title, introduction, and conclusion
	B	18–20	Clear plan related to thesis; plan developed with proportion, emphasis, logical order, and synthesis of ideas; paragraphs coherent, unified, and adequately developed; smooth transitions between paragraphs; effective title, introduction, and conclusion
	C	16–17	Conventional plan apparent but routinely presented; paragraphs adequately unified and coherent, but minimally effective in development; one or two weak topic sentences; transitions between paragraphs apparent but abrupt, mechanical, or monotonous; routine title, introduction, and conclusion
	D/F	5–15	Plan not apparent, inappropriate, undeveloped, or developed with irrelevance, redundancy, inconsistency, or inattention to logical progression; paragraphs incoherent, underdeveloped, or not unified; transitions between paragraphs unclear, ineffective, or nonexistent; weak or ineffective title, introduction, and conclusion
			Grammatical Form
	A	18–20	Sentences skillfully constructed, unified, coherent, forceful, effectively varied; deftness in coordinating, subordinating, and emphasizing ideas; harmonious agreement of content and sentence design; impressive use of grammatical structures
	B	16–17	Sentences accurately and coherently constructed with some variety; evident and varied coordination, subordination, and emphasis of ideas; no errors in complex patterns; effective and clear use of grammatical structures
	C	14–15	Sentences constructed accurately but lacking in distinction; clarity weakened by occasional awkward, incomplete, fused, and/or improperly predicated clauses and complex sentences; marginal to adequate use of grammatical structures
	D/F	1–13	Sentences marred frequently enough to distract or frustrate the reader; numerous sentences incoherent, fused, incomplete, and/or improperly predicated; monotonous, simple sentence structure; unacceptable use of grammatical structures
			Diction and Tone
	A	16–17	Diction distinctive; fresh, precise, concrete, economical, and idiomatic word choice; word form mastery; appropriate, consistent, and engaging tone
	B	14–15	Clear, accurate, and idiomatic diction; minor errors in word form and/or occasional weaknesses in word choice; generally clear, appropriate, and consistent tone
	C	12–13	Satisfactory diction; generally accurate, appropriate, and idiomatic word choice, though occasionally predictable, wordy, or imprecise; limited vocabulary; clarity weakened by errors in S–V and pronoun agreement, point of view, word forms; mechanical and/or inconsistent tone
	D/F	1–11	Diction unacceptable for a college-level essay; inappropriate, nonidiomatic, and/or inaccurate word choice that distracts the reader or obscures content; numerous word form errors; inappropriate and/or inconsistent tone
			Mechanics
	A	12–13	Clarity and effectiveness of expression enhanced by consistent use of conventional punctuation, capitalization, and spelling; appealing manuscript form
	B	10–11	Flow of communication only occasionally diverted by errors in conventional punctuation, capitalization, and spelling; attractive manuscript form
	C	8–9	Adequate clarity and effectiveness of expression, though diminished by punctuation, capitalization, and/or spelling errors; satisfactory manuscript form
	D/F	1–7	Communication hindered or obscured by frequent violations of punctuation, capitalization, and/or spelling conventions; manuscript form unattractive
			COMMENTS:
Total Score (out of 100)	Grade		

FIG. 8.3. Sample scoring rubric for a university NS/NNS freshman composition course.

grades or numeric values that, when summed, yield a score out of 100, thus obviating the need to assign "in-between" marks.

Analytic scoring is sometimes recommended as an alternative to holistic scoring for a number of reasons. A significant advantage is that analytic guides, by virtue of their explicit descriptors and weighting systems, facilitate the training of raters. Because consistent, reliable holistic scoring often requires regular (and sometimes extensive) norming, novice composition teachers may initially find an analytic scale easier to use than a holistic rubric because it allows them to isolate and rate specific textual features. Departments may request that their instructors use analytic scales as a way of standardizing rating procedures across sections and courses (Glenn et al., 2003; Weir, 1990). A further benefit of analytic scoring is that the procedure can guard against the conflation of two or more important text-based categories, a common drawback of holistic scoring (Weigle, 2002; Williamson & Huot, 1993).

In terms of instructional impact, analytic guides can reflect priorities assigned to specific aspects of written products and writing processes featured in the syllabus. Descriptors can be constructed to represent distinct discursive and linguistic course objectives (e.g., argumentative structure, figurative language, use of logical connectors, complex as opposed to simple syntax), and weightings for textual components can vary to encourage students to direct their efforts toward improving targeted skills (Fig. 8.3). For example, in a beginning- or intermediate-level course emphasizing idea development and fluency, the scoring guide might assign a 40% to 60% weighting to content development, with rhetorical structure and grammatical accuracy receiving proportionally lower weightings. Finally, the explicitness of analytic scoring offers teachers a valuable tool for providing writers with consistent, explicit feedback. Analytic guides can provide space for each component's score or rating and allow teachers to circle or underline descriptor items that apply to the essay being evaluated. When teachers use these options, complemented by text-specific comments (see chapters 5 and 7), component scores have meaning beyond mere numeric values or ranks. They are tied directly to identifiable text features and to explicit standards that apply equally to all student writers.

Critics of analytic scoring point out that the quality of a writing sample is much more than the sum of its parts. Measuring the effectiveness of a text by tallying subskill scores can diminish the interconnectedness of written discourse, conveying the false impression that writing can be understood and fairly assessed by analyzing separable text features (Casanave, 2004). Thus, component scales may not be used effectively according to their internal criteria, resulting in a halo effect in which one component score may positively or negatively influence another. A related disadvantage of analytic marking involves how raters operationalize overly simplified, misleading, ambiguous, or overlapping descriptors. Experienced essay judges sometimes find it difficult to assign numeric scores based on certain descriptors, even when they can refer to benchmark samples. Qualitative judgments of coherence, style, and similarly abstract textual characteristics are thus not always easily accommodated by analytic scoring methods (Brindley, 2000; Polio, 1997). Finally, analytic scoring may unfairly bias readers in favor of samples containing elements that are easily identified on the basis of the rubric's components and descriptors. Because grammatical errors are among the most salient characteristics of student writing for many readers, grammatical form may receive more attention from raters than text features such as idea development and rhetorical structure, even though the latter may be assigned heavier weighting in the scoring guide. The unfortunate result of such bias is that writers might not receive appropriate scores or truly beneficial feedback.

Primary and Multiple Trait Scoring

Holistic and analytic scoring rely on preexisting instruments and a priori criteria. In contrast, primary and multiple trait scoring presuppose that the quality of a writing sample can be judged accurately only with reference to a specific writing context (Brindley & Ross, 2001; Douglas, 2000; Hamp-Lyons, 1991c, 2003; Hamp-Lyons & Henning, 1991). Trait-based assessment "treats the construct of writing as complex and multifaceted," allowing teachers and testers "to identify the qualities or traits of writing that are important to a particular context or task type and to evaluate writing according to the salient traits in a specific context" (Hamp-Lyons, 2003, p. 176). Contextualization necessitates scoring guides that are unique to each prompt and the writing generated. The overarching goal of this approach is to develop criteria for successful writing on a given topic, in a selected genre, and in a meaningful context (Weigle, 2002). Teachers and writers alike focus on a narrow, identifiable range of textual aspects, or traits. We should emphasize that trait-based instruments "do not claim to assess every element of writing ability that may be manifested in the context," but rather "the most salient criteria or traits" associated with the task (Hamp-Lyons, 1991c, p. 248).

If a composing assignment aims to elicit persuasive writing, for example, scoring might focus on the development of an argument. The intentional emphasis on this feature would constitute primary trait scoring. In multiple-trait scoring, the principle is the same, except that several facets make up the scoring instrument. The procedure "is context sensitive at all stages and in all dimensions of the test development, implementation, scoring, and score reporting" (Hamp-Lyons, 2003, p. 176). In the case of an argumentative assignment, traits might include the directness of the position statement or proposition, the weight of persuasive evidence, the credibility of the writer's sources , the use of counterargument, the clarity of the warrant (the link between the claim and the evidence), and so on. A trait-based approach therefore focuses the reader's attention directly on the purposes of the writing task, as Fig. 8.4 illustrates. When used as part of the instructional cycle, trait-based guides offer the advantage of encouraging writers to limit their attention to a manageable set of topical resources, rhetorical strategies, and linguistic features as they compose and revise (Douglas, 2000).

The multiple trait scoring guide reproduced in Fig. 8.4 was developed to evaluate a timed writing in which advanced, college-level ESL writers compared two brief essays expressing opposing points of view. The students had completed assigned readings on technology's influence on education and the professions and were working toward an upcoming class debate on the topic. This assignment was explicitly designed to give the students extended, intensive practice analyzing and comparing written arguments and to extend their knowledge of the topic. The instructor had selected the topic and readings based on the students' majors and the next course in the literacy sequence, an interdisciplinary adjunct writing course entitled "Reading and Writing in the Applied Sciences." The prompt and scoring guide were thus constructed to reflect key dimensions of the assignment:

- its genre category and the rhetorical modes associated with it (e.g., explicit statement of the author's position, comparison)
- the subtasks associated with successfully completing the task (summarizing the two reading selections)
- the formal features elicited in the prompt (e.g., appropriateness of language, effective lexical use).

ENSL 24: Advanced Reading and Composing for Non-native Speakers
TIMED WRITING #3 – Comparative Analysis
Assignment

In their respective essays, Chang (2004) and Hunter (2004) express conflicting perspectives on how technology has influenced the education and training of the modern workforce. You will have 90 minutes in which to explain which author presents the most persuasive argument and why. On the basis of a brief summary of each author's point of view, compare the two essays and determine which argument is the strongest for you. State *your position* clearly, giving each essay adequate coverage in your discussion.

Scoring Guide for Timed Writing #3

Score	Rhetorical Structure	Summary Presentation and Comparison	Language Use
6	The writer's position is stated explicitly and substantiated with relevant references to the two essays.	The main idea of each essay is accurately captured and clearly represented; coverage of the two essays is symmetrically balanced.	Language is direct, fluid, and generally accurate; vocabulary use is sophisticated and varied.
5	The writer's position is stated clearly and supported with references to the two essays.	The paper effectively paraphrases each essay's main idea; coverage of the two essays is well balanced.	Language control is good; vocabulary use is nicely varied.
4	The writer's position is sufficiently explicit but could be stated more clearly; references to the two essays are adequate.	The paper paraphrases each essay's main idea with moderate effectiveness; coverage of the two essays is adequately balanced.	Language shows satisfactory but inconsistent control; vocabulary use shows adequate variety.
3	The writer's position is not sufficiently explicit; references to the two essays are sketchy.	The paper merely restates each essay's main idea or captures them inaccurately; coverage of the two essays is not satisfactorily balanced.	Language shows inconsistent control; vocabulary use shows a lack of variety.
2	The writer's position is either not explicit or is ineffectively developed; references to the two essays are minimal and inadequate.	The paper only partially restates each essay's main idea; minimal coverage of the two essays.	Language shows inconsistencies that distract the reader; vocabulary use is highly restricted.
1	The writer does not state a position; references to the two essays are unacceptable or nonexistent.	The paper fails to capture the main ideas of either essay.	Language control frequently distracts the reader; vocabulary use is highly restricted and/or inaccurate.
0	Not a ratable sample.	Not a ratable sample.	Not a ratable sample.

FIG. 8.4. Sample multiple-trait scoring guide (with prompt).

The descriptors in this scoring guide are geared toward measuring the academic and rhetorical skills specified in the course objectives (Hirvela, 1997). Furthermore, the scoring procedure is adapted to the context, purpose, and style of the writing to be elicited. Using this six-level scale, the rater assigns a single score to each trait to determine a cumulative score of 0 to 18. This total can be divided by three to arrive at a mean score on a scale of 1 to 6. For example, a writing sample may be assigned a 5 for rhetorical structure, a 4 for summary presentation, and a 6 for language use, yielding a cumulative score of 15/18, or 5.0 on a six-level scale.

Predictably, trait-based scoring involves several drawbacks: The time and effort required to construct and test a scoring guide for each writing assignment may exceed the limits of many classroom teachers. Moreover, a primary trait model cannot integrate writers' strengths and weaknesses. Even a sophisticated primary trait scale might award a lower score to an exemplary partial writing sample than to a truly weak sample that fully addresses the prompt. Furthermore, "even if the traits are specific to a local context, the raters may still fall back on traditional generalized concepts in their actual ratings" (Cohen, 1994, p. 323).

We can take basic steps to overcome the pitfalls of trait-based writing assessment. Because a trait-based scoring guide must be individualized to each writing assignment, we recommend incorporating rubric preparation directly into the task design process (see chapter 4). A primary or multiple-trait assessment tool should contain the following elements:

1. The task or prompt
2. A reference to the target genre and a description of the rhetorical trait or traits elicited by the task and featured in the scoring criteria
3. An interpretation of how the task or prompt will generate the expected writing performance
4. Identification of the relationship between the task and the trait or traits to be assessed
5. A scoring guide (Fig. 8.4)
6. Benchmark student texts representing each band or score value
7. A rationale for the scores assigned to the benchmark samples.

(Based on Hamp-Lyons, 1991c, 2003)

PORTFOLIO ASSESSMENT

The scoring methods addressed in the preceding sections offer classroom teachers a range of options from which to choose as they select response and evaluation methods for their courses and assignments. These summative procedures, used individually or in combination with one another, can easily serve for portfolio assessment, which is not an alternative scoring procedure, but rather a model for organizing writing processes and products for ongoing reflection, dialogue, and evaluation (Mabry, 1999). A portfolio system does not require any particular scoring procedure. In fact, some portfolio assessment models involve no scoring at all, although the process necessitates ongoing instructor response and evaluation (Casanave, 2004; Elbow, 1993). Portfolio assessment has become increasingly recognized as a valid and valuable tool for instruction and measurement in many contexts, including primary and secondary education, college composition, foreign language education, and professional training.[3] According to Hamp-Lyons and Condon (2000), "portfolios have spread like wildfire" (p. 15) in North America since the groundbreaking work of Belanoff and Elbow (1986), who pioneered portfolio-based writing assessment. Portfolio systems have also been introduced and successfully piloted in Australia and the United Kingdom.

Recognized widely as an "alternative" means of assessing learner achievement of all sorts (not just writing), portfolio assessment features "production rather than recognition, projects rather than items, and teacher judgment rather than mechanical scoring" (Calfee & Perfumo, 1996a, p. 63). When carefully planned and implemented, portfolio assessment crucially engages students and teachers in continual discussion, analysis, and evaluation of their processes and progress as writers, as reflected in multiple written products. Yancey (1992) argued that "reflection is perhaps the most critical feature distinguishing portfolios of writing from simple work folders": A meaningful portfolio consists of much more than "a set of unglossed rough and final drafts assembled willy-nilly" (p. 86).

Students, teachers, and administrators must bear these principles in mind if they expect a portfolio process to produce favorable outcomes. The following outlined principles, drawn from diverse sources, point toward the developmental nature of a valid portfolio assessment system.

1. *Collection.* A portfolio comprises a collection of work that is a subset of a larger archive, which represents the whole of a student's accomplishments. More frequently (and more practically), a portfolio represents a subset of artifacts completed in a course, program, or school (Yancey, 1992). Portfolios thus "allow readers to draw conclusions about writers, not only about the pieces of writing themselves. Collection . . . is the source of the portfolio's greater face validity, of its ability to represent the writer more fully than earlier forms of assessment allowed" (Hamp-Lyons & Condon, 2000, p. 33).

2. *Selection*. The process by which the subset emerges entails selection, a key dimension of portfolio assessment. Selection criteria vary according to the rhetorical situation contextualizing the portfolio, which may show only the writer's development, or which may demonstrate both growth and achievement. The writer's selection usually is guided by external criteria, although he or she is given options from which to select in compiling the collection, thereby promoting self-assessment (Glenn et al., 2003; Hirvela & Pierson, 2000). For Hamp-Lyons and Condon (2000), selection implies that "the assessor sees some evidence of a writer's ability to make extratextual choices, to present a selection that represents the writer well across the specified requirements for contents and the announced criteria for judgment" (p. 35).

3. *Communication*. Unique to the process of portfolio assessment is the principle of communication. Like any portfolio, a writing portfolio conveys something about the writer, his or her values, the literate contexts that the writer has come to know, and so forth (Brindley & Ross, 2001; Johns, 1997).

4. *Range*. Literacy instruction "should present frequent opportunities to write, in a variety of forms or genres, for a variety of purposes and a variety of audiences" (Hamp-Lyons & Condon, 2000, p. 33). Student writers consequently generate a range of writing from which they can select samples that display a range of their individual accomplishments (Murphy, 1999).

5. *Context richness*. Hamp-Lyons and Condon (2000) noted that "insofar as the contents of the portfolio represent the opportunities that a curriculum has presented . . . then the portfolio will be *context rich*" (p. 33). Unlike indirect assessment, a portfolio model presupposes that "writers bring their experiences, in the form of their writings, with them into the assessment, that the portfolio comprises samples of the writing produced in those learning experiences" (p. 34). A portfolio offers the potential of presenting not only student texts, but also the students' evolving roles as writers and the contexts in which they have learned to write (Johns, 1997).

6. *Delayed evaluation*. By delaying the appraisal of written products, selections, and self-assessments to the end of an academic term, a portfolio approach promotes revision, encouraging students to assume responsibility for their learning by giving them control over how they

manage their time. Portfolio instruments also move teachers "beyond judgments about students' competence, leading them to make judgments about the effectiveness of their course(s) as a whole" (Hamp-Lyons & Condon, 2000, p. 34).

7. *Writer-centered control.* Key facets of portfolio assessment are under the control of teachers and administrators (e.g., collection, range, and context, which reflect curricular goals and the demands of a literate community of practice). Nonetheless, a portfolio places "a large measure of control over success into the learner's hands" (Hamp-Lyons & Condon, 2000, p. 35). With the freedom to select portfolio entries, students exercise control over the "snapshot" that the portfolio will display. Because they receive feedback and revise their work as the portfolio evolves, students can improve the quality of their final collection as they see fit (Cole, 1999; Glenn et al., 2003; Mabry, 1999; Weigle, 2002).

8. *Evolution over time.* A hallmark of portfolios is that they expose the evolution of selected written products as they are revised, edited, and polished (Belanoff & Dickson, 1991; Reynolds, 2000). Writers typically present a series of drafts leading to an exemplary final product, enabling them to represent and scrutinize their processes as writers and readers as reflected in sequential iterations of their written products. Furthermore, "thinking about development over time . . . along specified parameters opens the door for surprises, allowing learners to exhibit and even to emphasize their development in ways or areas that the teacher may not have specified or even anticipated" (Hamp-Lyons & Condon, 2000, p. 37).

9. *Measured progress.* A portfolio system offers a means by which writers and teachers monitor learning over time, tracing "growth along specific parameters" (Hamp-Lyons & Condon, 2000, p. 36). Guidelines and criteria predetermine expectations concerning the quality of portfolio entries, as well as specifications for measuring skill development. Assessment criteria allow for evaluation of the extent to which learners have improved their literate skills and generated meaningful texts. Portfolio standards "allow students to show the extent of their progress toward exhibiting . . . characteristics of good writing and writers" (Hamp-Lyons & Condon, 2000, p. 37).

10. *Reflection.* By reflecting systematically on his or her products and processes, a writer explains his or her

learning, how portfolio entries were created, how entries compare with one another, how writing has enhanced his or her literacy skills, and so on (Elbow & Belanoff, 1997; Johns, 1997; Reynolds, 2000; Yancey, 1992). Guided self-assessment helps to "put control for learning into the learner's hands" (Hamp-Lyons & Condon, 2000, p. 36).

11. *Evaluation.* A portfolio naturally entails evaluation by demonstrating systematic appraisal. As they make selections, arrange entries, and articulate the strengths of their portfolio contents, students evaluate their work and provide the assessor with a cross section of products to examine and evaluate (Reynolds, 2000; Weigle, 2002; Yancey, 1992).

12. *Authenticity.* Because they exemplify direct assessment par excellence, portfolios represent learner performance and progress authentically. A complete portfolio contains artifacts that, when compiled sequentially, present an album of literacy performances. Unlike indirect writing assessments that at best provide single snapshots taken at often inopportune moments, portfolios allow writers to expose the genuine, iterative nature of their processes. Because they are embedded in genuine literacy contexts, portfolios are inextricably linked to socioliterate communities, their members, and the genres that they produce (Hirvela & Pierson, 2000; Johns, 1997).

Given these characteristics, it can easily be seen how a portfolio system can encourage the cyclical, heuristic, and recursive principles of composing pedagogy described and illustrated earlier in this book. Furthermore, the teacher–student transactions and dialogue entailed in portfolio assembly and evaluation underscore the vital role played by assessment in teaching and learning.

Portfolio assessment is naturally subject to limitations, particularly when used for large-scale performance evaluation. One such limitation concerns how raters fairly and reliably arrive at a single outcome for judging writing quality, particularly when the written products that students include in their portfolios vary widely in terms of genre and complexity (Hamp-Lyons & Condon, 1993). A related problem concerns comparability: How can grading equivalence be established when individual writers must select from a range of artifacts to include in their portfolios? How does one control the variation that might occur when different tasks assigned by different teachers necessitate the rating of portfolios that are not ostensibly comparable? For example, tasks created by some teachers might be more compelling and interesting than those assigned by others. A partial solution to this problem is to develop explicit instructions for students and instructors that ensure consistency and reliability in both the compilation and evaluation of portfolios (Herman, Gearhart, & Aschbacher, 1996).

A final aspect that should not be overlooked is authenticity: "How will ... portfolio raters know that the students actually wrote all the pieces in the portfolio, and when is editing and revising assistance from others too extensive to represent the student's own writing abilities?" (Grabe & Kaplan, 1996, p. 417). These are all challenges to be confronted directly as portfolio assessment becomes more widely practiced (Casanave, 2004; White, 1995, 1999). When implemented thoughtfully and systematically, however, a portfolio approach can furnish experienced and novice teachers with abundant "room to breathe and grow" (Burnham, 1986, p. 139).

A General Model

Far from being an easy way to grade student writing, portfolios require considerable planning and training for teachers and learners—to say nothing of continuous follow-through. Practitioners must also be alert to the danger of reducing portfolio assessment to a positivist method that trivializes writers and their processes. Hamp-Lyons and Condon (2000) warned that when the chief purpose of portfolios is to assess writing, practices may become "essentialized." That is, the focus becomes "what kind of portfolio this program or that program uses, how it is read and evaluated (in logistical terms) in a specific context, what local faculty's and students' reactions have been, and so forth" (p. 27).

With these dangers in mind, we present a general portfolio framework that, although developed for a specific educational context, illustrates ways in which portfolio assessment can function effectively within and across courses in a given setting. Clearly, the extent and complexity of portfolio systems vary widely. For example, many secondary and college writing programs require instructors to use program-wide portfolio assessment procedures and to participate in institutional portfolio rating sessions at specified intervals (e.g., at term end) (Glenn et al., 2003).

In such situations, each course syllabus may specify program-wide guidelines for students to follow in compiling their portfolios and for instructors to use in teaching, reviewing student work, and conducting conferences. Scoring criteria may likewise be standardized for multiple sections, thereby facilitating collaborative evaluation of students' portfolios, as instructors may judge their own students' work and participate in team grading of the work of students in other sections. Alternatively, teachers may be free to determine whether they will use portfolios at all. If they elect to implement a portfolio system, teachers may need to decide the weight of a portfolio in determining course grades, depending on the proportion of course goals that the portfolio will represent.

The model outlined next describes the portfolio process for a course in a multilevel college ESL program. Its structure is based on the systems pioneered by Burnham (1986), Elbow and Belanoff (1991), and Condon and Hamp-Lyons (2000), among others. Readers are encouraged to consult these and other sources for detailed descriptions of portfolio frameworks, procedures, evaluation methods, and learning outcomes. For purposes of illustration, we propose the following questions as a departure point for devising a portfolio process:

1. What are the purposes of the assessment?
2. What tasks and artifacts will be included in the portfolio document?
3. What are the performance standards and how will marking criteria be applied?
4. How will the instructor and raters ensure consistency in scoring and feedback?
5. To what extent will completed portfolios represent the performances reflected in course objectives and student goals? That is, will the portfolio product have content and construct validity?
6. How will the outcomes of the evaluation process (i.e., scores or grades, evaluative feedback) affect students' future learning?

Process Overview. The college program for which the following portfolio system was designed comprises four prefreshman composition ESL courses and two NNS-track composition courses that parallel the native speaker(NS)-track courses. The NNS freshman composition courses are taken in a two-semester sequence (COMP 120 and COMP 121). The prefreshman composition courses do not bear credit toward students' degrees, but are graded on a scale of A to E, as are the freshman composition courses, which bear full academic credit. Portfolio evaluation is used in all courses, with each course establishing required content and marking criteria appropriate to course objectives and student literacy profiles. We focus in this discussion on the portfolio model used in the first NNS freshman composition course, COMP 120.

The portfolio process for COMP 120 and all courses in the ESL writing program begins by acquainting instructors (regular faculty and graduate teaching associates) with the model's principles. The orientation for new instructors and periodic faculty-wide in-service workshops offer all instructors a thorough introduction to the program's goals, which include mastery of the structure and development of multiple forms of extended written discourse (i.e., discipline-specific academic and nonacademic written genres), research techniques, collaborative learning procedures, and the formal conventions of edited academic English. Although COMP 120 instructors design their own course outlines, the syllabus is negotiated before the start of each semester. To ensure consistency across sections, instructors agree on a common textbook, from which they choose readings and design writing assignments. Faculty also jointly establish the number and type of revised assignments and timed writings to be included in the COMP 120 portfolio. Deadlines for midterm and final portfolio documents also are determined collaboratively and announced in the syllabus.

The syllabus sets forth assessment criteria that are explicitly linked to course goals and assignment objectives, so that students and teachers alike have a clear understanding of how evaluation is to take place over the term (see chapter 3). Before students submit their first piece of revised writing, novice and experienced instructors participate in mandatory essay norming sessions to familiarize themselves with benchmark papers and the COMP 120 scoring rubric, which is very similar to the sample in Fig. 8.2. The purpose of this early workshop is twofold: (a) It increases the likelihood that marking criteria will be applied consistently across sections, and (b) it provides instructors with practice in giving feedback for revision (see chapters 5 and 7). Participants respond to sample papers for each band in the rubric and discuss options for written feedback and conducting conferences. Leaders emphasize providing students with formative commentary early in their composing processes, so that instructors demonstrate the use of the portfolio as an instrument of change, as opposed to a means of static, summative evaluation.

Vital to the success of a portfolio model is informing students of their responsibilities as portfolio compilers and of the specific benefits of engaging in the process. Before detailing procedures and policies, instructors should frame the portfolio assessment in terms of its primary advantages. One such advantage includes encouraging writers to show what and how much they have learned—progress that is difficult to measure when assignments are evaluated separately. Moreover, the portfolio entails built-in options from which students can choose, offering them latitude and personal choice in terms of the portfolio's contents. Writers therefore exercise autonomy and control as they select writing samples and make decisions about how to revise them.

In COMP 120, students are given a document on the first class day explaining the portfolio system, its rationale, and its procedures as an attachment to the syllabus. A portion of this document appears in Fig. 8.5. These guidelines, supplied along with the department's holistic scoring rubric, specify the portfolio's contents, ideas for selecting the most appropriate assignments, directions for commentaries and self-assessments, teacher and peer feedback procedures, revision policies, deadlines, and grading standards. In keeping with the precepts of personal growth, investment, and development, this handout also indicates that assignments given later in the semester will become more demanding, a clear signal that evaluation criteria will become more exacting.

Sequence, Procedures, and Instruments.   Once a portfolio system is formalized in writing as policy, it may take two or three drafting–feedback–revision cycles before students adapt to the rhythm of the process and assume responsibility for shaping their portfolios. In COMP 120, the portfolio process begins in a structured way, gradually becoming more flexible as students exercise autonomy as writers. For example, students must revise their first assignment twice and include it in their midterm portfolios. They may omit this assignment from their final portfolios, however. Subsequent papers may necessitate only a single revision, although the course requires that students revise all papers returned with a mark of "U" (Fig. 8.5). As the course progresses, students systematically add material to their portfolios, including paper drafts and revisions, peer feedback worksheets, quizzes, correspondence, self-assessment commentaries that front papers

COMP 120: ACADEMIC WRITING I FOR NON-NATIVE SPEAKERS

COMP 120 PORTFOLIO GUIDELINES
Fall Semester

Background and Rationale

The English Department and the Division of ESL have jointly developed a system of Portfolio assessment for all writing Courses in the 080, 090 (ESL Noncredit), 110 (Academic Writing), and 120 (Academic Writing for Non-native Speakers) series. The COMP 120 Portfolio is designed to help you meet its particular objectives, which include building your mastery of paragraph and essay development, research techniques, collaborative learning procedures, and the conventions of edited academic English. This course is thus designed to develop your academic literacy skills, including your ability to read and produce a range of scholarly texts. The COMP 120 syllabus therefore features texts drawn from literature, the social and physical sciences, and the popular media. You will write about topics using rhetorical techniques that include exposition, explanation, description, comparison, analysis, and persuasion. When completed, your COMP 120 Portfolio will demonstrate your control of these techniques and your progress as an academic writer.

For specific policies pertaining to the presentation and evaluation of Portfolios, please refer to the *Division of ESL/English Department Portfolio Policy Manual* (Revised edition), which is included as part of the syllabus for this course. The *Policy Manual* includes important information about procedures, confidentiality, grading, and so on. Please review the *Policy Manual* carefully and refer to it throughout the semester. Perhaps the best way to acquaint yourself with expectations for your COMP 120 Portfolio is to review successful Portfolios assembled by other students. Sample Portfolios are available for checkout from the University Library and from your instructor.

This Semester's COMP 120 Portfolio Requirements

As your syllabus and course outline indicate, COMP 120 will require four revised assignments and five timed writings this semester. *You must submit all of these assignments to your instructor on time and in the specified form (or satisfy the makeup policy) in order to earn a grade of "C" or higher in this course, as the Policy Manual specifies on page 7.* Assignments receiving a mark of "U" (Unsatisfactory) must be revised and resubmitted; only those assignments that receive a mark of "S" (Satisfactory) are eligible for inclusion in your Portfolio.

Please remember that the Midterm Portfolio and Final Portfolio are not separate documents: Your Midterm Portfolio is an in-progress version of your Final Portfolio. In Comp 120, 85% of your course grade is based on the quality of your Final Portfolio. Please review the *Policy Manual,* pages 9–12, for an explanation of how the contents of your Portfolio will be assessed. Included in the *Policy Manual* is a scoring rubric, "Explanation of Standards for Assessing Student Writing in COMP 120," which describes the specific features of writing assignments that earn marks of A, B, C, D, and E.

Checklist for the Midterm Portfolio

Your Midterm Portfolio will be due at the end of Week 8. Your instructor will not be authorized to accept your Midterm Portfolio unless it contains the items listed below:

❑ Assignment 1 (including all intermediate drafts, a peer response worksheet from at least one classmate, self-analysis cover sheets, and all written instructor feedback).

❑ Assignment 2 OR Assignment 3 (including all intermediate drafts, a peer response worksheet from at least one classmate, self-analysis cover sheets, and all written instructor feedback).

FIG. 8.5. Sample portfolio process guidelines for an NNS-track freshman composition course.

❑ One of your timed writings (including written instructor feedback). In addition, you may optionally include a revision of this timed writing.

❑ One to two pieces of informal, personal, or self-selected writing (e.g., a journal entry, a reading response, a letter to your instructor or a peer, a poem, an editorial for the campus newspaper).

❑ A one-page self-assessment of your performance and progress over the first 7 weeks of COMP 120. Please use the *Midterm Self-Assessment Guidelines* to compose this document, which should review your work and change as a writer. If you wish to receive a provisional, in-progress grade, please include this request at the end of your self-assessment.

The Final Conference

Final Conferences will be scheduled with your instructor during Weeks 12 and 13. You will submit a draft of your two-page final self-assessment to your instructor in advance of your conference, along with any other materials that he or she requests. In your Conference, you and your instructor will discuss your progress and the writing samples that you will include in your Final Portfolio.

Checklist for the Final Portfolio

Your Final Portfolio will be due at the end of Week 15. Your instructor will not be authorized to accept your Final Portfolio unless it contains the following items:

❑ Three revised assignments (each including intermediate drafts, at least one peer response worksheet, self-analysis cover sheets, and all written instructor feedback).

❑ Two of your timed writings (including written instructor feedback). You may also optionally include a revision of one of these timed writings, with an appropriate cover sheet. Your instructor will provide you with guidelines for preparing these cover sheets.

❑ Two pieces of informal, personal, or self-selected writing related to this course, to another course, or to activities outside school (e.g., a journal entry, a reading response, a letter to your instructor or a peer, a poem, an editorial for the campus newspaper).

❑ A two-page self-assessment of your performance and progress in COMP 120. Please use the *Final Self-Assessment Guidelines* to compose this document, which should review your work and growth as a writer. Your self-assessment should also explain why you have given yourself the grade you have indicated. If your instructor asks you to revise your self-assessment during your Final Conference, please include your initial draft as well.

General Reminders

• Please submit your Midterm and Final Portfolios in a rigid-cover, one-inch, three-ring binder, as instructed in the *Policy Manual*.

• Please check the *Policy Manual* for specific presentation requirements (i.e., cover sheet contents, typographic conventions, bibliographic style, word-processing formats, guidelines for headings, and so on).

FIG. 8.5.   Sample portfolio process guidelines for an NNS-track freshman composition course (Continued).

submitted for instructor feedback, personal and informal writing (e.g., reading responses, journal entries), and written feedback on their peers' assignments. Writers gradually assemble these materials over the term to facilitate preparation of midterm and final portfolios. Instructors consistently encourage students to include products that represent their best work and significant changes in their academic literacy skills, particularly composing.

An important additional component of the portfolio process involves interaction among writers and between student and teacher. Although group work, peer feedback sessions, and teacher–student conferences do not always lend themselves easily to the production of written samples for inclusion in the portfolio, these interactions are essential elements of the teaching-assessment cycle. In COMP 120, instructors meet individually with students for compulsory midterm and semester-end conferences, usually during scheduled class time. Semester-end conferences occur in the final weeks of the term so that instructors can assist students in selecting portfolio products. In addition to these formal meetings, instructors hold brief, periodic conferences with students to offer them guidance on individual drafts, revisions, and samples to include in their portfolios. Rather than provide extensive written feedback on all papers, instructors may instead hold miniconferences in which they respond orally to student writing, after which students revise these papers (see chapter 5).

Because of its academic course objectives, COMP 120 gives students the option of requesting provisional letter grades on revised assignments and on their midterm portfolios. All courses in the ESL program are graded on a scale of A to E, although for the purposes of ongoing assessment, instructors emphasize formative commentary and oral feedback over summative evaluation. To amplify the need for students to revise their work and to reflect on its quality, instructors report a mark of "S" or "U" on writing assignments submitted for possible inclusion in the portfolio. A mark of "U" represents a paper that is "unsatisfactory" for inclusion in the portfolio, whereas a mark of "S" suggests that the work satisfactorily meets minimum standards of quality. A paper assigned an "S" would earn at least a grade of "C" if it were to be assessed according to the holistic scoring guide. Thus, students who complete the minimum number of assignments on time and include in their portfolios only those products that the instructor has deemed satisfactory are assured of passing the course with a "C" or, depending on the context, a "B."

Instructors indicate traditional letter grades only when students request them—and only on assignments that have already been assigned a mark of "S." This practice is designed to promote the developmental aspect of the portfolio process and to downplay a strong product orientation in which summative grades preoccupy students at the expense of genuine growth (Casanave, 2004; Elbow, 1993; Moss et al., 1992; Murphy & Smith, 1999; Reynolds, 2000). These grades are reported to students as provisional: No course grade can be assigned until the portfolio is complete and has been evaluated by a team of raters. At the same time, the policy accommodates students who wish to have a more precise measure of their performance and standing (Burnham, 1986; Williams, 1996).

When designed efficiently, a portfolio system need not demand more work from the instructor than traditional summative evaluation of disconnected assignments. However, students may need time to adjust to taking charge of their own progress as writers. This process may necessitate allowing time at the beginning of the term for acquainting students with policies and procedures, training them to make their own decisions, and preparing them to make revisions independently. The COMP 120 syllabus requires three to six revised papers ranging in length from 500 to 2,000 words over a semester. The syllabus also includes several timed writings, one or more of which students may revise outside of class. Each of these assignments is read by the instructor and returned with written feedback or discussed in a conference. The number of revisions per assignment varies from term to term, from instructor to instructor, and from class to class. Nevertheless, the first assignment generally requires two revisions, for a total of at least three drafts. This first assignment usually is a required component of the midterm portfolio, when students meet with the instructor to discuss their progress since the first assignment (Fig. 8.5). At the midterm conference, the instructor compares his or her performance assessment with each individual's self-assessment, offering specific recommendations for improving students' products and strategies to complete the course successfully. Because many students routinely request a provisional course grade at this time, instructors should be prepared to report one, although students should be reminded that the final course grade can be determined only when the final portfolio is evaluated.

Because the curriculum and assignments in COMP 120 are revised frequently, and because new instructors teach the course every semester, midterm and final portfolios are evaluated collectively to ensure that the same objectives and standards are met across multiple sections. At midterm, instructors collect their students' midterm portfolios, completing an initial evaluation form that features written comments and a provisional grade. Experienced instructors are then paired with less experienced instructors. After portfolios are exchanged, they are given a second reading by the senior instructor, who also completes an evaluation form. Readings take place independently after a brief renorming with benchmark papers. Peer raters read holistically, focusing mainly (if not exclusively) on students' revised papers and commentaries, as opposed to initial and intermediate drafts (Belanoff & Elbow, 1991; Murphy & Smith, 1999). Teams next meet to compare results and to reconcile ambiguous, inconsistent, or divergent feedback. The level supervisor or program coordinator then meets with each team to resolve incompatible evaluations before individual instructors return portfolios and conduct midterm conferences. Although admittedly labor-intensive, this process reduces instructor bias, increases reliability, and lends face validity to the feedback that students receive in their midterm conferences, because it includes the evaluation of not one but two trained raters (Hamp-Lyons & Condon, 2000).

Given the high stakes involved, final portfolio evaluation necessitates more elaborate planning, but is ultimately intended to relieve challenges associated with determining course grades. Instructors hold conferences with students 2 to 3 weeks before the final deadline to discuss which assignments, projects, and samples to present. Before this conference, students submit a two-page draft self-assessment (Fig. 8.5). In this document, students systematically evaluate their portfolio contents, presenting a rationale for presenting the artifacts to be included. They also present arguments for which a particular grade is warranted. When the instructor's preliminary evaluation agrees with that of the student, the conference may focus on the steps the student will take to revise remaining work for final evaluation by the departmental scoring team. When the instructor's preliminary evaluation diverges from that of a student, the conference focuses on why the student's self-assessment is inflated or below target. In the former case, the instructor may ask the writer to review the grading criteria and to revise his or her work accordingly. Because time remains before the final deadline, students in such circumstances can sometimes make changes in their work that are significant enough to merit a higher overall grade. After the conference and before the submission deadline, students generally revise their written self-assessments.

The rating process for the final portfolios is similar to the midterm procedure, except that instructors do not read their own students' portfolios before they go to the evaluation team, which comprises two readers who are unfamiliar with the class. Again, less experienced raters are matched with more seasoned readers. Team members perform their readings independently, completing them within a 48- to 72-hour period. Raters compose only the briefest commentaries, which are submitted to the level supervisor or program coordinator. When no serious discrepancies emerge, the supervisor returns the portfolios and results directly to the instructor, who uses the outcomes to determine students' final course grades. When teams report discrepant written evaluations or grades, the supervisor meets with the raters to mediate a mutually agreeable result (Hughes, 1996). These arbitrated outcomes are then reported to the instructor at the time that portfolios are returned. Because portfolio contents have undergone preliminary scrutiny by the instructor in the process leading to (and perhaps following) the final conference, he or she is already familiar with the portfolio and its quality. Thus, the instructor is unlikely to need a final review of the entire dossier before assigning course grades, which may not be based solely on the portfolio (15% of the course grade in COMP 120 is based on student participation, attendance, on-time performance, and so forth).

The COMP 120 portfolio model represents one of many possible designs for a formative writing assessment system in which performance evaluation feeds back into teaching and instruments that hold writers and teachers accountable for their decisions (Hamp-Lyons & Condon, 2000). In some respects, portfolio systems such as the one just described reflect the general movement in language teaching and general education toward learner-centered assessment (Brown, 1998; Ekbatani & Pierson, 2000). In particular, portfolio assessment involves writers in managing their own processes (Bailey, 1998; Gottlieb, 2000; Hamp-Lyons, 2003; Hirvela & Pierson, 2000). An effective portfolio model also answers Elbow's appeal for more formative evaluation and less summative ranking: Portfolios engage teachers in a multifaceted response to their students' work. For Elbow (1993), sound evaluation entails going far beyond an initial response "that may be nothing but a kind of ranking ("I like it" or "This is better than that"), and instead looking carefully enough at the performance or person to make distinctions between parts or features or criteria" (p. 187). Portfolio evaluation is neither a panacea nor a universally accepted alternative to traditional assessment. Nonetheless, despite the challenges it presents (e.g., careful planning, serious commitment, labor-intensiveness, compromised reliability), portfolio assessment offers promising possibilities for instructors and student writers alike.

PRACTICAL CONCERNS IN ASSESSING STUDENT PERFORMANCE

This final section touches on practical issues in performance assessment that are often overlooked in composition teaching and teacher preparation. Some of these issues involve responding to written products, whereas others pertain to wider issues of management, scoring, and record keeping.

Managing the Workload

Responding efficiently to student writing is often the primary concern of novice and experienced teachers, for whom the workload can be simply overwhelming. Tarvers (1993) offered two obvious but frequently ignored pieces of advice: "Be realistic" and "don't make promises you can't keep" (p. 117). In other words, plan enough time to review the assignments you have given and allow adequate buffer time in your syllabus to accommodate delays. Novice teachers may spend 30 minutes or more on a 500-word sample, whereas experienced instructors may spend 15 to 20 minutes. Even at that rate, scoring 30 writing assignments can easily consume a full 8-hour workday or more. With practice, experience, and a reliable scoring instrument, grading time can be reduced to a manageable level.

Still, it may be necessary to restrict the time spent on each sample to a fixed period (e.g., 15 to 20 minutes per paper). Alternatively, you might divide your workload into smaller chunks, marking 5 to 10 samples per day over a 3- or 4-day period, rather than read a stack of papers in 1 day. Announce return dates based on a reasonable timetable. If assignments require revision, return them early enough to allow students several days before the revision due date. To minimize unproductive marking practices and maximize meaningful instructional time, we offer several additional suggestions for planning and handling student writing:

- Assign reading journals (see chapter 2) or writing logs that can be skimmed and commented on without editing or scoring.
- Assign informal writing such as journal entries, freewriting, and so forth that do not require instructor response (see chapters 2 and 3).
- Specify in the syllabus that not all writing tasks will be formally assessed.
- Construct formal writing assignments carefully, as recommended in chapter 4. Articulate writing tasks clearly in writing, providing sample benchmark papers to improve students' chances of producing successful assignments at the outset. Higher quality student writing necessitates less marking time.
- Reference performance criteria explicitly in the assignment description to allow you to identify each text's strengths and weaknesses efficiently.
- After learner training, instruct student writing groups to respond to early and middle drafts (see chapter 6).
- Resist excessive commentary, editing, and proofreading on early and middle drafts (see chapters 5, 6, and 7).
- Consider using a numeric or symbolic coding system that enables you to forgo extensive comments.
- Model and discuss the use of your scoring rubric to evaluate benchmark texts in class to reduce the need to comment extensively on individual assignments.
- Focus written comments on the central issues and textual conventions featured in the writing task and in students' cover sheets (see chapters 5 and 7).

Paper Grading Anxiety

Another important concern involves anxiety associated with assessing student writing for the first time. Although armed with an explicit scoring instrument, teachers may find it difficult to initiate the grading process, often because they fear making judgments that may be unfair, unjustified, and possibly damaging to student writers (Anson, 1999a; Glenn et al., 2003). These wholly natural apprehensions should not be treated lightly. Frequently, what teachers fear most are the results of crude, reductionist, and overly simple rankings (i.e., a "B" vs. a "C," or a "High Pass" vs. a "Pass") that do not convey a meaningful response to students. If we undertake evaluation in Elbow's (1993) sense, however, we do not stop at ranking. At the same time, ranking can be an excellent place to start when we are faced with a set of assignments to mark, and we obviously will not curtail our efforts at that point. Once we have read through a handful of papers—perhaps not even the whole set—we can rank-order them from most satisfactory to least satisfactory, and then examine our intuitive reactions.

Elbow (1993) pointed out that reflection on one's intuitions is part of judgment and that evaluation inherently involves judgment: We cannot avoid it, but we can make it more useful for ourselves and our students. Hirvela and Pierson (2000) noted that "the self-assessment procedures of portfolio pedagogy can enable students to learn from their self-analysis or reflection what otherwise might not have become apparent to them." Consequently, "students gain a deeper understanding of their performance and abilities as writers" (p. 113). Naturally, self-analysis and reflection can produce fruitful outcomes only if systematically scaffolded. Informative scaffolding questions might include the following: Why do I think writing sample Y is better than sample X? How do my reactions coincide with the descriptors on the rubric? How does my reading of sample Z affect my rereading of samples X and Y? If I read these texts tomorrow, will my rankings be different? By addressing such questions before assigning grades, we can move toward informative evaluation. Ideally, we also will calibrate our reading to some useful external standard (i.e., the task, the scoring rubric, benchmark samples, the quality of individual samples with respect to the others, and so forth).

Reporting grades often brings about discomfort. Teachers may find the process distressing because of insecurity about their objectivity and measurement skills. Most composition teachers also are highly sensitive and mindful of their students' personal investment in their written products. For ESL writers, assignment scores and course grades are frequently tied to their perceptions about how they are valued by authority figures such as teachers. To mitigate anxieties generated by the high stakes of educational measurement, we recommend that teachers regularly remind themselves and their students that formal assessment, when implemented according to the principles articulated in this chapter, should provide information about writing achievement, proficiency, and progress. Moreover, "it is almost impossible to assess adequately such intangible qualities as effort or sincerity"

(Peterson, 1995, p. 73). We should recall that writing instructors are expected to evaluate products, not the persons who author them. Moreover, systematic writing assessment provides a means of communicating honestly about writing quality. Explicit standards likewise enable us to "justify the grades we issue, so that we can monitor our own consistency and show students the criteria by which we evaluate their work" (Peterson, 1995, p. 73).

A further recommendation for reducing grading anxiety involves a simple reminder: Not all assignments have to be assessed. "Just because conventional institutions oblige us to turn in a single quantitative course grade at the end of every marking period, it doesn't follow that we need to grade individual papers" (Elbow, 1993, p. 191). This precept applies to settings in which teachers evaluate individual assignments summatively and to portfolio systems. As long as the syllabus allows for flexibility in terms of how many assignments are graded, teachers should take full advantage of their prerogative to focus essentially (or solely) on providing evaluative feedback on occasion, and not on traditional ranking, although we would argue that both methods are necessary and useful.

Assigning Course Grades

Determining individual course grades can be as anxiety provoking for teachers as marking student writing for the first time. Needless to say, the two processes should be undertaken with the same care. Arriving at fair, informative course grades need not, however, cause undue worry. As noted in chapter 3, the process of assigning grades can be facilitated by establishing clear assessment standards, weighting policies, and grade calculation procedures in the course syllabus. For example, in many postsecondary settings, weightings are fixed for certain courses. In others, individual instructors might have the freedom to assign variable weights to a certain percentage of the course grade. In many contexts, instructors may have complete freedom to weight grades as they wish.

When given options, teachers should first examine course goals and the aims of graded work. The weighting of assignments in grade calculation formulas should reflect their importance in the syllabus and the effort required for students to complete them satisfactorily (Glenn et al., 2003). For example, a multidraft research paper should legitimately receive more weight in the course grade if research writing is featured as a major course goal. It should likewise be weighted more heavily than a short review essay or timed writing. In a course requiring extensive reading, the grading scale might assign a corresponding weight to reading tasks such as journals and quizzes (see, for example, Appendix 3A).

A related concern involves rewarding students for their progress, particularly when the syllabus professes a process orientation and an emphasis on revision. Without compromising evaluation criteria, teachers can make room in their grading policies for fair assessment of both products and progress. This goal can be achieved by weighing assignments given later in the term more heavily than those given at the beginning. In a course that leads to the drafting and revision of an original research paper, for example, initial assignments might target skills necessary for composing and polishing that final product. Early assignments may require students to analyze and synthesize published sources as practice for extensive work with new material and a demanding research process later in the term. Initial assignments might be weighted 15% or 20%, whereas the final research paper might be weighted 30% or more to reflect increasing demands and the accretion of increasingly complex skills. Thus, students whose performance is initially weak still have opportunities to improve their marks over time. Meanwhile, students who begin with more solid skills still have ample incentive to complete the assigned work and improve their skills. Variable weighting can be a useful tool in both traditional courses and courses that feature portfolio assessment.

An additional recommendation for easing the distress of determining course grades is pragmatic: Keep current, accurate records of student performance, whether you use a gradebook, loose grade sheets, individual progress charts, or computer software. All assignments should be noted, with a score or evaluation recorded. The grade record should also track attendance, peer critiques, intermediate drafts, and so on if these components are assessed in your course or program. After marking student work, the results should be recorded in a form that will be converted easily to summative grades at the end of the term. For example, if your grading system is based on percentages (as in the case of analytic scoring) or numeric scores (as in the case of holistic and trait-based scoring), you should record these values instead of converting them to letter grades or symbols. Recording scores exactly as they are reported to students will obviate the need to reconstruct these notations later and facilitate the calculation

Letter Grade	Percentage Scale (Figs. 8.2 and 8.3)	Six-Point Scale (Fig. 8.4)	Five-Point scale (Fig. 8.1)
A	94–100%	6	5/4
A–	90–93%	6/5	
B+	87–89%	5	4/3
B	83–86%	5/4	
B–	80–82%	4/5	
C+	77–86%	4	2
C	73–75%	4/3	
C–	70–72%	3	
D+	67–69%	3/2	1
D	63–66%	2	
D–	60–62%	2/1	
E or F	0–59%	1/0	0

FIG. 8.6.   Numeric grade conversion scale.

of means and weighted scores. The conversion table shown in Fig. 8.6 presents suggested equivalencies. If course grades are weighted, organize the columns of your gradebook, charts, or computer database to reflect these categories. In this way, you can easily convert cumulative scores or means into weighted scores, which can subsequently be summed for calculation of a composite score or grade. Computer software for tracking student grades is remarkably flexible, easily accommodating weighted grades, an array of scoring scales, and qualitative comments.

SUMMARY

This chapter outlines principles of classroom-based writing assessment. It also describes theoretical and procedural aspects of holistic, analytic, and trait-based scoring methods. In addition to examining techniques for rating student writing, we present an overview of portfolio assessment in the context of ESL composition instruction. Finally, we offer specific suggestions for managing paper marking and facilitating student performance evaluation. Throughout this chapter, we emphasize the pedagogical role of assessment in the teaching of composition. In our view, responding to and evaluating student writing is as crucial to successful ESL writing instruction as careful materials design, course planning, and classroom teaching. Moreover, establishing clear, systematic scoring criteria is as useful for students as for teachers. Major points related to this generalization can be summarized in the following statements:

- Whatever scoring method or methods they select for marking student work, teachers should aim for the highest standards of validity and reliability.
- Each of the three scoring methods discussed here (holistic, analytic, and trait-based) presents advantages and disadvantages that must be weighed in light of each method's reliability and validity as well as how satisfactorily the method informs students about their writing performance and progress.
- Portfolio assessment offers distinct advantages over traditional, summative evaluation of individual writing assignments and can maximize the interactive, heuristic, recursive elements of process-based composing pedagogy introduced and explained throughout this book.
- Adopting efficient planning, paper-marking, record-keeping, and reporting practices facilitates fair, effective, and informative assessment of student performance and progress.

REFLECTION AND REVIEW

1. How do face, criterion (concurrent and predictive), content, and construct validity differ? Why are they relevant in ESL writing assessment?
2. Describe the relationship between validity and reliability. Why are both constructs important for classroom teachers to understand as they assess student writing and overall writing performance?
3. Identify and compare principles underlying holistic, analytic, and trait-based scoring. Of these three scoring

methods, which offers the greatest advantages for you in your teaching context? Why?

4. How can assessment criteria and scoring procedures be integrated into a writing course syllabus to promote positive washback? What advantages does such integration offer teachers and student writers?

5. To what extent can formative portfolio assessment be claimed as a more valid means of evaluating writing products and skills than traditional, summative evaluation? Explain.

6. Discuss scoring techniques and grading methods that you might adopt or adapt in your teaching context. Explain and justify your choices.

Application Activity 8.1: Holistic Essay Scoring Practice

Directions

1. Select several sample essays from those provided in Appendices 5B, 5C, 6B, or 7. Alternatively, select two or three sample assignments written by students in an ESL course at your institution. These samples should represent a diverse range of strengths.

2. Depending on the proficiency level of the students who composed the samples, rate the essays using the holistic rubric in either Fig. 8.1 or Fig. 8.2. Comment on a copy of the rubric or on the texts as you would if you were evaluating them in a classroom setting.

3. Make copies of your comments and scores for each of the samples, then distribute this material to one or more classmates for comparison.

4. In a pair or group discussion, compare your scores and comments with those of your peers. Use the following prompts to guide you:

   a. On what points did you agree or disagree? Why?
   b. If you disagreed, arrive at a consensus evaluation of each sample.
   c. Identify the sources of your agreement and disagreement, formulating a list of suggestions for using holistic scoring rubrics.

Application Activity 8.2: Analytic Essay Scoring Practice

Directions

1. As you did in Application Activity 8.1, select a set of student essays from those provided in Appendices 5B, 5C, 6B, or 7 (or two or three sample essays written by students in an ESL course at your institution). These samples should represent a diverse a range of quality.
2. Depending on the proficiency level of the writers, rate the samples using the analytic scoring rubric in Fig. 8.3. Make comments on a copy of the scoring sheet or on the sample essays as you would if you were evaluating the essays in a classroom setting.
3. Make copies of your comments and scoring sheet for each sample and distribute this material to one or more class-mates for comparison.
4. In a pair or group discussion, compare your component and composite scores as well as your comments with those of your peers. Use the following prompts to guide you:

   a. On what points did you agree or disagree? Why?
   b. Where you disagreed, arrive at a consensus evaluation of each of the essays.
   c. Identify the sources of your agreement and disagree-ment, formulating a list of suggestions for using and con-structing analytic scoring rubrics.

Application Activity 8.3: More Analytic Essay Scoring Practice

Directions

1. Using the same writing samples that you evaluated and discussed in Application Activity 8.1, rate and comment on these using the analytic scale in Fig. 8.3.
2. Follow the discussion and comparison guidelines outlined in Application Activity 8.2, items 2 to 4.
3. In your discussion (Application Activity 8.2, item 4), con-sider these questions:

   a. How well do your composite analytic ratings match with your holistic ratings?

b. Where do the two sets of scores and comments differ? Why?

c. Given the nature of the writing tasks that you evaluated, which of the two scales do you feel is most appropriate? Why?

d. How would you modify one or both of the scales to suit your educational setting?

Application Activity 8.4: Designing and Testing a Rubric or Scale

Directions

1. Identify a specific ESL or other composition course in your program or at a nearby institution. Individually or with a classmate, use this context to design one of the following:

   a. A holistic scoring rubric intended for systematic use in the course

   b. An analytic scoring scale intended for systematic use in the course

   c. A primary or multiple trait scoring scale intended for evaluating a specific writing assignment given in the course.

2. Use a model from Figs. 8.1 to 8.4 as a framework or consult other sources cited in this chapter for additional sample instruments. If you are not teaching the course, consult with the instructor to familiarize yourself with the students, course goals, and socioliterate context.

3. In addition to constructing the scoring guide itself, prepare a scoring "package" that includes essential elements such as benchmark papers for the bands in your scale, a rationale for the scores assigned to those papers, and an explanation of how the instrument reflects and promotes specific course goals (i.e., an analysis of the instrument's validity). If you construct a primary or multiple trait scale, also include the task or prompt, a description of the formal traits elicited, and an interpretation of how the task generates the expected writing performance.

4. If possible, pilot your instrument by using it to evaluate one or more sets of student papers. Use this experience to revise and refine your instrument for future use in this course or another one like it.

Application Activity 8.5: Designing a Writing Portfolio Plan

Directions

1. Select an ESL or mainstream composition course in your program or a nearby institution in which the current method of assessment relies on traditional summative evaluation of individual writing assignments.

2. Conduct a small study of the course design, syllabus, curriculum, and learner population (see Application Activities 3.1 and 3.2 for guidelines). Your fundamental goal is to assess the feasibility of integrating a portfolio system into the course.

3. On the basis of the portfolio model for COMP 120 described in this chapter (or in other sources on portfolio assessment), sketch a simple portfolio plan tailored to the writing course you have selected. In your proposal, include descriptions of the following elements: sequences, procedures, and instruments. Include a set of written guidelines for students similar to the sample materials shown in Fig. 8.5.

4. Share and discuss your proposal with your classmates, your instructor, and the instructor of the course under study. If you teach the course yourself, consider ways in which you might integrate your portfolio plan into the course and pilot it successfully.

NOTES

[1] Informative sources addressing research, theory, and practice in large-scale L2 writing assessment include Hamp-Lyons (2003), Hamp-Lyons and Kroll (1997), Kroll (1998), Kunnan (2000), and Weigle (2002).

[2] The following sources contain rubrics for scoring L2 writing: Bailey (1998); Bates, Lane, and Lange (1993), Cohen (1994), Educational Testing Service (1996), Graves (2000), Hamp-Lyons (1991a), and Weigle (2002).

[3] See, for example, Alatis and Barnhardt (1998), Black, Daiker, Sommers, and Stygall (1994), Belanoff and Dickson (1991), Calfee and Perfumo (1996b), Cole (1999), Mabry (1999), Murphy (1999), Reynolds (2000), White, Lutz, and Kamusikiri (1996), Yancey (1992), and Yancey and Weiser (1997).

Chapter **9**

Technology in the Writing Class: Uses and Abuses

Questions for Reflection

- *Do you use a computer regularly for your own writing? If so, do you do all of your planning, composing, revising, and editing at the computer? Do you undertake any of these tasks with pen and paper?*
- *If you use computers for writing, how has your writing benefited from word processing and other computer-based writing tools? What frustrations have you experienced?*
- *What do you think are the greatest advantages computers offer to L2 writers? What are potential drawbacks?*
- *What are your impressions concerning the ways in which computers and other technology might be part of future L2 writing courses you might teach?*

THE BRIEF, TUMULTUOUS HISTORY OF COMPUTER-ASSISTED WRITING RESEARCH AND INSTRUCTION

Writing about the effects of the personal computer on education, Bork (1985) asserted that "not since the invention of the printing press has a technological device borne such implications for the learning process" (p. 1). As computers became widely available during the 1980s in North American schools, colleges, and universities, writing teachers and researchers expressed almost limitless optimism and enthusiasm about the potential of word processing and other computer-based writing tools to facilitate students' writing processes and improve their end products. Within a few short years, however, this enthusiasm was tempered by caution. Some researchers (Barker, 1987; Haas, 1989; Hawisher, 1987) claimed that student writers planned less, revised less (or at least not more), and paid more attention to sentence-level concerns when composing with computers.

Faced with such a variety of negative evidence and conclusions, researchers in the early 1990s began to adopt a more moderate view of computer-assisted writing instruction, and a judicious middle ground for technology in literacy instruction was established. It is now understood that computers cannot teach novice writers how to think, plan, or revise nor can they magically transform inexperienced writers into proficient writers— or replace teachers' roles in providing instruction and feedback. Nonetheless, computers can make many dimensions of the writing process easier, rendering writing more enjoyable, improving student attitudes, and reducing anxiety about writing, particularly among ESL writers.

In summary, over the past two decades, composition researchers have been "either wildly enthusiastic or vehement in their rejection of the new medium" (Pennington, 1993a, p. 227). Today's literacy educators and researchers tend to hold a mostly positive view of computer-assisted writing that takes the conclusions of previous research and the inherent limitations of the medium into careful consideration. From this brief history, only one implication appears to be certain: Computers in education and in writing programs are here to stay, and "either we take the opportunity this new machine affords to rethink the ways we write and teach writing, or we soon risk seeming as anachronistic as a piece of parchment to our students" (Curtis, 1988, p. 344). Referring specifically to L2 writing, Pennington (2003), adopted the strong position that "those charged with instructing ESL students in writing cannot afford to remain outside these developments . . . , teachers should be prepared to bring computers into the center of their own pedagogical practice" (p. 287).[1]

RESEARCH TRENDS IN COMPUTER-ASSISTED WRITING INSTRUCTION

We need to begin this discussion with a word of caution. Empirical research investigating the effects of technology on ESL writers' processes, texts, and attitudes is scarce indeed. We can attest to an explosion of technological options and resources, even since this chapter was drafted in 1996 for the first edition of this book,[2] as well as many "how-to" articles and narrative reports of how teachers have used e-mail, the Internet, online discussions, interactive online exercises, and so forth in their writing courses. However, research on the nature and effects of these pedagogical alternatives has been slow to surface. Given the increasing interest in using technology in L2 writing instruction, we trust that such investigations are underway and will in time be disseminated. Currently, however, we can discuss only a handful of research findings for a limited number of subtopics, as we note later. We introduce a number of additional technological options for literacy teachers to consider, but it is important to acknowledge that, at this point, we cannot empirically assess their impact on student writers or their written production.

Computer-Assisted Writing Instruction: Potential Benefits and Drawbacks

Early reviewers and researchers outlined potential benefits and drawbacks to the use of computers for writing instruction (Fig. 9.1). Nonetheless, detractors (and proponents who are less enthusiastic about computers) pointed out that some studies have yielded less positive results. At the same time, as Pennington (2003) noted, most studies reporting negligible or negative results of word processing were conducted in the 1980s, when the technology itself was far less user-friendly and

Advantages	Disadvantages
• Increased motivation to revise (because of the ease of doing so) • Greater consciousness of writing as process • Quicker, more fluent, less self-conscious writing • Increased writing quantity	• Increased anxiety due to lack of familiarity with hardware or software • Unequal or limited student access to computers • Limited student typing and/or word processing abilities • Subversion of individual student writing processes (some prefer pen and paper; some are distracted by writing in a lab setting)
• Increased collaboration (teacher–student and student–student) in the computer writing lab • Greater motivation because writing is easier, more interesting, and more enjoyable (Teichman & Poris, 1989, p. 93)	• Increased student focus on surface features of texts because corrections are so easy (Balestri, 1988; Barker, 1987; Bernhardt et al., 1989, 1990; Bridwell-Bowles et al., 1987 Haas,1989; Hawisher, 1987)

FIG. 9.1. Potential advantages and disadvantages of computer-assisted writing.

available, and when students, their parents, and their teachers were completely unfamiliar with it. Pennington (2003) concluded that practitioners should be cautioned against assigning excessive weight to older studies of word processing effects, stating that teachers "are advised instead to base their decisions about computer use on more recent findings and the accumulated comparative evidence, which generally show a positive impact of word processing on students' writing" (pp. 291–292).

What Are the Effects of Word Processing?

Effects on the Writing Process: Planning, Revision, Collaboration. Studies of how computer-based writing affects the writing process have examined issues of planning, revision, and student–student collaboration. Whereas some early researchers (Bernhardt, Edwards, & Wojahn, 1989; Bridwell-Bowles, et al. 1987; Haas, 1989) suggested that the use of word processing could inhibit planning, others characterized this finding as reflective of a shift to a completely different drafting and composing process that is not only possible but also likely inevitable with the use of computers:

> [I]n a contrasting "computer writing style," the writer generally begins writing immediately, soon after a topic is decided—or even before it is decided. Instead of writing to fit a plan, computer writers plan as they are writing. . . . Planning thus becomes more of a middle stage than a beginning stage activity. . . . The sharp division of composing into the three stages of planning, revising, and writing breaks down in a computer context. (Pennington, 2003, pp. 290–291)

Pennington (2003) further observed that these effects have also been found among L2 writers (Akyel & Kamisli, 1999; Li & Cumming, 2001). In fact, this seamless, recursive planning–drafting–revising process might be "especially valuable for L2 writers" because of its potential to reduce the stress and memory load that particularly challenges those composing in an L2 (Pennington, 2003, p. 291). It also is important to offer the qualification that "the relationship of planning to text quality has not been established. It is not clear . . . if the differences in planning . . . would result in texts of lower judged quality" (Haas, 1989, p. 202). In other words, the simple fact that student writers spend less observable time planning when using word processors does not at all demonstrate that their writing processes or subsequent products will be negatively affected by this shift.

Researchers also have examined whether word processing leads to more extensive and effective revisions. Such studies presuppose, of course, that computers naturally facilitate revision because word processors make the mechanics of text changes so much easier. Nevertheless, as Curtis (1988) noted, assuming that "given word processors and sent out on their own, inexperienced student writers will compose better essays . . . is similar to assuming that, given a two horsepower table saw, writing teachers will build credenzas" (p. 338). In fact, empirical studies have found that students exhibit improved or superior revision behaviors when using computers: They do more revision on a computer (Chadwick & Bruce, 1989; Li & Cumming, 2001; Phinney & Khouri, 1993), and they are more likely to make meaning-level changes (Daiute, 1985; McAllister & Louth, 1988; Pennington, 1993a; Pennington & Brock, 1992; Susser, 1993). Finally, Pennington (2003) suggested that students' surface-level editing also may be facilitated by computer use, because only small portions of text are visible on the screen at any given moment.

Again, as with planning, computers fundamentally change the nature of the writing process, making the overlapping stages of planning, drafting, revising, and editing even less discrete and linear. As Cochran-Smith (1991) reminded us, "excluding the revisions made as a text is initially shaped is probably tantamount to excluding the very aspect of writing with word processing that makes it unusual" (p. 126). Advances in technology—software that enables us to capture and track online revisions—should make it easier for researchers to examine the various iterations of revision that occur between hard copy drafts submitted to a teacher. Such investigations would mirror, in a sense, studies of the writing process that have used students' think-aloud protocols. Studies that track online revisions would be superior to think-aloud studies because the methodology would not artificially interfere with students' thinking and writing processes.

Empirical findings also conflict with regard to whether conducting writing courses in computer writing labs leads to more or less collaboration in the form of peer interaction. Computer enthusiasts initially believed that interaction and collaboration would increase and be greatly facilitated by the lab setting because of the open, informal atmosphere of the computer lab, and because collaboration is made so easy with technology. That is, partners and groups can gather around a screen and send one another files over electronic mail or over a local area network (LAN). In addition, word processed texts are more attractive and easier to read than handwritten drafts. However, Bernhardt et al. (1989) and Bernhardt, Wojahn, and Edwards (1990) actually reported decreased peer collaboration in the lab because of time pressures and students' lack of interest in doing anything but their own writing (see also Conway, 1995). On the other hand, Sullivan (1993) reported that the use of a computer network to provide peer feedback improved student motivation, participation, interaction, and collaboration, concluding that electronic discussion groups were "freer of risk than a traditional teacher-centered classroom" (p. 34). Sullivan (1993) further claimed that computer-mediated peer feedback relieved ESL students of their anxieties about being understood and using culturally inappropriate language (see also Barker, 1987; Brady, 1990; Braine, 1997; Selfe & Wahlstrom, 1986; Teichman & Poris, 1989). Of course, whether in or out of the computer lab, peer response activities must be carefully planned and executed: "Networking student writers electronically does not guarantee better writing" (Pennington, 2003, p. 299; see chapter 6).

Effects on Text Quality. Again, it was initially taken as a given that student writing would automatically improve with the use of computers because they make the process of writing presumably easier, and because students tend to be more highly motivated to write using a keyboard, screen, and central processing unit (CPU). Studies of L2 writers have consistently indicated that students spend more time writing and produce longer texts when using a computer, and in most studies of L2 text quality, "longer" nearly always significantly correlates with "better" (in terms of quality ratings) (Brock & Pennington, 1999; Chadwick & Bruce, 1989; Pennington & Brock, 1992). However, as Pennington (2003) emphasized, the evolving informality of the medium, influenced by students' increasing buy-in to e-mail and chat rooms, can lead writers to produce texts that are "unconstrained and experimental . . . long strings of loosely constrained strands of ideas" (p. 14). Given time, this "unfinished intermediate work" may result in a "high-quality product" (p. 289). However, Pennington cautioned that teachers need to communicate their values to students carefully so that the medium does not overshadow the message. Similarly, teachers must ensure that students do not spend so much time on ancillary issues (hypertext, Internet applications, illustrations, and so on) that they do not produce good quality writing.

In summary, it seems clear that technology offers great potential for enhancing many aspects of the writing process. These enhancements include more integrated planning, more extensive revisions, more (and better) collaboration, more time on task, and higher quality end products. A number of studies have, in fact, reported such positive effects. However, research, experience, and intuition also demonstrate that teachers cannot assume that students' processes and texts will be magically transformed for the better by the introduction of technology into writing instruction. In fact, if teachers do not carefully think through the possible pitfalls and the ways in which the writing task is fundamentally different with computers, there is at least an equal likelihood that the use of technology could do more harm than good. We return to this point later in the chapter.

Effects on Student Attitudes. One area of inquiry in which there is comparatively little disagreement involves the issue of student reactions to word processing. Early student complaints involved long waits to use computer labs (Bernhardt et al., 1989; Dalton & Hannafin, 1986), unfamiliarity with hardware and software (Barker, 1987; Bernhardt et al., 1989), difficulty with rereading because of small screen size (Barker, 1987; Haas, 1989), and lack of typing skills (Brady, 1990; Dalton & Hannafin, 1986). Despite these areas of student dissatisfaction, "almost all researchers in word processing note that using a word processor improves student attitudes" (Barker, 1987, p. 112).

It appears that ESL writers in particular reap tremendous affective benefits from word processing (Jones & Fortescue, 1987; Neu & Scarcella, 1991; Pennington, 1990, 1991, 1993a, 1993b; Pennington & Brock, 1992; Phinney, 1989, 1991; Phinney & Mathis, 1990; Piper, 1987). Specifically, students' attitudes toward, and motivations for, writing in English appear to benefit from computer use (Neu & Scarcella, 1991; Phinney, 1989; Piper 1987; Warschauer, 1996). Moreover, their anxieties appear to decrease because computers reduce the fear of errors and worries about legibility (Phinney, 1989). Pennington (1993b) pointed out that word processors may also "free up some of the novice writer's time and attention, making it easier to concentrate on the nonmechanical aspects of composing" (p. 151). Because writing at a computer is faster and easier (in most cases) for L2 writers, than writing by hand, word processing may encourage writers to produce more text over longer periods (Pennington, 1993b; Phinney, 1989). Additionally, the mechanical ease of the computer benefits L2 students who may at first struggle to master the Roman alphabet and those who face cognitive and memory overloads while trying to compose in their L2. Computer memory supplements the human brain's storage capacity (Betancourt & Phinney, 1988; Jones & Tetroe, 1987; Pennington, 1993b).

Effects on Writing Instruction. Several researchers have examined the differences between class sessions conducted in a computer lab setting and those conducted in traditional classroom environments (Bernhardt et al., 1989; Bernhardt, Wojahn, & Edwards, 1990). The findings of these studies, coupled with evidence from other reports, reflect clear differences between writing instruction in traditional classes and computer lab sessions:

- The time spent writing in a computer lab can greatly decrease the proportion of teacher-fronted instructional time.
- More one-on-one time between teacher and students is possible in the computer lab.

> - Students in the lab setting may be less willing to attend to administrative announcements, do exercises, and participate in discussion.
> - Some teachers may be less comfortable than others in adapting to the computer lab setting.

Although research evidence on these points is also scarce, outcomes indicate that writing instructors who wish to use computer labs or online instruction extensively must carefully consider the advantages and disadvantages of doing so. Educators also must realize that the shift will necessitate modifying their teaching practices and expectations to maximize the potential benefits for their students.

Beyond Word Processing: What Are the Effects of Other Types of Technology on L2 Writing?

Although word processing is the most frequently studied and used computer application in composition research and instruction, many other computer-based writing tools are also available. Such tools include interactive, adaptive software, the best known of which is the Daedulus program published by the University of Texas. (Another well-known application, CommonSpace, has recently become unavailable.) These software applications walk students through various aspects of the composing process by providing invention heuristics, organization tools, revision questions, and so forth. They similarly offer text analyzers that check written production for spelling, grammar, and style. Response components enable teachers and peers to insert comments and corrections into student files (see Swaffar, et al., 1998, for a collection of papers on the use of Daedulus with L2 writing students). Finally, the ever-increasing availability of electronic mail and the Internet has created new options for teachers and students, potentially affecting all aspects of the composing process (see Egbert & Hanson-Smith, 1999; Warschauer, 1995; and Warschauer, Shetzer, and Meloni, 2000, for excellent reviews of the issues and pedagogical implications.)

Text Analyzers. Once student texts have been generated in a word processing file, text analysis applications can search and examine documents for various features, count them, and give the writer or teacher quantitative information about the distribution of textual features. Most word processing packages include spelling, grammar, and style checkers that flag errors in diction and usage such as clichés, wordiness, and mechanical problems (capitalization errors, double words, and so on). These packages also include counters, which can tabulate the number of words in a text, the average word or sentence length, punctuation marks, and so on. Text counters also may include standards or thresholds against which the writer can measure his or her text, such as readability scores. Beyond the commercially available features of word processors, more specialized programs can tag and count various parts of speech and lexical features (Biber, 1988; Biber, Conrad, & Reppen, 1998). Because some studies have suggested that particular types and combinations of syntactic and lexical features in student texts may be positively correlated with text quality or L2 proficiency (Ferris, 1994; Grant & Ginther, 2000; Jarvis, 2002; Jarvis, Grant, Bikowskia, & Ferris 2003), such analyses may be useful to teachers and program administrators.

On the other hand, experts have expressed considerable ambivalence concerning the value of grammar, style, and spelling checkers for student writers, as well as outright alarm about their potential harm to L2 writers. For instance, in a review of three popular grammar and style checkers, Lewis and Lewis (1987) concluded that these applications "use fixed grammatical rules and canned phrases when analyzing a document and are limited by their inability to 'understand' context or logic" (p. 246). Consequently, these tools are fallible, and most effectively used by "users with enough knowledge of grammar to sort accurate advice from misplaced assertions" (p. 246). Nelson (1987) similarly characterized style checkers as "far too rule-bound to serve higher forms of communication" (p. 49). Thus, two potentially irreconcilable problems with grammar and style checkers must be recognized: (a) They are at once too simple, in that they apply formulaic, limited, prescriptive rules uncritically to all texts regardless of the genre, content, or context, and (b) they are too difficult to use because they require a great deal of sophistication on the part of the user to separate good advice from bad.

Even more troubling than the limitations of the software applications may be their effects on novice L2 writers. Pennington and Brock (1990) reported that when ESL students used a text analyzer alone without feedback from a teacher, the results were shorter sentences, shorter drafts, and fewer revisions. They also noted that writers tended to accept the analyzer's suggestions, even when those alternatives were inappropriate. Writers also failed to correct errors that the analyzer did not flag. Furthermore, students became increasingly dependent on feedback, a finding that casts doubts on claims that such computer programs promote self-monitoring and self-correction. Poulsen (1991) similarly reported that although a spell checker caught about 80% of student spelling errors, the ESL students did not always use the correct form suggested by the spell checker. In addition, if a correct alternative was not offered, students rarely tried to solve the problems in other ways. In the face of such concerns and problems, Sampson and Gregory (1991) warned that ESL writing teachers cannot simply proscribe or ignore the use of spelling and grammar checkers by ESL students, observing that many students are computer literate and aware of the existence of these aids, which tend to be widely available in campus computer labs in North American educational institutions. Instead of "leading these students down the technological primrose path," teachers need to engage in frank discussions with their students concerning the advantages, drawbacks, and pitfalls of using text analyzers (Sampson & Gregory, 1991, p. 36).

It also could be argued that spelling and grammar checkers actually are more harmful to student writers than to experienced writers. Because they may lack confidence, linguistic proficiency, and rhetorical sophistication, novice writers are more likely to accept uncritically the suggestions, prescriptions, and corrections offered by an apparently all-knowing computer application. We have found this tendency to apply consistently to our own ESL student writers, who lack confidence in their metalinguistic and editing abilities. Such learners are even more likely than their native speaker (NS) peers to trust the computer's advice. Finally, L2 writing errors are more idiosyncratic and even harder to classify than L1 errors (Brock, 1990a, 1990b; Ferris, 1993).

In summary, a vast array of computer-based resources is available to L2 writing teachers and their students. (see Fig. 9.2) Access to these resources can be both exciting and intimidating. The average L2 writing instructor (at least at this stage in our history) may be far less technology proficient than his or her ESL students. To maximize the benefits of the technology, teachers need to become comfortable with these tools and then sort through the options thoughtfully and carefully. Although it may be tempting to throw up our hands in despair because of too much information, or to take an attitude of self-righteous moral superiority ("Students need to be reading, writing, and developing critical thinking skills, not playing with computers and surfing the Internet"),

Term/Acronym	Description
Asynchronous CMC	Delayed-time or saved communication, such as e-mail, discussion lists, newsgroups, and bulletin boards
Bulletin board	Similar to a discussion list except that instead of receiving e-mail messages, the user goes to a specific Web site to read messages. A bulletin board also can be set up for a particular class or group of students.
CAI/CALL/CAW/CAWI	Computer-assisted instruction, computer-assisted language learning, computer-assisted writing, computer-assisted writing instruction
Chat	Real-time discussions among users on LAN or Internet sites.
CMC	Computer-mediated communication
Discussion list	Group that communicates by e-mail about specific topics, available only to subscribers. Teachers can create lists for particular classes, open only to the enrolled students and their instructor (Listserv capacity is available at many schools; some e-mail packages have the capability to create lists; or teachers can go to a free list-making site such as www.egroups.com.)
Hypertext/hypermedia	A "nonlinear, multilayered system of information in which files (of text, graphics, or audiovisual elements) are linked to each other and are accessed by pointing to or choosing particular references" (Warschauer et al., 2000, p.171)
LAN	Local area network (such as in a campus computer lab)—a group of linked computers wired to communicate with each other
MUD or MOO	Multi-user domains; multi-user domains, object-oriented: Web sites where students can participate in real-time discussions similar to simulations. Students can assume imaginary identities as they participate. A well known MOO for ESL students is called schMOOze University (http://schmooze.hunter.cuny.edu:8888/)
Newsgroup	Similar to a discussion list except that it is managed through a service called Usenet
OWL	Online writing lab, usually offered through university writing centers, which contains handouts, exercises, classroom presentations, and resource links to helpful Web sites for teachers and students
Synchronous CMC	Real-time or live communication, such as chats, live discussions over LANs, MUDs, and MOOs

FIG. 9.2. Important terms and acronyms.

we owe it to our students to familiarize ourselves with the possibilities and then to exploit the technology for the ways it can be truly helpful to our students. These benefits include improving revision and editing skills, conducting purposeful Internet research, communicating via e-mail, engaging in online collaboration with instructors and classmates, and so on. It also could be argued that we do not serve our students well if we become condescending about such issues and neglect to acknowledge the ways that technology can help writing to be more fun. Anything that helps L2 students to see writing as engaging and motivating cannot, after all, be entirely bad.

PEDAGOGICAL ISSUES IN COMPUTER-ASSISTED WRITING INSTRUCTION

From this review of the research on various aspects of computer use in L2 writing classes, several generalizations emerge: (a) ESL writers who use word processing can enjoy many potential benefits; (b) These benefits are unlikely to materialize without careful preparation and instruction by the writing instructor, and (c) because of the many pitfalls in the uses of other types of writing software with L2 students, especially text analyzers, teachers must be alert to the possible dangers and communicate these drawbacks to their learners. Considering these issues, ESL writing teachers who wish to use computers as an integral part of their writing courses have several practical decisions to make. Figure 9.3 encapsulates these decisions in question form.

1	What model of CAI will you select (lab, traditional class with out-of-class computer use, online/Web-based course)?
2	How can you best prepare yourself to teach ESL composition using technology?
3	How will you (a) assess students' familiarity with the technology and (b) train them to use specific applications for your course?
4	Will you incorporate technology into your own responding practices, and if so, how?
5	Will you use CMC for peer response, and if so, in what way(s)?
6	Will you use the Internet for (a) computer-assisted instruction (course Web pages, OWLs, ESL Web sites) and (b) for student research? If so, how will you evaluate the Internet sources and help students to navigate them effectively?
7	How will you help students to understand the advantages and disadvantages of the spell/grammar check on their word processor, electronic or online dictionaries, and online thesauruses?
8	How will you guard against abuses or dangers of technology—plagiarism; excessive or inappropriate Internet use at the expense of reading, thinking, and writing; informal language use similar to that used in e-mail and chat rooms; and so on?

FIG. 9.3. Pedagogical options and questions to consider.

How Frequently and in What Ways Will Word Processing and Computer-Assisted Instruction Be Used?

Four general models of computer-assisted writing instruction can be distinguished:

1. Class sessions are taught exclusively in a computer laboratory.
2. Class sessions are divided between traditional classrooms and computer labs, with the computer lab used regularly (e.g., once per week).
3. Class sessions are held exclusively in a conventional classroom, but students are expected to use computers (on their own time) for their writing assignments.
4. The course is taught wholly or partially online.

The quantitative and microethnographic studies conducted by Bernhardt et al. (1989, 1990) demonstrated that the first two models entail strengths and weaknesses (also see Mayers, 1996). Class sessions conducted entirely in a computer lab tend to function as writers' workshops. That is, students see class sessions as a time to write rather than to receive explicit instruction in writing. Such sessions may be characterized by a great deal of informal teacher–student interaction as the teacher moves about the lab to help individual students. However, peer interaction may be minimal because students tend to be more interested in completing their own writing projects than in responding to others' work.

The second model, in which the class alternates between a conventional classroom and a computer lab (as in the Bernhardt et al. [1989, 1990] studies), has the potential of providing the best and the worst of both worlds. Students benefit from receiving both in-class instruction (in the regular classroom) and in-class writing time (in the lab), but students and teachers may feel that they do not have enough time for either priority and thus do nothing well.

Structuring Instruction Within the Computer Setting

Once a teacher decides to use a computer lab for classroom instruction, whether for all or part of the class time, experts agree that lab time should be carefully planned. Unstructured lab time offers certain benefits. For one, it offers students extended periods to write while offering teachers time to conduct individual conferences. Nonetheless, we must acknowledge several important drawbacks to relinquishing the class time spent in the lab to free writing. First, students may feel resentful that their time is being used (or "wasted") because they are not doing anything in class. Alternatively, they may prefer to do their thinking and writing at a different time of day, in a quieter setting, and for longer or shorter blocks of time (Bernhardt et al., 1989, 1990). Thus, students may object to being forced to write in conditions that are not optimal for them.

Second, researchers concur that computers cannot and should not replace instruction by the teacher. Novice writers need instruction, modeling, and practice in various aspects of the composing process and the technical aspects of writing (citing sources, editing, and so on). These needs are especially salient for ESL students, who need more extensive introduction to the linguistic and rhetorical forms of written English than do NSs (Ferris, 1994; Leki, 1990a; Reid, 1994; Silva, 1993). Phinney (1989) warned that "without specific instruction in using the computer to facilitate the writing process, from prewriting to revision, the computer alone appears to have little effect in changing writing behavior . . . whether [students] are writing in their first or second language" (p. 87).

Although instructors can and probably should allow students unstructured free writing time in the computer lab, they can take steps to use computer lab time for maximal benefit. Experts such as Phinney (1989) and Pennington (1990) advised that ESL writers be given instruction and practice early in the term in the use of computers, the specifics of the word processing package they are using, e-mail applications, and Internet browsers.[3] Moreover, the curriculum should be designed so that students can progressively develop their computer writing skills over the course of a semester or longer. Phinney (1989) suggested that the teacher develop or adapt exercise files to be made available on course web pages or through links to specific Web sites. These files should provide "writing heuristics, suggestions for strategies in content generation and organization, revision and editing exercises, and exercises which teach various aspects of the software" (p. 87). Figure 9.4 provides an example of such an exercise, which could also, of course, be done on paper. Generally, "almost anything that can done with pencil and paper can be transferred to a computer" (Phinney, 1989, p. 88). The advantage of this practice

Note: This activity is connected to an assignment in which students choose a reading from a selection, analyze it, and then relate the author's ideas to their own experiences or opinions (Spack, 1996). It is assumed that before this lab activity, students will have selected the reading and identified its main points.

Complete the following prewriting activities. When you have answered the questions, be sure to save your file with a name such as "Essay 1 Prewrite," print out a copy, and e-mail it to your writing group members and your instructor.

Essay 1 Prewriting Activities

1. *5–7 minutes:* Send a brief (one-paragraph) e-mail message to the members of your writing group and to your teacher that answers the following questions:
   a. Which reading did you choose?
   b. Why did you choose it?
   c. What are the author's main points?

2. *20 minutes:* Now take some time to look through the reading(s) you have selected for Essay 1. Complete the chart below.

The Reading	Your Experience and Ideas
Main idea of entire reading	*What your reaction is to the main idea?*
Author's Point #1 (quote or paraphrase)	*Your examples or opinions*
Author's Point #2 (quote or paraphrase)	*Your examples or opinions*
Author's Point #3 (quote or paraphrase)	*Your examples or opinions*
Conclusion: How does the author end his or her story? What did she or he learn from it ?	*Now that you have compared the reading and your own experiences, what do you think about the topic you have discussed? Did the reading change your views in any way? Did it strengthen your opinions?*

3. *20 minutes:* Now participate in an electronic discussion with your group members by completing the following steps:
   a. *5 minutes:* Write 1–3 sentences that introduce your topic (what your paper is about), your opinion about the topic, and whether you agree or disagree with the author's viewpoints in the reading you selected (or whether your experiences are similar to or different from that of the authors). E-mail this to your group members and instructor.
   b. *15 minutes (5 minutes per group member)*: Now discuss each group member's topic and ideas in turn. Ask any questions and make any suggestions. Each writer should save the questions and comments from group members along with other notes from today's lab session. You will use all of these ideas as you write your first draft.

FIG. 9.4.   Computer lab exercise: Sample student prewriting activity.

is that working through writing activities on the computer saves time, because students can write more quickly and give copies to their teacher or classmates more easily. The practice also builds familiarity and comfort with the computer while nurturing efficient composing skills.

Whatever the teacher decides to introduce during computer lab sessions, (e.g., word-processing instruction, composing activities, freewriting, online peer response, teacher–student conferences), it is essential that lab time be planned carefully. We should not simply assume that a traditional lesson plan can be transferred to a computer lab with little or no modification (see chapter 3). As Bernhardt et al. (1990) pointed out, "teaching in a computer lab is a more pressured situation than teaching a regular classroom, and . . . teachers need to approach the new environment deliberately and with ample planning" (p. 372). Specifically, teachers need to limit classroom administration talk (collecting homework, discussing assignments, and so on) by making efficient announcements at the beginning of the class before students become distracted by the computers (and possibly miss important information). Teachers also should promote the instructional strategy of using the computer lab by helping learners "understand why class time is being given to writing and what the expectations are for both preparation and participation" (Bernhardt et al., 1990, p. 365).

Computers as a Supplement to Classroom Instruction

Probably the most common model of computer-based writing instruction is for class sessions to be held in a traditional classroom, with the students and teacher using computers outside class to complete the coursework. In most U.S. colleges and universities, instructors do not accept handwritten work. Students are expected to word process, proofread, and spell check their papers before submitting them for feedback or grading, whether printed out in hard copy or sent via e-mail to the instructor or peers. In this model, teachers may also integrate various other technological components that we have already discussed:

- Requiring use of the Internet for research for assigned writing projects
- Giving students feedback via e-mail
- Requiring students to give and receive peer feedback online

- Sending students to appropriate Web sites for extra instruction and practice exercises (e.g., on grammar points)
- Encouraging or requiring students to participate in a class discussion list or newsgroup or to participate in chats designed for ESL students.

Depending on which of the preceding options the teacher uses and on the students' familiarity with the technology, the teacher may wish to schedule several classroom sessions in a campus computer lab to familiarize the students with procedures and answer any questions.

Web-Based Composition Courses

Many institutions have begun to offer online writing courses taught partially or entirely over the Web using delivery systems such as WebCT. In this model, the teacher posts all course materials—syllabus, assignments, worksheets, exercises, presentations of material—on the course Web site and interacts with students via e-mail, discussion lists, real-time chats, and online conferencing. Teachers can even create a "paperless class" using electronic portfolio submissions (Forbes, 1996; Moore, 1996; Purves, 1996; Wall & Peltier, 1996). Practically speaking, the structure of such a course is parallel to that of a course held in a computer lab on campus. The instruction and interaction simply take place online and away from campus. A modified version of this approach has students coming to a traditional classroom or computer lab occasionally for explicit instruction, exams, teacher–student conferences, and peer response sessions, but completing the rest of the course outside a classroom.

It is only candid to say that we (along with many other L1 and L2 composition specialists) are extremely dubious of online composition courses as a prevailing pedagogical model. We find that important components of writing instruction are best delivered in a live, face-to-face, interactive mode (teacher ↔ students; students ↔ students), and that "virtual" instruction, collaboration, and interaction offer a poor substitute for the "real thing." Not wishing to be entirely closed-minded, however, we acknowledge that such alternative delivery models may well meet the practical needs of many students who might have trouble getting to campus because of time, distance, transportation, and family responsibilities. Moreover, some students undoubtedly work well independently and on their own schedules. Such learners may prefer this option to a traditional literacy course. We also concede that using online instruction can be an excellent supplement to a traditional composition course (or what is known as a "Web-enhanced" as opposed to a Web-based course), and we certainly encourage teachers to consider its many advantages seriously.

Response to Student Writing in Computer-Mediated Environments

As already noted, word processors and other software packages offer teachers a range of options in responding to student writing:

- Teachers can complete essay checklists and compose summary endnotes on the computer (see chapter 5), thereby saving time—assuming the teacher types faster than he or she writes! Computer-mediated feedback also obviates problems with handwriting legibility. Teachers also can easily insert links to Web sites that they would like students to consult during revision and editing, as another way of individualizing feedback and grammar instruction (as discussed in chapters 5 and 7).

- Teachers can insert comments directly into student texts that have been e-mailed to them as attached word-processing files, using different color fonts and highlighters to call students' attention to specific passages. Teachers can also use the "Comment" function (available in some word processing packages such as Microsoft Word) so that the student text appears unmarked except for a small icon (much like a footnote), thus enabling the student to choose when to make the teacher's comments visible.

- Teachers and students can engage in an interactive dialogue by posing and responding to questions inserted into the student's text (Gurevich, 1995; Sirc, 1995). Thus, rather than a teacher simply reading and responding to a completed draft once, the teacher and writer can take a number of turns via e-mail (or electronic conferencing) as the student revises.[4]

- Teachers can train and require students to use the "Track Changes" feature available in word processing applications as they compose and revise. Students can submit drafts thus marked along with their drafts in folders of ongoing writing projects. This technique can help teachers assess the effects of their feedback and their students' revision processes.

• Teachers can use the highlighter function and design macros with pop-up correction codes so that they can provide computerized error feedback (see Holmes [2000] for an impressive-looking sample of this practice). We have found such manuevers to be more cumbersome and time-consuming than simply marking student errors by hand. Nevertheless, we see a point in inserting corrections into the student's computerized writing. Inserted corrections might be helpful in the short term and in the long term, namely, for tracking student progress in editing (see chapter 7). We encourage more adventurous teachers to give it a try.

We also encourage teachers to experiment with peer response options conducted online and via e-mail. Instructors may opt for a compromise approach, in which papers are exchanged, read, and responded to online and then discussed during live class sessions. Teachers may also opt to conduct the entire peer feedback process outside class. A disadvantage to this approach is that students might help one another too much or perhaps expect too much and take unfair advantage of classmates. This potential abuse can lead to either resentment or confusion regarding individual students' contributions to their own papers. Teachers can forestall such problems by carefully structuring peer review tasks (see chapter 6), and by requiring students to copy him or her on all e-mail discussions or to submit hard copies of all drafts, peer feedback, and subsequent revisions.

As Pennington (2003) pointed out, the computer also can facilitate other types of peer collaboration, for example, in-group writing and presentation projects, shared editing of texts, and so forth. Furthermore, as with traditional peer response modes, teachers should not feel that a peer review task should be limited only to reading peers' completed drafts. "Virtual" peer response tasks also can be assigned during the prewriting and editing stages as well as for between-draft revision suggestions.

Grammar and Style Checkers and Other Dangers

As previously discussed, L2 computer writing experts warn against encouraging ESL writers to use grammar checkers because these tools tend to be inaccurate in assessing L2 text. Moreover, students become excessively dependent on them, to the

~~~~~~

The following student paper was written in 50 minutes on the following topic: "Lies—are they always harmful or sometimes appropriate?"

1. Read the paper and highlight any grammar errors you find (verbs, nouns, sentence structure, articles, word choice).

Lying is not always wrong, if it is used for good intentions. Lying can be very manipulative, yet that particular quality, Goodrich mentioned, "is also exciting". Instead of using it for evil, lying can be a vital source for good, whether it from sparing a child feelings or doing it just to get something out of it. There are numerous explanations why people would create white lies. One reason why people lie is to surprise or distract a love one. Another reason why people do it is to create a diversion, in order to escape the difficulties that may take place by telling the truth.

There is no greater rush than getting away with a good, harmless lie. For example, on one occasion, I have used lies for good intention. My close friend birthday was coming up. My friends and I were planning a surprise birthday. We did not want the birthday girl to know of this, so we manipulated her into thinking that we did not remember her birthday. Making up stories that we were busy on that day, to convince her so. Seeing the hurt in her eyes further greaten our smile. Like Goodrich said, "even though people lie for good reason, lying can be harmful". My friends and I knew that by lying to her, the surprise party would be a total success. Yes, our way of springing the party on her was wrong, but when the surprise was successful, seeing the joy on her face gave everyone involve a great rush, and that is exciting___

When Goodrich said that, "everyone lie" it could very well be the truth. People lie constantly to avoid difficult situation by telling the truth. For instant, I was at my friends' house for dinner. His mother was cooking her best dish that took hours to make. During the course of the meal she asked me how was it. The truth is that I didn't like it, maybe is because I hate shrimp, but to avoid being an unwanted guess, I bit my lips and told her that the meal was excellent. Besides my stomach hurting from the shrimp, no feelings got hurt.

To conclude, small, harmless ies can be exciting and fun. Not knowing if you will get caught in a lie, or knowing that you just got away with a lie is a great thrill. The truth is, some lies can be damaging when it is discovered, but if done properly, lies can be very benificial. No one really likes to lie, but not everyone is aware that they are lying. Lying is not always wrong.

FIG. 9.5. Grammar check: Awareness exercise.

2. Now you will examine the same paper after it has been analyzed by a grammar checker. (*Note*: The paper with analysis may be found in Appendix 9.) Compare your analysis with the computer's suggestions:
   a. What was the same?
   b. What was different? Did you mark errors that were not marked by the computer? Did the computer mark errors that you did not?
   c. In places where you and the computer disagreed, who do you think was right? (If you are not sure, discuss the problem with your classmates and instructor.)
3. After completing this exercise, discuss with your classmates and teacher whether you think grammer checkers are helpful for student writers . If not, why not? If so, what can a student do to avoid the problems you discovered in this exercise?

FIG. 9.5. (Continued).

detriment of developing their own editing strategies. However, it is probably naïve, especially in college and university settings where such programs are widely available on campus networks, to forbid students to use grammar checkers. Teachers should meet this problem head-on by candidly discussing with students the problems and pitfalls of grammar checkers. This practice can involve showing students the results from a grammar checker's analysis of a sample ESL student paper and pointing out what errors were overlooked by the software and ways that suggested corrections might actually lead students astray (Brock, 1990a; Sampson & Gregory, 1991). Figure 9.5 provides an example of such an exercise. Although L2 writing experts are less wary of spell checker and thesaurus use by ESL writers, students may use them more accurately and effectively if teachers point out their strengths and limitations during a regular class session (Fig 9.6).

A related technological topic concerns students' use of electronic and online dictionaries and thesauruses. Although the same benefits and pitfalls of such reference tools exist as for their print counterparts, the technology's ease of use and appeal may encourage students to use the electronic versions more frequently (Wechsler & Pitts, 2000; Yonally & Gilfert, 2000). Thus, it is probably wise for writing instructors to discuss the effective use of these resources with their students as well. Finally, if Internet research is allowed or required for course assignments, students may need guidance on how to use search engines, how to evaluate sources, and how to cite them appropriately in their texts and bibliographies. Many recent composition textbooks and handbooks offer a great deal of helpful information on Internet research, as do reference librarians (see also Warschauer et al. [2000] and Windeatt, Hardisty, & Eastment, [2000]).

~~~~~~

Note: The student paper below was written in 35 minutes on the topic of "culture shock."

1. Read the paper and circle or highlight any spelling errors that you find. You may ignore other types of errors. For the errors you circled, suggest correct spellings.

> When I first came to America, it was five years ago. I was only thirteen years old, and I experience a lot of "culture shock".
> There are a lot of things that were totally strange to me. For example, the (1) **chees**, rock music, and even people kissing on the street.
> The thing that (2) effect me the most is the language different. I only have taken one year of basic English class before I came to America. When I want to talk to the teacher in class, I have to use hand sign to help, so that teacher can understand what I'm trying to say.
> Also, the food is another problem. I have never taste (3) chees before I came to America, and it seem to me that my stomach does not (4) fited too (5) will to American food. So about once a week, I have to go to chinese (6) resturan for some "home taste."
> Also, the people kissing, hugging in public place was also a (7) unbelieveable thing in my country.
> But, as times (8) gose by now I can solve all this problems.

Spell Check Results:
(1) The correct choice "cheese" was #2 of nine options.
(2) The correct choice "affect" was the only option offered.
(3) See (1).
(4) The correct choice "fitted" was #1 of ten options.
(5) Not marked by spell check (actual English word).
(6) The correct choice "restaurant" was #1 of eight options.
(7) The correct choice "unbelievable" was the only option.
(8) The correct choice "goes" was the first of three options.

2. Now compare your analysis with the computer's suggestions. What was the same and what was different?

3. Discuss with your classmates and teacher whether you think spell checkers are helpful for student writers. If not, why not? If so, what can a student do to avoid the problems or deal with the limitations (like the "will/well" problem) that you discovered?

~~~~~~

FIG. 9.6.   Spell check awareness exercise.

Another potential abuse of computer-assisted writing involves cheating and plagiarism. Writing teachers often complain about student paper networks for essays, term papers, and other projects. Assuming that such networks exist (and both authors have seen evidence of them during their teaching careers), they become even more problematic when papers can be quickly copied from a floppy disk, hard drive, or CD-ROM, then e-mailed from one student to another or downloaded from Internet "term paper mills." The student can easily make a few changes and print the paper for submission. On the bright side, search engines are also available for instructors to use in checking student writing for evidence of plagiarism and other forms of academic dishonesty (e.g., www.plagiarism.org).

Teachers can take several precautions against computer-assisted cheating, such as requiring parts of each assignment to be composed in class. Teachers can monitor assignments as they develop and perhaps initial draft printouts. We also recommend requiring that preliminary drafts be submitted in a folder with the final version so teachers can note sudden, dramatic changes in content, style, or accuracy by observing the "fossil record" of the assignment. Teachers should also collect some baseline and periodic samples of each student's in-class writing so that if computer-facilitated peer-tutoring sessions result in excessive correction by a classmate or friend, they can compare the in- and out-of-class writing samples. Although L1 and L2 students occasionally cheat (and do so regardless whether a computer is being used), this knowledge should inform, but not control, instructors' pedagogical choices. The mere fact that some forms of dishonesty may be facilitated by the use of computers should not, in and of itself, discourage teachers from using them.

SUMMARY

It is tempting for literacy educators simply to dismiss computers from their instructional plans, even if they are devoted computer users themselves. The logistical problems may discourage them from attempting to incorporate computer technology into the writing curriculum. These problems may include provision of adequate computer facilities and training, increased constraints on lesson planning, and a perceived increase in student dishonesty that may follow from computer-assisted writing. Moreover, for teachers who are not especially computer literate, the challenge of developing computer-based activities may seem overwhelming.

Nonetheless, the evidence is strong that computer use improves student attitudes, confidence, and motivation, and that these benefits may be even more significant for L2 writers. Clearly, as Bernhardt et al. (1989) pointed out, not all teachers are comfortable or effective in a computer lab setting. However, we encourage readers whose students have adequate computer facilities available to consider holding some computer lab sessions as part of their writing course. The intervention may be as minimal as a session or two to show students how to perform simple operations, such as saving and printing files; blocking, moving, adding, and deleting text; and using spelling and grammar checkers. This assistance can surely help a number of students write for longer durations, write more frequently, write longer drafts, and ultimately write better. Regardless how much or how little the computer lab is used, if at all, it is important to recognize that novice writers still need the teacher to plan the instructional time so that they can improve their composing and word-processing skills. Finally, teachers who are just beginning to introduce computer-assisted writing to their students should remember that "the effects of computers on writing ability may not be a matter of quick transfer, but of subtle and incremental evolution over the life of a writer" (Bernhardt et al., 1989, p. 129).

REFLECTION AND REVIEW

1. Identify the advantages and disadvantages of the various models of computer-assisted writing instruction discussed in this chapter (computer lab, traditional instruction with outside computer use, Web-based, Web-enhanced). Assuming you had the opportunity to choose among these models in your teaching practice, which model or combination of models would you choose, and why?

2. Reflect on your own experience and review the findings presented in this chapter. What do you think is the single greatest potential benefit for students in a computer-assisted composition or literacy course? Can you think of conditions or circumstances that could prevent this advantage from being realized?

3. On the basis of your own experience and your reading of this chapter, identify the single greatest potential drawback for students in a computer-assisted composition or literacy course. What steps might a teacher take to solve this problem or prevent it from occurring?

4. Imagine that you are about to teach an ESL writing course and have decided to conduct all or some of your sessions in

a computer lab (or wholly or partially online). What effects do you think this decision might have on

a. your syllabus
b. your day-to-day lesson plans
c. your choice of textbook or textbooks and other materials
d. your interactions with students, including your responses to their writing
e. peer interaction
f. the ratio of in-class to out-of class writing?

5. Consider some of the in-class activities illustrated in chapters 2 through 4 and 6 through 8 (or the Application Activities you completed in conjunction with these chapters). Could these activities be adapted for use on a computer? If so, what changes might you make, and why?

6. Consider the principles and examples of written and oral teacher response discussed in chapter 5 (or the Application Activities you completed in conjunction with these chapters). How would you adapt written feedback or teacher–student conferencing to a computer-assisted environment? If you do not think you could adapt your feedback strategies, why not?

Application Activity 9.1: Reflecting on Your Own Computer-Assisted Writing Process

Directions

1. Choose a writing task that you undertake regularly and in which you can engage at two different times (e.g., letters, journal entries, course assignments, lesson plans, classroom materials). Complete two separate examples of the task (e.g., two different letters) at different times. Prepare one example using pen and paper and the other using a computer.

2. As you complete the two tasks, audio- or videotape yourself as you think aloud about how you are carrying out the task (or have a partner observe you as you write and think aloud). You may wish to consult Bridwell-Bowles, Johnson, & Brehe, (1987) and Haas (1989) for examples and analyses of think-aloud data. For the computer version, turn on

the "Track Changes" feature in your word processor and keep copies of your evolving document. For the handwritten version, keep all notes and drafts (including revisions and corrections) that you produce.

3. On the basis of your own observations, your taped think-aloud (or partner's notes), and the two texts you produced, reflect on your experience of writing using the two media:

   a. How much and what types of planning did you do before beginning your writing?
   b. What revisions did you make, and when in the process did you make them?
   c. Did you produce a longer text using either medium? Do you feel that one text is of higher quality than the other?
   d. How did you feel as you completed the two tasks? Did you find one more enjoyable, rewarding, difficult, challenging, frustrating than the other?
   e. How would you feel if you were a writing student forced to use one medium exclusively?

4. Compose a paper in which you discuss your analysis, relating it to the research and ideas presented in this chapter and explaining how the experience will or will not affect your present or future teaching of writing.

Application Activity 9.2: Adapting Lesson Plans and Syllabi for Computer-Assisted Environments

Directions

1. Obtain a lesson plan created for a traditional L2 writing class setting (or use the example in Appendix 3B). Examine it carefully, thinking through the principles and ideas discussed in this chapter. Make a list of specific ways in which you might adapt the lesson for a lab or online course. Choose at least one lesson or set of activities and practice creating or adapting materials for a lab or online session. Share your ideas with your classmates and instructor, discussing what you think the differences would be between a traditional and computer-assisted lesson on this topic.

2. Obtain two syllabi for the same course at the same institution: one taught in a traditional classroom setting and

one taught either online or in a computer lab. Compare and contrast the syllabi, looking carefully at course goals, assignments, topics for instruction, and course procedures (e.g., how papers are submitted). Identify and evaluate the strengths and weaknesses of each syllabus (you might use Figs. 3.3 and 3.4 as a reminder of issues to consider). If possible, interview one or more instructors at that institution who have taught the same course in both traditional and computer-assisted environments, asking about their experiences with each instructional model: Discuss advantages, drawbacks, preferences, and so forth. Share your findings with your classmates and instructor. As a current or future L2 literacy educator, consider how this exercise has affected your thinking about computer-based writing instruction.

Application Activity 9.3: Evaluating Internet Resources for L2 Writing Instruction

Directions

1. Using the resources mentioned in this chapter or others of which you are aware, visit at least three OWLs with ESL links or ESL Web sites. Choose a specific topic (e.g., introductory passages, quotations, commas), and for each site, carefully examine the instructional materials (explanations given in handouts or PowerPoint presentations) and the follow-up exercises or quizzes provided. Evaluate each source, considering the following criteria:

   a. User-friendliness and site navigability
   b. Clarity and appropriateness of instructional materials (you might use the textbook evaluation criteria outlined in Fig. 4.1 and the minilesson guidelines discussed in chapter 7 as resources)
   c. Accuracy and clarity of practice exercises and quizzes.

2. After evaluating each source and comparing and contrasting the three, prepare to discuss

   a. whether you would or would not direct ESL literacy students to this particular source, and why
   b. Whether the materials on these Web sites might be more appropriate for a particular student audience (consider

proficiency levels, student backgrounds [e.g., eye/ear learners], course goals, and so forth).

3. To extend this assignment, you might consider these follow-up activities:

   a. Compare the Web site materials with one or more print sources (textbooks, teacher handouts) on the same topic. What are the advantages, if any, of the Web materials?

   b. If you are teaching or tutoring an ESL student and the materials you have reviewed are appropriate for his or her proficiency level and needs, ask him or her to examine the materials and complete the exercises. Ask the student to give you an evaluation of which source she or he found most helpful.

Application Activity 9.4: "Cybertutoring" an ESL Student Writer

Directions. Identify an ESL student writer currently enrolled in a composition course who has access to a computer and e-mail. After obtaining permission from the classroom teacher and the cooperation of the student, complete the following steps to become a cybertutor:

1. If the student is not computer literate or experienced with using e-mail, meet with him or her to introduce the basics of sending and receiving e-mail messages and attaching, uploading, and downloading word processed documents. If the student is already an experienced e-mail user, you can skip this step.

2. Instruct the student to e-mail you a partial or completed draft of an assignment that he or she is developing for his or her course.

3. Respond online to the paper's ideas and organizational structure by inserting comments either in the margins or between paragraphs (whatever your word processor will accommodate) and by writing a summary comment (like a brief letter) at the end of the paper. Respond to the paper according to the principles for written response discussed in chapter 5. E-mail the annotated paper back to the student.

4. Ask the student to send you a follow-up message indicating

   a. What comments were most helpful

   b. Feedback that was confusing

   c. Comments with which he or she disagreed.

Also ask the student to e-mail you revisions of the paper so that you can assess the student's progress and the effects of your comments.

5. Reflect on the experience. Did you find responding online different from handwriting comments on paper or commenting in a face-to-face writing conference? What did you like about communicating with the student in this way? What did you find difficult?

6. You might extend or adapt this project in the following ways:

   a. Exchange additional draft–comment–revision iterations with the same student.

   b. Repeat the process with other student writers, noting variation across students.

   c. Ask your student to send you texts from other class activities on which you provide feedback (e.g, journal entries, responses to readings).

   d. Exchange messages with the student in which he or she poses questions about grammar, vocabulary, organization, the writing process, and so on, and in which you provide tutoring through your answers.

NOTES

[1] We have observed that, far more often, teachers rather than students display resistance to learning new technology, which limits its progress in implementation. We include ourselves in this indictment.

[2] This chapter received the most criticism by far in the reviews of the first edition, and understandably so. The nature of the comments, which were not at all mean-spirited, was along the lines of "Nice try, but already way out of date." We suspect that such legitimate criticism will always apply to any chapter on this topic, regardless of how many editions we undertake!

[3] We note again that this training may be less necessary for some L2 students than for their writing instructors.

[4] The potential drawbacks of this possibility should be immediately apparent. Teachers definitely risk increasing their workloads by inviting several rounds of e-mail discussion over a particular student draft. On the other hand, this practice could be considered a form of (asynchronous) virtual conferencing, saving in-person office time and easing scheduling difficulties.

APPENDIX 9: SAMPLE STUDENT PAPER WITH SPELLING AND GRAMMAR ANALYSIS

Lying is not always wrong, if it is used for good intentions. Lying can be very manipulative, yet that particular quality, Goodrich mentioned, "is also exciting." Instead of using it for evil, lying can be a vital source for good, whether it from sparing *a child feelings* or doing it just to get something out of it. There are numerous explanations why people would create white lies. One reason why people lie is to surprise or distract *a love one*. Another reason why people do it is to create a diversion, in order to escape the difficulties that may take place by telling the truth.

There is no greater rush than getting away with a good, harmless lie. For example, on one occasion, I have used lies *for good intention*. My *close friend birthday* was coming up. My friends and I were planning *a surprise birthday*. We did not want the birthday girl to know of this, so we manipulated her into thinking that we did not remember her birthday. *Making up stories that we were busy on that day, to convince her so.* Seeing the hurt in her eyes further *greaten* our smile. Like Goodrich said, "even though people lie for good reason, lying can be harmful." My friends and I knew that by lying to her, the surprise party would be a total success. Yes, our way of springing the party on her was wrong, but when the surprise was successful, seeing the joy on her face gave everyone *involve* a great rush, and that *is* exciting__

When Goodrich said that, "everyone **lie**[1]" it could very well be the truth. People lie constantly to avoid difficult *situation* by telling the truth. For instant, I was at my friends' house for dinner. His mother was cooking her best dish that took hours to make. During the course of the meal she asked me *how was it*. The truth is that I didn't like it, maybe *is* because I hate shrimp, but to avoid being an unwanted *guess*, I bit my lips and told her that the meal was excellent. Besides my stomach hurting from the shrimp, no feelings got hurt.

To conclude, small, harmless **ies**[2] can be exciting and fun. Not knowing if you will get caught in a lie, or knowing that you just

---

[1]Grammar check offered one (correct) comment: That the error was in subject–verb agreement and that the correct form was "lies."

[2]Spell check offered 10 suggestions, of which the correct choice ("lies") was #5.

got away with a lie is a great thrill. The truth is, some lies can be damaging when *it is* discovered, but if done properly, lies can be very **benificial**[3]. No one really likes to lie, but not everyone is aware that they are lying. Lying is not always wrong.

Note: Spelling and grammar check performed using Word 2000.

Analysis: The spelling and grammar checks of this document were accurate, *as far as they went.* Two of the three **errors marked (in bold in the text)** offered only one choice, the correct one. The third (*"ies"*) had 10 alternative spellings offered, with the correct one being fifth on the list. However, given the topic, it is likely that the student could correct the spelling error given time to proofread or the spell check suggestions.

The more problematic issue, of course, is how much the checkers *missed (in italics in the text).* A whole range of L2 errors—from missing plural and possessive markers on nouns, to tense and form errors on verbs, to word order, sentence boundaries, and word choice—went completely undetected. The student writer could easily correct the three errors marked by the word processor and continue on in blissful ignorance of the many others.

(Source of student paper: Ferris, Kennedy, & Senna, 2004 research corpus (Text 1). Used with student permission.)

---

[3]Spell check offered one suggestion, the correct one ("beneficial").

References

Adam, C., & Artemeva, N. (2002). Writing instruction in English for academic purposes (EAP) classes: Introducing second language learners to the academic community. In A. M. Johns (Ed.), *Genre in the classroom: Multiple perspectives* (pp. 179–196). Mahwah, NJ: Lawrence Erlbaum Associates.

Aebersold, J. A., & Field, M. L. (1997). *From reader to reading teacher: Issues and strategies for second language classrooms.* New York: Cambridge University Press.

Akyel, A., & Kamisli, S. (1999). Word processing in the EFL classroom: Effects on writing strategies, attitudes, and products. In M. C. Pennington (Ed.), *Writing in an electronic medium: Research with language learners* (pp. 27–60). Houston: Athelstan.

Alatis, J., & Barnhardt, S. (Eds.). (1998). *Portfolio assessment in the foreign language classroom.* Washington, DC: National Capital Language Resource Center.

Alderson, J. (1984). Reading in a foreign language: A reading problem or a language problem? In J. Alderson & A. Urquhart (Eds.), *Reading in a foreign language* (pp. 1–27). New York: Longman.

Allaei, S. K., & Connor, U. (1990). Using performative assessment instruments with ESL student writers. In L. Hamp-Lyons (Ed.), *Assessing second language writing in academic contexts* (pp. 227–240). Norwood, NJ: Ablex.

Allaei, S. K., & Connor, U. (1991). Using performative assessment instruments with ESL student writers. In L. Hamp-Lyons (Ed.), *Assessing second language writing in academic contexts* (pp. 227–240). Norwood, NJ: Ablex.

Allwright, D., & Bailey, K. M. (1991). *Focus on the language classroom: An introduction to classroom research for language teachers.* Cambridge, UK: Cambridge University Press.

Amsel, E., & Byrnes, J. P. (Eds.). (2002). *Language, literacy, and cognitive development.* Mahwah, NJ: Lawrence Erlbaum Associates.

Anderson, N. (1999). *Exploring second language reading: Issues and strategies.* Boston: Heinle.

Angelova, M., & Riazantseva, A. (1999). "If you don't tell me, how can I know?": A case study of four international students learning to write in the U. S. way. *Written Communication, 16*, 491–525.

Anson, C. M. (Ed.). (1989). *Writing and response.* Urbana, IL: National Council of Teachers of English.

Applebee, A. N. (1978). Teaching high-achievement students: A survey of the winners of the 1977 NCTE Achievement Awards in writing. *Research in the Teaching of English, 1*, 41–53.

Arndt, V. (1993). Response to writing: Using feedback to inform the writing process. In M. N. Brock & L. Walters (Eds.), *Teaching composition around the Pacific rim: Politics and pedagogy* (pp. 90–116). Clevedon, UK: Multilingual Matters.

Ascher, A. (1993). *Think about editing*. Boston: Heinle.

Ashwell, T. (2000). Patterns of teacher response to student writing in a multiple-draft composition classroom: Is content feedback followed by form feedback the best method? *Journal of Second Language Writing, 9,* 227–258.

Atkinson, D. (1997). A critical approach to critical thinking in TESOL. *TESOL Quarterly, 31,* 71–94.

Atkinson, D. (1999). Culture in TESOL. *TESOL Quarterly, 33,* 625–654.

Atkinson, D. (2000). On Peter Elbow's response to "Individualism, academic writing, and ESL writers," by Vai Ramanathan and Dwight Atkinson. *Journal of Second Language Writing, 9,* 72–76.

Atkinson, D. (Guest Ed.). (2003a). L2 writing in the postprocess era [Special issue]. *Journal of Second Language Writing, 12*(1), 49–63.

Atkinson, D. (2003b). L2 writing in the postprocess era: Introduction. *Journal of Second Language Writing, 12,* 3–15.

Atkinson, D., & Ramanathan, V. (1995). Cultures of writing: An ethnographic comparison of L1 and L2 university writing/language programs. *TESOL Quarterly, 29,* 539–568.

Atwell, N. (1998). *In the middle: New understandings about writing, reading, and learning* (2nd ed.). Portsmouth, NH: Boynton/Cook Heinemann.

August, D., & Hakuta, K. (Eds.). (1997). *Improving schooling for language-minority children*. Washington, DC: National Academy Press.

Babin, E. H., & Harrison, K. (1999). *Contemporary composition studies: A guide to theorists and terms*. Westport, CT: Greenwood Press.

Bachman, L. (1990). *Fundamental considerations in language testing*. Oxford: Oxford University Press.

Bachman, L., & Palmer, A. (1996). *Language testing in practice: Designing and developing useful language tests*. Oxford: Oxford University Press.

Bailey, K. M. (1996). The best laid plans: Teachers' in-class decisions to depart from their lesson plans. In K. M. Bailey & D. Nunan (Eds.), *Voices from the language classroom* (pp. 15–40). Cambridge, UK: Cambridge University Press.

Bailey, K. M. (1998). *Learning about language assessment: Dilemmas, decisions, and directions*. Boston: Heinle.

Bailey, K. M., Curtis, A., & Nunan, D. (2001). *Pursuing professional development: The self as source*. Boston: Heinle.

Bakhtin, M. (1981). *The dialogic imagination*. M. Holquist, (Ed.), and C. Emerson (Trans.). Austin: University of Texas Press.

Balestri, D. P. (1988). Softcopy and hard: Wordprocessing and writing process. *Academic Computing, 2*(1), 14–17, 41–45.

Bamberg, B. (2003). Revision. I. Clark (Ed.), *Concepts in composition: Theory and practice in the teaching of writing* (pp. 108–140). Mahwah, NJ: Erlbaum.

Barker, T. T. (1987). Studies in word processing and writing. *Computers in the Schools, 4* (1), 109–121.

Barnett, T. (2002). *Teaching argument in the composition course: Background readings*. Boston: Bedford/St. Martin's.

Bartholomae, D., & Petrosky, A. (Eds.). (1986). *The language of teaching and learning*. Portsmouth, NH: Heinemann.

Bates, L., Lane, J., & Lange, E. (1993). *Writing clearly: Responding to ESL compositions*. Boston: Heinle.

Bazerman, C. (1985). Physicists reading physics: Schema-laden purposes and purpose-laden schema. *Written Communication, 2,* 3–24.

Bazerman, C. (1988). *Shaping written knowledge: The genre and activity of the experimental article in science.* Madison, WI: University of Wisconsin Press.

Bazerman, C. (1994). Systems of genres and the enactment of social intentions. In A. Freedman & P. Medway (Eds.), *Genre and the new rhetoric* (pp. 79–101). London: Taylor & Francis.

Bazerman, C. (1998). *The languages of Edison's light.* Chicago: University of Chicago Press.

Beach, R., & Liebman-Kleine, J. (1986). The writing/reading relationship: Becoming one's own best reader. In B. T. Petersen (Ed.), *Convergences: Transactions in reading and writing* (pp. 64–81). Urbana, IL: National Council of Teachers of English.

Belanger, J. (1987). Theory and research into reading and writing connections: A critical review. *Reading-Canada-Lecture, 5,* 10–18.

Belanoff, P., & Dickson, M. (Eds.). (1991). *Portfolios: Process and product.* Portsmouth, NH: Heinemann/Boynton Cook.

Belanoff, P., & Elbow, P. (1986). Using portfolios to increase collaboration and community in a writing program. *Writing Program Administration, 9,* 27–40.

Belcher, D. (1997). An argument for nonadversarial argumentation: On the relevance of the feminist critique of academic discourse to L2 writing pedagogy. *Journal of Second Language Writing, 5,* 1–21.

Belcher, D., & Braine, G. (Eds.). (1995). *Academic writing in a second language.* Norwood, NJ: Ablex.

Belcher, D., & Hirvela, A. (Eds.). (2001a). *Linking literacies: Perspectives on L2 reading–writing connections.* Ann Arbor: University of Michigan Press.

Belcher, D., & Hirvela, A. (Eds.). (2001b). Voice in L2 writing [Special issue]. *Journal of Second Language Writing, 10*(1).

Bell, J. C. (1995). The relationship between L1 and L2 literacy: Some complicating factors. *TESOL Quarterly, 29,* 687–704.

Benesch, S. (1987, March). *Word processing in English as a second language: A case study of three non-native college students.* Paper presented at the Conference on College Composition and Communication, Atlanta, GA (EDRS No. ED 281 381).

Benesch, S. (Ed.). (1988). *Ending remediation: Linking ESL and content in higher education.* Washington, DC: TESOL.

Benesch, S. (1995). Genres and processes in a sociocultural context. *Journal of Second Language Writing, 4,* 191–195.

Benesch, S. (1996). Needs analysis and curriculum development in EAP: An example of a critical approach. *TESOL Quarterly, 30,* 723–738.

Benesch, S. (2001). *Critical English for academic purposes: Theory, politics, and practice.* Mahwah, NJ: Lawrence Erlbaum Associates.

Benesch, S., Rakijas, M., & Rorschach, B. (1987). *Academic writing workshop.* Belmont, CA: Wadsworth.

Bereiter, C., & Scardamalia, M. (1984). Learning about writing from reading. *Written Communication, 1,* 163–188.

Bereiter, C., & Scardamalia, M. (1987). *The psychology of written composition.* Hillsdale, NJ: Lawrence Erlbaum Associates.

Berg, E. C. (1999). The effects of trained peer response on ESL students' revision types and writing quality. *Journal of Second Language Writing, 8,* 215–241.

Berger, V. (1990). The effects of peer and self-feedback. *CATESOL Journal, 3*, 21–35.

Berkenkotter, C., & Huckin, T. (1995). *Genre knowledge in disciplinary communication.* Hillsdale, NJ: Lawrence Erlbaum Associates.

Berlin, J. (1984). *Writing instruction in nineteenth century American colleges.* Carbondale, IL: Southern Illinois University Press.

Berlin, J. (1987). *Rhetoric and reality: Writing instruction in American colleges, 1900–1985.* Carbondale, IL: Southern Illinois University Press.

Berlin, J., & Inkster, R. (1980). Current-traditional rhetoric: Paradigm and practice.*Freshman English News, 8*, 1–5, 14.

Berlin, J. A. (1988). Rhetoric and ideology in the writing class. *College English, 50*, 477–494.

Bernhardt, E. B. (1991). *Reading development in a second language: Theoretical, empirical, and classroom perspectives.* Norwood, NJ: Ablex.

Bernhardt, E. B., & Kamil, M. L. (1995). Interpreting relationships between L1 and L2 reading: Consolidating the linguistic threshold and the linguistic interdependence hypotheses. *Applied Linguistics, 16*, 15–34.

Bernhardt, S. A., Edwards, P. R., & Wojahn, P. G. (1989). Teaching college composition with computers: A program evaluation study. *Written Communication, 6*, 108–133.

Bernhardt, S. A., Wojahn, P. G., & Edwards, P. R. (1990). Teaching college composition with computers: A timed observation study. *Written Communication, 7*, 342–374.

Betancourt, F., & Phinney, M. (1988). Sources of writing block in bilingual writers. *Written Communication, 5*, 461–478.

Bhatia, V. K. (1993). *Analysing genre: Language use in professional settings.* London: Longman.

Bhatia, V. K. (1999). Integrating products, processes, purposes, and participants in professional writing. In C. N. Candlin & K. Hyland (Eds.), *Writing: Texts, processes, and practices* (pp. 21–39). London: Longman.

Biber, D. (1988). *Variation across speech and writing.* Cambridge, UK: Cambridge University Press.

Biber, D., Conrad, S., & Reppen, R. (1998). *Corpus linguistics: Investigating language structure and use.* Cambridge: Cambridge University Press.

Birch, B. M. (2002). *English L2 reading: Getting to the bottom.* Mahwah, NJ: Lawrence Erlbaum Associates.

Birnbaum, J. (1982). The reading and composing behavior of selected fourth- and seventh-grade students. *Research in the Teaching of English, 16*, 241–260.

Bishop, W., & Ostrom, H. (Eds.). (1997). *Genre and writing: Issues, arguments, alternatives.* Portsmouth, NH: Boynton/Cook.

Bizzell, P. (1987). Language and literacy. In T. Enos (Ed.), *A sourcebook for basic writing teachers* (pp. 125–137). New York: Random House.

Bizzell, P. (1992). *Academic discourse and critical consciousness.* Pittsburgh: University of Pittsburgh Press.

Black, L., Daiker, D. A., Sommers, J., & Stygall, G. (Eds.). (1994). *New directions in portfolio assessment: Reflective practice, critical theory, and large-scale scoring.* Portsmouth, NH: Boynton/Cook.

Blanton, L. (1993). Reading as performance: Reframing the function of reading. In J. Carson, & I. Leki (Eds.), *Reading in the composition classroom: Second language perspectives* (pp. 234–246). Boston: Heinle.

Blanton, L. L., Kroll, B., Cumming, A., & Erickson, M. (2002). *ESL composition tales: Reflections on teaching.* Ann Arbor: University of Michigan Press.

Bloch, J. (2001). Plagiarism and the ESL student: From printed to electronic texts. In D. Belcher & A. Hirvela (Eds.), *Linking literacies: Perspectives on L2 reading–writing connections* (pp. 209–228).Ann Arbor: University of Michigan Press.

Bloom, L. Z., Daiker, D. A., & White, E. M. (Eds.). (1997). *Composition in the 21st century: Crisis and change.* Carbondale, IL: Southern Illinois University Press.

Borich, G. (1999). *Observation skills for effective teaching* (3rd ed.). Upper Saddle River, NJ: Merrill/Prentice Hall.

Bork, A. (1985). *Personal computers for education.* New York: Harper & Row.

Bosher, S. (1998). The composing process of three Southeast Asian writers at the postsecondary level: An exploratory study. *Journal of Second Language Writing, 7*, 205–241.

Bossers, B. (1991). On thresholds, ceilings, and short-circuits: The relation between L1 reading, L2 reading, and L2 knowledge. *AILA Review, 8*, 45–60.

Bowden, D. (1999). *The mythology of voice.* Portsmouth, NH: Heinemann.

Bowden, D. (2003). Voice. In I. Clark (Ed.), *Concepts in composition: Theory and practice in the teaching of writing* (pp. 285–303). Mahwah, NJ: Lawrence Erlbaum Associates.

Brady, L. (1990). Overcoming resistance: *Computers in the writing classroom. Computers and Composition, 7*(2), 21–33.

Braine, G. (1996). ESL students in first-year writing courses: ESL versus mainstream classes. *Journal of Second Language Writing, 5*, 91–107.

Braine, G. (1997). Beyond word-processing: Networked computers in ESL writing classes. *Computers and Composition, 14*, 45–58.

Brannon, L., & Knoblauch, C. H. (1982). On students' rights to their own texts: A model of teacher response. *College Composition and Communication, 33*, 157–166.

Bräuer, G. (Ed.). (2000). *Writing across languages.* Stamford, CT: Ablex.

Brice, C. (1995, March). *ESL writers' reactions to teacher commentary: A case study.* Paper presented at the 30th Annual TESOL Convention, Long Beach, CA (ERIC Document Reproduction Service No. ED394 312).

Brice, C., & Newman, L. (2000, September). *The case against grammar correction in practice: What do students think?* Paper presented at the Symposium on Second Language Writing, Purdue University, West Lafayette, IN.

Brindley, G. (Ed.). (2000). *Studies in immigrant English language assessment.* Sydney, Australia: National Centre for English Language Teaching and Research, Macquarie University.

Brindley, G., & Ross, S. (2001). EAP assessment: Issues, models, and outcomes. In J. Flowerdew & M. Peacock (Eds), *Research perspectives on English for academic purposes* (pp. 148–166). Cambridge, England: Cambridge University Press.

Bridwell-Bowles, L., Johnson, P., & Brehe, S. (1987). Composing and computers: Case studies of experienced writers. In A. Matsuhashi (Ed.), *Writing in real time: Modelling production processes* (pp. 81–107). Norwood, NJ: Ablex.

Briggs, C. L., & Bauman, R. (1992). Genre, intertextuality, and social power. *Journal of Linguistic Anthropology, 2*, 131–172.

Brinton, D., & Master, P. A. (Eds.). (1997). *New ways in content-based instruction.* Alexandria, VA: TESOL.

Brinton, D., Snow, M. A., & Wesche, M. B. (1989). *Content-based second language instruction.* Boston: Heinle.

Brisk, M. E., & Harrington, M. M. (2000). *Literacy and bilingualism. A handbook for ALL teachers.* Mahwah, NJ: Lawrence Erlbaum Associates.

Brock, M. N. (1990a). Can the computer tutor? An analysis of a disk-based text analyzer. *System, 18,* 351–359.

Brock, M. N., and Pennington, M. C. (1999). A comparative study of text analysis and peer tutoring as input to writing on computer in an ESL context. In M. C. Pennington (Ed.), *Writing in an electronic medium: Research with language learners* (pp. 61–94). Houston: Athelstan.

Brock, M. N. (1990b). Customizing a computerized text analyzer for ESL writers: Cost versus gain. *CALICO Journal, 8*(2), 51–60.

Brown, H. D. (2000). *Principles of language learning and teaching* (4th Ed.). Englewood Cliffs, NJ: Prentice-Hall Regents.

Brown, H. D. (2001). *Teaching by principles: An interactive approach to language pedagogy* (2nd ed.). White Plains, NY: Longman.

Brown, J. D. (1995). *The elements of language curriculum: A systematic approach to program development.* Boston: Heinle.

Brown, J. D. (Ed.). (1998). *New ways of classroom assessment.* Alexandria, VA: TESOL.

Browning, G. (1996). Challenges facing California ESL students and teachers across the segments. *CATESOL Journal, 9,* 15–46.

Bruffee, K. A. (1986). Social construction, language, and the authority of knowledge: A bibliographical essay. *College English, 48,* 773–790.

Burnham, C. (1986). Portfolio evaluation: Room to breathe and grow. In C. Bridges (Ed.), *Training the new teacher of college composition* (pp. 125–139). Urbana, IL: National Council of Teachers of English.

Buzan, T., & Buzan, B. (1993). *The mind map book.* London: BBC Books.

Byram, M. (1997). *Teaching and assessing intercultural communicative competence.* Clevedon, UK: Multilingual Matters.

Byrd, P. (2001). Textbooks: Evaluation for selection and analysis for implementation. In M. Celce-Murcia (Ed.), *Teaching English as a second or foreign language* (3rd ed.) (pp. 415–427). Boston: Heinle.

Byrd, P., & Nelson, G. (1995). NNS performance on writing proficiency exams: Focus on students who failed. *Journal of Second Language Writing, 4,* 273–285.

Calfee, R., & Perfumo, P. (1996a). A national survey of writing portfolio practice: What we learned and what it means. In R. Calfee & P. Perfumo (Eds.), *Writing portfolios in the classroom: Policy and practice, promise and peril* (pp. 63–81). Mahwah, NJ: Lawrence Erlbaum Associates.

Calfee, R., & Perfumo, P. (Eds.). (1996b). *Writing portfolios in the classroom: Policy and practice, promise and peril.* Mahwah, NJ: Lawrence Erlbaum Associates.

Camp, R. (1993). Changing the model for direct assessment of writing. In M. Williamson & B. Huot (Eds.), *Holistic scoring: Theoretical foundations and validation research* (pp. 56–69). Cresskill, NJ: Hampton Press.

Canagarajah, S. (2002). *A geopolitics of academic writing.* Pittsburgh: University of Pittsburgh Press.

Carnicelli, T. (1980). The writing conference: A one-to-one conversation. In T. R. Donovan & B. W. McClelland (Eds.), *Eight approaches to teaching composition* (pp. 101–131). Urbana, IL: National Council of Teachers of English.

Carrell, P. L. (1983a). Three components of background knowledge in reading comprehension. *Language Learning, 33,* 183–207.

Carrell, P. L. (1983b). Background knowledge in second language comprehension. *Language Learning and Communication, 2,* 25–34.

Carrell, P. L. (1987). Text as interaction: Some implications of text analysis and reading research for ESL composition. In U. Connor & R. Kaplan (Eds.),

Writing across languages: Analysis of L2 text (pp. 47–56). Reading, MA: Addison-Wesley.

Carrell, P. L. (1991). Second language reading: Reading ability or language proficiency? *Applied Linguistics, 12*, 159–179.

Carrell, P. L., Devine, J., & Eskey, D. (Eds.). (1988). *Interactive approaches to second language reading.* New York: Cambridge University Press.

Carrell, P. L., & Eisterhold, J. C. (1983). Schema theory and ESL reading pedagogy. *TESOL Quarterly, 17*, 553–574.

Carrell, P. L., & Monroe, L. (1995). ESL composition and learning styles. In J. Reid (Ed.), *Learning styles in the ESL/EFL classroom* (pp. 148–157). Boston: Heinle.

Carson, J. E. (1993). Reading for writing: Cognitive perspectives. In J. G. Carson, & I. Leki (Eds.), *Reading in the composition classroom: Second language perspectives* (pp. 85–104). Boston: Heinle.

Carson, J. E., Carrell, P. L., Silberstein, S., Kroll, B., & Kuehn, P. A. (1990). Reading–writing relationships in first and second language. *TESOL Quarterly, 24*, 245–266.

Carson, J. E., & Leki, I. (Eds.). (1993). *Reading in the composition classroom: Second language perspectives.* Boston: Heinle.

Carson, J. G. (2001). A task analysis of reading and writing in academic contexts. In D. Belcher & A. Hirvela (Eds.), *Linking literacies: Perspectives on L2 reading–writing connections* (pp. 48–83). Ann Arbor: University of Michigan Press.

Carson, J. G., & Nelson, G. L. (1994). Writing groups: Cross-cultural issues. *Journal of Second Language Writing, 3*, 17–30.

Carson, J. G., & Nelson, G. L. (1996). Chinese students' perceptions of ESL peer response group interaction. *Journal of Second Language Writing, 5*, 1–19.

Carter, R., & McRae, J. (Eds.). (1996). *Language, literature, and the learner: Creative classroom practice.* London: Longman.

Casanave, C. P. (2002). *Writing games: Multicultural case studies of academic literacy practices in higher education.* Mahwah, NJ: Lawrence Erlbaum Associates.

Casanave, C. P. (2003). Looking ahead to more sociopolitically oriented case study research in L2 writing scholarship (But should it be called "post process"?). *Journal of Second Language Writing, 12*, 85–102.

Casanave, C. P. (2004). *Controversies in second language writing: Dilemmas and decisions in research and instruction.* Ann Arbor: University of Michigan Press.

Celce-Murcia, M., & Olshtain, E. (2000). *Discourse and context in language teaching: A guide for language teachers.* Cambridge, UK: Cambridge University Press.

Chadwick, S., & Bruce, N. (1989, April). The revision process in academic writing: From pen and paper to word processor. *Hong Kong Papers in Linguistics and Language Teaching, 12*, 1–27.

Chambers, F. (1997). Seeking consensus in coursebook evaluation. *ELT Journal, 51*, 29–35.

Chaney, S. J. (1999). *The effect of error types on error correction and revision.* Unpublished M.A. thesis, California State University, Sacramento, Department of English.

Chang, M.-C. (2004). *On the inevitability of technological infiltration in education and the professions.* Unpublished manuscript, Monterey Institute of International Studies.

Chaudron, C. (1983, March). *Evaluating writing: Effects of feedback on revision.* Paper presented at the 17th annual TESOL Convention, Toronto, Canada (EDRS No. ED 227 706).

Chen, H., & Graves, M. F. (1995). Effects of previewing and providing background knowledge on Taiwanese college students' comprehension of American short stories. *TESOL Quarterly, 29,* 663–686.

Chiang, S. Y. (1999). Assessing grammatical and textual features in L2 writing samples: The case of French as a foreign language. *Modern Language Journal, 83,* 219–232.

Ching, R., McKee, S., & Ford, R. (1996). Passages between the community college and the California State University. *CATESOL Journal, 9,* 79–98.

Christie, F. (1993). The "received tradition" of literacy teaching: The decline of rhetoric and corruption of grammar. In B. Green (Ed.), *The insistence of the letter: Literacy studies and curriculum theorizing* (pp. 75–106). London: Falmer.

Christie, F. (1995). Genre-based approaches to teaching literacy. In M. L. Tickoo (Ed.), *Reading and writing: Theory into practice* (pp. 300–320). Singapore: SEAMEO Regional Language Centre.

Christie, F., & Martin, J. R. (Eds.). (1997). *Genre and institutions: Social processes in the workplace and school.* London: Continuum.

Clark, I. (2003a). Audience. In I. Clark (Ed.), *Concepts in composition: Theory and practice in the teaching of writing* (pp. 141–160). Mahwah, NJ: Lawrence Erlbaum Associates.

Clark, I. (Ed.). (2003b). *Concepts in composition: Theory and practice in the teaching of writing.* Mahwah, NJ: Lawrence Erlbaum Associates.

Clark, I. (2003c). Invention. In I. Clark (Ed.), *Concepts in composition: Theory and practice in the teaching of writing* (pp. 72–93). Mahwah, NJ: Lawrence Erlbaum Associates.

Clark, I. (2003d). Process. In I. Clark (Ed.), *Concepts in composition: Theory and practice in the teaching of writing* (pp. 1–19). Mahwah, NJ: Lawrence Erlbaum Associates.

Cochran-Smith, M. (1991). Word processing and writing in elementary classrooms: A critical review of related literature. *Review of Educational Research, 61,* 107—155.

Coe, R. M. (1987). An apology for form: Or who took the form out of process? *College English, 49,* 13–28.

Cohen, A. (1987). Student processing of feedback on their compositions. In A. L. Wenden & J. Rubin (Eds.), *Learner strategies in language learning* (pp. 57–69). Englewood Cliffs, NJ: Prentice-Hall.

Cohen, A. (1994). *Assessing language ability in the classroom* (2nd ed.). Boston: Heinle.

Cohen, A. (1998). *Strategies in learning and using a second language.* London: Longman.

Cohen, A. (2001). Second language assessment. In M. Celce-Murcia (Ed.), *Teaching English as a second or foreign language* (3rd ed.) (pp. 515–534). Boston: Heinle.

Cohen, A., & Cavalcanti, M. (1990). Feedback on written compositions: Teacher and student verbal reports. In B. Kroll (Ed.), *Second language writing: Research insights for the classroom* (pp. 155–177). Cambridge: Cambridge University Press.

Cohen, A. D., & Robbins, M. (1976). Toward assessing interlanguage performance: The relationship between selected errors, learners' characteristics, and learners' expectations. *Language Learning, 26,* 45–66.

Cole, D. J. (1999). *Portfolios across the curriculum and beyond.* Thousand Oaks, CA: Corwin.

Connor, U. (1996). *Contrastive rhetoric: Cross-cultural aspects of second language writing.* New York: Cambridge University Press.

Connor, U. (2003). Changing currents in contrastive rhetoric: Implications for teaching and research. In B. Kroll (Ed.), *Exploring the dynamics of second language writing* (pp. 218–241). Cambridge: Cambridge University Press.

Connor, U., & Asenavage, K. (1994). Peer response groups in ESL writing classes: How much impact on revision? *Journal of Second Language Writing, 3,* 257–276.

Connor, U., & Kaplan, R. B. (Eds.). (1987). *Writing across languages: Analysis of L2 text.* Reading, MA: Addison-Wesley.

Connor-Linton, J. (1995). Crosscultural comparison of writing standards: American ESL and Japanese EFL. *World Englishes, 14,* 99–115.

Connors, R., & Lunsford, A. (1993). Teachers' rhetorical comments on student papers. *College Composition and Communication, 44,* 200–223.

Conrad, S. M., & Goldstein, L. M. (1999). ESL student revision after teacher-written comments: Text, contexts, and individuals. *Journal of Second Language Writing, 8,* 147–180.

Conway, G. (1995). "What are we doing today?" High school basic writers collaborating in a computer lab. *Computers and Composition, 12*(1), 79–95.

Cope, B., & Kalantzis, M. (Eds.). (1993). *The powers of literacy: A genre approach to teaching writing.* Pittsburgh: University of Pittsburgh Press.

Cope, B., & Kalantzis, M. (Eds.). (2000). *Multiliteracies: Literacy learning and the design of social futures.* London: Routledge.

Corder, S. P. (1967). The significance of learners' errors. *International Review of Applied Linguistics (IRAL), 5*(4), 161–170.

Corson, D. (2001). *Language diversity and education.* Mahwah, NJ: Lawrence Erlbaum Associates.

Crandall, J., & Kaufman, D. (Eds.). (2001). *Content-based instruction: Case studies in TESOL practice series.* Alexandria, VA: TESOL.

Cruickshank, D. R., Bainer, D. L., Metcalf, K. K. (1999). *The act of teaching* (2nd ed.). Boston: McGraw-Hill.

Cumming, A. (1985). Responding to the writing of ESL students. *Highway One, 8,* 58–78.

Cumming, A. (1989). Writing expertise and second language proficiency. *Language Learning, 39,* 81–141.

Cumming, A. (1990). Expertise in evaluating second language compositions. *Language Testing, 7,* 31–51.

Cumming, A. (1998). Theoretical perspectives on writing. *Annual Review of Applied Linguistics, 18,* 61–78.

Cumming, A. (2001). Learning to write in a second language: Two decades of research. In R. M. Manchón (Ed.), *International Journal of English Studies 1*(2), 1–23.

Cumming, A. (2003). Experienced ESL/EFL writing instructors' conceptualizations of their teaching: Curriculum options and their implications. In B. Kroll (Ed.), *Second language writing: Research insights for the classroom* (pp. 71–92). Cambridge, UK: Cambridge University Press.

Cumming, A., Kantor, R., & Powers, D. E. (2002). Decision making while rating ESL/EFL writing tasks: A descriptive framework. *Modern Language Journal, 86,* 67–96.

Cumming, A., Kantor, R., & Powers, D. E. (2003). *Scoring TOEFL essays and TOEFL 2000 prototype writing tasks: An investigation into raters' decision making and development of a preliminary analytic framework.* Princeton, NJ: Educational Testing Service.

Cumming, A., Kantor, R., Powers, D., Santos, T., & Taylor, C. (2000). *TOEFL 2000 writing framework: A working paper.* Princeton, NJ: Educational Testing Service.

Cumming, A., & Riazi, A. (2000). Building models of adult second language writing instruction. *Learning and Instruction, 10,* 55–71.

Cummins, J. (1981). The role of primary language development in promoting educational success for language minority students. In *Schooling and language minority students: A theoretical framework* (pp. 3–49). Los Angeles: California State University Evaluation, Dissemination, and Assessment Center.

Cummins, J. (1984). *Bilingualism and special education.* San Diego, CA: College Hill.

Currie, P. (1993). Entering a disciplinary community: Conceptual activities required to write for one introductory university course. *Journal of Second Language Writing, 2,* 101–118.

Curtis, M. S. (1988). Windows on composing: Teaching revision on word processors. *College Composition and Communication, 39,* 337–344.

Cziko, G. (1978). Differences in first and second language reading: The use of syntactic, semantic, and discourse constraints. *Canadian Modern Language Review, 34,* 473–489.

Daiute, C. (1985). *Writing and computers.* Reading, MA: Addison-Wesley.

Dalton, D. W., & Hannafin, M. J. (1986). The effects of word processing on written composition. *Journal of Educational Research, 80,* 338–342.

Day, R. R. (Ed.). (1993). *New ways in teaching reading.* Alexandria, VA: TESOL.

Day, R. R., & Bamford, J. (1998). *Extensive reading in the second language classroom.* New York: Cambridge University Press.

de Larios, J., Murphy, L., & Marín, J. (2002). A critical examination of L2 writing process research. In S. Ransdell & M.-L. Barbier (Eds.), *New directions for research in L2 writing* (pp. 11–47). Dordrecht, The Netherlands: Kluwer.

Delpit, L. (1988). The silenced dialogue: Power and pedagogy in educating other people's children. *Harvard Educational Review, 58,* 280–298.

Delpit, L. (1998). The politics of teaching literate discourse. In V. Zamel & R. Spack (Eds.), *Negotiating academic literacies: Teaching and learning across languages and cultures* (pp. 207–218). Mahwah, NJ: Lawrence Erlbaum Associates.

DeLuca, G., Fox, L., Johnson, M. A., & Kogen, M. (Eds.). (2001). *Dialogue on writing: Rethinking ESL, basic ESL writing, and first-year composition.* Mahwah, NJ: Lawrence Erlbaum Associates.

DeRemer, M. (1998). Writing assessment: Raters' elaboration of the rating task. *Assessing Writing, 5,* 7–29.

Devine, J. (1993). The role of metacognition in second language reading and writing. In J. G. Carson & I. Leki (Eds.), *Reading in the composition classroom: Second language perspectives* (pp. 105–127). Boston: Heinle.

Dias, P. Freedman, A., Medway, P., & Paré, A. (Eds.). (1999). *Worlds apart: Acting and writing in academic and workplace contexts.* Mahwah, NJ: Lawrence Erlbaum Associates.

Dias, P., & Paré, A. (Eds.). (2000). *Transitions: Writing in academic and workplace settings.* Cresskill, NJ: Hampton Press.

Dobson, B., & Feak, C. (2001). A cognitive modeling approach to teaching critique writing to nonnative speakers. In D. Belcher & A. Hirvela (Eds.), *Linking literacies: Perspectives on L2 reading-writing connections* (pp. 186–199). Ann Arbor: University of Michigan Press.

Dong, Y. R. (1998). From writing in their native language to writing in English: What ESL students bring to our writing classrooms. *College ESL, 8,* 87–104.

Doughty, C., & Varela, E. (1998). Communicative focus on form. In C. Doughty & J. Williams (Eds.), *Focus on form in classroom SLA* (pp. 114–138). New York: Cambridge University Press.

Doughty, C., & Williams, J. (Eds.) (1998). *Focus on form in classroom second language acquisition.* New York: Cambridge University Press.

Douglas, D. (2000). *Assessing languages for specific purposes.* New York: Cambridge University Press.

Doyle, W. (1983). Academic work. *Review of Educational Research, 52,* 159–199.

Dubin, F., Eskey, D. E., & Grabe, W. (Eds.). (1986). *Teaching second language reading for academic purposes.* Reading, MA: Addison-Wesley.

Dubin, F., & Olshtain, E. (1986). *Course design: Developing programs and materials for language learning.* Cambridge, UK: Cambridge University Press.

Dudley-Evans, T., & St. John, M. J. (1998). *Developments in English for specific purposes: A multidisciplinary approach.* Cambridge, UK: Cambridge University Press.

Duff, P. (1986). Another look at interlanguage talk: Taking task to task. In R. Day (Ed.), *Talking to Learn* (pp. xx–xx). Newbury House.

Dupuy, B., Tse, L., & Cook, T. (1996). Bringing books into the classroom: First steps in turning college-level ESL students into readers. *TESOL Journal, 5*(4), 10–15.

Duszak, A. (Ed.). (1997). *Culture and styles of academic discourse.* Berlin: Mouton.

Edelsky, C. (1982). Writing in a bilingual program: The relation of L1 and L2 texts. *TESOL Quarterly, 16,* 211–228.

Ediger, A. (2001). Teaching children literacy skills in a second language. In M. Celce-Murcia (Ed.), *Teaching English as a second or foreign language* (3rd ed.) (pp. 153–169). Boston: Heinle.

Educational Testing Service. (1996). *Test of written English guide* (4th ed.). Princeton, NJ: Educational Testing Service.

Egbert, J., & Hanson-Smith, E. (Eds.) (1999). *CALL environments: Research, practice, and critical issues.* Alexandria, VA: TESOL.

Eisterhold, J. C. (1990). Reading–writing connections: Toward a description for second language learners. In B. Kroll (Ed.), *Second language writing: Research insights for the classroom* (pp. 88–101). Cambridge, UK: Cambridge University Press.

Ekbatani, G., & Pierson, H. (Eds.). (2000). *Learner-directed assessment in ESL.* Mahwah, NJ: Lawrence Erlbaum Associates.

Elbow, P. (1973). *Writing without teachers.* Oxford: Oxford University Press.

Elbow, P. (1981a). *Embracing contraries: Explorations in learning and teaching.* New York: Oxford University Press.

Elbow, P. (1981b). *Writing with power: Techniques for mastering the writing process.* New York: Oxford University Press.

Elbow, P. (1993). Ranking, evaluating, and liking: Sorting out three forms of judgment. *College English, 55,* 187–206.

Elbow, P. (1999). Individualism and the teaching of writing: Response to Vai Ramanathan and Dwight Atkinson. *Journal of Second Language Writing, 8,* 327–338.

Elbow, P., & Belanoff, P. (1989). *Sharing and responding.* London: Random House.

Elbow, P., & Belanoff, P. (1991). SUNY Stony Brook portfolio-based evaluation program. In P. Belanoff & M. Dickson (Eds.), *Portfolios: Process and products* (pp. 3–16). Portsmouth, NH: Boynton/Cook.

Elbow, P., & Belanoff, P. (1997). Reflections on an explosion: Portfolios in the '90s and beyond. In K. B. Yancey & I Weiser (Eds.), *Situating portfolios: Four perspectives* (pp. 21–33). Logan: Utah State University Press.

Elley, W. (1991). Acquiring literacy in a second language: The effect of book-based programs. *Language Learning, 41,* 375–411.

Elley, W., & Mangubhai, F. (1983). The impact of reading on second language learning. *Reading Research Quarterly, 19*, 53–67.

Ellis, R. (1991). The interaction hypothesis. In E. Sadtono (Ed.), *Language acquisition and the second/foreign language classroom* (pp. 179–211). Singapore RELC.

Ellis, R. (1994). *The study of second language acquisition.* Oxford: Oxford University Press.

Ellis, R. (1998). Teaching and research: Options in grammar teaching. *TESOL Quarterly, 32*, 39–60.

Ellis, R. (2002). Does form-focused instruction affect the acquisition of implicit knowledge? A review of the research. *Studies in Second Language Acquisition, 24*, 223–236.

Ellis, R., Basturkmen, H., & Loewen, S. (2001). Learner uptake in communicative ESL lessons. *Language Learning, 51*, 281–318.

Emig, J. (1971). *The composing processes of twelfth graders.* Urbana, IL: National Council of Teachers of English.

Emig, J. (1983). *The web of meaning.* Upper Montclair, NJ: Boynton/Cook.

Enginarlar, H. (1993). Student response to teacher feedback in EFL writing. *System, 21*, 193–204.

Erdosy, M. U. (2001). The influence of prior experience on the construction of scoring criteria for ESL composition: A case study. In R. M. Manchón (Ed.), *International Journal of English Studies, 1*(2), 175–196.

Eskey, D. E. (1983). Meanwhile, back in the real world. . . . Accuracy and fluency in second language teaching. *TESOL Quarterly, 17*, 315–323.

Eskey, D. E. (1993). Reading and writing as both cognitive process and social behavior. In J. Carson, & I. Leki (Eds.), *Reading in the composition classroom: Second language perspectives* (pp. 221–233). Boston: Heinle.

Faigley, L. (1986). Competing theories of process: A critique and a proposal. *College English, 48*, 527–542.

Faigley, L., & Witte, S. (1981). Analyzing revision. *College Composition and Communication, 32*, 400–414.

Fairclough, N. (1995). *Critical discourse analysis.* London: Longman.

Fairclough, N. (2000). Multiliteracies and language: Orders of discourse and intertextuality. In B. Cope & M. Kalantzis (Eds.), *Multiliteracies: Literacy learning and the design of social futures* (pp. 162–181). London: Routledge.

Fakhri, A. (1994). Text organization and transfer: The case of Arab ESL learners. *International Review of Applied Linguistics, 32*, 78–86.

Fathman, A., & Whalley, E. (1990). Teacher response to student writing: Focus on form versus content. In B. Kroll (Ed.), *Second language writing: Research insights for the classroom* (pp. 178–190). Cambridge: Cambridge University Press.

Feagles, S. (Ed.). (1997). *A guide to educational systems around the world.* New York: NAFSA/Association of International Educators.

Feez, S. (1998). *Text-based syllabus design.* Sydney, Australia: NCELTR Publications, Macquarie University.

Feez, S. (2002). Heritage and innovation in second language education. In A. M. Johns (Ed.), *Genre in the classroom* (pp. 47–68). Mahwah, NJ: Lawrence Erlbaum Associates.

Ferris, D. R. (1993). The design of an automatic analysis program for L2 text research: Necessity and feasibility. *Journal of Second Language Writing, 2*, 119–129.

Ferris, D. R. (1994). Rhetorical strategies in student persuasive writing: Differences between native and non-native English speakers. *Research in the Teaching of English, 28*, 45–65.

Ferris, D. R. (1995a). Can advanced ESL students be taught to correct their most serious and frequent errors? *CATESOL Journal, 8*, 41–62.

Ferris, D. R. (1995b). Student reactions to teacher response in multiple-draft composition classrooms. *TESOL Quarterly, 29*, 33–53.

Ferris, D. R. (1995c). Teaching ESL composition students to become independent self-editors. *TESOL Journal, 4*(4), 18–22.

Ferris, D. R. (1997). The influence of teacher commentary on student revision. *TESOL Quarterly, 31*, 315–339.

Ferris, D. R. (1999a). One size does not fit all: Response and revision issues for immigrant student writers. In L. Harklau, K. Losey, & M. Siegal (Eds.), *Generation 1. 5 meets college composition* (pp. 143–157). Mahwah, NJ: Lawrence Erlbaum Associates.

Ferris, D. R. (2001a). Teaching "writing for proficiency" in summer school: Lessons from a foxhole. In J. Murphy & P. Byrd (Eds.), *Understanding the courses we teach: Local perspectives on English language teaching* (pp. 328–345). Ann Arbor: University of Michigan Press.

Ferris, D. R. (2002a). Introduction. In L. L. Blanton & B. Kroll (Eds.), *ESL composition tales* (pp. 1–15). Ann Arbor: University of Michigan Press.

Ferris, D. R. (2002b). *Treatment of error in second language student writing.* Ann Arbor: University of Michigan Press.

Ferris, D. R. (2003a). Responding to writing. In B. Kroll (Ed.), *Exploring the dynamics of second language writing* (pp. 119–140). Cambridge: Cambridge University Press.

Ferris, D. R. (2003b). *Response to student writing: Implications for second language students.* Mahwah, NJ: Lawrence Erlbaum Associates.

Ferris, D. R. (2004). The "Grammar Correction" Debate in L2 Writing: Where are we, and where do we go from here? (and what do we do in the meantime. . . ?) *Journal of Second Language Writing, 13*, 1–14.

Ferris, D. R., Chaney, S. J., Komura, K., Roberts, B. J., & McKee, S. (2000, March). *Does error feedback help student writers? New evidence on the short- and long-term effects of written error correction.* Paper presented at the 34th Annual TESOL Convention, Vancouver, B.C.

Ferris, D., Kennedy, C., & Senna, M. (2004, April). *Generations 1.5 and 2.0 in college composition.* Paper presented at the 38th Annual TESOL Convention, Long Beach, CA.

Ferris, D. R., Pezone, S., Tade, C. R., & Tinti, S. (1997). Teacher commentary on student writing: Descriptions and implications. *Journal of Second Language Writing, 6*, 155–182.

Ferris, D. R., & Roberts, B. (2001). Error feedback in L2 writing classes: How explicit does it need to be? *Journal of Second Language Writing, 10*, 161–184.

Ferris, D. R., & Tagg, T. (1996). Academic oral communication needs of EAP learners: What subject matter instructors actually require. *TESOL Quarterly, 30*, 31–58.

Findlay, C. A., & Nathan, L. A. (1980). Functional language objectives. *TESOL Quarterly, 14*, 221–231.

Finocchiaro, M., & Brumfit, C. (1983). *The functional–notional approach: From theory to practice.* Oxford: Oxford University Press.

Flahive, D., & Bailey, N. (1993). Exploring reading–writing relationships in adult second language learners. In J. G. Carson & I. Leki (Eds.), *Reading in the composition classroom: Second language perspectives* (pp. 128–140). Boston: Heinle.

Flower, L. (1979). Writer-based prose: A cognitive basis for problems in writing. *College English, 41*, 19–38.

Flower, L. (1985). *Problem-solving strategies for writing* (2nd ed.). San Diego: Harcourt Brace Jovanovich.

Flower, L. (1989). *Problem-solving strategies for writing* (3rd ed.). San Diego: Harcourt Brace Jovanovich.

Flower, L. (1994). *The construction of negotiated meaning: A social cognitive theory of writing*. Carbondale, IL: Southern Illinois University Press.

Flower, L. S., & Hayes, J. R. (1980). The cognition of discovery: Defining a rhetorical problem. *College Composition and Communication, 31*, 21–32.

Flower, L. S., & Hayes, J. R. (1981). A cognitive process theory of writing. *College Composition and Communication, 32*, 365–387.

Flower, L. S., Long, E., & Higgins, L. (2000). *Learning to rival: A literate practice for intercultural inquiry*. Mahwah, NJ: Lawrence Erlbaum Associates.

Flower, L. S., Stein, V., Ackerman, J., Kantz, M., McCormick, K., & Peck, W. (1990). *Reading-to-write: Exploring a cognitive and social process*. New York: Oxford University Press.

Flowerdew, J. (1993). An educational, or process, approach to the teaching of professional genres. *ELT Journal, 47*, 305–316.

Flowerdew, J. (2002). Genre in the classroom: A linguistic approach. In A. M. Johns (Ed.), *Genre in the classroom: Multiple perspectives* (pp. 91–102). Mahwah, NJ: Lawrence Erlbaum Associates.

Forbes, C. (1996). Cowriting, overwriting, and overriding in portfolio land online. *Computers and Composition, 13*(2), 195–205.

Fox, L. (1992). *Focus on editing*. London: Longman.

Freedman, A. (1993). Show and tell? The role of explicit teaching in the learning of new genres. *Research in the Teaching of English, 27*, 222–251.

Freedman, A. (1994). "Do as I say": The relationship between teaching and learning new genres. In A. Freedman & P. Medway (Eds.), *Genre and the new rhetoric* (pp. 191–210). London: Taylor & Francis.

Freedman, A., & Adam, C. (2000). Bridging the gap: University-based writing that is more than simulation. In P. Dias & A. Paré (Eds.), *Transitions: Writing in academic and workplace settings* (pp. 129–144). Cresskill, NJ: Hampton.

Freedman, A., & Medway, P. (Eds.). (1994a). *Genre and the New Rhetoric*. London: Taylor & Francis.

Freedman, A., & Medway, P. (1994b). Locating genre studies: Antecedents and prospects. In A. Freedman & P. Medway (Eds.), *Genre and the New Rhetoric* (pp. 1–20). London: Taylor & Francis.

Freedman, A., & Medway, P. (Eds.). (1994c). *Learning and teaching genre*. Portsmouth, NH: Boynton/Cook.

Freire, P. (1970). *Pedagogy of the oppressed*. New York: Continuum.

Freire, P. (1985). *The politics of education*. South Hadley, MA: Bergin & Garvey.

Freire, P. (1994). *Pedagogy of hope*. New York: Continuum.

Freire, P., & Macedo, D. (1987). *Literacy: Reading the word and the world*. South Hadley, MA: Bergin & Garvey.

Fries, C. (1945). *Teaching and learning English as a second language*. Ann Arbor: University of Michigan Press.

Frodesen, J. (1991). Grammar in writing. In M. Celce-Murcia (Ed.), *Teaching English as a second or foreign language* (2nd ed., pp. 264–276). Boston: Heinle & Heinle.

Frodesen, J. (1995). Negotiating the syllabus: A learning-centered, interactive approach to ESL graduate writing course design. In D. Belcher & G. Braine (Eds.), *Academic writing in a second language: Essays on research and pedagogy* (pp. 331–350). Norwood, NJ: Ablex.

Frodesen, J. (2001). Grammar in writing. In M. Celce-Murcia (Ed.), *Teaching English as a second or foreign language* (3rd ed., pp. 233–248). Boston: Heinle.

Frodesen, J., & Holten, C. (2003). Grammar and the ESL writing class. In B. Kroll (Ed.), *Exploring the dynamics of second language writing* (pp. 141–161). Cambridge: Cambridge University Press.

Fromkin, V., Rodman, R., & Hyams, N. (2003). *An introduction to language* (7th ed.). Boston: Heinle.

Garrison, R. (1974). One-to-one tutorial instruction in freshman composition. *New Directions for Community Colleges, 2,* 55–84.

Gaskill, B. (1996). Articulation agreements between intensive ESL programs and postsecondary institutions. *CATESOL Journal, 9,* 117–127.

Gass, S. M., & Selinker, L. (2001). *Second language acquisition: An introductory course* (2nd ed.). Mahwah, NJ: Lawrence Erlbaum Associates.

Gauntlett, J. (1978). Project WRITE and its effect on the writing of high school students. *Dissertation Abstracts International, 38,* 7189-A.

Gebhard, J. G., & Oprandy, R. (1999). *Language teaching awareness: A guide to exploring beliefs and practices.* New York: Cambridge University Press.

Gee, J. P. (1992). *The social mind: Language, ideology, and social practice.* New York: Bergin & Garvey.

Gee, J. P. (1996). *Social linguistics and literacies: Ideology in Discourses* (2nd ed.). London: Taylor & Francis.

Gee, J. P. (1998). What is literacy? In V. Zamel & R. Spack (Eds.), *Negotiating academic literacies: Teaching and learning across languages and cultures* (pp. 51–59). Mahwah, NJ: Lawrence Erlbaum Associates.

Gee, J. P. (1999). *An introduction to discourse analysis: Theory and method.* London: Routledge.

Geertz, C. (1983). *Local knowledge: Further essays in interpretive anthropology.* New York: Basic Books.

Geisler, C. (1994). *Academic literacy and the nature of expertise.* Hillsdale, NJ: Lawrence Erlbaum Associates.

Glenn, C., Goldthwaite, M. A., & Connors, R. (2003). *St. Martin's guide to teaching writing* (5th ed.). Boston: Bedford/St. Martin's.

Goldman, S. (1997). Learning from text: Reflections on the past and suggestions for the future. *Discourse Processes, 23,* 357–398.

Goldman, S., & Trueba, H. (Eds.). (1987). *Becoming literate in English as a second language.* Norwood, NJ: Ablex.

Goldstein, L. M. (1993). Becoming a member of the "teaching foreign languages" community: Integrating reading and writing through an adjunct/content course. In J. Carson & I. Leki (Eds.), *Reading in the composition classroom: Second language perspectives* (pp. 290–298). Boston: Heinle.

Goldstein, L. M., & Conrad, S. (1990). Student input and the negotiation of meaning in ESL writing conferences. *TESOL Quarterly, 24,* 443–460.

Gottlieb, M. (2000). Portfolio practices in elementary and secondary schools: Toward learner-directed assessment. In G. Ekbatani & H. Pierson (Eds.),

Learner-directed assessment in ESL (pp. 89–104). Mahwah, NJ: Lawrence Erlbaum Associates.

Gottschalk, K., & Hjortshoj, K. (2004). *The elements of teaching writing: A resource for instructors in all disciplines.* Boston: Bedford/St. Martin's.

Grabe, W. (1991). Current developments in second language reading research. *TESOL Quarterly, 25,* 375–406.

Grabe, W. (2001a). Reading–writing relations: Theoretical perspectives and instructional practices. In D. Belcher & A. Hirvela (Eds.), *Linking literacies: Perspectives on L2 reading–writing connections* (pp. 15–47). Ann Arbor: University of Michigan Press.

Grabe, W. (2001b). Notes towards a theory of second language writing. In T. Silva & P. K. Matsuda (Eds.), *On second language writing* (pp. 39–57). Mahwah, NJ: Lawrence Erlbaum Associates.

Grabe, W. (2002). Narrative and expository macro-genres. In A. M. Johns (Ed.), *Genre in the classroom: Multiple perspectives* (pp. 249–267.). Mahwah, NJ: Lawrence Erlbaum Associates.

Grabe, W. (2003). Reading and writing relations: Second language perspectives on research and practice. In B. Kroll (Ed.), *Exploring the dynamics of second language writing* (pp. 242–262). Cambridge: Cambridge University Press.

Grabe, W., & Kaplan, R. (1996). *Theory and practice of writing.* London: Longman.

Grabe, W., & Kaplan, R. (1997). The writing course. In K. Bardovi-Harlig & B. Hartford (Eds.), *Beyond methods: Components of second language teacher education* (pp. 172–197). New York: McGraw-Hill.

Grabe, W., & Stoller, F. (2001). Reading for academic purposes: Guidelines for the ESL/EFL teacher. In M. Celce-Murcia (Ed.), *Teaching English as a second/foreign language* (3rd ed.) (pp. 187–203). Boston: Heinle.

Grabe, W., & Stoller, F. (2002a). *Applied linguistics in action: Researching reading.* New York: Longman.

Grabe, W., & Stoller, F. (2002b). *Teaching and researching reading.* Harlow, England: Pearson Education.

Grady, K. (1997). Critically reading an ESL text. *TESOL Journal, 6* (4), 7–10.

Grant, L., & Ginther, A. (2000). Using computer-tagged linguistic features to describe L2 writing differences. *Journal of Second Language Writing, 9,* 123–145.

Grant, N. (1987). *Making the most of your textbook.* London: Longman.

Graves, K. (Ed.). (1996). *Teachers as course developers.* Cambridge, UK: Cambridge University Press.

Graves, K. (2000). *Designing language courses: A guide for teachers.* Boston: Heinle.

Graves, R. L. (Ed.). (1990). *Rhetoric and composition: A sourcebook for teachers and writers* (3rd ed.). Portsmouth, N: Boynton Cook/Heinemann.

Graves, R. L. (Ed.). (1999). *Writing, teaching, learning: A sourcebook.* Portsmouth, NH: Boynton/Cook.

Gronland, N. E. (1985). *Stating objectives for classroom instruction* (3rd ed). New York: Macmillan.

Grosjean, F. (1982). *Life with two languages.* Cambridge, MA: Harvard University Press.

Guleff, V. (2002). Approaching genre: Prewriting as apprenticeship to communities of practice. In A. M. Johns (Ed.), *Genre in the classroom: Multiple perspectives* (pp. 211–223). Mahwah, NJ: Lawrence Erlbaum Associates.

Gunderson, L. (1991). *ESL literacy instruction: A guidebook to theory and practice.* Englewood Cliffs, NJ: Regents/Prentice-Hall.

Gurevich, N. (1995). Teacher–student writing conferences via e-mail. In M. Warschauer (Ed.), *Virtual connections: Online activities and projects for networking language learners* (pp. 211–215). Honolulu: University of Hawaii, Second Language Teaching and Curriculum Center.

Haas, C. (1989). How the writing medium shapes the writing process: Effects of word processing on planning. *Research in the Teaching of English, 23*, 181–207.

Hadfield, J., & Hadfield, C. (2000). *Simple writing activities.* Oxford, England: Oxford University Press.

Hafernik, J. J., Messerschmitt, D. S., & Vandrick, S. (2002). *Ethical issues for ESL faculty: Social justice in practice.* Mahwah, NJ: Lawrence Erlbaum Associates.

Hafiz, F., & Tudor, I. (1989). Extensive reading and the development of language skills. *ELT Journal, 43*, 1–13.

Hairston, M. (1986). On not being a composition slave. In C. W. Bridges (Ed.), *Training the new teacher of college composition* (pp. 117–124). Urbana, IL: NCTE.

Hakuta, K., & D'Andrea, D. (1992). Some properties of bilingual maintenance and loss in Mexican background high-school students. *Applied Linguistics, 13*, 72–99.

Halliday, M. A. K., & Hasan, R. (Eds.). (1989). *Language, context and text: Aspects of language in a social semiotic perspective.* Oxford, UK: Oxford University Press.

Hammond, J., & Macken-Horarik, M. (1999). Critical literacy: Challenges and questions for ESL classrooms. *TESOL Quarterly, 33*, 528–544.

Hamp-Lyons, L. (Ed.). (1991a). *Assessing second language writing in academic contexts.* Norwood, NJ: Ablex.

Hamp-Lyons, L. (1991b). Basic concepts. In L. Hamp-Lyons (Ed.), *Assessing second language writing in academic contexts* (pp. 5–15). Norwood, NJ: Ablex.

Hamp-Lyons, L. (1991c). Scoring procedures for ESL contexts. In L. Hamp-Lyons (Ed.), *Assessing second language writing in academic contexts* (pp. 241–276). Norwood, NJ: Ablex.

Hamp-Lyons, L. (2003). Writing teachers as assessors of writing. In B. Kroll (Ed.), *Second language writing: Research insights for the classroom* (pp. 162–189). Cambridge, UK: Cambridge University Press.

Hamp-Lyons, L., & Condon, W. (1993). Questioning assumptions about portfolio-based assessment. *College Composition and Comunication, 44*, 176–190.

Hamp-Lyons, L., & Condon, W. (2000). *Assessing the portfolio: Principles for practice, theory, and research.* Cresskill, NJ: Hampton Press.

Hamp-Lyons, L., & Henning, G. (1991). Communicative writing profiles: An investigation of the transferability of a multiple-trait scoring instrument across ESL writing assessment contexts. *Language Learning, 41*, 337–373.

Hamp-Lyons, L., & Kroll, B. (1996). Issues in ESL writing assessment. *College ESL, 6*(1), 52–72.

Hamp-Lyons, L., & Kroll, B. (1997). *TOEFL 2000—Writing: Composition, community, and assessment.* Princeton, NJ: Educational Testing Service.

Hamp-Lyons, L., & Mathias, S. P. (1994). Examining expert judgments of task difficulty on essay tests. *Journal of Second Language Writing, 3*, 49–68.

Hansen, J. G. (2000). Interactional conflicts among audience, purpose, and content knowledge in the acquisition of academic literacy in an EAP course. *Written Communication, 17*, 27–52.

Hasan, R. (1996). Literacy, everyday talk and society. In R. Hasan & G. Williams (Eds.), *Literacy in society* (pp. 394–424). London: Longman.

Harklau, L., Losey, K. M., & Siegel, M. (Eds.). (1999). *Generation 1.5 meets college composition.* Mahwah, NJ: Lawrence Erlbaum Associates.

Harris, M. (1986). *Teaching one-to-one: The writing conference*. Urbana, IL: National Council of Teachers of English.

Hartwell, P. (1985). Grammar, grammars, and the teaching of grammar. *College English, 47*, 105–127.

Haswell, R. H. (1998). Searching for Kiyoko: Bettering mandatory ESL writing placement. *Journal of Second Language Writing, 7*, 133–174.

Hawisher, G. E. (1987). The effects of word processing on the revision strategies of college freshmen. *Research in the Teaching of English, 21*, 145–159.

Hayes, J. R. (1996). A new framework for understanding cognition and affect in writing. In C. M. Levy & S. Ransdell (Eds.), *The science of writing: Theories, methods, individual differences, and applications* (pp. 1–27). Mahwah, NJ: Lawrence Erlbaum Associates.

Hayes, J. R., & Flower, L. (1983). Uncovering cognitive processes in writing: An introduction to protocol analysis. In P. Mosenthal, L. Tamar, & S. A. Walmsley (Eds.), *Research in writing* (pp. 206–220). New York: Longman.

Hayes, J. R., & Nash, J. G. (1996). On the nature of planning in writing. In C. M. Levy & S. Ransdell (Eds.), *The science of writing: Theories, methods, individual differences, and applications* (pp. 121–142). Mahwah, NJ: Lawrence Erlbaum Associates.

Hedgcock, J. (2002). Toward a socioliterate approach to language teacher education. *Modern Language Journal, 86*, 299–317.

Hedgcock, J. (in press). Taking stock of research and pedagogy in L2 writing. In E. Hinkel (Ed.), *Handbook of research in second language teaching and learning*. Mahwah, NJ: Lawrence Erlbaum Associates.

Hedgcock, J., & Atkinson, D. (1993). Differing reading–writing relationships in L1 and L2 literacy development. *TESOL Quarterly, 27*, 329–333.

Hedgcock, J., & Lefkowitz, N. (1992). Collaborative oral/aural revision in foreign language writing instruction. *Journal of Second Language Writing, 4*, 51–70.

Hedgcock, J., & Lefkowitz, N. (1994). Feedback on feedback: Assessing learner receptivity to teacher response in L2 composing. *Journal of Second Language Writing, 3*, 141–163.

Hedgcock, J., & Lefkowitz, N. (1996). Some input on input: Two analyses of student response to expert feedback on L2 writing. *Modern Language Journal, 80*, 287–308.

Hedgcock, J., & Pucci, S. (1993). Whole language applications to ESL in secondary and higher education. *TESOL Journal, 3*(2), 22–26

Heller, M. F. (1999). *Reading–writing connections: From theory to practice* (2nd ed.). Mahwah, NJ: Lawrence Erlbaum Associates.

Hendrickson, J. M. (1980). The treatment of error in written work. *Modern Language Journal, 64*, 216–221.

Henning, G. (1991). Issues in evaluating and maintaining an ESL writing assessment program. In L. Hamp-Lyons (Ed.), *Assessing second language writing in academic contexts* (pp. 279–291). Norwood, NJ: Ablex.

Herman, J. L., Gearhart, M., & Aschbacher, P. R. (1996). Portfolios for classroom assessment: Design and implementation issues. In R. Calfee & P. Perfumo (Eds.), *Writing portfolios in the classroom: Policy and practice, promise, and peril* (pp. 27–59). Mahwah, NJ: Lawrence Erlbaum Associates.

Hillocks, G., Jr. (1986). *Research on written composition: New directions for teaching*. Urbana, IL: National Conference on Research in English.

Hillocks, G., Jr. (1995). *Teaching writing as reflective practice*. New York: Teachers College Press.

Hinds, J. (1983a). Contrastive rhetoric: Japanese and English. *Text, 3*, 183–195.

Hinds, J. (1983b). Linguistics in written discourse in particular languages: Contrastive studies in Japanese and English. In R. B. Kaplan (Ed.), *Annual review of applied linguistics, III* (pp. 78–84). Rowley, MA: Newbury House.

Hinds, J. (1987). Reader vs. writer responsibility: A new typology. In U. Connor & R. B. Kaplan (Eds.), *Writing across languages: Analysis of L2 text* (pp. 141–152). Reading, MA: Addison-Wesley.

Hinkel, E. (2002). *Second language writers' text: Linguistic and rhetorical features.* Mahwah, NJ: Lawrence Erlbaum Associates.

Hirvela, A. (1997). "Disciplinary portfolios" and EAP writing instruction. *English for Specific Purposes, 16*, 83–100.

Hirvela, A. (1999). Collaborative writing instruction and communities of readers and writers. *TESOL Journal, 8*(2), 7–12.

Hirvela, A. (2001). Connecting reading and writing through literature. In D. Belcher & A. Hirvela (Eds.), *Linking literacies: Perspective on L2 reading–writing connections* (pp. 109–134). Ann Arbor: University of Michigan Press.

Hirvela, A., & Belcher, D. (2001). Coming back to voice: The multiple voices and identities of mature multilingual writers. *Journal of Second Language Writing, 10*, 83–106.

Hirvela, A., & Pierson, H. (2000). Portfolios: Vehicles for authentic self-assessment. In G. Ekbatani & H. Pierson (Eds.), *Learner-directed assessment in ESL* (pp. 105–126). Mahwah, NJ: Lawrence Erlbaum Associates.

Holliday, A. (1994). *Appropriate methodology and social context.* Cambridge: Cambridge University Press.

Holmes, V. L., & Moulton, M. R. (1995). A contrarian view of dialogue journals: The case of a reluctant participant. *Journal of Second Language Writing, 4*, 223–251.

Holmes, M. (2000). Marking student work on the computer. *The Internet TESL Journal, 6*(5). Accesssed at http://iteslj.org/

Holyoak, S., & Piper, A. (1997). Talking to second language writers: Using interview data to investigate contrastive rhetoric. *Language Teaching Research, 1*, 122–148.

Horowitz, D. (1986a). The author responds to Liebman-Kleine. *TESOL Quarterly, 20*, 788–790.

Horowitz, D. (1986b). Process, not product: Less than meets the eye. *TESOL Quarterly, 20*, 141–144.

Horowitz, D. (1986c). What professors actually require: Academic tasks for the ESL classroom. *TESOL Quarterly, 20*, 445–462.

Huang, S. (1994). Learning to critique and revise in English-as-a-foreign-language university writing class. *Dissertation Abstracts International, 55*(10), 3120–A.

Hudson, T. (1998). Theoretical perspectives on reading. *Annual Review of Applied Linguistics, 18*, 43–60.

Hughes, W. K. (1996). Combined assessment model for EAP writing workshops: Portfolio decision making, criterion-referenced grading, and contract negotiation. *TESL Canada Journal, 14*, 21–33.

Hughey, J., Wormuth, D., Hartfiel, F., & Jacobs, H. (1983). *Teaching ESL composition: Principles and techniques.* Rowley, MA: Newbury House.

Hulstijn, J. (1991). How is reading in a second language related to reading in a first language? *AILA Review, 8*, 5–14.

Hunter, J. M. (2004). *Myths and misperceptions: How technology undermines our public lives.* Unpublished manuscript, Monterey Institute of International Studies.

Huot, B. (1993). The influence of holistic scoring procedures on reading and rating student essays. In M. Williamson & B. Huot (Eds.), *Validating holistic scoring for writing assessment* (pp. 206–236). Cresskill, NJ: Hampton Press.

Hutchinson, T., & Waters, A. (1987). *English for specific purposes.* Cambridge, UK: Cambridge University Press.

Hyland, F., & Hyland, K. (2001). Sugaring the pill: Praise and criticism in written feedback. *Journal of Second Language Writing, 10*(3), 185–212.

Hyland, K. (2000). *Disciplinary discourses: Social interactions in academic writing.* London: Longman.

Hyland, K. (2002). Genre: Language, context, and literacy. *Annual Review of Applied Linguistics, 22,* 113–135.

Hyland, K. (2003). Genre-based pedagogies: A social response to process. *Journal of Second Language Writing, 12,* 17–29.

Hyon, S. (2002). Genre and ESL reading: A classroom study. In A. M. Johns (Ed.), *Genre in the classroom: Multiple perspectives* (pp. 121–141). Mahwah, NJ: Lawrence Erlbaum Associates.

Irwin, J., & Doyle, M. (Eds.). (1992). *Reading/writing connections.* Newark, DE: International Reading Association.

Ivanic, R. (1998). *Writing and identity: The discoursal construction of identity in academic writing.* Amsterdam: John Benjamins.

Jabbour, G. (2001). Lexis and grammar in second language reading and writing. In D. Belcher & A. Hirvela (Eds.), *Linking literacies: Perspectives on L2 reading–writing connections* (pp. 291–308). Ann Arbor: University of Michigan Press.

Jacobs, G. M., Curtis, A., Braine, G., & Huang, S. (1998). Feedback on student writing: Taking the middle path. *Journal of Second Language Writing, 7,* 307–318.

Jacobs, H. L., Zingraf, S., Wormuth, D., Hartfiel, V., & Hughey, J. (1981). *Testing ESL composition: A practical approach.* Rowley, MA: Newbury House.

James, C. (1998). *Errors in language learning and use: Exploring error analysis.* London: Longman.

Janopoulos, M. (1986). The relationship of pleasure reading and second language writing proficiency. *TESOL Quarterly, 20,* 763–768.

Jarvis, S. (2002). Short texts, best-fitting curves, and new measures of lexical diversity. *Language Testing, 19,* 57–84.

Jarvis, S., Grant, L., Bikowskia, D., and Ferris, D. (2003). Exploring multiple profiles of highly rated learner compositions. *Journal of Second Language Writing, 12*(4), 377–403.

Jensen, L. (2001). Planning lessons. In M. Celce-Murcia (Ed.), *Teaching English as a second or foreign language* (3rd ed.), (pp. 403–414). Boston: Heinle.

Johns, A. M. (1988). The discourse communities dilemma: Identifying transferable skills for the academic milieu. *English for Specific Purposes, 7,* 55–60.

Johns, A. M. (1990). L1 composition theories: Implications for developing theories of L2 composition. In B. Kroll (Ed.), *Second language writing: Research insights for the classroom* (pp. 24–36). Cambridge, UK: Cambridge University Press.

Johns, A. M. (1993). Reading and writing tasks in English for academic purposes classes: Products, processes, and resources. In J. Carson & I. Leki (Eds.), *Reading in the composition classroom: Second language perspectives* (pp. 274–289). Boston: Heinle.

Johns, A. M. (1995a). Genre and pedagogical purposes. *Journal of Second Language Writing, 4,* 181–190.

Johns, A. M. (1995b). The reading/writing relationship: Implications for ESL teaching. In P. Hashemipour, R., Maldonado, & M. van Naerssen (Eds.), *Studies in language learning and Spanish linguistics in honor of Tracy D. Terrell* (pp. 185–200). New York: McGraw-Hill.

Johns, A. M. (1995c). Teaching classroom and authentic genres: Initiating students into academic cultures and discourses. In D. Belcher & G. Braine (Eds.), *Academic writing in a second language: Essays on research and pedagogy* (pp. 277–291). Norwood, NJ: Ablex.

Johns, A. M. (1997). *Text, role, and context: Developing academic literacies.* New York: Cambridge University Press.

Johns, A. M. (2002a). Destabilizing and enriching novice students' genre theories. In A. M. Johns (Ed.), *Genre in the classroom: Multiple perspectives* (pp. 237–246). Mahwah, NJ: Lawrence Erlbaum Associates.

Johns, A. M. (Ed.). (2002b). *Genre in the classroom: Multiple perspectives.* Mahwah, NJ: Lawrence Erlbaum Associates.

Johns, A. M. (2003). Genre and ESL/EFL composition instruction. In B. Kroll (Ed.), *Exploring the dynamics of second language writing* (pp. 195–217). Cambridge: Cambridge University Press.

Johns, A. M., & Price-Machado, D. (2001). English for specific purposes: Tailoring courses to student needs—and to the outside world. In M. Celce-Murcia (Ed.), *Teaching English as a second or foreign language* (3rd ed.), (pp. 43–54). Boston: Heinle.

Johnson, K. E. (1996). The role of theory in L2 teacher education. *TESOL Quarterly, 30,* 765–771.

Jones, C., & Fortescue, S. (1987). *Using computers in the classroom.* London: Longman.

Jones, C., Turner, J., & Street, B. (Eds.). (1999). *Students' writing in the university: Cultural and epistemological issues.* Amsterdam: John Benjamins.

Jones, S. (1985). Problems with monitor use in second language composing. In M. Rose (Ed.), *Studies in writer's block and other composing process problems* (pp. 96–118). New York: Guilford.

Jones, S., & Tetroe, J. (1987). Composing in a second language. In A. Matsuhashi (Ed.), *Writing in real time: Modeling production processes* (pp. 34–57). Norwood, NJ: Ablex.

Jordan, R. R. (1997). *English for academic purposes: A guide and resource book for teachers.* Cambridge, UK: Cambridge University Press.

Joseph, P. B., Bravmann, S. L., Windschitl, M. A., Mikel, E. R., & Green, N. S. (2000). *Cultures of curriculum.* Mahwah, NJ: Lawrence Erlbaum Associates.

Just, M., & Carpenter, P. (1987). *The psychology of reading and language comprehension.* Boston: Allyn & Bacon.

Kachru, Y. (1995). Contrastive rhetoric in world Englishes. *English Today, 41,* 21–21.

Kaplan, R. B. (1966). Cultural thought patterns in intercultural communication. *Language Learning, 16,* 1–20.

Kaplan, R. B. (1987). Cultural thought patterns revisited. In U. Connor & R. B. Kaplan (Eds.), *Writing across languages: Analysis of L2 text* (pp. 9–27). Reading, MA: Addison-Wesley.

Kaplan, R. B. (1988). Contrastive rhetoric and second language learning. Notes toward a theory of contrastive rhetoric. In A. C. Purves (Ed.), *Writing across languages and cultures: Issues in contrastive rhetoric* (pp. 275–304). Newbury Park, CA: Sage.

Kaplan, R. B. (2001). Foreword. In C. G. Panetta (Ed.), *Contrastive rhetoric revisited and redefined* (vii–xx). Mahwah, NJ: Lawrence Erlbaum Associates.

Kasper, L. F. (Ed.). (2000). *Content-based college instruction.* Mahwah, NJ: Lawrence Erlbaum Associates.

Kellogg, R. T. (1993). Observations on the psychology of thinking and writing. *Composition Studies, 21,* 3–41.

Kent, T. (Ed.). (1999). *Postprocess theory: Beyond the writing-process paradigm.* Carbondale, IL: Southern Illinois University Press.

Kepner, C. G. (1991). An experiment in the relationship of types of written feedback to the development of second-language writing skills. *Modern Language Journal, 75,* 305–313.

Kirkpatrick, A. (1997). Using contrastive rhetoric to teach writing: Seven principles. *Australian Review of Applied Linguistics, 14,* 89–102.

Kirsch, G., & Ritchie, J. S. (1995). Beyond the personal: Theorizing a politics of location in composition research. *College Composition and Communication, 46,* 7–30.

Knoblauch, C. H., & Brannon, L. (1981). Teacher commentary on student writing: The state of the art. *Freshman English News, 10* (Fall, 1981), 1–4.

Knoblauch, C. H., & Brannon, L. (1984). *Rhetorical traditions and the teaching of writing.* Upper Montclair, NJ: Boynton/Cook.

Kobayashi, H., & Rinnert, C. (1996). Factors affecting composition evaluation in an EFL context: Cultural rhetorical pattern and readers' background. *Language Learning, 46,* 397–437.

Koffolt, K., & Holt, S. L. (1997). Using the "writing process" with non-native users of English. In D. L. Sigsbee, B. W. Speck, & B. Maylath (Eds.), *Approaches to teaching non-native English speakers across the curriculum* (pp. 53–60). San Francisco: Jossey-Bass.

Komura, K. (1999). *Student response to error correction in ESL classrooms.* MA thesis. Sacramento: California State University.

Kramsch, C. (1993). *Content and culture in language teaching.* Oxford, UK: Oxford University Press.

Krapels, A. R. (1990). An overview of second language writing process research. In B. Kroll (Ed.), *Second language writing: Research insights for the classroom* (pp. 37–56). Cambridge, UK: Cambridge University Press.

Krashen, S. D. (1984). *Writing: Research, theory, and application.* Oxford, UK: Pergamon.

Krashen, S. D. (1985a). *The input hypothesis: Issues and implications.* New York: Longman.

Krashen, S. D. (1985b). *Inquiries and insights: Second language teaching, immersion and bilingual education, literacy.* Englewood Cliffs, NJ: Alemany/Prentice Hall Regents.

Krashen, S. D. (1988). Do we learn to read by reading? The relationship between free reading and reading ability. In D. Tannen (Ed.), *Linguistics in context: Connecting observation and understanding* (pp. 269–298). Norwood, NJ: Ablex.

Krashen, S. D. (1989). We acquire vocabulary and spelling by reading: Additional evidence for the input hypothesis. *Modern Language Journal, 73,* 440–464.

Krashen, S. D. (1993). *The power of reading.* Englewood, CO: Libraries Unlimited.

Krashen, S. D. (1994). *The pleasure hypothesis.* Paper presented at the Georgetown Round Table on Language and Linguistics, Washington, DC.

Kress, G. (1993). Genre as social process. In B. Cope & M. Kalantzis (Eds.), *The powers of literacy: A genre approach to teaching writing* (pp. 22–37). Pittsburgh: University of Pittsburgh Press.

Kroll, B. (1993). Teaching writing IS teaching reading: Training the new teacher of ESL composition. In J. G. Carson, & I. Leki (Eds.), *Reading in the composition classroom: Second language perspectives* (pp. 61–81). Boston: Heinle.

Kroll, B. (1998). Assessing writing abilities. *Annual Review of Applied Linguistics, 18*, 219–240.

Kroll, B. (2001). Considerations for teaching an ESL/EFL writing course. In M. Celce-Murcia (Ed.), *Teaching English as a second or foreign language* (3rd ed., pp. 219–232). Boston: Heinle.

Kroll, B. (2003b). Introduction: Teaching the next generation of second language writers. In B. Kroll (Ed.), *Exploring the dynamics of second language writing* (pp. 1–10). Cambridge, England: Cambridge University Press.

Kroll, B., & Reid, J. (1994). Guidelines for designing writing prompts: Clarifications, caveats, and cautions. *Journal of Second Language Writing, 3*, 231–255.

Kubota, R. (1997). A reevaluation of the uniqueness of Japanese written discourse. *Written Communication, 14*, 460–480.

Kubota, R. (1999). Japanese culture constructed by discourses: Implications for Applied Linguistics research and ELT. *TESOL Quarterly, 33*, 9–35.

Kumaravadivelu, B. (2003). *Beyond methods: Macrostrategies for language teaching.* New Haven, CT: Yale University Press.

Kunnan, A. (Ed.). (2000). *Fairness and validation in language assessment.* Cambridge, UK: Cambridge University Press.

Lai, F.-K. (1993). The effect of a summer reading course on reading and writing skills. *System, 21*, 87–100.

Lalande, J. F. II (1982). Reducing composition errors: An experiment. *Modern Language Journal, 66*, 140–149.

Lally, C. G. (2000a). First language influences in second language composition: The effect of prewriting. *Foreign Language Annals, 33*, 428–432.

Lally, C. G. (2000b). Writing across English and French: An examination of strategy use. *The French Review, 73*, 525–538.

Lane, J., & Lange, E. (1993, 1999). *Writing clearly: An editing guide.* Boston: Heinle.

Larimer, R., & Schleicher, L. (Eds.). (1999). *New ways in using authentic materials in the classroom.* Alexandria, VA: TESOL.

Lave, J., & Wenger, E. (1991). *Situated learning: Legitimate peripheral participation.* Cambridge: Cambridge University Press.

Lazar, G. (1993). *Literature and language teaching: A guide for teachers and trainers.* Cambridge, UK: Cambridge University Press.

Lee, J. F., & VanPatten, B. (2003). *Making communicative language teaching happen* (2nd ed.). Boston: McGraw-Hill.

Leeds, B. (Ed.). (1996). *Writing in a second language: Insights from first and second language teaching and research.* New York: Longman.

Leki, I. (1990a). Coaching from the margins: Issues in written response. In B. Kroll (Ed.), *Second language writing: Research insights for the classroom* (pp. 57–68). Cambridge: Cambridge University Press.

Leki, I. (1990b). Potential problems with peer responding in ESL writing classes. *CATESOL Journal, 3*, 5–19.

Leki, I. (1991a). The preferences of ESL students for error correction in college-level writing classes. *Foreign Language Annals, 24*, 203–218.

Leki, I. (1991b). Twenty-five years of contrastive rhetoric: Text analysis and writing pedagogies. *TESOL Quarterly, 25,* 123–143.

Leki, I. (1991c). Twenty-five years of contrastive rhetoric: Text analysis and writing pedagogies. *TESOL Quarterly, 25,* 123–143.

Leki, I. (1992). *Understanding ESL writers: A guide for teachers.* Portsmouth, NH: Boynton/Cook.

Leki, I. (1995). Coping strategies of ESL students in writing tasks across the curriculum. *TESOL Quarterly, 29,* 235–260.

Leki, I. (1997). Cross-talk: ESL issues and contrastive rhetoric. In C. Severino, J. C. Guerra, & J. E. Butler (Eds.), *Writing in multicultural settings* (pp. 234–244). New York: Modern Language Association.

Leki, I. (2000). Writing, literacy, and applied linguistics. *Annual Review of Applied Linguistics, 20,* 99–115.

Leki, I. (2001). Material, educational, and ideological challenges of teaching EFL writing at the turn of the century. In R. M. Manchón (Ed.), *International Journal of English Studies, 1*(2), 197–209.

Leki, I. (2003). A challenge to second language writing professionals: Is writing overrated? In B. Kroll (Ed.), *Exploring the dynamics of second language writing* (pp. 315–331). Cambridge, England: Cambridge University Press.

Leki, I., & Carson, J. (1994). Students' perceptions of EAP writing instruction and writing needs across the disciplines. *TESOL Quarterly, 28,* 81–101.

Lewin, K. (1951). *Field theory in social science.* New York: Harper Torchbooks.

Lewis, B., & Lewis, R. (1987). Do style checkers work work? *PC World, 5,* 247–252.

Lewis, J. (2001). *Academic literacy: Readings and strategies* (2nd ed.). Boston: Houghton Mifflin.

Li, J., & Cumming, A. (2001). Word processing and second language writing: A longitudinal case study. *International Journal of English Studies, 1*(2), 127–152.

Lightbown, P. (1998). The importance of timing in focus on form. In C. Doughty & J. Williams (Eds.), *Focus on form in classroom SLA* (pp. 177–196). Cambridge, UK: Cambridge University Press.

Lightbown, P., & Spada, N. (1999). *How languages are learned* (2nd ed.). Oxford: Oxford University Press.

Lippman, J. N. (2003). Assessing writing. In I. Clark (Ed.), *Concepts in composition: Theory and practice in the teaching of writing* (pp. 199–220). Mahwah, NJ: Lawrence Erlbaum Associates.

Littlejohn, A. (1998). The analysis of language teaching materials: Inside the Trojan horse. In B. Tomlinson (Ed.), *Materials development in language teaching* (pp. 190–216). Cambridge, UK: Cambridge University Press.

Liu, J., & Hansen, J. G. (2002). *Peer response in second language writing classrooms.* Ann Arbor: University of Michigan Press.

Lockhart, C., & Ng, P. (1995a). Analyzing talk in ESL peer response groups: Stances, functions, and content, *Language Learning, 45,* 605–655.

Lockhart, C., & Ng, P. (1995b). Student stances during peer response in writing. In M. L. Tickoo (Ed.), *Reading and writing: Theory into practice* (pp. 118–132). Singapore: SEAMEO Regional Language Centre/RELC. London: Longman.

Long, M. H., & Porter, P. A. (1985). Group work, interlanguage talk, and second language acquisition. *TESOL Quarterly, 19,* 207–227.

Lumley, T., & McNamara, T. (1995). Rater characteristics and rater bias: Implications for training. *Language Testing, 12,* 54–71.

Lyster, R., & Ranta, L. (1997). Corrective feedback and learner uptake: Negotiation of form in communicative classrooms. *Studies in Second Language Acquisition, 19*, 37–66.

Ma, G., & Wen, Q. (1999). The relationship of second-language learners' linguistic variables to second-language writing ability. *Foreign Language Teaching and Research, 4*, 34–39.

Mabry, L. (1999). *Portfolios plus a critical guide to alternative assessment.* Thousand Oaks, CA: Corwin.

MacGowan-Gilhooly, A. (1991). Fluency first: Reversing the traditional ESL sequence. *Journal of Basic Writing, 10*, 21–34.

Macrorie, K. (1984). *Writing to be read* (rev. 3rd ed.). Portsmouth, NH: Boynton/ Cook Heinemann.

Mager, R. F. (1975). *Preparing instructional objectives.* Belmont, CA: Fearon-Pitman.

Manchón, R. M. (2001). Trends in the conceptualizations of second language composing strategies: A critical analysis. In R. M. Manchón (Ed.), *International Journal of English Studies, 1*(2), 47–70.

Manchón-Ruiz, R. (1997). Learners' strategies in L2 composing. *Communication and Cognition, 30*, 91–114.

Mangelsdorf, K. (1989). Parellels between speaking and writing in second language acquisition. In D. M. Johnson & D. H. Roen (Eds.), *Richness in writing: Empowering ESL students* (pp. 134–145). New York: Longman.

Mangelsdorf, K. (1992). Peer reviews in the ESL composition classroom: What do the students think? *ELT Journal, 46*, 274–284.

Mangelsdorf, K., & Schlumberger, A. L. (1992). ESL student response stances in a peer-review task. *Journal of Second Language Writing, 1*, 235–254.

Mannes, S., & St. George, M. (1996). Effects of prior knowledge on text comprehension: A simple modeling approach. In B. K. Britton & A. C. Graesser (Eds.), *Models of understanding text* (pp. 115–139). Mahwah, NJ: Lawrence Erlbaum Associates.

Markee, N. (1997). *Managing curricular innovation.* Cambridge, UK: Cambridge University Press.

Martin, J. R. (2002). A universe of meaning: How many practices? In A. M. Johns (Ed.), *Genre in the classroom: Multiple perspectives* (pp. 269–283). Mahwah, NJ: Lawrence Erlbaum Associates.

Masuhara, H. (1998). What do teachers really want from coursebooks? In B. Tomlinson (Ed.), *Materials development in language teaching* (pp. 239–260). Cambridge, UK: Cambridge University Press.

Matsuda, P. K. (1998). Situating ESL writing in a cross-disciplinary context. *Written Communication, 15*, 99–121.

Matsuda, P. K. (1999). Composition studies and ESL writing: A disciplinary division of labor. *College Composition and Communication, 50*, 699–721.

Matsuda, P. K. (2003a). Process and postprocess: A discursive history. *Journal of Second Language Writing, 12*, 65–83.

Matsuda, P. K. (2003b). Second language writing in the twentieth century: A situated historical perspective. In B. Kroll (Ed.), *Exploring the dynamics of second language writing* (pp. 15–34). Cambridge: Cambridge University Press.

Matsuda, P. K., & Silva, T. (1999). Cross-cultural composition: Mediated integration of U.S. and international students. *Composition Studies, 27*, 15–30.

Mavor, S., & Trayner, B. (2001). Aligning genre and practice with learning in higher education: An interdisciplinary perspective for course design and teaching. *English for Specific Purposes, 20*, 345–366.

Mayers, T. (1996). From page to screen (and back): Portfolios, Daedalus, and the "transitional classroom." *Computers and Composition, 13*, 147–154.

McAllister, C., & Louth, R. (1988). The effect of word processing on the quality of basic writers' revisions. *Research in the Teaching of English, 22*, 417–427.

McKay, S. L. (1993). *Agendas for second language literacy.* Cambridge, UK: Cambridge University Press.

McKay, S. L. (1994). Developing ESL writing materials. *System, 22*, 195–203.

McKay, S. L. (2001). Literature as content for ESL/EFL. In M. Celce-Murcia (Ed.), *Teaching English as a second or foreign language* (3rd ed.) (pp. 319–332). Boston: Heinle.

McLaughlin, B. (1987). Reading in a second language: Studies with adult and child learners. In S. Goldman, & H. Trueba (Eds.), *Becoming literate in English as a second language* (pp. 57–70). Norwood, NJ: Ablex.

McNamara, T. (1996). *Measuring second language performance.* London: Longman.

McNamara, T. (2000). *Language testing.* Oxford, UK: Oxford University Press.

McQuillan, J. (1994). Reading versus grammar: What students think is pleasurable for language acquisition. *Applied Language Learning, 5*, 95–100.

Mendonça, C. O., & Johnson, K. E. (1994). Peer review negotiations: Revision activities in ESL writing instruction. *TESOL Quarterly, 28*, 745–769.

Milanovic, M., Saville, N., & Shuhong, S. (1996). A study of the decision-making behavior of composition markers. In M. Milanovic & N. Saville (Eds.), *Studies in language testing 3: Performance testing, cognition, and assessment* (pp. 92–111). Cambridge, UK: Cambridge University Press.

Miller, C. R. (1994a). Genre as social action. In A. Freedman & P. Medway (Eds.). *Genre and the new rhetoric* (pp. 23–42). London: Taylor & Francis.

Miller, C. R. (1994b). Rhetorical community: The cultural basis of genre. In A. Freedman & P. Medway (Eds.). *Genre and the new rhetoric* (pp. 67–78). London: Taylor & Francis.

Mitchell, R., & Myles, F. (1998). *Second language learning theories.* London: Arnold.

Mittan, R. (1989). The peer review process: Harnessing students' communicative power. In D. M. Johnson & D. H. Roen (Eds.), *Richness in writing: Empowering ESL students* (pp. 207–219). New York: Longman.

Mohan, B. (1986). *Language and content.* Reading, MA: Addison-Wesley.

Moore, L. (1986). Teaching students how to evaluate writing. *TESOL Newsletter, 20*(5), 23–24.

Moran, P. R. (2001). *Teaching culture: Perspectives in practice.* Boston: Heinle.

Moss, P. A., Beck, J. S., Ebbs, C., Matson, B., Muchmore, J., Steele, D., et al. (1992). *Educational Measurement: Issues and Practice, Fall*, 12–21.

Moxley, J. (1989). Responding to student writing: Goals, methods, alternatives. *Freshman English News, 17* (Spring, 1989), 3–4, 9–10.

Murphy, S. (1999). Assessing portfolios. In C. R. Cooper & L. Odell (Eds.), *Evaluating writing: The role of teachers' knowledge about text, learning, and culture* (pp. 114–135). Urbana, IL: National Council of Teachers of English.

Murphy, S., & Smith, M. A. (1999). Creating a climate for portfolios. In C. R. Cooper & L. Odell (Eds.), *Evaluating writing: The role of teachers' knowledge about text, learning, and culture* (pp. 325–343). Urbana, IL: National Council of Teachers of English.

Murray, D. E. (1992). Collaborative writing as a literacy event: Implications for ESL instruction. In D. Nunan (Ed.), *Collaborative language learning and teaching* (pp. 100–117). Cambridge, UK: Cambridge University Press.

Murray, D. E. (1996). Is remediation an articulation issue? *CATESOL Journal, 9,* 175–182.

Murray, D. M. (1978). Write before writing. *College Composition and Communication, 29,* 375–382.

Murray, D. M. (1985). *A writer teaches writing* (2nd ed.). Boston: Houghton Mifflin.

Murray, D. M. (1986). *Colleague in the classroom.* New York: Houghton Mifflin.

Murray, D. M. (1987). *Write to learn.* New York: Holt, Rinehart, & Winston.

Mustafa, Z. (1995). The effect of genre awareness on linguistic transfer. *English for Specific Purposes, 14,* 247–256.

Myers, G. (1990). *Writing biology: Texts in the social construction of scientific knowledge.* Madison: University of Wisconsin Press.

Nelson, G., & Burns, J. (2000). Managing information for writing university exams in American history. In M. Pally (Ed.), *Sustained content teaching in academic ESL/EFL* (pp. 132–157). Boston: Houghton Mifflin.

Nelson, G. L. (1997). How cultural differences affect written and oral communication: The case of peer response groups. In D. L. Sigsbee, B. W. Speck, & B. Maylath (Eds.), *Approaches to teaching non-native English speakers across the curriculum* (pp. 77–84). San Francisco: Jossey-Bass.

Nelson, G. L., & Carson, J. G. (1998). ESL students' perceptions of effectiveness in peer response groups. *Journal of Second Language Writing, 7,* 113–132.

Nelson, G. L., & Murphy, J. M. (1992). An L2 writing group: Task and social dimensions. *Journal of Second Language Writing, 1,* 171–193.

Nelson, G. L., & Murphy, J. M. (1992/1993). Writing groups and the less proficient ESL student. *TESOL Journal, 2*(2), 23–26.

Nelson, G. L., & Murphy, J. M. (1993). Peer response groups: Do L2 writers use peer comments in revising their drafts? *TESOL Quarterly, 27,* 135–142.

Nelson, N., & Calfee, R. (Eds.). (1998). *The reading–writing connection.* Chicago: National Society for the Study of Education.

Nelson, R. (1987, August). Let's hear it for CAW. *Personal Computing, August,* 49–52.

Neu, J., & Scarcella, R. (1991). Word processing in the ESL classroom: A survey of student attitudes. In P. Dunkel (Ed.), *Computer-assisted language learning and testing: Research issues and practice* (pp. 169–187). Rowley, MA: Newbury House.

New, E. (1999). Computer-aided writing in French as a foreign language: A qualitative and quantitative look at the process of revision. *Modern Language Journal, 83,* 80–97.

Newell, G., Garriga, M. C., & Peterson, S. S. (2001). Learning to assume the role of author: A study of reading-to-write one's own ideas in an undergraduate ESL composition course. In D. Belcher & A. Hirvela (Eds.), *Linking literacies: Perspectives on L2 reading–writing connections* (pp. 164–185). Ann Arbor: University of Michigan Press.

Newkirk, T. (1984). Direction and misdirection in peer response. *College Composition and Communication, 35,* 301–311.

Newkirk, T. (1995). The writing conference as performance. *Research in the Teaching of English, 29,* 193–215.

Nieto, S. (2002). *Language, culture, and teaching: Critical perspectives for a new century.* Mahwah, NJ: Lawrence Erlbaum Associates.

Norton, B. (1997). Language, identity, and the ownership of English. *TESOL Quarterly, 31,* 409–429.

Nunan, D. (1989). *Designing tasks for the communicative classroom.* Cambridge, UK: Cambridge University Press.

Nunan, D. (1991a). *Language teaching methodology.* London: Prentice-Hall.

Nunan, D. (1991b). *The learner-centered curriculum.* Cambridge, UK: Cambridge University Press.

Nunan, D. (1991c). *Syllabus design.* Oxford: Oxford University Press.

Nunan, D. (2001). Syllabus design. In M. Celce-Murcia (Ed.), *Teaching English as a second or foreign language* (3rd ed., pp. 55–65). Boston: Heinle.

Olsen, S. (1999). Errors and compensatory strategies: A study of grammar and vocabulary in texts written by Norwegian learners of English. *System, 27,* 191–205.

Olshtain, E. (2001). Functional tasks for mastering the mechanics of writing and going just beyond. In M. Celce-Murcia (Ed.), *Teaching English as a second or foreign language* (3rd ed., pp. 207–217). Boston: Heinle.

Olson, M., & DiStephano, P. (1980). Describing and testing the effectiveness of a contemporary model for in-service education in teaching composition. *English Education, 12,* 69–76.

Omaggio Hadley, A. (2001). *Teaching language in context* (3rd ed.). Boston: Heinle.

Orr, T. (Ed.). (2002). *English for specific purposes.* Alexandria, VA: TESOL.

Oxford, R. L. (1990). *Language learning strategies: What every teacher should know.* New York: Newbury House.

Oxford, R. L., & Ehrman, M. (1993). Second language research on individual differences. *Annual Review of Applied Linguistics, 13,* 188–205.

Pally, M. (Ed.). (2000). *Sustained content teaching in academic ESL/EFL.* Boston: Houghton Mifflin.

Paltridge, B. (2001). *Genre and the language learning classroom.* Ann Arbor: University of Michigan Press.

Paltridge, B. (2002). Genre, text type, and the English for Academic Purposes (EAP) classroom. In A. M. Johns (Ed.), *Genre in the classroom: Multiple perspectives* (pp. 73–90). Mahwah, NJ: Lawrence Erlbaum Associates.

Panetta, C. G. (2001). *Contrastive rhetoric revisited and redefined.* Mahwah, NJ: Lawrence Erlbaum Associates.

Pang, T. T. T. (2002). Textual analysis and contextual awareness building: A comparison of two approaches to teaching genre. In A. M. Johns (Ed.), *Genre in the classroom: Multiple perspectives* (pp. 145–161). Mahwah, NJ: Lawrence Erlbaum Associates.

Parry, K. (1996). Culture, literacy, and L2 reading. *TESOL Quarterly, 30,* 665–692.

Patthey-Chávez, G. G., & Ferris, D. R. (1997). Writing conferences and the weaving of multivoiced texts in college composition. *Research in the Teaching of English, 31,* 51–90.

Paulus, T. (1999). The effect of peer and teacher feedback on student writing. *Journal of Second Language Writing, 8,* 265–289.

Pecorari, D. (2001). Plagiarism and international students: How the English-speaking university responds. In D. Belcher & A. Hirvela (Eds.), *Linking literacies: Perspectives on L2 reading–writing connections* (pp. 229–245). Ann Arbor: University of Michigan Press.

Pennington, M. C. (1990). An evaluation of word processing for ESL writers. *University of Hawaii Working Papers in ESL, 9*(1), 77–113.

Pennington, M. C. (1991). Positive and negative potentials of word processing for ESL writers. *System, 19,* 267–275.

Pennington, M. C., and Brock, M. N. (1992). Process and product approaches to computer-assisted composition. In M. C. Pennington and V. Stevens (Eds.), *Computers in applied linguistics: An international perspective* (pp. 79–109). Clevedon, UK: Multilingual Matters.

Pennington, M. C. (1993a). A critical examination of word processing effects in relation to L2 writers. *Journal of Second Language Writing, 2*, 227–255.

Pennington, M. C. (1993b). Exploring the potential of word processing for nonnative writers. *Computers and the Humanities, 27*, 149–163.

Pennington, M. C. (2003). The impact of the computer in second language writing. In B. Kroll (Ed.), *Exploring the dynamics of second language writing* (pp. 287–310). Cambridge: Cambridge University Press.

Pennington, M. C., & Brock, M. N. (1990). Process and product approaches to computer-assisted composition. In M. C. Pennington & V. Stevens (Eds.), *Computers in applied linguistics* (pp. 79–109). Clevedon: Multilingual Matters.

Pennycook, A. (1996). TESOL and critical literacies: Modern, post, or neo? *TESOL Quarterly, 30*, 163–171.

Pennycook, A. (2001). *Critical applied linguistics: A "critical" introduction.* Mahwah, NJ: Lawrence Erlbaum Associates.

Peregoy, S. F., & Boyle, O. F. (1997). *Reading, writing, and learning in ESL: A resource book for K–12 teachers* (2nd ed.). New York: Longman.

Pérez, B. (Ed.). (1998). *Sociocultural contexts of language and literacy.* Mahwah, NJ: Lawrence Erlbaum Associates.

Perfetti, C., Rouet, J.-F., & Britt, M. (1999). Toward a theory of documents representation. In H. van Oostendorp & S. Goldman (Eds.), *The construction of mental representations during reading* (pp. 99–122). Mahwah, NJ: Lawrence Erlbaum Associates.

Perl, S. (1979). The composing process of unskilled college writers. *Research in the Teaching of English, 13*, 317–339.

Peterson, R. (1995). *The writing teacher's companion: Planning, teaching, and evaluating in the composition classroom.* Boston: Houghton Mifflin.

Peyton, J. K., & Reed, L. (1990). *Dialogue journal writing with nonnative English speakers: A handbook for teachers.* Alexandria, VA: TESOL.

Phinney, M. (1989). Computers, composition, and second language teaching. In M. C. Pennington (Ed.), *Teaching languages with computers: The state of the art* (pp. 81–96). La Jolla, CA: Athelstan.

Phinney, M. (1991). Computer-assisted writing and apprehension in ESL students. In P. Dunkel (Ed.), *Computer-assisted language learning and testing: Research issues and practice* (pp. 189–204). Rowley, MA: Newbury House.

Phinney, M., & Khouri, S. (1993). Computers, revision, and ESL writing: The role of experience. *Journal of Second Language Writing, 2*, 257–277.

Phinney, M., & Mathis, C. (1990). ESL student responses to writing with computers. *TESOL Newsletter, 24*(2), 30–31.

Pica, T., Young, R., & Doughty, C. (1987). The impact of interaction on comprehension. *TESOL Quarterly, 21*, 737–758.

Piper, A. (1987). Helping learners to write: A role for the word processor. *ELT Journal, 41*, 119–125.

Polio, C. (1997). Measures of linguistic accuracy in second language writing research. *Language Learning, 47*, 101–143.

Polio, C. (2003). Research on second language writing: An overview of what we investigate and how. In B. Kroll (Ed.), *Exploring the dynamics of second language writing* (pp. 35–65). Cambridge: Cambridge University Press.

Polio, C., Fleck, C. & Leder, N. (1998). "If only I had more time": ESL learners' changes in linguistic accuracy on essay revisions. *Journal of Second Language Writing, 7*, 43–68.

Poulsen, E. (1991). Writing processes with word processing in teaching English as a foreign language. *Computers in Education, 16*, 77–81.

Pratt, D. (1980). *Curriculum design and development.* New York: Harcourt Brace Jovanovich.

Pressley, M. (1998). *Reading instruction that works: The case for balanced teaching.* New York: Guilford.

Prior, P. A. (1995a). Redefining the task: An ethnographic examination of writing and response in graduate seminars. In D. Belcher & G. Braine (Eds.), *Academic writing in a second language: Essays on research and pedagogy* (pp. 47–82). Norwood, NJ: Ablex.

Prior, P. A. (1995b). Tracing authoritative and internally persuasive discourses: A case study of response, revision, and disciplinary enculturation. *Research in the Teaching of English, 29*, 288–325.

Prior, P. A. (1998). *Writing/disciplinarity: A sociohistoric account of literate activity in the academy.* Mahwah, NJ: Lawrence Erlbaum Associates.

Prior, P. A. (2001). Voices in text, mind, and society: Sociohistoric accounts of discourse acquisition and use. *Journal of Second Language Writing, 10*, 55–81.

Purgason, K. B. (1991). Planning lessons and units. In M. Celce-Murcia (Ed.), *Teaching English as a second or foreign language* (2nd ed., pp. 419–431). New York: Newbury House.

Purves, A. C. (Ed.). (1988). *Writing across languages and cultures: Issues in contrastive rhetoric.* Newbury Park, CA: Sage.

Purves, A. C. (1996). Electronic portfolios. *Computers and Composition, 13*, 135–146.

Quindlen, A. (1988, April 28). Life in the 30s. *The New York Times,* C1, C3.

Radecki, P., & Swales, J. (1988). ESL student reaction to written comments on their written work. *System, 16*, 355–365.

Raimes, A. (1983). *Techniques in teaching writing.* New York: Oxford University Press.

Raimes, A. (1985). What unskilled ESL students do as they write: A classroom study of composing. *TESOL Quarterly, 19*, 229–258.

Raimes, A. (1987). Language proficiency, writing ability, and composing strategies: A study of ESL college student writers. *TESOL Quarterly, 19*, 229–258.

Raimes, A. (1991). Out of the woods: Emerging traditions in the teaching of writing. *TESOL Quarterly, 25*, 407–430.

Raimes, A. (1992). *Grammar trouble spots.* New York: St. Martin's.

Raimes, A. (1993). *How English works.* New York: St. Martin's.

Raimes, A. (1998). Teaching writing. *Annual Review of Applied Linguistics, 18*, 142–167.

Raimes, A. (2002). *Keys for writers: A brief handbook* (3rd ed.). Boston: Houghton Mifflin.

Ramanathan, V., & Atkinson, D. (1999b). Individualism, academic writing, and ESL writers. *Journal of Second Language Writing, 8*, 45–75.

Ramanathan, V., & Kaplan, R. B. (1996a). Audience and voice in current composition textbooks: Implications for L2 student writers. *Journal of Second Language Writing, 5*, 21–34.

Ramanathan, V., & Kaplan, R. B. (1996b). Some problematic channels in the teaching of critical thinking in current L1 composition textbooks: Implications for L2 student writers. *Issues in Applied Linguistics, 7*, 225–249.

Rampton, B. (1995). *Crossing: Language and ethnicity among adolescents.* London: Longman.

Ransdell, S., & Berbier, M.-L. (2002a). Introduction. In S. Ransdell & M.-L. Barbier (Eds.), *New directions for research in L2 writing* (pp. 1–10). Dordrecht, The Netherlands: Kluwer.

Ransdell, S., & Barbier, M.-L. (Eds.). (2002b). *New directions for research in L2 writing.* Dordrecht, The Netherlands: Kluwer.

Reagan, T. (1996). *Nonwestern educational traditions: Alternative approaches to educational thought and practice.* Mahwah, NJ: Lawrence Erlbaum Associates.

Reid, J. M. (1989). English as a second language composition in higher education: The expectations of the academic audience. In D. Johnson & D. Roen (Eds.), *Richness in writing: Empowering ESL students* (pp. 220–234). New York: Longman.

Reid, J. M. (1993a). Historical perspectives on writing and reading in the ESL classroom. In J. G. Carson, & I. Leki (Eds.), *Reading in the composition classroom: Second language perspectives* (pp. 33–60). Boston: Heinle.

Reid, J. M. (1993b). *Teaching ESL writing.* Englewood Cliffs, NJ: Regents/Prentice-Hall.

Reid, J. M. (1994). Responding to ESL students' texts: The myths of appropriation. *TESOL Quarterly, 28,* 273–292.

Reid, J. M. (1995a). Environmental writing inventory. In J. M. Reid (Ed.), *Learning styles in the ESL/EFL classroom* (pp. 218–219). Boston, MA: Heinle.

Reid, J. M. (Ed.). (1995b). *Learning styles in the ESL/EFL classroom.* Boston, MA: Heinle.

Reid, J. M. (1998a). "Eye" learners and "ear" learners: Identifying the language needs of international student and U.S. resident writers. In P. Byrd & J. M. Reid (Eds.), *Grammar in the composition classroom: Essays on teaching ESL for college-bound students* (pp. 3–17). Boston: Heinle.

Reid, J. M. (1998b). Responding to ESL student language problems: Error analysis and revision plans. In P. Byrd & J. M. Reid (Eds.), *Grammar in the composition classroom: Essays on teaching ESL for college-bound students* (pp. 118–137). Boston: Heinle.

Reid, J. M. (2002). Ask! In L. L. Blanton & B. Kroll (Eds.), *ESL composition tales* (pp. 83–103). Ann Arbor: University of Michigan Press.

Reid, J. M., & Kroll, B. (1995). Designing and assessing effective classroom writing assignments for NES and ESL students. *Journal of Second Language Writing, 4,* 17–41.

Reid, J. M., & Lindstrom, M. (1985). *The process of paragraph writing.* Englewood Cliffs, NJ: Prentice-Hall.

Rennie, C. (2000). *Error feedback in ESL writing classes: What do students really want?* MA thesis. Sacramento: California State University.

Reppen, R. (1994/1995). A genre-based approach to content writing instruction. *TESOL Journal, 4*(2), 32–35.

Resh, C. A. (1994). A study of the effect of peer responding on the responder as writer-reviser. *Dissertation Abstracts International, 55*(12), 3771A–3772A.

Reynolds, N. (2000). *Portfolio teaching: A guide for instructors.* Boston: Bedford/St. Martin's.

Richards, J., & Lockhart, C. (1994). *Reflective teaching in second language classrooms.* Cambridge: Cambridge University Press.

Richards, J. C., & Rodgers, T. S. (1987). Method, approach, design, and procedure. In M. H. Long & J. C. Richards (Eds.), *Methodology in TESOL: A book of readings* (pp. 133–160). New York: Newbury House.

Rivers, W. (1968). *Teaching foreign language skills.* Chicago: University of Chicago Press.

Robb, T., Ross, S. & Shortreed, I. (1986). Salience of feedback on error and its effect on EFL writing quality. *TESOL Quarterly, 20,* 83–93.

Roberts, B. J. (1999). *Can error logs raise more than consciousness? The effects of error logs and grammar feedback on ESL students' final drafts.* MA thesis. Sacramento: California State University.

Robinson, D. W. (2000). Building consensus on the scoring of students' writing: A comparison of teacher scores versus native informants' scores. *The French Review, 73,* 667–688.

Robinson, P. (1991). *ESP today: A practitioner's guide.* Hemel Hempstead, UK: Prentice-Hall International.

Rodby, J. (1992). *Appropriating literacy: Writing and reading in English as a second language.* Portsmouth, NH: Boynton/Cook.

Romaine, S. (1995). *Bilingualism* (2nd ed.). Cambridge, MA: Blackwell.

Rooks, G. (1988). *Share your paragraph.* Englewood Cliffs, NJ: Prentice-Hall.

Rose, M. (1980). Rigid rules, inflexible plans, and the stifling of language: A cognitivist analysis of writer's block. *College Composition and Communication, 31,* 389–401.

Rose, M. (Ed.). (1985). *Studies in writer's block and other composing process problems.* New York: Guilford Press.

Rothschild, D., & Klingenberg, F. (1990). Self- and peer evaluation of writing in the intensive ESL classroom. *TESL Canada Journal, 8*(1), 52–65.

Rouet, J.-F., Favart, M., Britt, M., & Perfetti, C. (1997). Studying and using multiple documents in history: Effects of discipline expertise. *Cognition and Instruction, 15,* 85–106.

Rumelhart, D. E., & McClelland, J. L. (1982). An interactive activation model of the effects of context in perception. *Psychological Review, 89,* 60–94.

Saito, H. (1994). Teachers' practices and students' preferences for feedback on second language writing: A case study of adult ESL learners. *TESL Canada Journal, 11*(2), 46–70.

Sakyi, A. (2000). Validation of holistic scoring for ESL writing assessment: How raters evaluate ESL compositions. In A. Kunnan (Ed.), *Fairness and validation in language assessment* (pp. 129–152). Cambridge, UK: Cambridge University Press.

Sampson, D. E., & Gregory, J. F. (1991). A technological primrose path? ESL students and computer-assisted writing programs. *College ESL, 1*(2), 29–36.

Sasaki, M. (2000). Toward an empirical model for EFL writing processes: An exploratory study. *Journal of Second Language Writing, 9,* 259–291.

Savignon, S. (1997). *Communicative competence: Theory and classroom practice.* New York: McGraw-Hill.

Savignon, S. (2001). Communicative language teaching for the twenty-first century. In M. Celce-Murcia (Ed.), *Teaching English as a second or foreign language* (3rd ed., pp. 13–28). Boston: Heinle.

Scarcella, R. C., & Oxford, R. L. (1992). *The tapestry of language learning: The individual in the communicative classroom.* Boston: Heinle.

Scarcella, R. (1996). Secondary education in California and second language research. *CATESOL Journal, 9*(1), 129–152.

Schleppegrell, M. J., & Colombi, M. C. (Eds.). (2002). *Developing advanced literacy in first and second languages: Meaning with power.* Mahwah, NJ: Lawrence Erlbaum Associates.

Schmid, L. M. (1999). *The effects of peer response on essay drafts.* MA thesis. Sacramento: California State University.

Schunk, D. (2000). *Learning theories: An educational perspective* (3rd ed.). Upper Saddle River, NJ: Merrill.

Scollon, R. (1997). Contrastive rhetoric, contrastive poetics, or perhaps something else? *TESOL Quarterly, 31,* 352–358.

Scollon, R., & Scollon, S. B. (1981). *Narrative, literacy, and face in interethnic communication.* Norwood, NJ: Ablex.

Selfe, C. L., & Wahlstrom, B. J. (1986). An emerging rhetoric of collaboration: Computers, collaboration, and the composing process. *Collegiate Microcomputer, 4*(4), 289–295.

Semke, H. (1984). The effects of the red pen. *Foreign Language Annals, 17,* 195–202.

Shanahan, T. (1984). Nature of the reading–writing relation: An exploratory multivariate analysis. *Journal of Educational Psychology, 76,* 466–477.

Shanahan, T. (Ed.). (1990). *Reading and writing together: New perspectives for the classroom.* Norwood, MA: Christopher-Gordon.

Shanahan, T., & Tierney, R. (1990). Reading–writing connections: The relations among three perspectives. In J. Zutell & S. McCormick (Eds.), *Literacy theory and research: Analyses from multiple paradigms* (pp. 13–34). Chicago: National Reading Conference.

Sharples, M. (1999). *How we write: Writing as creative design.* London: Routledge.

Shaugnessy, M. (1977). *Errors and expectations: A guide for the teacher of basic writing.* New York: Oxford University Press.

Shi, L. (2001). Native- and nonnative-speaking EFL teachers' evaluation of Chinese students' English writing. *Language Testing, 18,* 303–325.

Shih, M. (1998). ESL writers' grammar editing strategies. *College ESL, 8,* 64–86.

Silberstein, S. (1994). *Techniques and resources in teaching reading.* New York: Oxford University Press.

Silva, T. (1988). Comments on Vivian Zamel's "Recent research on writing pedagogy." *TESOL Quarterly, 22,* 517–519.

Silva, T. (1990). Second language composition instruction: Developments, issues, and directions in ESL. In B. Kroll (Ed.), *Second language writing: Research insights for the classroom* (pp. 11–23). Cambridge: Cambridge University Press.

Silva, T. (1993). Toward an understanding of the distinct nature of L2 writing: The ESL research and its implications. *TESOL Quarterly, 27,* 657–677.

Silva, T. (1997). On the ethical treatment of ESL writers. *TESOL Quarterly, 31,* 359–363.

Silva, T., Leki, I., & Carson, J. G. (1997). Broadening the perspective of mainstream composition studies. *Written Communication, 14,* 398–428.

Sirc, G. (1995). The twin worlds of electronic conferencing. *Computers and Composition, 12,* 265–277.

Skehan, P. (1989). *Individual differences in second language learning.* London: Arnold.

Skehan, P. (1991). Individual differences in second language learning. *Studies in Second Language Acquisition, 13,* 275–298.

Skehan, P. (1996). A framework for the implementation of task-based instruction. *Applied linguistics, 17,* 38–62.

Skehan, P. (1998). *A cognitive approach to language learning.* Oxford: Oxford University Press.

Skutnabb-Kangas, T., & Cummins, J. (1988). *Minority education: From shame to struggle.* Clevedon: Multilingual Matters.

Smith, D. (2000). Rater judgments in the direct assessment of competency-based second language writing ability. In G. Brindley (Ed.), *Studies in immigrant English language assessment* (pp. 159–189). Sydney, Australia: National Centre for English Language Teaching and Research, Macquarie University.

Smith, F. (1984). *Reading like a writer.* Victoria, BC: Abel Press.

Smith, F. (1988). *Joining the literacy club: Further essays into education.* Portsmouth, NH: Heinemann.

Smith, F. (1994). *Writing and the writer* (2nd ed.). Mahwah, NJ: Lawrence Erlbaum Associates.

Snow, M. A. (1998). Trends and issues in content-based instruction. *Annual Review of Applied Linguistics, 18,* 243–267.

Snow, M. A. (2001). Content-based and immersion models for second and foreign language teaching. In M. Celce-Murcia (Ed.), *Teaching English as a second or foreign language* (3rd ed., pp. 303–318). Boston: Heinle.

Snow, M. A., & Brinton, D. (1988). The adjunct model of language instruction: An ideal EAP framework. In S. Benesch (Ed.), *Ending remediation: ESL and content in higher education* (pp. 33–52). Washington, DC: TESOL.

Snow, M. A., & Brinton, D. M. (Eds.). (1997). *The content-based classroom: Perspectives on integrating language and content.* New York: Longman.

Sokmen, A. A. (1988). Taking advantage of conference-centered writing. *TESOL Newsletter, 22*(1), 1–5.

Sommers, N. (1982). Responding to student writing. *College Composition and Communication, 33,* 148–156.

Song, B., & Caruso, L. (1996). Do English and ESL faculty differ in evaluating the essays of native English-speaking and ESL students? *Journal of Second Langauge Writing, 5,* 163–182.

Soven, M. I. (1999). *Teaching writing in middle and secondary schools: Theory, research, and practice.* Boston: Allyn & Bacon.

Spack, R. (1984). Invention strategies and the ESL college composition student. *TESOL Quarterly, 18,* 649–670.

Spack, R. (1988). Initiating ESL students into the academic discourse community: How far should we go? *TESOL Quarterly, 22,* 29–52.

Spack, R. (1993). Student meets text, text meets student: Finding a way into academic discourse. In J. Carson, & I. Leki (Eds.), *Reading in the composition classroom: Second language perspectives* (pp. 183–196). Boston: Heinle.

Spack, R. (1990, 1996). *Guidelines: A cross-cultural reading/writing text.* New York: St. Martin's Press.

Spack, R. (1997a). The acquisition of academic literacy in a second language. *Written Communication, 14,* 3–62.

Spack, R. (1997b). The rhetorical construction of multilingual students. *TESOL Quarterly, 31,* 765–774.

Sperling, M., & Freedman, S. W. (1987). A good girl writes like a good girl: Written responses to student writing. *Written Communication, 4,* 343–369.

Stanley, J. (1992). Coaching student writers to be effective peer evaluators. *Journal of Second Language Writing, 1,* 217–233.

Stapleton, P. (2003). Critiquing voice as a viable pedagogical tool in L2 writing: Returning the spotlight to ideas. *Journal of Second Language Writing, 11,* 177–190.

Stewart, D. (1993). *Immigration and education: The crisis and the opportunities.* New York: Lexington Books.

Stotsky, S. (1983). Research on reading/writing relationships: A synthesis and suggested directions. *Language Arts, 60,* 627–642.

Straub, R. (1996). The concept of control in teacher response: Defining the varieties of directive and facilitative commentary. *College Composition and Communication, 47,* 223–251.

Straub, R. (1997). Students' reactions to teacher comments: An exploratory study. *Research in the Teaching of English, 31,* 91–119.

Straub, R., & Lunsford, R. F. (1995). *Twelve readers reading: Responding to college student writing.* Creskill, NJ: Hampton.

Sudol, R. A., & Horning, A. S. (Eds.). (1999). *The literacy connection.* Cresskill, NJ: Hampton Press.

Sullivan, N. (1993). Teaching writing on a computer network. *TESOL Journal, 3*(1), 34–35.

Susser, B. (1993). ESL/EFL process writing with computers. *CAELL Journal, 4*(2), 16–22.

Swaffar, J., Arens, K., & Byrnes, H. (1991). *Reading for meaning.* Englewood Cliffs, NJ: Prentice-Hall.

Swales, J. M. (1990). *Genre analysis: English in academic and research settings.* Cambridge: Cambridge University Press.

Swales, J. M. (1998). *Other floors, other voices: A textography of a small university building.* Mahwah, NJ: Lawrence Erlbaum Associates.

Tarvers, J. K. (1993). *Teaching writing: Theories and practice* (4th ed.). New York: HarperCollins.

Teichman, M., & Poris, M. (1989). Initial effects of word processing on writing quality and writing anxiety of freshman writers. *Computers and the Humanities, 23,* 93–101.

Thorson, H. (2000). Using the computer to compare foreign and native language writing processes: A statistical and case study approach. *Modern Language Journal, 84,* 155–169.

Tickoo, M. L. (Ed.). (1995). *Reading and writing: Theory into practice.* Singapore: SEAMEO Regional Language Centre.

Tobin, L. (Ed.). (1994). *Taking stock: The writing process movement in the '90s.* Portsmouth, NH: Heinemann.

Tomasello, M., & Herron, C. (1989). Feedback for language transfer errors. *Studies in Second Language Acquisition, 11,* 385–395.

Trimbur, J. (1994). Taking the social turn: Teaching writing postprocess. *College Composition and Communication, 45,* 108–118.

Truscott, J. (1996). The case against grammar correction in L2 writing classes. *Language Learning, 46,* 327–369.

Truscott, J. (1999). "The case for grammar correction in L2 writing classes": A response to Ferris. *Journal of Second Language Writing, 8,* 111–122.

Tsang, W. (1996). Comparing the effects of reading and writing on writing performance. *Applied Linguistics, 17,* 210–233.

Tsui, A. B. M. (1996). Learning how to teach ESL writing. In D. Freeman & J. Richards (Eds.), *Teacher learning in language teaching* (pp. 97–119). Cambridge, UK: Cambridge University Press.

Ur, P. (1996). *A course in language teaching.* Cambridge: Cambridge University Press.

Urquhart, A. H., & Weir, C. (1998). *Reading in a second language: Process, product, and practice.* New York: Longman.

Valdés, G. (1992). Bilingual minorities and language issues in writing. *Written Communication, 9,* 85–136.

Valdés, G. (2000). Nonnative English speakers: Language bigotry in English mainstream classrooms. *ADE Bulletin, 124,* 12–17.

Vandrick, S. (1994). Feminist pedagogy and ESL. *College ESL, 4*(2), 69–82.

Vandrick, S. (1995). Privileged ESL university students. *TESOL Quarterly, 29,* 375–380.

Vandrick, S. (2003). Literature in the teaching of second language composition. In B. Kroll (Ed.), *Exploring the dynamics of second language writing* (pp. 263–283). Cambridge: Cambridge University Press.

van Lier, L. (1994). Some features of a theory of practice. *TESOL Journal, 4*(1), 6–10.

van Lier, L. (1996). *Interaction in the language curriculum: Awareness, autonomy, and authenticity.* London: Longman.

Vaughan, C. (1991). Holistic assessment: What goes on in the rater's mind? In L. Hamp-Lyons (Ed.), *Assessing second language writing in academic contexts* (pp. 111–125). Norwood, NJ: Ablex.

Verhoeven, L., & Snow, C. E. (Eds.). (2001). *Literacy and motivation: Reading engagement in individuals and groups.* Mahwah, NJ: Lawrence Erlbaum Associates.

Villamil, O. S., & de Guerrero, M. C. M. (1996). Peer revision in the L2 classroom: Social-cognitive activities, mediating strategies, and aspects of social behavior. *Journal of Second Language Writing, 5,* 51–76.

Vygotsky, L. (1986). *Thought and Language.* (A. Kozulin, Trans. & Ed.). Cambridge, MA: MIT Press. (Original work published 1962)

Wajnryb, R. (1992). *Classroom observation tasks.* Cambridge: Cambridge University Press.

Walker, D. F. (2003). *Fundamentals of curriculum: Passion and professionalism.* Mahwah, NJ: Lawrence Erlbaum Associates.

Wall, B. C., & Peltier, R. F. (1996). "Going public" with electronic portfolios: Audience, community, and the terms of student ownership. *Computers and Composition, 13,* 207–217.

Warschauer, M. (1995). *E-mail for English teaching.* Alexandria, VA: TESOL.

Warschauer, M., Schetzer, H., & Meloni, C. (2000). *Internet for English teaching.* Alexandria, VA: TESOL.

Watson-Reekie, C. (1982). The use and abuse of models in the ESL writing class. *TESOL Quarterly, 16,* 5–14.

Way, D., Joiner, E., & Seaman, M. (2000). Writing in the secondary foreign language classroom: The effects of prompts and tasks on novice learners of French. *Modern Language Journal, 84,* 171–184.

Weaver, C. (1994). *Reading process and practice* (2nd ed.). Portsmouth, NH: Heinemann.

Weaver, C. (1996). *Teaching grammar in context.* Portsmouth, NH: Boynton/Cook Heinemann.

Weese, K. L., Fox, S. L., & Greene, S. (Eds.). (1999). *Teaching academic literacy: The uses of teacher research in developing a writing program.* Mahwah, NJ: Lawrence Erlbaum Associates.

Weigle, S. C. (1999). Investigating rater/prompt interactions in writing assessment: Quantitative and qualitative approaches. *Assessing Writing, 6,* 145–178.

Weigle, S. C. (2002). *Assessing writing.* Cambridge, UK: Cambridge University Press.

Weinstein, G. (2001). Developing adult literacies. In M. Celce-Murcia, M. (Ed.), *Teaching English as a second or foreign language* (3rd ed., pp. 171–186). Boston: Heinle.

Weir, C. J. (1990). *Communicative language testing.* New York: Prentice-Hall International.

Wells, G. (1999). *Dialogic inquiry: Towards a sociocultural practice and theory of education.* New York: Cambridge University Press.

Weschler, R., & Pitts, C. (2000). An experiment using electronic dictionaries with EFL students. *The Internet TESL Journal 6*(8). Accessed at http://iteslj.org/

White, E. M. (1994). *Teaching and assessing writing: Recent advances in understanding, evaluating, and improving student performance* (2nd rev. ed.). San Francisco: Jossey-Bass.

White, E. M. (1999). *Assigning, responding, evaluating: A writing teacher's guide* (3rd ed.). Boston: Bedford/St. Martin's.

White, E. M., Lutz, W. D., & Kamusikiri, S. (Eds.). (1996). *Assessment of writing: Politics, policies, practices.* New York: Modern Language Association.

White, R. (Ed.). (1995). *New ways in teaching writing.* Alexandria, VA: TESOL.

Williams, J. D. (1996). *Preparing to teach writing.* Mahwah, NJ: Lawrence Erlbaum Associates.

Williams, M., & Burden, R. L. (1997). *Psychology for language teachers: A social constructivist approach.* Cambridge, UK: Cambridge University Press.

Williamson, M., & Huot, B. (Eds.). (1993). *Validating holistic scoring for writing assessment.* Cresskill, NJ: Hampton Press.

Windeatt, S., Hardisty, D., & Eastment, D. (2000). *The Internet.* Oxford: Oxford University Press.

Witbeck, M. C. (1976). Peer correction procedures for intermediate and advanced ESL composition lessons. *TESOL Quarterly, 10,* 321–326.

Wu, S.-Y., & Rubin, D. L. (2000). Evaluating the impact of collectivism and individualism on argumentative writing by Chinese and North American college students. *Research in the Teaching of English, 35,* 148–178.

Yancey, K. B. (Ed.). (1992). *Portfolios in the writing classroom.* Urbana, IL: National Council of Teachers of English.

Yancey, K. B., & Weiser, I. (Eds.). (1997). *Situating portfolios: Four perspectives.* Logan, UT: Utah State University Press.

Yates, R., & Muchisky, D. (2003). On reconceptualizing teacher education. *TESOL Quarterly, 37,* 135–146.

Yonally, D., & Gilfert, S. (2000). Electronic dictionaries in the classroom!? Bah, humbug! *The Internet TESL Journal, 6*(5). Accessed at http://iteslj.org/

Zamel, V. (1976). Teaching composition in the ESL classroom: What we can learn from research in the teaching of English. *TESOL Quarterly, 10,* 67–76.

Zamel, V. (1982). Writing: The process of discovering meaning. *TESOL Quarterly, 16,* 195–209.

Zamel, V. (1983). The composing processes of advanced ESL students: Six case studies. *TESOL Quarterly, 17,* 165–187.

Zamel, V. (1985). Responding to student writing. *TESOL Quarterly, 19,* 79–102.

Zamel, V. (1987). Recent research on writing pedagogy. *TESOL Quarterly, 21,* 697–715.

Zamel, V. (1992). Writing one's way into reading. *TESOL Quarterly, 26,* 463–485.

Zamel, V. (1993). Questioning academic discourse. *College ESL, 3*(1), 28–39.

Zamel, V. (1997). Toward a model of transculturation. *TESOL Quarterly, 31,* 341–352.

Zamel, V., & Spack, R. (Eds.). (1998). *Negotiating academic literacies: Teaching and learning across languages and cultures.* Mahwah, NJ: Lawrence Erlbaum Associates.

Zamel, V., & Spack, R. (Eds.). (2002). *Enriching ESOL pedagogy: Readings and activities for engagement, reflection, and learning.* Mahwah, NJ: Lawrence Erlbaum Associates.

Zebroski, J. (1986). The uses of theory: A Vygotskian approach to composition. *The Writing Instructor, 5,* 57–67.

Zhang, Q. (1997). Academic writing in English and Chinese: Case studies of senior college students. *Dissertation Abstracts International, 58,* 3909.

Zhang, S. (1995). Reexamining the affective advantage of peer feedback in the ESL writing class. *Journal of Second Language Writing, 4,* 209–222.

Zhang, S. (1999). Thoughts on some recent evidence concerning the affective advantage of peer feedback. *Journal of Second Language Writing, 8,* 321–326.

Author Index

415

Subject Index